Poland into the New Millennium

ECONOMIES AND SOCIETIES IN TRANSITION

General Editor: Ronald J. Hill
Professor of Comparative Government
and Fellow of Trinity College
Dublin, Ireland

Economies and Societies in Transition is an important series which applies academic analysis and clarity of thought to the recent traumatic events in Eastern and Central Europe. As many of the preconceptions of the past half century are cast aside, newly independent and autonomous sovereign states are being forced to address long-term, organic problems which had been suppressed by, or appeased within, the Communist system of rule.

The series is edited under the sponsorship of Lorton House, an independent charitable association which exists to promote the academic study of communism and related concepts.

Poland into the New Millennium

Edited by

George Blazyca and Ryszard Rapacki

ECONOMIES AND SOCIETIES IN TRANSITION

Edward Elgar
Cheltenham, UK • Northampton, MA, USA

Published by
Edward Elgar Publishing Limited
Glensanda House
Montpellier Parade
Cheltenham
Glos GL50 1UA
UK

Edward Elgar Publishing, Inc.
136 West Street
Suite 202
Northampton
Massachusetts 01060
USA

A catalogue record for this book
is available from the British Library

Library of Congress Cataloguing in Publication Data

Poland into the new millennium / edited by George Blazyca and Ryszard Rapacki.
p. cm.— (Economies and societies in transition)
Includes index.
1. Poland—Economic conditions—1990– 2. Poland—Economic policy—1990– 3. Poland—Social conditions—1980– 4. Poland—Foreign relations. I. Rapacki, Ryszard. II. Blazyca, George. III. Series.

HC340.3 .P64383 2001
330.9438—dc21

2001023648

ISBN 1 84064 639 X

Printed and bound in Great Britain by MPG Books Ltd, Bodmin, Cornwall

Contents

List of figures

List of tables

List of contributors

Marek Belka (mbelka@prezydent.pl) is economic adviser to Polish President Aleksander Kwaśniewski. In 1997 he served in the Polish government as deputy prime minister and minister of finance. Professor Belka also advises the prime minister of the Republic of Albania and is consultant to the World Bank. He is based at the Institute of Economics of the Polish Academy of Sciences in Warsaw. He has written several books and many articles in Poland and abroad on macroeconomic theory and policy, anti-inflation policy in developed countries as well as macroeconomic policy and enterprise restructuring in transition economies. Professor Belka is vice-president of the board of the 'Know-How Fund' for Poland and also serves as member and adviser to the supervisory boards of various agencies and Polish and foreign companies.

George Blazyca (george@blazyca.freeserve.co.uk) is professor of economics in the Paisley Business School and co-ordinates the work of the Centre for Contemporary European Studies at the University of Paisley in Scotland. He is an economist with a special interest in Poland and has published widely on Polish economic and political developments, post-communist transformation and EU enlargement. He has contributed to the *Poland Country Report* of the London-based Economist Intelligence Unit since the early 1980s.

Christopher Bobiński (bobinski@it.com.pl) is Warsaw correspondent of the *Financial Times* for whom he has covered Polish business and political developments since 1976. In 1998 he was a founding editor and publisher of the Warsaw-based, *Unia & Polska* magazine (www.unia-polska.pl).

Barbara Gąciarz (matey@kki.net.pl) is based at the Institute of Philosophy and Sociology, Polish Academy of Sciences in Warsaw and the Institute of Social Sciences, Academy of Mining and Metallurgy in Kraków. She has researched and written extensively on economic sociology and post-communist transformation especially with regard to Poland, Georgia and Ukraine.

Marek Góra (marek_gora@mpips.gov.pl) led the team that prepared Poland's 1999 pension reform and headed the government office for social security reform. He has also advised the Macedonian and Slovakian governments on pension reform. He is based at the Warsaw School of Economics and has been visiting researcher in a number of European and US universities. He worked with the OECD Directorate for Education, Labour and Social Affairs in 1992–93. He has published widely in the fields of pension economics, labour economics, unemployment, labour market policies and the macro- and microeconomic problems of transition.

Marian Górski (gorski@mail.wz.uw.edu.pl) is professor and head of the finance and capital markets department at the Warsaw University School of Management where he was dean of faculty in 1990–96. His research interests focus on the financial and banking sector, monetary policy and comparative economics. He is an adviser to the state treasury and a member of the expert advisory team to the minister of education. From 1991 he served as member, and from 1995 as chair, of the board of the *Wielkopolski Bank Kredytowy (WBK SA),* a state bank privatised in 1993 with Allied Irish Bank as strategic investor. He also chairs, as state treasury representative, other supervisory boards.

Grzegorz Gorzelak (gorzelak@kki.net.pl) is professor of regional studies and director of the University of Warsaw-based European Institute for Regional and Local Development. He has published widely on regional aspects of Poland's transformation and is active in the Polish section of the Regional Studies Association. He was a founding editor in 2000 of the new regional studies periodical, *Studia Regionalne i Lokalne*, designed to bridge the gap between theory and practice in Polish regional development.

Tadeusz Kowalik (tkowalik@wspiz.edu.pl) is professor of economics and humanities at the Institute of Economics, Polish Academy of Sciences in Warsaw. He is a member of the government advisory body, the Council for Socio-economic Strategy (*Rada Strategii Społeczno-Gospodarczej*). His academic interests span the political economy of socialism, economic history and contemporary issues of post-communist transformation and globalisation. He is editor of the collected works of Oskar Lange, published in English in *Economic Theory and Market Socialism – The Selected Works of Oskar Lange* (Edward Elgar, 1996) and co-editor of Michal Kalecki's collected works. His most recent Polish book, *Współczesne systemy* ekonomiczne (Contemporary Economic Systems), was published in 2000. Professor Kowalik is a member of the left-wing Polish Labour Party (*Unia Pracy*).

Jan Macieja (macieja@pixel.mg.gov.pl) is a researcher at the Institute of Economics, Polish Academy of Sciences, with many publications and a special interest in industrial economics, regulation and privatisation. He served in the first Solidarity government as a general director in the industry ministry and has spent time as a research fellow in a number of US and UK universities and institutions.

Witold M. Orłowski (nobe-wmo@lodz.pdi.net) is professor and director at the Research Centre for Statistical and Economic Studies (ZBSE) in Warsaw and founder of the Independent Centre for Economic Studies (NOBE), one of Poland's leading economic think-tanks. His research interests include the economics of transition, European integration, economic modelling and forecasting. Professor Orłowski has also acted as consultant to various national and international organisations, including the World Bank, EBRD, FAO, and the European Commission. He is a member of the finance minister's advisory macroeconomic council and adviser to Poland's chief EU negotiator.

Włodzimierz Pańków (wpankow@ifispan.waw.pl) is professor at the Institute of Philosophy and Sociology, Polish Academy of Sciences, and the '*Collegium Civitas*' both in Warsaw. In 1989-92 he was co-ordinator of the Centre of Trade Union Studies in the Warsaw region of 'Solidarity'. He has researched and written widely on organisational sociology, industrial relations and post-communist transformation especially focused on Poland, Georgia, Ukraine and Russia.

Ryszard Rapacki (rrapacki@sgh.waw.pl) is professor and head of the economics department at the Warsaw School of Economics (SGH). He also lectures at Poland's National School of Public Administration. His research interests focus on systemic transformation in Poland and East–Central Europe, especially macroeconomic policy, microeconomic adjustment and privatisation. He has researched and lectured extensively in the UK, Canada and the USA where he was a Fulbright Scholar at Michigan State University. In Poland Professor Rapacki has been adviser to the minister of education and the president of the foreign investment agency. He has also been actively involved in the Polish privatisation process as consultant and as a member of the board of one of Poland's mass privatisation (NFI) funds. He has acted as consultant on behalf of UNIDO and UNDP to governments in Albania, Jamaica, Sudan, Uganda, Zambia and Zimbabwe.

Aleks Szczerbiak (a.a.szczerbiak@sussex.ac.uk) lectures at the Sussex European Institute (SEI) of the University of Sussex in the UK. His main research interests are in post-communist Central and East European politics and he specialises in contemporary Polish political developments. He has published widely on Polish electoral politics and party development.

Jerzy Wilkin (wilkin@wne.uw.edu.pl) is professor of economics at Warsaw University, where he was dean of the economics faculty in 1996–99. He is author of many articles and books on agrarian and rural development. He has served as consultant to the OECD, the World Bank and the European Commission. He is chairman of the committee for agricultural economics in the Polish Academy of Sciences.

Edmund Wnuk-Lipiński (ewlip@isppan.waw.pl) is based in the Institute of Political Studies, Polish Academy of Sciences, Warsaw. He has been involved in many international comparative research projects on the transition to democracy and has written several books and many journal articles on social structure, inequality and radical social change. He also contributes to graduate and undergraduate programmes at *Collegium Civitas*, Warsaw University, the College of Europe and the National School of Public Administration. He is involved in the management of a number of academic institutions and serves on governmental committees for European integration and the civil service.

Preface

Much has been written on post-communist transformation but with the passage of time it becomes perhaps slightly easier to detect underlying patterns of social, political and economic change. In the first 10 years of system transformation many early, perhaps too hastily made judgements have had to be revised, some substantially so. The move from defunct central planning to some kind of market mechanism has not been smooth and is by no means complete (whatever that may mean). Political transformation also continues with no neat or clear mapping of group 'interests' onto party politics. Societies long used to stultifying stability, sometimes comfortable, more often not, have had adjust to a host of new tensions including 'transformation recession', strong inflation, high unemployment, fast-growing regional and income inequality, alongside the release of powerful new entrepreneurial energies and reintegration into the international economy.

In this book we have invited a group of social scientists and other well informed observers with a special interest in Poland to describe and comment on some of the key features of that country's post-1989 transformation. We have also encouraged, however tentatively, exploration of likely future developments – where is Polish economy and society heading in the new millennium? The answers are by no means straightforward but it will come as no surprise that EU entry figures as a dominating issue alongside a broad optimism that might be expected from those who have played an active role in transformation. We hope that the collection of essays in this volume conveys something of the flavour of transformation, from a largely Polish (although by no means uniform) perspective. The reader will judge whether our labour has been worthwhile.

As always, the finished product represents the efforts of a collective that goes beyond the team of authors. But first the editors must thank those authors for their patience in responding to the many requests we made for revisions and clarifications of material in our attempts to make essays clearer for the largely Western audience at which we aim. In addition, a special thanks to Karen Buchanan, Jean Finn and the secretarial staff in the Paisley Business School for their hard work in preparing the camera-ready copy. We are grateful too for the support of the Centre for Contemporary European Studies at Paisley University in funding translations from Polish to English (special thanks here are owed to Stephen Green and John Bates from the Department of Slavonic Studies at

Glasgow University as well as Michał Białkowski from Wrocław and Paisley). The Economics Department of the Warsaw School of Economics facilitated, through its KBN research grant, staff exchanges between Poland and Scotland, which played an important part in shaping this book. A special thanks also to Krystyna Budniewska for providing a marvellous research base in the Saska Kępa diatrict of Warsaw. The editors also thank Wendy Blazyca and Anna Rapacka for their forbearance and support during a time-consuming, indeed at times almost *all*-consuming, eighteen months of work on this project.

Lastly, Christopher Saunders, a former director of research at the UNECE in Geneva, with a long-standing interest in Central Europe, died in early 2000 in his ninety-second year. Christopher had a special and lively interest in Poland throughout a retirement that was as long as a working life. He helped shape the thinking and writing of one of the editors in particular and that contribution, acknowledged here, will be very much missed in the future.

1. Poland into the new millennium: introduction and overview

George Blazyca and Ryszard Rapacki

INTRODUCTION

It is widely reckoned that the Polish experience of system transformation following the final collapse of 'real socialism' in 1989 is one of the 'best'. While this book is devoted to studying the dynamic of Polish social and economic change through the 1990s, with an eye of course on the future, it is certainly *not* the editors' intention to offer any triumphalist account – notwithstanding the country's frequent description as 'pioneer' or 'soaring eagle'. Instead we have asked a group of well informed observers (in many cases 'activists') to describe key aspects of system transformation to help us better understand the nature of the processes released in economy and society since 1989, what has been achieved (and not achieved) so far. The accounts will, we hope, give the reader a solid feel for where Polish economy and society is heading as well as some inkling of the problems that may lie ahead in a transformation that is by no means complete. Although we have grouped contributions in three parts to make the story easier to digest, the material in our collection forms in reality a continuum. It will not escape the reader's attention that sometimes sharp differences of opinion exist among authors but the collection should be viewed as a contribution to on-going debate and we hope, in this spirit, that it encourages a wider discussion across social science perspectives.

PART I: POLITICAL ECONOMY, SOCIETY AND POLITICS

While we focus in this book on economic change we have been careful not to exclude social and political matters since the interrelationships are self-evident and particularly strong in the circumstances of system transformation. The scene is set in the first part of the collection, where the focus is on political economy, society and politics, by Marek Belka, one of our 'observer/activists' (finance minister in 1996–97 and also the chief economic adviser to Poland's president, Aleksander Kwaśniewski from 1997 through to 2000). Belka's background means that he is superbly equipped to assess the experience of economic transformation and here he traces the broad sweep of economic policy in the 1990s, drawing attention to a strong element of pragmatism notwithstanding 'simplistic foreign advice' and 'ultra liberal rhetoric'. He emphasises the need for a fast rate of 'sustainable economic growth', a key condition of meeting the challenges (especially EU accession) that lie ahead, but warns too of the dangers of overlooking the need for social cohesion in transformation – the 'Kuroń factor' was as important, argues Belka, as the 'Balcerowicz factor' in creating the basis for Polish transformation success. In his view Polish achievements were underpinned by a 'broad consensus' which if strengthened bodes well for the future. It is easy however for policy makers to get things wrong especially when the awkward problem of 'time dislocation' between policy impacts is recognised: speedy macroeconomic stabilisation but delayed microeconomic adjustment can generate, says Belka, a 'transition cycle'; a key lesson from the 1990s experience is to try to make policy 'time consistent'.

Tadeusz Kowalik, another 'observer/activist', a self-confessed socialist (in tradition of the Solidarity Left rather than the Communist party) pulls no punches in his view of transformation where its 'ugly side' gets a good 'going-over'. Kowalik's political economy of transformation leads him to ask what sort of system is taking shape in Poland and whose interests does it serve? He picks up and explores in detail a point made in passing by Belka ('transition has brought great achievements. Unprecedented success for some, justified hopes for many others, but also disappointment for the least fortunate') and notes that transformation has had high costs in terms of mass unemployment, poverty, steadily increasing inequalities in income distribution (some of the worst Gini coefficients this side of Russia, says Kowalik) and widespread corruption. Like Belka, Kowalik, has much time for the role played in early transformation by Kuroń although this 'legend of the Polish non-communist left' does not get off so lightly in the Kowalik account. Returning to his main theme, Kowalik doubts very much that IMF experts, if they examined Polish capitalism under the microscope, would find something either recognisable to them or which they could (or should) really approve of. In his view a kind of 'crony capitalism' is the outcome of the first 10 years of transformation where 'the transformation classes' have done exceedingly well but, as he sees it, the bulk of society (industrial workers, public sector employees, farmers) has lost out.

It is not a view shared by Edmund Wnuk-Lipiński, a sociologist and political scientist much quoted in the Polish press, who gives what he considers to be the historic-sociological background needed to understand contemporary Poland. He concedes however the curious but perhaps not unexpected outcome that there was no neat mapping from Solidarity's initial make-up to eventual winners and losers in transformation ('many who were initially against reform gained whereas many who promoted reform lost'). As Solidarity inevitably fragmented so too did more narrow group interests begin to dominate any notion of 'long-term benefits for all of society' leading, as Wnuk-Lipiński puts it, to 'a significant growth of social pessimism, disappointment and frustration', 'a speedy erosion of the common belief in a better future', 'a narrowing of perspectives'. Yet despite all, he sticks to a basically optimistic view where the 'new system' is 'consolidating itself'. It will, he continues, survive the numerous conflicts that are likely to appear as the strongly internationally integrated economy is buffeted by shocks (inevitable sooner or later) in the global system, as restructuring continues, and as the EU debate intensifies within the country.

From a view on society (and solidarity with a small 's') at Wnuk-Lipiński's macro-level we move to a complementary micro analysis of collective bargaining and industrial relations at the level of the enterprise. Here the striking features are trade union weakness, incapacity, and falling membership (down from 6 million in the early 1990s to no more than 3.5 million at the end of the decade, with less than one quarter of men and only 14% women in trade unions). It is a picture that may surprise many Western readers given the sometimes intense and highly charged level of worker (and in the late 1990s also farmer) protests in Poland. The detailed research of Włodzimierz Pańków and Barbara Gąciarz (from the Polish Academy of Sciences Institute for Philosophy and Sociology) shows that trade unions do *not* have a high profile in the workplace, are *not* greatly respected by workers (with the exception of the activists themselves) and tend to reveal their *weaknesses* in the means of protest they select (the 'strike threat' and quick recourse in disputes to broad, sector-wide appeals for support). Especially noticeable is the low regard of workers for institutions, notably parliament, 'saturated' with former trade unionists. There is, say Pańków and Gąciarz, little evidence to back up the suggestion frequently made by management (indeed also by some contributors to this collection), and amplified through the media, of aggressive wage-bargaining. Instead, at the level of the enterprise the social atmosphere is mainly calm, interest groups tend to co-operate rather than conflict but unions are weak with management tending towards an 'enlightened paternalism'. What all of this means for the future is hard to say. Perhaps Polish industrial relations reflect, say the authors, aspects of early capitalism and a stronger trade union development is yet to appear, one that may be given a boost by EU labour law?

Aleks Szczerbiak, a UK based political scientist, concludes Part I of the collection with a thumbnail sketch of the sometimes complex, and often confusing, political situation in the country. Szczerbiak carefully describes the major actors on the political stage while arguing too that party politics in Poland, even after 10 years of post-communist transformation, remains fluid, as he puts it, only 'partially consolidated'. His suggestion is that group *interests* are not yet mapped firmly onto parties and so *values* still play a distinctive role in forming political attachments and identity. Polish politics in the 1990s was a politics of 'them and us', 'post-communism versus post-Solidarity' and a key question for the future is just how long that fundamental division will last?

PART II: ECONOMIC PERFORMANCE, INSTITUTIONAL AND SECTORAL TRANSFORMATIONS

At this point, to launch the second part of the collection with its focus on economic performance, institutional and sectoral transformations we return to a review of economic events and processes. Ryszard Rapacki, a close observer of the economic scene, based at the Warsaw School of Economics, gives a detailed account of the trajectory of GDP in the 1990s from both the perspective of demand- and supply-side (including factor use and productivity) developments. Readers will find here much systematically gathered and carefully presented data charting the economy's post-transformation course alongside some disturbing suggestions as regards investment (little medium–high technology investment as compared with other transforming economies), innovation (domestic capacity declined in the 1990s) and human capital (where despite improvement the gap with the developed West remains wide). All this stimulates some doubt as to the current and future competitiveness of the economy and Rapacki concludes with a daunting list of problems yet to be resolved but, like most other contributors, he is inclined towards optimism, largely because of the discipline forced by the imperative of EU accession.

Jan Macieja offers a microeconomic account of transformation concentrating on developments as between the fast growing and, in the 1990s, highly successful private sector (formal and informal) and the increasingly poorly performing state sector. In his view almost all weaknesses of Polish economic performance in the 1990s can be ascribed to too slow structural change and a pace of privatisation dented by interest groups determinedly hanging on to privilege. Macieja believes that successes of state firms in the early transformation period 'were blown out of proportion by the World Bank'. He also links the state's still, as he sees it, too extensive embrace of economic activity to a steady increase in party political 'clientism' (post-communism *and* post-Solidarity are held equally to blame) and plain corruption. One wonders however how easy it will be for the initial surge in entrepreneurialism to continue, especially given that a sudden switch from 'real socialism' liberated energies that may be, to some extent, 'once-for-all'. Experience in the West (at least in some countries, not least Scotland!) shows that enterprise and small firm growth needs encouragement but is by no means straightforward and is, moreover, an area in which the state has a positive role to play. The reader will judge whether Macieja's strong commitment to 'economic Darwinism' looks like a plausibly winning strategy for the new millennium but the editors have some reservations regarding the view that 'only the threat of losing one's property, coupled with the natural desire to increase one's possessions, guarantees rational decisions'.

Marian Górski is another 'observer/activist', an academic and part-time chairman of the supervisory board of the Poznań based, but Irish-owned, WBK bank, someone well-placed therefore to give a first hand review of banking and financial sector developments in Poland in the 1990s. The reader with specialist interests will find here much useful background information as well as a definitive account of the development of central banking, commercial banking (including its regulatory framework and the role of foreign capital) and the capital markets. If the financial sector, due to its weakness, had relatively little impact on the real economy in the first decade of transformation, as Górski suggests, this is something that the author believes will change markedly in the period ahead as Poland draws closer to the EU and as banking sector competition intensifies. Marek Góra's contribution, telling the story of pension reform in Poland, is closely linked to Górski's description of capital markets' evolution since the new private sector pension funds that came into existence after 1999 are expected to play a key role in generating savings and stimulating investment. Of course, they also defuse the pensions time bomb that threatened to explode Poland's bankrupt Pay-As-You-Go (PAYG) pensions system. Góra, one of the authors of the 1999 reform, makes the point that on pensions reform Poland has stolen a march on most EU members, many of which face as yet unresolved difficulties with PAYG pensions.

In terms of broad structural problems we decided to cover two key areas: uneven regional development and agriculture. We chose the former because Poland, due to its size, can expect to see substantial differences open up across its economic space, creating new and potentially dangerous tensions for the future. Agriculture, as is well known, has a special place in the domestic economy, not to mention the EU accession process, and no book on Polish economy and society at the start of the new millennium would be complete without some discussion of matters rural/agricultural. We invited two leading Polish specialists to discuss those issues: Grzegorz Gorzelak describes regional policy and regional development while Jerzy Wilkin covers agriculture. Gorzelak's account vests greatest hope for the future of Polish regions in a self-activity that seems rooted in a neo-liberalism which cautions 'no one can expect the state, in implementing an overall regional policy [to] attend to the situation in individual regions, [its] role is to ensure the development of the entire national economy and to support its global competitiveness'. So the regions, it seems, have to look after themselves. Gorzelak appears resigned to the idea that some may not do well, at least in the early phases of transformation when, in his view, 'efficiency' considerations should take precedence over those of 'equity'. Later, he suggests, the balance may be redressed. Meanwhile Jerzy Wilkin, agreeing that farmers as a socio-economic group lost out badly in the first transformation decade, goes on to probe closely Poland's rural/agriculture structure. He identifies a core farming group (400,000 out of Poland's 2 million farms) likely to be viable in the longer term and constituting 'the main CAP "clients" after Poland joins the EU'. The Polish countryside needs, he believes (along with many of our authors), a comprehensive socio-economic development strategy that goes beyond farming. However, he continues, an institutional hiatus means that no existing agency in Poland is up to that task. There is little doubt that the countryside (with 38% of the population) and agriculture (with, according to various estimates, anything from 12% to 27% of employment) deserve special attention if Poland is to sustain its broadly successful 1990s economic performance.

PART III: INTERNATIONAL DIMENSIONS OF POLAND'S TRANSFORMATION

The final part of the collection begins with a review by George Blazyca (a UK based observer of Polish economic development) of Poland's changing place in the international economy. The author draws attention to the key transformations of the 1990s (where the rapidity of the shift in the geography of trade from East to West was particularly impressive) and asks what these may mean for the future. The collapse of central planning (or, in Poland, a species thereof) led to immediate trade openness with huge adjustment problems for Polish enterprise. Exactly what happened to the 'skills content' of Polish exports in the 1990s is not clear. Meanwhile the country's current account deficit (7.6% of GDP in 1999) looked to be becoming a particularly serious problem for the future. From 1989 investment openness existed too but Poland only began to benefit substantially in the later 1990s perhaps suggesting that a multinational corporation (MNC) sponsored restructuring has only just started and may have a more decisive impact in shaping Polish trade in the years ahead (as occurred in Hungary from the mid-1990s).

Witold Orłowski is an economist and GUS statistician as well as perhaps the best known of Polish specialists on the economics of EU integration, and in his contribution he examines carefully the costs and benefits of accession, drawing lessons from earlier enlargement, particularly to southern Europe in the 1980s. In his view the lesson from history is clear: prudent macroeconomic policy is critical in ensuring that membership advantages are not squandered. Orłowski (like Belka and others) also reminds us that 'real convergence' (of income levels) is of great importance and Polish macro policy must be geared to achieving the relatively faster growth that the country needs to reduce the gap (32 years in 1996 in his estimate) between Poland and the EU.

Christopher Bobiński, the *Financial Times* Warsaw correspondent since 1976, brings the volume to a close with his timely vignette built around an attempt to tease out the views of all the prime ministers (seven of them) who served in the 1990s on what is surely the big issue of the new decade, EU accession. In May 2000 Bobiński launched, with colleagues from the publication, *Unia&Polska*, the so-called 'Bristol Appeal' in which the question was directly put (to the seven PMs), 'Can Polish political leaders work together on EU accession?'. The detailed answer can be found in the pages Bobiński has written and we will not spoil the reader's enjoyment by giving it away earlier. As he concludes the book, Bobiński reminds us however of many of the key features that will shape Polish social, economic and political developments in the new millennium. They include the glaring need for a real strategy for agricultural/rural modernisation as well as intriguing suggestions regarding the politics of a future Polish referendum on EU membership.

LOOKING AHEAD

Looking ahead is not the easiest thing to do and our attempts will be modest. The first 10 years of post-communist transformation have brought very many surprises across the region and it is clear that transformation processes are far from complete if indeed the notion has any sense at all. We have seen great 'successes' (Russian and Czech privatisations come to mind) turn into famous failures. There have been financial crises and currency collapses. If inflation in its suppressed form always existed in the centrally planned economies, the post-1989 move to the market brought some new market-type infections, and apart from deepening inequalities, unemployment was probably the worst problem to be faced. In Russia and most of the CIS, economies whose importance for Poland should not be overlooked, GDP growth has stubbornly refused decisively to pick up. Perhaps throughout the region the clearest success has been the easiest one to achieve, the simple release of latent entrepreneurial energy, the release, as it might have been called in an earlier period, of 'hidden reserves'. Meanwhile, perhaps one of the greatest mistakes in transformation was the early determination (encouraged by a prevailing, but now changed, climate in the West) to run down the role of the state in shaping, not just the business environment, but developments in key economic sectors (agriculture, regions) as well as in education and R&D.

No one is certain what kind of capitalism is emerging in transformation economies but most agree that deepening social and regional differentiation is one of its defining aspects and it must be reasonable to ask if this process may not become dangerous and to some extent destructive? A striking feature of post-communism was what some have called 'transformation recession', a fate from which many formerly Soviet-type economies had yet to escape even as the 1990s drew to a close. Poland was luckier. The country recovered more quickly and no doubt very particular circumstances helped.

(Most) Polish eyes are now set on EU accession as the next major step in a comprehensive social and economic remodelling that has proceeded in the 1990s at a great speed. It is apparent however, even within this collection of essays, that the views of (mainly Polish) social scientists differ considerably on major issues, including the likely impact of EU membership (will the investment inducing aspects of membership of a premier international business club outweigh what some of our authors perceive to be the undesirable added costs of its mandatory social welfare provision?). Perhaps the pace of system change is also becoming just too fast given the state of the social fabric, as Wnuk-Lipiński seemed ready to believe after the poor social reception of the four 1999 reforms in local government, pensions, health and education?

So what about a highly speculative look into the future?

First, macroeconomic balance may prove difficult to maintain. Poland needs fast growth for 'real convergence' with the EU but has still high inflation and a disturbingly weak current account balance. Those dangers are compounded by the complication of high unemployment just as a demographic bulge brings a surge of new young workers on to the labour market. The acceleration in FDI in the late 1990s will most probably continue and help to soften some of those problems. It will also speed up economic restructuring and lock Polish trade into the production profile of the multinational company. Another factor, a potential source of macro imbalance, is that political pressures in an extended election period (presidential then parliamentary) may lead to a weakening of fiscal control.

Second, the trend towards decentralisation will deepen; regions will grow in importance, although not at equal pace, becoming more varied across indicators of economic performance – both a source of strength but also possibly of new tensions. Overarching the regional issue is the rural/agricultural question where, with EU assistance, it is not hard to imagine a comprehensive strategy for modernisation emerging.

Third, turning to Poland's emerging capitalism, one aspect is its highly unequal income distribution, potentially a source of economic, social and political problems; another is its 'cronyism', by no means an oligarchic capitalism of the Moscow variety, but one that many observers believed lacked the transparency the market mechanism should have.

Fourth, there is a fair chance that Polish political life will cease to be dominated by confessions of faith with regard to August 1980 or the events of 1989 and that 'interests' may come to dominate 'values' in making political choices.

Lastly (and here the editors risk all), Brussels will yield to pressure on firming an EU entry date in 2001 and Poland will join the Union in 2005 but remain outside EMU until 2010 when sectoral restructuring is substantially complete – unless of course major upsets occur in the meantime!

PART I

Political Economy, Society and Politics

2. Lessons from the Polish transition

Marek Belka

INTRODUCTION

After the first ten years of transition from socialist central planning to a market economy in Poland enough experience has been accumulated to permit us to synthesise and draw conclusions for our own future and for other reforming countries of the region. Poland has been frequently quoted, particularly in the 1990s, as an example of successful reform. High economic growth rates and a general consistency of economic policy earned us a reputation as one of the front-runners in the process of transition. Both statistical data and political facts, such as Poland's admission to the OECD in 1996, NATO membership in 1999 and the beginning of the accession negotiations with the EU, confirm this positive assessment. More importantly, political and economic changes in recent years seem to have commanded the broad support of Polish society, as shown in virtually all opinion polls concerning its attitudes towards the market economy, democracy and Poland's integration with Western institutions. Notwithstanding the more complicated economic and social situation that developed in 1999–2000 transformation in Poland is an indisputable success. This is the general assumption underlying the remarks we present below.

TEN YEARS OF TRANSITION: STYLISED FACTS

Early 1990s starting point

The starting point for reforms was in many respects highly unfavourable. The Polish economy suffered from all the typical deficiencies of central planning: it had deeply distorted structures, including prices, pervasive shortages, massive misallocation of resources and state enterprises lacked inventiveness. On top of this, and contrary to most of its neighbours in the region, Poland inherited from the command economy a huge foreign debt and high inflation, approaching, in late 1989, hyperinflation. In sum, Poland entered transition not only as a stagnant, but also a destabilised economy. Due to the unsuccessful attempts to reform the previous system, dating back to the mid-1950s, and repeated with a surprising regularity every 10 years or so, the government had no credibility in terms of economic policy making and implementation. This added to a deep sense of demoralisation among both the managers and the workers in state firms. The task of economic reform appeared, in 1989–90, to be paralysingly difficult.

On the one hand, the miserable state of economic affairs combined with the popular enthusiasm over the fall of the communist rule created a unique opportunity for a radical change. The people were ready to make sacrifices and accept whatever the *Solidarność*-dominated government of late 1989 would propose. Political opposition was virtually absent, branch lobbies were temporarily silenced, trade unions had lost their usual social role, and the external environment was unequivocally positive. On the other hand, courage, determination and vision, coupled with a minimum initial knowledge of what in fact had never before been tried by anyone was provided by the team of reformers led by the then deputy prime minister Leszek Balcerowicz. A golden opportunity existed but, unlike some other countries and as may have happened in Poland, it was not lost.

The January 1990 stabilisation package

The dual challenge of the new economic policy was to stabilise the economy and start building the institutions of a market economy. The January 1990 stabilisation package is usually associated with what was later labelled 'shock therapy' or the Polish 'big bang'. The package contained liberalisation measures, which in fact created the foundations of a market economy, and fairly routine stabilisation policies aimed at equilibrating the economy. Most prices were immediately set free, rationing of goods and foreign exchange was eliminated, the złoty was made internally convertible. The state enterprise suddenly found that individual tax concessions (one of the most perverse characteristics of the late socialist economy) and most subsidies were done away with. State budget expenditure was reduced and monetary policy dramatically tightened. A new restrictive tax on excess wage growth was designed as a back-up measure to strengthen fiscal austerity and protect the embattled enterprises from the wage demands of their own workers. The fragile convertibility of the currency was supported by an up front 50% złoty devaluation and foreign financial assistance provided in a special stabilisation fund. The exchange rate was fixed against the $US at a rate that the authorities promised to maintain for half a year in a move designed to rebuild confidence in the national currency and strengthen the credibility of economic policy.

The main goal of these harsh measures was to reduce the extent of macroeconomic disequilibrium as reflected in inflation and the state budget deficit. The first two years, 1990–91, were marked by falling output and national income as well as by high 'corrective' inflation, the latter the result of price liberalisation. Real wages (as measured statistically) were reduced by more than 20%, and unemployment – a phenomenon unknown in a centrally planned economy – appeared and quickly exceeded 10% of the labour force. Kornai labelled the experience 'transformation recession'.

These were extremely difficult years as the reality turned out to be much gloomier than the rather optimistic official scenarios. Only later did we realise that the Polish recession was the mildest among all transition countries (see Rapacki in this volume for the relevant data). It was moreover partially a statistical illusion (as redundant output was eliminated alongside a scaling down of excessive inventories and the overuse of energy and transportation services and so on). High unemployment, however, was for real. So was the high inflation that proved to be much more difficult to stem than we all expected. Most importantly this first stage of transition produced extremely positive results in three respects. First, basic price distortions were eliminated permitting the market to send correct signals to firms and households. The three most critical categories of prices (interest rates, the foreign exchange rate and energy prices) were set at realistic levels leading to consequential adjustments to all other prices. Sensible price relations allowed sensible decision making on resource allocation. Second, złoty convertibility was introduced and maintained. A lengthy process of rebuilding confidence in the national currency was initiated and the dominant position of the US dollar was undermined. This in fact was the real opening of the Polish economy, a factor stimulating an unprecedented growth of newly established private firms. Third, a radical reduction of the scale of subsidisation coupled with the beginning of privatisation changed the philosophy of the way of doing business. Even though most large and medium-size companies were state-owned at that time their managers started to realise that without proper adjustment they would not survive in the market. In sum, the greatest achievement of the first phase of transition was the fact that the economy became manageable and people started to react to the instruments of economic policy in a predictable manner.

The enterprise sector response

The success of 'shock therapy' depended very much on the reaction of large state-owned enterprises (SOEs), on how fast and how deeply they would adjust to the new situation. Many observers were afraid that without immediate privatisation these companies would quickly degenerate, their assets would be squandered on a massive scale, a 'business as usual' attitude would be adopted and prevail and then collapse would soon follow. At best many thought that

SOEs would engage in barter trade, extending to each other unofficial commercial credit so temporarily overcoming the liquidity crunch, but making the ultimate industrial crisis more serious or forcing the government to carry out a big bail-out operation. In consequence, the whole stabilisation programme would be derailed.

The microeconomic dimension of the early transition proved, however, to be quite different from those dark expectations. The January 1990 'big bang' was indeed a huge blow for existing companies. It came both from the demand and supply sides. Those particularly hard hit were traditional exporters to the USSR and Comecon markets as so-called 'protocol trade' collapsed entirely. On the whole, the enterprise sector managed to survive 1990 quite well. More surprisingly, companies registered record profits, due to the inflated value of their foreign currency deposits and artificially low (historical) value of inventories accumulated in earlier years. This was reflected in unexpectedly high tax revenues and paper profits that could not last for long. One danger here was that managers might be misled by these signals as to the true state of their enterprises. Moreover managers might also be misled about the seriousness of the government's commitment to reform. One has to remember that the credibility of economic policy, particularly of any reform attempts, was still to be established.

The immediate reaction of most SOEs, in typical monopolist fashion, was to cut output and raise prices. Those who were able tried to repay outstanding bank credits because the level of interest rates became prohibitive overnight. The financial situation of most enterprises deteriorated by the end of 1990 and further administrative price increases in January 1991 together with the final collapse of Comecon markets delivered a decisive blow. The industrial sector fell into a full-fledged crisis, with consumer goods producers, traditional suppliers of the Soviet market and companies with heavy credit burdens from the past suffering most. Even if they did not react immediately, SOEs began adjusting to the new situation relatively early. Virtually all aspects of their functioning underwent changes. Internal organisation was modified: marketing and sales departments were created and reinforced, redundant assets were disposed of gradually, unused machinery sold to the new private firms, free space rented out, social assets closed down or separated from main activities, the excess labour force was laid off. Enterprises had to rebuild domestic distribution channels as the state wholesale network was the first to go bankrupt due to high interest rates.

One of most serious challenges was to deal with the accumulation of overdue payables and receivables, potentially leading to a massive payments jam and generating a barter economy. It is rightly believed that the consistent macroeconomic policy that was pursued forced firms to control their finances and prevent leads and lags from reaching unmanageable proportions. In my opinion this was one of the most convincing pieces of evidence showing that meaningful restructuring was taking place in Polish state-owned enterprises in that period. Another was a successful reorientation of exports from the former Comecon to the EU countries (see Blazyca, in this volume). All in all, SOEs did much to change from being producers and insatiable users of inputs (as in socialism) to become sellers and asset managers in a very short period of time.

Restructuring was thus very broad, covering a majority of firms and most dimensions of their activities. However, it was also rather shallow, not involving the deeper technological change that was badly needed and, by definition, not yet touching on changes in ownership. Whatever adjustments they made, without privatisation state firms remained virtually incapable of attracting sufficient external financing and gaining indispensable flexibility. Restructuring was mostly of a 'defensive' character, to use a term coined by Wendy Carlin, as opposed to the strategic response that would enable them to prosper in a longer time horizon.

One could legitimately ask, why in the absence of massive privatisation, did state firms bother to adjust at all? Two factors seem to have been decisive: the consistent and increasingly credible macroeconomic policy and the promise that privatisation *would* happen. The first factor reduced hopes for any automatic bail-out, even for large state companies, as illustrated early on by numerous near-bankruptcies in the textile sector. Without making an effort to adjust to the new circumstances the chances of survival were limited. The second factor made the acting managers think about their reputation and its role in shaping their future professional careers. Thus a powerful mechanism of industrial restructuring was set in motion at an early stage.

Banks in transition[1]

An important dimension at the microeconomic level of transformation was the evolution of bank behaviour. An important concern regarding the state banks, parallel to that of state enterprises, was that they would carelessly extend credit to defunct companies either due to lack of expertise or through a certain kind of conspiracy or 'cronyism' among nomenklatura managers in banks and non-financial institutions. No matter how exotic these allegations sound now they seemed to pose a serious problem for the early reformers. To strengthen credit controls, lending ceilings for individual banks were introduced and the Ministry of Finance encouraged banks to concentrate on the private sector. The latter measure proved however to be rather naive as many newly established small private firms turned out to be too weak to repay their obligations and banks accumulated a large volume of bad loans not only related to the large SOEs (as feared) but also (perhaps more unexpectedly) to the new private firms. Indeed the banking sector's health deteriorated significantly in 1990–91. The share of poor credits (lost and doubtful) in all bank credit outstanding climbed to 30–40% in some of the most important banks. A full-scale crisis was in sight. Moreover, some studies (most notably Pinto, Belka and Krajewski) showed a negative correlation between firms' dependence on bank credit and their profitability. 'Good' enterprises tried to avoid external financing because it was too expensive while 'bad' enterprises had to 'double the stakes' to stay in business. A massive market collapse looked highly likely.

Luckily however the reaction of the authorities was proper and timely. In late 1991 a programme of bank privatisation was announced. At the same time a bank restructuring scheme was designed. It provided banks with additional capital in the form of special bonds and required them, in return, to clean up their assets portfolio. Banks were helped to establish new departments dealing with these issues. In dealing with the bad debt problem they could follow one of several routes. They could (a) sell their assets on the market; (b) initiate bankruptcy procedures for insolvent debtors; or (c) initiate a so-called 'bank conciliatory procedure'. The latter permitted an embattled but prospectively viable enterprise to obtain cancellation or rescheduling of its debt upon presentation of a sensible and realistic restructuring programme. The scheme probably helped some manufacturing firms to survive the worst times although analysts' views on this differ. That said, no one has ever denied that the 'Law on Financial Restructuring' was beneficial for the banks. It helped increase their capital base, added new expertise and, most important of all, changed their attitude towards creditors. In fact, Polish banks earned a reputation of becoming overly conservative rather than lenient in their relations with enterprises. The result, after 10 years of transition, is that the Polish banking sector may still be undercapitalised, fragmented and not sufficiently modern and cost-efficient, but it is certainly not haunted by bad loans and opaque ownership structures. In consequence, the privatisation of state banks proceeded smoothly and the most prestigious financial institutions have competed fiercely to acquire shares in their equity.

Institution building

The dominant position of *private ownership* – a mainstay of a market economy – was the first institutional aspect that had to be established and strengthened. The expansion of the new private sector was made possible by the radical liberalisation of business activity (with freedom of entry) that happened even in 1989 but was stimulated further by the abolition of the state monopoly of foreign trade and by the introduction of złoty convertibility. In fact it transpired that this grass-roots privatisation became the most powerful engine of growth for the whole decade. The privatisation of state-owned enterprises turned out to be much more difficult and time-consuming. Indeed, after 10 years, Poland remained only halfway through this process. We return to this later.

It was understood early on that the *financial system* would be decisive for a proper functioning of a resource allocating market mechanism. The pre-transition mono-bank was broken down as early as in 1988 and 'commercial' banks created. More important, independent bank supervision was established and located in the structure of the National Bank of Poland, whose independence from the government was declared and gradually strengthened (also in the new Constitution of 1997). Very soon, important auxiliary institutions, such as a clearing house, a national register of collaterals and others, were created. In parallel, the capital market was developed. The Warsaw Stock Exchange (WSE) was inaugurated in 1991, and the Securities Commission, a watchdog of the market, began to perform its duties. This paved the way for a stepwise, orderly expansion of a capital market that became capable of absorbing new companies and new money market instruments. The rather tough regulatory framework might have at times slowed down its quantitative growth but saved it from many disruptions so characteristic of newly born institutions of this kind.

The *tax system* in the command economy was based on a complicated turnover tax levied on the sales of (state) enterprises. Due to its high degree of non-neutrality it was entirely inconsistent with the exigencies of a market economy. The rates of turnover tax were randomly differentiated. It may have also been very sensitive to the swings in economic activity. In 1992–93 a new system was introduced: personal income tax (PIT) and corporate income tax (CIT) were put in place in 1992 and VAT in mid-1993. Both income taxes were relatively simple with a moderate top marginal rate of 40% so that the collection rate was high from the very beginning. The newly introduced PIT was very comprehensive, the standard deduction was minimal, the lowest rate rather high (20%) and virtually all incomes, including social benefits, were taxable. Because the pre-transition period's flat 20% wage tax was replaced by a moderately progressive personal tax, lower income earners were protected from a net income reduction and the entire tax burden increase was placed on the better-off. The PIT thus turned out to be easily socially acceptable. Poland, with the notable exception of farmers, became a normal taxpayers' society.

Privatisation

Privatisation was immediately declared to be one of the highest priorities of transition. It could proceed basically in two ways: through the expansion of new private firms (so called grass-roots or bottom-up privatisation) and through the disposal of state assets (or top-down privatisation). Liberalisation of economic activity, stabilisation and convertibility of the domestic currency, accompanied by lifting of travel restrictions to the West, created favourable conditions for a real explosion of private entrepreneurship. Selling off state companies turned out to be much more difficult. In mid-1990, the Law on Privatisation of state-owned enterprises was passed providing a broad spectrum of methods of disposing of state assets. To win the support of trade unions 10% (later increased to 15%) of equity stock was to be distributed free of charge among the employees of the privatised company. SOEs could be sold to foreign and domestic investors, could be bought out by employees and management or could be subject to an initial public offering (IPO) on the Warsaw Stock Exchange. The Law on Financial Restructuring of Banks and Enterprises of 1993 allowed firms' debts to be swapped for equity. Finally, in 1994 a limited mass privatisation programme was initiated via the National Investment Funds (NIFs) experiment.

Disposal of state assets proved to be a technically difficult and politically loaded process. On top of this the demand for Polish companies on the part of foreign investors turned out to be low at the beginning of the decade. 'Case by case' privatisation is always time-consuming even in the most favourable economic and political circumstances. In Poland, powerful labour unions often resisted an ownership change in 'their' companies. Moreover the political will to act vigorously was erratic and sometimes weak (particularly under the governments of Jan Olszewski in early 1992 and Waldemar Pawlak in 1993–94). In sum, privatisation was treated by many as a fight for power. In consequence the privatisation process was marked by the following features:

- it was dominated by so-called 'insider privatisation' either in the form of employee leasing schemes in smaller and medium-sized SOEs or management-dominated buyouts of foreign trade organisations, many of which were transformed into industrial conglomerates (for example, the electrical engineering trading concern Elektrim, and the metals trader Impexmetal);
- there was only a small number of outside investors, especially foreign, in early privatisation;
- there was a virtual lack of privatisation in 'strategic' industries due to political sensitivity, the often ambivalent behaviour of managers, the resistance of special interest groups (for example, in the oil industry) and the moderate interest of foreign investors in the early 1990s.

The slow pace of privatisation, or more correctly, its slower than needed and expected pace, resulted in a more limited microeconomic restructuring, sufficient only to carry a rather brisk revival from the early transition recession but leaving the Polish enterprise sector vulnerable to external shocks and lagging in its efforts to adjust to EU standards. This critical assessment should, however, be supplemented by the following observations:

- the temptation to use 'shortcuts', that is, doubtful forms of mass privatisation, was largely avoided, thus leaving ownership and corporate governance structures relatively sound and transparent;
- the properly designed and regulated capital market could in many instances be used as a channel facilitating ownership changes in a number of ways. It enabled employee-dominated companies to go public and acquire new

investors. It permitted IPO-privatised SOEs to move to outsiders' control and for NIFs to become full-fledged investment funds;

- the scale of actual privatisation is largely underestimated, because the majority of ailing SOEs, before formal liquidation or bankruptcy, tended to dispose of much of their assets (space, machinery, labour) that stimulated the expansion of newly established private firms.

Thus it is tenable to say that Poland managed to avoid major mistakes in the privatisation process. We may, it is true, have lost many opportunities, but acceleration is possible when political and economic circumstances allow.

An economic cycle in transition?

Business activity in Poland after 1989 can roughly be divided into four phases: *transformation recession* in 1990–92, the *early revival* of mid-1992 to late 1994, *acceleration* between 1994 and mid-1998 and subsequent *slowdown*.

The *transformation recession* resulted from the introduction of the stabilisation package of 1990, followed by the collapse of Comecon trade. Recorded GDP fell by around 18%, which turned out to be the least in the region, but real wages (again statistically recorded) decreased by 30% and the unemployment rate climbed from what was perceived as 0% to over 10%. Households were the first to take a blow while enterprises felt the pinch after some delay as they fell back on the 'shallow' reserves inherited from the previous system but these were used up, in most cases, within a year. Bank credit contracted drastically and investment was duly reduced. For many it seemed to be the end of the world, but also the beginning of a painful but ultimately, in many cases, rewarding adjustment process. Ten years later I tend to consider that the first two years represented a huge 'cleansing' operation. Most price distortions were eliminated or reduced but other structural imbalances survived as some important industries managed to build institutional shields from market competition (some recentralisation occurred, import tariffs were raised, softer budget constraints in the form of tax arrears appeared, and so on).

The period of *early revival* started in the second quarter of 1992. Manufacturing industry rebounded first followed with a considerable lag by construction. Almost nobody believed the revival was sustainable. First, investment expenditure stagnated. Second, there was a fear that growth was fuelled by the expansion of inter-firm arrears, the infamous 'payments logjam'. With the benefit of hindsight we can say that 'stagnation' in investment masked positive adjustment in the enterprise sector. Early growth was based on rearrangement of existing assets and some marginal new modernisation. It should be remembered that state-owned firms entered transition with excesses of largely redundant space, working capital, machinery and labour. The issue was thus how to rationalise – rather than expand. Investment outlays in new construction were conspicuously absent. As to inter-firm payments arrears, it turned out that credible macroeconomic policy convinced the SOEs that bankruptcy, or at least financial trouble and not an easy bail-out, was the typical consequence that non-viable debtors could expect. As a result, the extent of the inter-firm payment arrears problem remained largely under control and never assumed a scale dangerous for the economy.

Growth acceleration over 1995–98 produced rates of GDP expansion in the range of 6–7% annually. Poland entered a phase of intensive modernisation. Real investment outlays grew regularly at rates surpassing 20% per annum, albeit from a relatively low level. After the final resolution of foreign debt rescheduling (London Club in 1994) FDI started flowing in (see Blazyca in this volume). For the first time in decades Poland regained a status as an attractive location for investment. It became widely regarded as one of the most promising emerging markets in the world and a leader of post-communist transformation. Growth was accompanied by falling inflation and unemployment. Rising consumption fuelled optimism. Success however brought a certain degree of complacency as the urgency of a tough restructuring effort and quick privatisation became somewhat overshadowed by the flow of good macroeconomic news. The bright picture was spoiled a little by signs of a widening trade deficit. Mitigated by a positive balance of cross-border trade the current account deficit looked much better but nevertheless touched 4% of GDP in late 1996. Real appreciation of the złoty coupled with a strong demand for imported investment goods inevitably resulted in a growing current account deficit. Monetary restrictions and budgetary discipline helped arrest its growth to just 3.1% of GDP in 1997 but two years later it expanded to over 7%. Clearly, external disequilibrium needs to be cured before the situation becomes unsustainable.

Growth slowdown took place in late 1998 but GDP for the whole year grew by a healthy 4.8% before decelerating further in 1999 to just 4.1%. It is difficult to say whether this was fully the consequence of the Russian crisis and the subsequent loss of export markets in the rouble-related area or whether the 1998 macroeconomic policy stance (aimed at cooling the economy) was the reason. With the impact of Russia largely digested by late 1999, the Polish economy found itself in a delicate position. The current account deficit was clearly not decreasing and needed to be tackled by effective macroeconomic management. In this regard tight monetary policy is easy to use but may also be self-defeating as high interest rates attract portfolio investments, pushing the exchange rate of the domestic currency upwards, causing the current account deficit to grow further, precisely the opposite of what was, and is, needed. A proper response hinges on fiscal adjustment – that is, on strengthening budgetary discipline. This is, however, close to impossible in a period of dramatic structural reforms reinforced by equally sweeping tax reform.

Looking at the experience of other successful transition countries, especially Hungary and the Czech Republic, one can notice certain similarities that suggest a common pattern, a *sui generis* transition cycle. Market-orientated reforms in these countries have two linked but conceptually separate dimensions: macroeconomic stabilisation and microeconomic adjustment. Both aspects of transformation are mutually reinforcing. Macro stability provides an environment of a hard budget constraint that is necessary to stimulate micro adjustment. Privatisation and restructuring of enterprises and institutional reform provides for economic dynamism and competitiveness. Lack of it can derail stabilisation efforts. The key issue is to keep both developments time-consistent. It is difficult, as by nature microeconomic adjustment takes more time and always lags behind macro stabilisation. Even worse, the more successful a national economy is in terms of fighting inflation, restoring fiscal stability and so forth, the more attractive it becomes for foreign investors, the more pronounced is the appreciation pressure on domestic currency. The pressure on domestic companies grows the more effective macroeconomic management is and, paradoxically, the more efficient they are in restructuring themselves. There is thus a constant disequilibrating force that acts to derail the transition process. No matter how fast we privatise, a setback may always occur. Hungary is a good example. This is of course not an argument against fast-track privatisation and restructuring, but a reminder that transition is not a smooth process. To attenuate a possible crisis two things are needed. First, a realistic exchange rate policy, or more generally, realistic policy targets should be set. Second, transparency in policy making should be considered a highest priority. Hiding problems will always backfire (as in the Czech republic).

'Four reforms' at the end of the 1990s

The end of the 1990s was marked by important reforms in the neglected sphere of social services financed predominantly from the budget. The so-called 'budgetary sector' to a large extent survived as a non-market enclave with characteristic immanent inefficiency and stagnation. High cost and poor quality services, a feature that prevailed throughout the Polish economy before transition and which the 'productive' sector gradually overcame, largely continued to dominate the public health service, education and social security. On top of this, a bold decision was made to promote an administrative reform that provided for introducing a new intermediate level of local government (the *powiat*) and promised a significant decentralisation of the state functions (see Góra, chapter 10 of this book, for a comprehensive review).

Reform of the *pension system* in Poland boils down to replacing a traditional state-run, monopolistic pay-as-you-go (PAYG) system by a multi-pillar scheme borrowing from best international experience, notably that of Sweden and Chile. The reform was launched in 1999 following years of preparatory work. It has three pillars: a defined-contribution pay-as-you-go first pillar; a mandatory defined-contribution, privately managed second pillar; and a voluntary employee pension plan in the third pillar. Its introduction was accompanied by attempts to purge from the old system sectoral privileges and all sorts of special treatment, privileges enjoyed by more than a third of the Polish labour force. The pension reform, it is hoped, will bring many positive consequences both for the insured and for the public finances. The nature of the labour market should change in some important respects, as a strong link between contributions and benefits is introduced. The capital market will also benefit by the establishment of pension funds and, hopefully, by an increase in the propensity to save, or at least by an increase in the supply of long-term savings. The reform entails significant fiscal cost, as employees switching from the state system to the pension funds divert part of their social security contributions to the latter institutions. The resultant deficit in the social insurance fund (FUS) in the order of 1–1.5% of GDP throughout the first 10–12 years has to be covered by the state budget although this deficit is not inflationary in the same sense as other public expenditures. The bulk of this will have to be financed from privatisation proceeds in the coming decade. All in all, pensions reform seems to be well designed and should have a positive impact on the overall functioning of the Polish economy. On top of the expected cost (non-inflationary as we stress) the implementation of the reform resulted in painful slippages. It turned out that the state social insurance office (ZUS) responsible for the (by 2000 already deeply reformed) first pillar of the system was not able to introduce a new information system on time. In consequence it failed to collect contributions in 1999 to the order of 1–1.5% of GDP, endangering the entire fiscal position of the public sector.

The Polish *health system* has long suffered from many serious diseases: low quality of services, cost explosion, underfunding from public sources, waste, inefficiency and corruption. From the purely fiscal point of view, the complete lack of discipline in managing public resources by medical units was probably the most dangerous aspect. Taking only a narrowly financial point of view, the reform of the health sector consisted of two main elements. First, most of the medical units were transferred (following cancellation of their accumulated past debts) to local government structures that were supposed to take over control and responsibility for their future obligations. Second, regional health administration institutions were established (*kasy chorych,* similar to German *krankenkassen*, a 'health insurance fund' is probably the best English translation) that are supposed to contract out medical services for the insured citizens. These institutions become thus intermediaries between patients and health units. Their role is to distribute scarce resources coming from personal income taxes and supplementary budget funding in the most efficient way among the most productive service-providers. Health reform is certainly very difficult from a logistical point of view. Most problems arise however from its social consequences. If the cost explosion is to be contained some hospitals should close, redundant personnel should be laid off and carelessness in managing expenditures eradicated. The doctors and nurses are not happy with the reform, especially since resources are limited and wages cannot grow too much. Uncertainty prevails about what will happen as health funds' payments arrears emerge, with the possible bankruptcies of medical units, not to mention health service privatisation.

Education reform is probably the least spectacular social reform, but nevertheless is one that is crucially important for the country's future. Its aim is to improve the curricula, adjusting the education path to the changing situation on the labour market (particularly replacing the traditional vocational secondary schools with more generally orientated educational institutions), lowering the obligatory school age from 7 to 6 years, and introducing performance-linked incentives into the teachers' pay. The immediate budgetary impact of educational reform is limited and needs no further elaboration here. What has to be observed however is that, as in the health sector, the changes here aim at bringing labour relations closer to the exigencies of a market system, at stimulating rationality and innovation. Social tensions are thus a natural and inevitable consequence.

Decentralisation of state functions began in Poland as early as 1990 when first-level local government units, the communes (*gminas*), were created. Later, numerous functions (for example administration of primary education) were added to their responsibilities, along with additional funding and big cities were entrusted with a certain autonomy. In 1999, two other local government levels, *powiat* and *województwo*, or county and region, were created. They received some specific financial resources, mainly shares in general tax revenues, and were allocated precisely defined responsibilities. The tendency to strengthen local government is very favourable for the 'activism' of local communities (important particularly in view of future EU membership), expansion of civil society, entrenching democracy and political stabilisation in general. It is also hoped that decentralisation will eventually result in more efficient use of public resources and in a better quality of public service. In the shorter run it may however cause serious problems for financial discipline. Local governments are desperately short of money (if only in their subjective assessment) and will try to acquire new funds either through incurring debts on the capital market and/or by squeezing more resources from the central budget. Administrative reform, very much as other institutional changes initiated in recent years, is a good investment in the future of Poland but its financial cost carries a destabilising potential for fiscal equilibrium. The financial consequences of these 'four reforms' (there are more – including coal mining, railways restructuring, reform of the judiciary) are serious and pose a difficult dilemma that government(s) will have to face in the coming years. This is a necessity to reconcile the need to maintain, or rather continuously strengthen, financial discipline as reflected in a reduced public sector deficit, and find resources to co-finance a comprehensive modernisation effort as in the four institutional reforms described above.

SOURCES OF RELATIVE SUCCESS

Poland remains a poor country, at least compared to the EU. Per capita GDP in the year 2000 did not exceed 40% of the average West European level (in PPP terms). The international competitiveness of Polish firms is low although improving. Export potential is limited. The infrastructure is better but is still underdeveloped in many respects. More than a quarter of the working population is employed in agriculture. Ten years of rapid change cannot undo decades, or even centuries, of turbulent history, backwardness and poverty. On the other hand, resolute reform efforts and clear EU membership prospects make Poland one of the most promising 'emerging markets', an attractive location for foreign investment and an increasingly important regional player. Beyond doubt Poland is one of the most successful transition countries. The success however is relative as it is increasingly frequently measured against the achievements of the more recent EU entrants like Portugal, Spain, Greece or Ireland. From the 'transition' class Poland graduated to the class 'EU prospects' and its further progress will be verified not by the distance from the slow-reforming countries of Eastern Europe but by the smoothness of integration with the EU.

The Polish transition success is, in my view, due to *five* main factors: the success of shock therapy; good relations with the international organisations; Polish pragmatism; social sensitivity; and EU entry ambitions. For most commentators the famous 1990 'shock therapy' or the early stabilisation package implemented by Leszek Balcerowicz was the key source of subsequent positive developments in the Polish economy. I share this view entirely, but let me elaborate on its significance. First, as noted earlier, it was a huge 'cleansing' operation. Most price distortions were eliminated and the rules of the economic game were abruptly changed. Second, it was an attempt to begin restoring the credibility of economic policy, or more broadly, of the state itself. One must remember that Poland entered transition as a highly destabilised economy, the result, among others, of numerous failed attempts to reform the socialist system. In consequence, SOE managers had learned how to survive 'reforms' in the past and nothing short of a 'shock' could convince them about the seriousness of the government. Third, the 1990 package set out a very forceful and comprehensive agenda of market reforms, that no one later dared challenge let alone reverse. Thus, from the very onset of transition, Polish reformers did not lose time looking for a 'third way'; instead they introduced measures and solutions tested in advanced countries.

The relations between the international financial institutions and the Polish authorities were very good throughout the whole period of transition. Poland was always considered in the 1990s to be the 'best pupil' in the class, a faithful follower of the IMF-tailored stabilisation programme, and eventually one of the few examples of the success of IMF-inspired adjustment strategy. There is no doubt that international assistance and policy advice played a significant and positive role in the implementation of Polish reforms. It must be added, however, that the most simplistic foreign advice, sometimes ascribed to the IMF, the famous recipe, 'privatise, liberalise and fight inflation – the rest will be taken care off by market mechanism', was in practice largely ignored. Mass privatisation was reduced to a manageable scale, capital flows liberalisation was phased in gradually and an overly ambitious policy of a fixed exchange rate regime was replaced early on by a pre-announced crawling peg. A carefully sequenced process of institution building was initiated. As a result the newly emerging market structures had some time to mature and the embattled companies some time to adjust to the new situation.

The early reformers in Poland, alongside Leszek Balcerowicz, rightly earned a reputation of being liberal and consistently pursuing free market solutions. They avoided any search for a 'third way' and never used the argument of 'unique conditions' in Poland. At the same time, the policies applied were quite frequently much more pragmatic than one might expect from their ultra-liberal rhetoric. Credit ceilings were installed in 1990, as nobody believed that (state) commercial banks would immediately start applying efficiency criteria to their credit activity, a tax on excessive growth of wages (the so-called *popiwek*) was introduced to protect firms from fast growing wage demands. A Law on Financial Restructuring of Banks and Enterprises was prepared and passed in early 1993 when it became evident that without help from the state a widespread banking crisis was in sight. These were measures that could not be considered to be entirely in line with liberal orthodoxy but helped to strengthen the implementation of a liberal strategy. Policies are always more pragmatic than programmes and declarations, so my observation may seem almost banal. However, pragmatism can sometimes be dangerous, particularly when the policy agenda remains vague and the politicians unconvinced and unconvincing. Then, pragmatism can degenerate into opportunism. This was not the case in Poland, where clear vision and a pragmatic day-to-day attitude generated a blend of policies that worked.

Shock therapy applied in 1990 brought severe hardship to the population. Increased job insecurity and falling real wages were only partially compensated for by a better supply of goods and services of higher quality. Those people approaching retirement age and workers in 'single-company towns' and rural areas were particularly hard hit. The early transition is often described, particularly by its critics, as totally ignoring the social consequences of reforms and completely disregarding the precarious situation of the poor and weak. The patience and restraint shown in Poland is thus explained only by the unique political circumstances after the fall of communism. This story does not capture, in my opinion, one important factor, which I call the 'Jacek Kuroń factor'. Jacek Kuroń, a legendary figure of the anti-communist opposition, became employment minister in the first Solidarity-dominated government from 1989. Understanding the hardships of transformation he managed to introduce some measures to ameliorate them, notably early retirement benefits and more generous indexation of social security benefits. In fact when we look at the statistical record of the 1990s we find that the share of social expenditures in the state budget increased sharply at the beginning of the decade. Equally important Kuroń was skilful in using the media to communicate with society, explaining the essence of the changes and trying to project the prospects of a better life in a market-orientated, democratic society. His policies often diluted the necessary budget discipline that Balcerowicz was adamant to keep. Little wonder that he was not a favourite of the 'economists' in the team of reformers. With the benefit of hindsight, and looking at the bad experience of some countries in the region, the consideration for social needs that Kuroń added to the transformation process in Poland may well have strengthened (and not weakened) the reform process. This important factor is almost uniformly overlooked in the assessments of Polish reforms.

From the very beginning of transition Poland declared its strategic goal to become a member of the European Union. An association agreement, the Europe Agreement, was signed as early as 1991 (ratified in 1993). It provided, among other things, for an asymmetric trade liberalisation, modest financial assistance in the form of PHARE, and most important, an obligation for Poland to adjust all new legal regulations to EU standards. No matter how naive it sounded to our Western partners, we considered it a first step towards membership. All of the Polish political elite and a vast majority of the population stood firmly behind the idea of joining the Union as early as possible. The reasons for that clear orientation were more geopolitical (national security) and, in my view, instinctive reactions rather than purely economic. We wanted to be a part of a stable, democratic and prosperous world. The question of the accession to the unified market was secondary. So was the perspective of financial assistance. Of course priorities change over time, the understanding of the consequences of EU membership deepens, and popular support dwindles somewhat as the evident costs become visible. Nevertheless after 10 years of transition this pro-European orientation emerges as one of the key sources of success, a key engine driving the system forward in a positive manner. Here a number of features are worth highlighting. First, the association agreement with its *acquis communautaire* related provisions may well reduce national sovereignity in economic policy *but* it also reduces our freedom to commit serious mistakes. It has served as a guideline for reforms. Second, it has mobilised a political will to reform, helped stem natural resistance to change and increased the level of policy discourse in the country. Third, intensified contacts with the EU provided a massive inflow of policy-related know-how, and last, but by no means least, association status finally (after some years of hesitation) resulted in a significant increase in the FDI inflow into Poland.

LESSONS FROM TRANSITION: SOME NON-ORTHODOX REMARKS

The experience of the last decade both in Poland and in other countries in the region shows that transition is an inherently unstable process. This is not only an exercise in building and rebuilding institutions, in changing our behaviour and our mindset, but also in catching up with the most advanced societies. A technically and socially difficult reform process has thus to be accompanied by fast economic growth. I have previously pointed to the complex linkage between the macroeconomic and microeconomic dimensions of transition, between the exigencies of equilibrium and growth. We have therefore to be prepared for setbacks and recurrent imbalances and should not expect the process of transformation to be smooth. Having this in mind we have to avoid setting over-ambitious targets, to avoid underestimating difficulties and to avoid the desperate search for shortcut solutions. In terms of policy making we have to be bold but cautious and even conservative in our planning. Unrealistic exchange rate policies, budgets built on overoptimistic assumptions do not serve well the ultimate goal of transition – catching up with the best. Transparency is important to avoid misperceptions. Covering up problems and diminishing the extent of difficulties is counterproductive on two accounts. First, it encourages people to expect too much, so eventually they become bitterly disappointed. Second, there is a danger that foreign investors are induced to behave in a more erratic way. Both can result in detrimental instabilities, either social or financial. Transition is a holistic process. To succeed, no important element can be ignored. It is not enough to proceed on one field, say in currency stabilisation, but then neglect structural reforms. It is not enough to introduce a modern tax system if the restructuring of troubled sectors is hopelessly slow. Even more, an unbalanced mix of reforms, consisting of advanced, ambitious measures in some dimensions and complete failure on other accounts, can be particularly harmful to the sustainability of the reform process. This means that you do not need to be perfect in all respects; what is important is to avoid major mistakes. In fact, a detailed analysis of Polish developments in the 1990s could lead to the conclusion that it has been characterised by a streak of failures or, at best, very limited success. Privatisation was too slow and dominated by insiders, inflation permanently higher than in other successful transition countries, restructuring of coal mining delayed, agricultural policies inconsistent. Nevertheless, Poland succeeded in building up a reasonably well-functioning market economy because the main elements of this process – consistent and carefully sequenced macroeconomic policy, gradual microeconomic adjustment and basic institutions, were not neglected.

One of the key premises of success in reforms is political stability. This should not, however, be confused with lack of change on the political scene. What really counts is the continuity that results from a broad consensus over major goals. Looking at Poland (and Hungary) one may even say that frequent changes in power may, under certain circumstances, speed up reforms. The more parties who take part in the policy making process, developing a necessary expertise and sense of responsibility at the same time, the more evenly are inevitable political costs of transformation spread over the whole spectrum of parties. A highly petrified structure of power (as in the Czech Republic for many years) leaves the opposition alienated from the realities of painful decisions and largely unprepared to continue necessary policies. We must remember, however, that a high turnover in the political leadership and at the steering wheel of the economy avoids chaos only if a broad consensus over the general course of reforms is secured. In Poland, as I mentioned before, this was provided by the widely shared European orientation of the political elite.

UNFINISHED BUSINESS: TOUGH CHOICES FOR THE FUTURE

The coming decade will not bring relief to the economic policy makers. On the contrary, it seems that the challenges ahead are equally formidable. How are we to combine successful EU accession with consolidation of reforms and, probably most important, with the high rate of growth necessary to close the gap between Poland and our West European partners? The main dilemma is how to reconcile fast growth with both economic and social equilibrium. In other words, it is how to reconcile fiscal discipline with the need to co-finance a modernisation effort and maintain some degree of social cohesion. We have dwelled extensively on the issue of inherent instability of the transition process. Fiscal restraint is one of very few short-run instruments in the hands of the authorities to reduce the gap between savings and investment. As long as we do not create institutions stimulating private saving (and this is a time-consuming process linked to the recently initiated social security reform) and as long as the wave of investment does not produce more exports, there will always be a strong pressure to reduce the budget deficit or indeed to build up a surplus. At the same time, public funds have to be provided to co-finance industrial restructuring (mining, metallurgy, agriculture), to modernise the technical infrastructure (highways) and improve the environment. Also, structural funds from the EU have to be partially matched by a domestic component. Fundamental reforms of the expenditure side of the budget coupled with drastic cuts in non-essentials are the only way to reconcile these two exigencies. Recent experience shows, however, that when you undertake a deep reform, as happened with the health sector and local government, prospective efficiency gains are preceded by increased costs. You have to invest first and only later can you reap the benefits.

Fast growth does not automatically solve acute social problems. Excessive income disparities, regional differences and poverty have to be tackled or the situation may get out of hand. Fiscal austerity makes it all but impossible to try to build a generous welfare-state-type social policy. There will always be pressure to better streamline expenditures, eliminate 'waste' and restrict spending programmes to the very basic level. Such prudence may be salutary since it is evident that poverty and social exclusion have never been properly addressed, let alone solved, by carelessness in public spending. However, intelligent methods of fighting poverty have to be used. These include, in my opinion, massive investment in education, particularly in rural areas, as well as support for small and medium-sized enterprises. Poverty is linked to unemployment and jobs are created almost exclusively in the SME sector. Lack of education makes people unemployable even if demand for labour is rising. Thus, the recipe seems obvious. It requires a certain budgetary support and knowledge of how to spend public money in the most efficient way.

In the short run, sustainable growth is jeopardised by an inconsistent macro policy mix. A constant need to keep the economy from overheating and the current account deficit from widening too much leads the central bank to monetary restrictions. High interest rates policy – necessary to stimulate savings and curb domestic demand – may become a self-defeating policy when an interest rate differential attracts excessive inflows of foreign portfolio capital. This results in an appreciation of the domestic currency and a higher trade deficit the exact opposite of the aim of the central bank. This inconsistency can be tackled, in theory, if fiscal policy is sufficiently tight. However, as was mentioned earlier, a too dramatic shift in the budget may be impossible, not only because of political ramifications, but also due to economic exigencies. This is another dimension of what I call the inherently unstable character of transition.

Summing up, transition in Poland has so far brought great achievements. Unprecedented success for some, justified hopes for many others, but also disappointment for the least fortunate. And yet transition is far from over. Reconstruction of the entire agricultural sector, the further restructuring of sunset industries, reform of the labour market and judiciary are among some of the most difficult challenges facing Poland in its drive to join the European Union. So far, success has largely been due to a broad consensus across the political elite, and indeed, society at large, concerning strategic goals. As long as that consensus is strengthened by common sense in the policy-implementation process we can look to the future with optimism.

NOTE

1 Górski, in his contribution to this book, gives a detailed account of the major milestones and institutional aspects underpinning the development of the Polish banking sector from 1989.

REFERENCE

Pinto B., Belka, M. and Krajewski, S. (1993), 'Transforming state enterprises in Poland: Microeconomic evidence on adjustment', *Brookings Papers on Economic Activity,* 1.

3. The ugly face of Polish success: social aspects of transformation

Tadeusz Kowalik

INTRODUCTION

The tenth anniversary of Poland's transformation is not only an opportunity for detailed analysis but also an occasion for a more general review from the viewpoint of chances taken and chances lost in economic and social development. The basic question we pose here is what kind of capitalism is emerging in Poland? Our aim is not however to discuss the problems of the economic mechanism from the viewpoint of major elements of the system ('how much market?', 'how much state?', 'what type of financial system exists?' and so on – these are in any case questions discussed in depth in other contributions to this book) but rather it is an attempt to consider the problem as expressed by one sociologist at the beginning of the transformation:

> Polish citizens are interested in the restoration of capitalism to the extent, at least in its Polish version … , that it guarantees in a relatively short time an improvement of standards of living for society as a whole, or at least for a significant majority. Any conception where improvement is only for a small minority cannot count on lasting support. (Dziewięcka-Bokun, 1990)

The questions here are clear. Who pays for the new system and whom does it serve? Can it count on continuing support? In the opinion of the sociologist quoted above people always judge systems in terms of capacity to satisfy their individual and collective needs, both material and spiritual.

THE GLOOMY SIDE OF POLISH SUCCESS

Before trying to answer these questions we outline Polish achievements thus far. This is necessary since public opinion in the West is nursed on stories of Polish economic success. It is true that for the seven years (1992–99) the average annual rate of growth of GDP was around 5% and it was, for this long period, the fastest growth rate among all the formerly communist countries. The inflation rate fell from several hundreds of percent in the early 1990s to less than 10% by the end of the decade. Throughout most of the mid to late 1990s it was the excessive appreciation of the złoty that was the greatest cause for concern. Nevertheless, it is indisputable that these successes were accompanied by a series of negative phenomena which emerged with greater intensity in Poland than in any other country in Central Europe. Although their extent has been documented by many researchers, both foreign and Polish, in the official propaganda – and especially its exported part – they have been played down or even ignored. Here are a few examples. Poland has the highest average rate of unemployment (in 1997 it peaked at 16% and in spring 2000 it was around 14%) and less than 25% of the registered unemployed receive benefits. Moreover, a significant extra portion of unemployment was concealed by early and (very easy to get) invalidity and retirement pensions, as a result of which Poland is one of those countries with the lowest ages for retirement. The decline in the unemployment rate of a few percentage points in recent years finds a weak reflection on employment statistics since it was connected to a large extent with tightening the benefits and registration criteria. There is much to suggest too that unemployment is set to rise in the years ahead since the state has no programme (other than cutting taxes for business and the wealthy) to manage the exceptionally large number of school-leavers entering the jobs market – the result of the last big ‘demographic wave’. Perhaps worst of all, the authorities seem to be becoming accustomed to mass and permanent unemployment. This is reflected in the public assertion of the employment minister (Longin Komołowski – previously a leader of the trade union Solidarity) that in Polish circumstances the ‘natural rate of unemployment’ lies between 8% and 10% and so a radical reduction should not be expected (Komołowski, 1999).

Poland also leads the way with regard to the depth and breadth of poverty. Researchers use various criteria for identifying the poor. It is however striking that so much of the latest Polish and foreign research (for example from the World Bank and UNICEF) unanimously agrees that in the 1990s the number of people living in poverty more than doubled. According to a comparative study from Vienna (Beskid, 1998a) the percentage of households living on less than half average income per head was as follows:

Poland	18.3%
Hungary	9.3%

Slovakia	6.7%
Czech Republic	6.1%
Former East Germany	6.6%

These data cover the period 1993–95. It is however disturbing that despite rapid GDP growth in the years that followed, the range and depth of poverty in Poland did not change. There is also a strong basis for the belief (although here a comparison is considerably more difficult) that the proportion of poor people in Poland is one of the greatest, if not the greatest, of all European countries west of the Ukraine.

Mass unemployment and widespread poverty are accompanied by an exceptionally large and uneven differentiation of earnings and incomes. Research shows that, as in the case of unemployment and poverty, the spread of incomes in Poland is higher than in all other Central European countries. It is high even in comparison with West European countries. For example, the income share of the bottom decile is, in Poland, around one half that found in Hungary, the Czech Republic, Slovakia and eastern Germany (Milic-Czerniak, 1998). Further evidence of workers' impoverishment is provided by the fact that even towards the end of 1996, and therefore in the fifth year of the economic boom (Żienkowski, 1998; Jacukowicz, 1997), real wages were approximately 20% lower than in 1989. And since the 1980s were characterised in this respect by stagnation, they were that much lower than in 1981! Much is hidden in 'averages' but it is easy to deduce the fact that many workers were earning in the mid 1990s one-third less than they did 10 to 15 years earlier. In the intervening years the workforce has undergone an especially high level of stratification. According to Golinowska (1999a) the Gini coefficient for earnings increased in the years 1989–99 from 0.18 to 0.34, 'placing us amongst the most unequal countries in Europe'. Golinowska adds that 'in 1999 Poland found itself in the group of countries with the greatest degree of income inequality, similar to that in the USA and, in Western Europe – Italy. A greater degree of "uncivilised" differentiation occurs only in Albania and Russia' (1999b).

At the other end of the scale we find a greedy managerial group where earnings can reach 60 times the average wage – as in the USA some time ago. In addition, managers' perks are expanding rapidly, an area where directors of state firms often make the running[1]. A situation like this could not have arisen without the silent acquiescence of both the previous (SLD-PSL) administration with its leftist logo and the post-1997 (AWS-UW) authorities alike. One effect of the recently implemented health reforms, even in this still state-run sector, reveals a degree of inequality rarely met anywhere in the world where a nurse earns barely one-thirtieth of the salary of the (admittedly highest paid) director of the newly created state-run health care insurance funds and care providers (*kasy chorych*).[2] As far as pay equality for working women is concerned, Poland fares poorly here also in comparison with other countries. International comparative research shows that Polish women's monthly earnings (from a main job plus additional work) reached in the mid 1990s not quite 57% of men's earnings. This was moreover the worst indicator among the six countries studied, not only worse than Hungary and the Czech Republic, which would be understandable, but worse also than Slovakia, Bulgaria, and even Russia! Figures based purely on earnings from principal employment are not much better (although Poland does at least come ahead of Russia on this measure) (see Domański, 1996, p. 124). Despite this an attempt in 1999 to set up a special parliamentary commission which would look at problems of sexual discrimination ended in failure (see Luxmoore, 1999). Discrimination against women stems largely from the traditionalism and conservatism of the Polish Catholic Church whose doctrine is pretty much the official ideology of the post-1997 government authorities. These and other data have led one economist/sociologist to conclude that 'Poland has the most unequal income distribution … to put it in other words, against all other countries of central Europe Poland is pursuing the most elitist model of income distribution' (Beskid, 1998b).

The neglect of house building has led to a situation which experts (even government experts) describe as catastrophic. For local authority provided housing the average length of the queue was between 5 and 8 years in the late 1990s (see Kowalik, 1999). Although in the 1980s the housing situation was already considered intolerable, in the mid-1990s Poland was building only one-third of the number of houses that were under construction at the end of that decade. This is one of the areas where inequalities appear most acutely.[3] The official preference in housing policy was to award large tax breaks for individuals building houses – available to all those building villas surrounded by high security fencing – with negligible support for building affordable rented accommodation. Another feature of the new system is an increasing number of homeless due, among other things, to a draconian law passed during the reign of the centre-left coalition.

Agricultural decline has resulted in the almost complete pauperisation of the peasantry. In the first phase of transformation private farmers' incomes fell by almost half and were only partially restored in the following years. Social mobility was also restricted (according to a *Polityka* report based on official data, only one of every 140 peasant children gets to university: see Wróblewski and Nowakowska, 1998) With no 'home-grown' programme for agriculture all hopes for agricultural modernisation lie in the framework of the European Union.

The crisis in the welfare state and the erosion of social security is also more acute in Poland than in the other Central European states, especially the Czech Republic, Slovakia and Hungary. Even if we reject extreme views many unfortunate developments remain.[4] The demise of enterprises' social security provision has accompanied cuts in state spending on health, education and science. The 'wild' privatisation of the state health service (a 'grey' area of economic life even in the past) and the latest reforms with their commercial character have made access to these services much more differentiated. Frequent changes in principles of funding and access to benefits, together with the recent reform of pensions creating strong links to the financial market, have created a feeling of uncertainty amongst workers who fear unemployment, as well as among the elderly. Although the state's share in GDP expenditure has fallen by only a couple of percentage points during the past few years (it stood at round 47% in the late 1990s) the popular feeling is that the welfare state has been almost completely dismantled.

It is worthwhile, finally, to turn our attention to privatisation. Economists tend to focus exclusively on privatisation of the public sector according to the legal processes in force. That does not however exhaust the rich problems linked to the broader issues associated with ownership change. The legalities and the economics are possibly even less important than the social consequences of privatisation. In the first instance it is worth drawing attention to the uncontrolled (yet strongly state supported) process of private sector expansion that preceded the formal privatisation of the state sector on a greater scale. In the first period of transformation, over barely three years the number of registered private enterprises (outside agriculture) rose from 800,000 to more than 1.6 million (and to over 2 million by 1999). To this should be added the significant number of firms which operate in the 'grey sphere'. The sudden loosening of restrictions on international trade, official consent for market (*bazaar*) and street trade, alongside the ease of tax evasion all created a veritable Eldorado for the expansion of small private firms.[5]

Of course for society this has meant enriching market supply and a sudden sea change in the ease of making purchases – of shopping. At the same time it has brought some undesirable phenomena including the decline of many services. Handicrafts and co-operative trading networks, unable to cope with duty-free imports or the effectively tax-free bazaar trade, went into decline. The sudden influx of foreign goods meant that the previously highly regulated co-operative movement simply had no opportunity to restructure and break free of state control. Most important, however, the private sector was home to industrial relations that can best be described as 'nineteenth century'. In this sector, especially in new enterprises, regulations on hygiene and safety at work were usually not observed and written contracts of employment, required by law, were not adhered to. In regions of high unemployment and/or immigration in the east and south of the country wages were, and are, frequently below the legal minimum. Frequently, the establishment or activity of trade unions is not permitted. Initially this could have been explained by the inexperience of new entrepreneurs, the uniqueness of the situation, reorganisation, and the paralysis of state regulatory and tax bodies. It is a disturbing fact however that even with the passage of time the annual State Employment Inspection Reports show not an improvement but rather a deterioration in conditions of employment (see

Państwowa Inspekcja Pracy, 1998, 1997). Hope, therefore, of more civilised conditions in the private sector is dangerously receding.[6] Authoritarian industrial relations at the micro level in private enterprises and the appropriation of the trade unions by alternate governing political parties at the macro level has led to a dramatic fall in trade union power and an equally dramatic fall in union membership (as the study in chapter 5 of this volume shows). Some researchers claim that in this respect Poland is already taking the lead among European countries.

The privatisation of state enterprises in accordance with written legal procedure is one of the few areas of Poland's transformation where both the positive and negative social consequences can be readily assessed from a social (and not purely economic) viewpoint. It is of course a process, as the sociologist Jacek Kurczewski (1995) has excellently put it, 'of redistribution of the title deeds' in part, a 'war over power, ownership and capital [in which] absolutely everyone is taking part'. This 'redistribution' proceeded, for the most part, either on the borders of legality or corruptly in diverse forms. Two of these are of particular interest here. The first was the interception and seizure of part of the productive apparatus by newly created private firms which could be labelled 'nomenklatura partnerships'. This game had the following features: part of the capital of state firms, at reduced prices, was conveyed into partnerships with private individuals; sales were struck at a reduced price or in the absence of the supposedly obligatory tendering procedures; long-term leasing contracts on machinery or buildings were concluded but failed to include indexation clauses; information on business contacts was released free of charge giving the recipients a privileged competitive position. Such practices became the norm also for the new, 'post-Solidarity nomenklatura' (more of which below). The second relied on the legal privatisation of firms with the support of state credit. Stocks or shares in privatised firms were bought with credit granted on easy terms by banks that, at that time, were still state owned. Later the profits of these firms were used for repayments although part of the credit was never repaid. [7]

The most innovative idea of the 'Gdańsk Liberals' and the first two Solidarity governments – the concept of general (or mass) privatisation, promoted as a form of 'popular enfranchisement' – ended in fiasco and fraud. The 'mouse' (the so-called National Investment Funds – *Narodowe Fundusze Inwestycyjne* – NFI) that emerged from the government's 'mountain' brought neither the proclaimed 'democratisation' of ownership nor 'peoples' capitalism', nor did it contribute significantly to the modernisation of participating firms. It became instead a vehicle for conveying a part of national wealth into the hands of a few Polish and foreign owners (fortunately not on any great scale and it was this that turned out to be the chief merit of this programme).

The only clear feature, from the viewpoint of social justice and possibly also acceptable industrial relations, was the permission for state firms to convert into workers' or management–workers' companies. These companies were initially 'unwanted children', rejected by the authorities as a kind of crypto-socialism. However, under pressure from employees, and particularly the autonomous workers' self-management movement, which was both real and active in Poland in 1980 and in 1990, they were accepted by the highest authorities (at least as an interim construct en route to 'real' joint stock companies). It is worth emphasising that workers' buy-outs dominated, by number, the privatisation process.[8] They were, and remain, characterised by mildly paternalistic industrial relations and less severe pay inequalities than found elsewhere – a situation that is changing. To the surprise of many politicians and economic theorists, workers' buy-outs or, with increasing frequency, management–workers' buy-outs based on leasing arrangements, turned out to be one of the most effective privatisation routes. Their profitability alternated between being slightly worse or slightly better than firms privatised via the 'capital' route (those with so-called strategic investors either foreign or domestic).

THE REJECTED REJECT THE SYSTEM

Poland with its high growth rate disproves the well-known 'trickle down' theory. Wide social groups, and certainly the majority of society, do not benefit, or else benefit only to a minimal extent from economic growth. Growth serves only those, described by Roy Harrod (1958) (see Hirsch 1977) as the 'oligarchy of the wealthy' in a process he thought was the antithesis of democracy.[9] Branko Milanovic of the World Bank also observed this in 1995 (somewhat paradoxically given that this 'development' Bank was partly responsible for the distorted character of development). Milanovic wondered whether further economic growth would bring improvement or deterioration in income equality. He suggested that all depended on the nature of future growth, noting that, 'if growth occurs first at the top and in the middle of the income distribution, inequality will continue to rise and poverty will remain stable' (see Milanovic, 1995). Turning to Poland in its third year of fast GDP growth Milanovic suggested that this was just what was happening – with significant GDP growth and slightly slower growth of private incomes (10% and 7% respectively) – 'the poverty rate in 1994 was about the same as in 1992 and inequality had risen'. Data for the following years confirm this tendency continues. However by the late 1990s the World Bank had changed its views. Broad equality was no longer seen as conflicting with efficiency. The Bank began to recommend development policies promoting simultaneously greater equality and growth. The experience of the 'Asian tigers' reinforced those conclusions (see Stiglitz, 1998).

The result of transformation was to create a system pregnant with social conflict, conflicts softened initially by the social acceptance of 'shock therapy' and then by fast economic growth. Another factor softening the situation was the hope created by the frequency with which parliamentary elections changed governing teams. Yet another was the belief in the myth of the 'leap to European affluence'. In the long run, however, and crucially for the future of the system, a lack of acceptance may appear amongst important social groups who become more convinced of its permanent instability and even of the need for its fundamental reform. An extremely valuable resource in examining social responses and attitudes to transformation is the survey information collected by Polish sociologists in the *Polacy '95* studies.[10] The editor of this collection summing up many years of survey research notes on *workers*:

> workers constituted almost half of the total labour force now however their numbers have declined significantly and they are scattered across the public/private sectors of the economy. Yet they are still distinguished by the greatest level of trade union organisation – and remain the only influential social class of society not reconciled to the status offered them by the newly developing system.

Reading the volume carefully suggests however that workers are not, as Professor Adamski states, the only class which is decidedly unhappy with the new system. As it turns out farmers' level of satisfaction is even lower:

> Merely 19% of farmers perceive the changes currently taking place as opening new possibilities – this is the lowest optimism ranking in the entire population ... Farmers also figure among those who have serious doubts in the likelihood of improvements in living conditions in the next few years. Meanwhile those for whom the past evokes great sentiment are also full of anxiety and scepticism. In their attachment for both socialist ideology and socialist realities alike they have no equals in society.[11]

The events of the first months of 1999 (stormy demonstrations, blockaded roads) showed that the peasantry has become a second 'influential group' (to use Adamski's phrase) knowing how to demand its rights. What is more, the first signs of alliance between these two large social groups started to appear. The peasantry is ceasing to be the proverbial (as Marx once put it) 'sack of potatoes'. To the already considerable dissatisfied strata of society should be added at least two other large professional groups: health service workers (in the summer of 1999, at the time of writing, nurses were involved in a several weeks, long rotating hunger strike) and teachers. We can therefore boldly risk stating that the majority of Polish society does not accept the new socio-economic system. In these conditions the first recession faced by the new system may make a prophecy out of Jacek Kuroń's warning of revolt.[12] For this reason it is worthwhile examining changes in Poland in the comparative perspective of various other systems and to start thinking today not just about the alternatives that could have been but also to look for the road to the sort of system that will serve well the vast majority of society.

A DANGEROUS UMBRELLA

The question arises as to the reasons why the authorities' actions fail so spectacularly to coincide with the aspirations of society. It is worth considering here the views of Jacek Kuroń, in our view the only politician with governmental experience who strives to understand and elucidate this problem heedless of critics and criticism. But we should not forget that even this politician, a hero of the democratic opposition and the non-communist left, openly suspended his personal left-wing credo at the time when the foundations of a capitalist economy were being laid.[13] The first occasion was as early as the summer of 1989 when enthusiastic support was given to Jeffrey Sachs' argument in favour of a sudden jump to a market economy. A couple of years later it became clear to Kuroń that the government's fundamental error (as well as his own personally) was its withdrawal from the path of social accord and of co-operation with the workers' self-management and trade union movements. In 1994 Kuroń discussed Solidarity's 1993 defeat at the polls, when a post-communist coalition won, in the following manner

> Solidarity's defeat occurred because the state authorities it gave rise to, instead of leading a mass movement for social transformation, acted above society. An etatist-technocratic programme was implemented over the head of society and this pushed the majority to the left, all the more radically the more acutely they felt the cost of the fall of Communism. (Kuroń, 1994)

It was also apparent to Kuroń that in the years 1989–93 'the Solidarity movement was being destroyed by the government and administration'. To some extent Kuroń tried to make good this error but, unfortunately, not until shortly before the fall of the Suchocka government in which he had been reappointed employment minister. As labour minister Kuroń pushed forward the idea that government and unions could reach an understanding in an 'enterprise pact' (*pakt o przedsiębiorstwie*) as a key element of transformation. He himself however admitted that the *pakt* had two shortcomings: 'It did not go far enough in transferring administrative power to the people. Secondly it was implemented far too late. It should have been signed at the very beginning of 1990' (Kuroń, 1997). In this manner the initial actions of the government, and the blatant corruption of Polish capitalism (more of which below), created the conviction in a large section of society that 'These are not their [society's] reforms. They are the authorities' reforms and ... they serve the authorities alone.' In retrospect Kuroń suggests that the trade union Solidarity and especially the workers' self-management movement should have been seen as partners. Activists in the self-management movement (*samorządowcy*) were 'pretty well schooled, they knew how an enterprise operated, understood economic processes ... if they knew it was their factory ... they would act rationally ... . Those people from self-management could have been elite in the transformation process.'

Kuroń does not however make clear how it was possible for the social movement Solidarity, until recently with a membership of 10 million, to allow the launch of a programme which so severely attacked those who were responsible for the collapse of communism. Many factors played a part (see Modzelewski, 1993; Kowalik, 1995) but three in particular seem most important. First, the mass exodus of Solidarity activists, especially its intellectuals, to the government apparatus, to administration and to business greatly weakened a movement that was just emerging from an underground existence. Second, at the time when the Balcerowicz plan was passing through parliament and then when it was launched, a significant section of society believed in the necessity of drastic (although short-term) sacrifices in the name of a better future. The plan was neither publicly discussed nor negotiated with the trade unions – not that negotiations were even demanded – after all it was thought that 'our people, tested in battle and in prison are in the government!'. When it realised that the 'better future' was constantly receding the union movement suffered a massive loss of trust in the government and began to question the wisdom of holding a protective parasol over it. Third, it was this very umbrella – the possibility of applying shock therapy to society without negotiation – that permitted a truly drastic programme to be launched.

Here was a fundamental difference between the governments of Vaclav Klaus and Tadeusz Mazowiecki. Since in Czechoslovakia the anti-communist opposition was very weak, no social movement existed which could hold such a protective umbrella over the government. In these circumstances Klaus had to put some effort into winning social support. Although he employed the rhetoric of Margaret Thatcher and Milton Friedman he proceeded very carefully. He clearly did not want to have to manage mass unemployment and widespread poverty. The early stages of transformation witnessed something of a paradox. The new Polish elite, at first appealing to the values of syndicalist-social democracy, and later to the example of the German 'social market economy', nevertheless conducted a neo-liberal policy leap to the free market.[14] Kuroń – we repeat – a legend of the Polish non-communist left, played the role of anaesthetist to society, numbing the social pain of a rather rough operation. As he himself put it: 'If Balcerowicz appears in this metaphor as a skilled surgeon then I am the anaesthetist and as such I am able temporarily to soothe my patients with kind words' (Kuroń, 1997, p. 79). Vaclav Klaus, on the other hand, at that time an extreme liberal, was forced by circumstance to adopt a style of politics closer to that of social democratic moderation.[15] In each case rhetoric was a useful political tool. Klaus's neoliberal rhetoric legitimised his economic policy in the eyes of the West. Mazowiecki's social-market rhetoric (and even that of another Solidarity prime minister, Hanna Suchocka) legitimised Balcerowicz's neoliberal policies. But it also created a barrier, making it difficult to absorb the real essence of the West German model since it helped to mystify and hide the fundamental and real breach of the social contract to which representatives of Solidarity in government were supposedly bound.

The Polish tradition, even from 1980, was to find social agreements through negotiated compromise as the means for building the new social-economic order. If the contracts negotiated later at the 1989 round table had been adhered to, as voters had surely expected when they went to the polls in June of that year, then the new social-economic system would necessarily have looked completely different. The Balcerowicz plan would have stood no chance of acceptance in the form we now know it. Of course, some sort of mini-shock with effects similar to those that the government had actually anticipated in 1990 was inevitable, but not the unprecedented (in post-war Europe) recession that did take place and which was most certainly not foreseen by the authorities, nor the great shift of incomes from poor to rich.[16]

It is worthwhile clarifying two common misconceptions. Discussion on the great cost to society of transformation has frequently been stopped in its tracks by the argument that compared to other countries Poland is a success story. 'Just look', they say, 'at the Ukraine, Russia and even Bulgaria and Romania.' Of course in Poland too things could have turned out much worse, especially if in panic it had backed out of draconian reforms. We tend to forget however that with the possible exception of Hungary during the Kadar period Poland was known as the 'warmest barracks in the Soviet camp'. During the 1980s Poland had the fastest growing private sector. Until Janos Kornai achieved international celebrity Poland had also the best known economists (Oskar Lange and Michał Kalecki). From the start of the 1970s it was the most open to the West. All of this predestined Poland for a pioneering role and for economic success. The second misconception is that there was no alternative to the Balcerowicz plan: the opposite was true. Poland was the only country, before the collapse of communism, to have ready to hand an outline programme of radical reform the foundations of which were negotiated during the 1989 'round table'. It did of course have shortcomings (the greatest of which was far too high indexation). Nevertheless it could have provided the basis for an improved working programme for the new government had that government not intended to tear up the existing accords and depart from the path of social compromise and negotiation embarked on in 1980. The basis for an alternative existed had the leaders and advisers of Solidarity not performed a complete U-turn.[17] It is therefore hard to understand where the idea comes from that no alternatives existed.

WHAT KIND OF CAPITALISM: MANAGERIAL OR 'CRONY'?

Thus far we have concentrated attention chiefly on one end of the social transformation – noting and discussing mass unemployment and poverty, the sudden decline in private farmers' incomes, the sluggish growth in real average wage (still lower in 1999 than 10 years ago), the exceptionally high differentiation of wages, Poland's nineteenth century standards in industrial relations and its cuts in welfare spending. In order however to answer the question posed in our introduction – what kind of capitalism is emerging in Poland? – we must also look at the other end of the spectrum. The influential stratum based on power and property may be less numerous but is certainly more visible. If the first social groups are the passive objects of change, the second represent the beneficiaries of restructuring. Some sociologists (see Gardawski and Gilejko, 1999) draw attention to (besides managers and wealthy individuals) two other evolving social groups: people holding political and state administrative power and the *petit bourgeois* whose base is small business.

In spite of the authorities' promise (as in the Balcerowicz plan) to withdraw the state from the economy and limit its size, state administration has grown particularly fast in the 1990s. The whole state administration employed 159,000 people in 1990 and only six years later that number had increased to 290,000. The state central administration (not counting its regional branches) has been growing even faster, more than doubling in size, yet the central administrative apparatus has grown faster still, by more than 250% in the same period. To understand the character of the new system it is important above all to understand the social role of groups involved in public administration. These groups are sometimes referred to sociologically as the 'transformation classes'. They are entitled (in their opinion) to 'transformation rents', which is their polite term for what others might call corruption and cronyism. Many sociologists have written about corruption and 'clientism' yet they admit that systematic research on these matters can be problematic. While it is easy to agree with this it is useful to return here to Kuroń who, once again, offers a penetrating analysis of these phenomena. It is worth adding that this politician is known not only for his perceptiveness and sensitivity to authority-based pathologies but also for his readiness to reveal its mechanisms quite brutally. He does not shy away from (sometimes exaggerating) his shared culpability. We mentioned earlier the transformation of a significant section of the old nomenklatura of businessmen. Kuroń recalls the early stages of this exploitation of the apparatus of power at the end of the 1980s and adds:

> it was the beginning of a massive transfer of wealth which took place right before our very eyes. Alongside the slogan 'get rich', with the country in general turmoil, unbridled 'wild privatisation' began. It will surely never be possible to know just how

much money state enterprises lost, the managers of which negotiated contracts with friendly nomenklatura partnerships, causing losses to the enterprises in question, but with enormous profits for the partners. Of course there were swindles but the law turned out to be useless against them. (Kuroń, 1997, p. 119)

These procedures later became known as 'red spiders' webs'. In contrast however to many right-wing politicians who think that these phenomena relate only to the old post-communist nomenklatura Kuroń has indicated on many occasions that this pattern, the pattern of self-enfranchisement by the new elite in authority, remains to the present day. Recalling that the first non-communist cabinet was formed in this way through networks, with the prime minister's closest aides looking up the names of contacts in filo-faxes, he writes:

That method survived throughout the following months and years when staff had to be found for banks, companies, local authorities, embassies and state media companies ... . The Polish middle-class, while at first sight leading post PRL capitalism, in reality failed to consolidate its position in the market. For its greater part – and particularly for those who acquired significant wealth – it was not the free market which turned out to be of greatest importance but contacts. It follows that if those who profited are defending anything, it's the 'filo-fax' – connections, agreements, quotas, governmental customers, limits, price barriers, monopolies – to which they owe their current positions. That's the Polish drama. (Kuroń, 1997, pp. 91–92)

Kuroń has no doubts that 'this phenomenon is of key significance in the development of democracy and the market economy in Poland' (p. 127). Those remarks date back to early 1997. In the autumn of that year a post-Solidarity coalition came to power on, in part, an anti-corruption ticket. In less than two years corruption and its milder form – cronyism (*klientelizm*) – had become one of the most important topics of daily debate. Sociologists are in no doubt that these two practices are both surviving and expanding. One sociologist and politician (a former senator and Freedom Union member of parliament) closes his general account of corruption with the statement that his attempts at intervention on these matters as high up as the procurator general as a rule disappeared without so much as an acknowledgement (Celiński, 1999). In circles around the political elite it was considered impolite to raise this topic.[18] Another sociologist writing on this theme notes that after the latest (1999) reforms on regional decentralisation the members of these new structures show themselves to be:

effective builders of the next nomenklatura ... . At local self-government level, all positions – starting, for example, at nursery school directors in a district – are political, which means they are appointed without regard to competence,

> qualifications and previous service to society. Hope for effectiveness and justice has probably completely evaporated … . (Krzemiński, 1999)

To sum up, Polish capitalism is characterised by mass unemployment, a large stratum of people living in poverty, great and steadily increasing wage and income differentiation. At the other end of the spectrum lies a stratum of society differentiated by its wealth and ownership of assets, disposing also of power, where cronyism or open corruption rules. Both of these poles of society are not so much products of spontaneous market processes as the result of deliberate acts of the authorities and administration in the broadest possible sense. From such an understanding of Polish capitalism we can see that the idea of 'managerial capitalism' could be too narrow for the Polish context. A group of Californian sociologists suggested that in Central Europe a managerial strain of capitalism was emerging rather than one based on ownership or politics. This was, they said, 'capitalism without capitalists' in the sense that it was not dominated by great owners. In the briefest summary the concept goes as follows:

> the most distinctive characteristic of post-communist social structure in East Central Europe is the absence of a capitalist class. Private property rights are in place, markets in labour and capital exist, these economies are open to world markets, and they have strong relationships with international financial institutions. However, there is no organised group of major capitalists. There are no interlocking corporate directorates based on ownership and there is no class organisation through networks of family property. Indeed, the result of privatisation in most of the region has been highly diffused property rights. This is the puzzle we seek to understand. (Eyel et al. 1997, p. 60)

In contrast to Western countries, especially the USA, where the economically dominant class forms the recruitment base for the political elite, in Poland, the Czech Republic and Hungary this base belongs to various social circles. With the collapse of communism the technocratic-managerial elite was able:

> to occupy the command positions of the economy, but it was not in a position to make a bid for political power. The key positions of political power were captured by humanistic intellectuals. They quickly organized a tight ruling group, or politocracy, which only later formed an alliance with the new technocratic-managerial elite.

Initially this description seemed accurate, corresponding in general and roughly with Polish realities. Now however it would seem better to say, more cautiously, that it is *not in contradiction* with that reality, but only because those holding central power are indeed 'humanistic intellectuals', especially if we bestow the term 'humanistic' on economics professors.[19] In light of the above description of a system characterised by mutual exchange of services and profits, attempts to explain basic differences between these two groups, and to define the system using one group, is of little real help in understanding the character of the system as a whole. It worth noting too that many 'humanists', professors of economics and law, have a direct stake in the state authorities, in management boards of various 'foundations' and in treasury owned enterprises. What is however most important is that as the role of managerial professionalism gets magnified it also reduces the state-bureaucratic character of the system and meanwhile the social aspects of the system are also eroded. There is not much sense in distinguishing the managerial group from the wider collective that has authority as well as human and material capital.

It seems that underpinning the sociological view that managers form a 'dominating class' is the belief that this class rules through its appropriation of decision making authority – it can rule by taking a small number of important decisions, those that affect current and future economic policy. But at the same time the transformation process, especially privatisation, is more complex. It is a question of tens, if not hundreds of thousands of decisions affecting personnel, credit, tax, tariffs (and also eliminating certain 'perks', for example, outstanding credit, tax breaks, national insurance contribution arrears, duties, preventing illegal house building). These create close ties between the apparatus of authority, from central to local state administration right down to the lowest level, with businesses both big and small. They are also less visible and more difficult to examine than, for example, basic policy directions as declared by the government or by parliament.

Nor does it seem that there was any specific time sequence, as some claim, between the founding of the 'politocracy' and the moment of forging a 'union' with the technocratic-managerial cadre. All the more so, since the initially glaring conflicts between the aims of the authorities and the interests of the 'proto-technostructure' were short-lived. Wesołowski (1993) describes the initial actions of the authorities as representing 'transgressive interests' to do with the introduction of organisation and legal regulation of a healthy capitalist economy based on free competition, with wealth creation based on enterprise, innovation and competent management. Since there was no distinct capitalist class the authorities acted in the name of an 'imagined' middle class to create the basis for a liberal democratic order. Leszek Balcerowicz very frequently enumerates the qualities of such an imaginary system, one in harmony with the standards of the Washington consensus, and some foreign commentators mistakenly assume that this is a description of the *actual* situation. This vision of an ideal system corresponds more with abstract orthodox Western economic thinking rather than the actually existing situation, with a domestic business that leans heavily towards protectionism. It is more interested in subsidies, reliefs and so on than liberalisation and hard budget constraints.

There is however a large swathe of economic policy which has no hint of any 'transgressive' character. In at least three fields the clearly declared aims of the authorities coincide absolutely with the interests of the new propertied class: tax cuts for business and the wealthy, attempts to cut back on the welfare state, and further labour market deregulation.

NOTES

1 According to Wyżnikiewicz (1997, p. 62), in 1996 'The average earnings of directors of state enterprises rose by 72%, directors of state treasury owned firms by 49% and directors of private firms by 36%'.
2 According to press reports the average wage of a nurse in 1999 was between zł 500 and zł 700 per month. The highest earnings of a director of a *Kasa Chora* were reported to be zł 23,000 per month. In early 2000 parliament ratified a law limiting managers' salaries in state firms and organisations.
3 After noting 'the diverse villas, and palaces', belonging to the new 'Polish owners', Jacek Kuroń described the opposite end of Polish housing thus: 'In my area, as in many parts of Warsaw, places where the council builds are broken up and where previously wild hedgerows stood – in recent years emerged houses stuck together with various pieces of rubbish, corrugated iron, and the remains of old furniture' (Kuroń, 1997).
4 See my debate with Maurice Glasman (Kowalik, 1994). Jacek Kochanowicz (1999, p. 197) begins his study on this theme with the following two sentences: 'In post-communist countries the welfare state seems already to be a thing of the past. Part of it has simply collapsed and that which remains requires reform.'
5 Even in 1993 (and therefore after the greatest wave of 'bottom-up' private sector expansion) state firms paid on average three times more tax contributions than privately owned firms and more than 15 times more than certain large private firms (mainly through negotiated tax vacations) (Krajewska, 1994). Small firms' proprietors also pay about half in the way of insurance premiums. Given these circumstances it seems a touch naive to attribute the expansion of the private sector simply to 'the elimination of the barrier for enterprising people' or to 'deregulation at the stroke of a pen' which 'frees peoples' initiative' (Winiecki, 1994, pp. 55–59).
6 It is possible that one of the prime factors contributing to the backwardness of industrial relations is the large proportion of unskilled workers among the owners of private firms. Unskilled and skilled workers are becoming by far the largest group among new entrepreneurs (two and a half times greater by number than in those from an intelligentsia or managerial background) (Domański, 1997).
7 The former (twice) minister of privatisation, Janusz Lewandowski, admitted that at the start of the 1990s he was not aware that 'state funds were utilised

in this way. It simply escaped from the field of view' (Lewandowski, 1997, as cited by Bałtowski, 1998, p. 138).

8 The law permitted this form of transformation for small and medium-sized enterprises only. While more than 1200 of these partnerships exist they employ barely 2% of the workforce with around 2–5% of fixed assets.

9 Harrod, an otherwise rather conservative economist, warned that an 'unbridgeable gulf' existed between the oligarchy of the wealthy and a democratic system. The oligarchy of the wealthy is associated with an oligarchic democracy. However, politics designed to help the poor (increasingly popular of late) merely supports the system of inequality, rather than bringing it down. This is the essence of the 'paradox of redistribution' (Korpi and Palme, 1997).

10 See Adamski, 1998. Note that although the social survey data refer to 1995, contributors to the volume invariably use later evidence in their comments.

11 See K. Szafraniec, 'Rolnicy polscy aktorzy czy klienci transformacji?' quoted in (ibid).

12 'When large social groups get the feeling that society has pushed them aside, that they are deprived of the chance to participate in normal life, that the opportunity to achieve their aspirations has been taken away from them, they begin to rebel against such an order, and can bring about its downfall' (Kuroń, 1997).

13 Kuroń has described his address to the inaugural meeting of the Freedom Union's predecessor (the ROAD organisation) as a 'stupid and fundamental error'. He said then that he would like to be a 'decent social democrat in a decent capitalist system, but unfortunately there is no decent capitalism, we must therefore start by building a decent capitalism'. On the other hand he was not able 'to formulate the fundamental question: who, in particular, is responsible for building this capitalism?' (ibid., p. 79).

14 *Die Soziale Marktwirtschaft* had its creator in Ludwig Erhard, and the Polish prime minister, Tadeusz Mazowiecki, said that he was looking for his own Erhard to run the economy.

15 There is no opportunity here to elaborate the reasons for the Czech Republic's current economic difficulties. Suffice to say that in our view it is a mistake to locate the source of these difficulties in Klaus's socially moderate politics (we ignore the, to a high degree, only apparent and yet highly corrupt scheme of coupon privatisation). It is also a mistake to attribute Poland's high rate of economic growth mainly to the drastic nature of the Balcerowicz plan.

16 The 'overshooting' was colossal. Forecasts and predictions were frequently out by several hundred per cent. Here are some of the widest divergences:

- Yearly inflation was to be in single digits by the end of 1990. This result was only achieved after nine years. In 1990 inflation reached nearly 600%.
- In 1990 GDP was to fall by 3% but in fact fell by 11%.
- In 1990 industrial production was expected to fall by 5% but fell by 25%. These were the main effects of the drastic 30% fall in production in the first month of the programme's implementation.
- Unemployment was expected to rise temporarily to approximately 400,000. In the first year of the plan it actually rose to over 1 million, to 2 million in the second year, and close to 3 million the year after that. The large number of people taking early retirement and those who gained access to invalidity benefit far too easily should be added to this figure.
- In 1990 wages fell by more than a third instead of the few percentage points predicted and continued falling right up until 1994. Due to a steep decline in agricultural produce prices (in comparison to industrially manufactured goods) farmers incomes fell by more than more than 50% in 1990 and by a further 20% in 1991. Even by 1999 real wages did not reach the levels they had before 'shock therapy' and farmers' incomes rose at all hardly.

It all seems to be a confirmation of the undesirability (following Karl Popper) of global sociotechnics.

17 'To this day I am amazed at the ease with which the elite which evolved from the workers' movement did a complete 180 degree turn and rejected the value of what had been acknowledged, up until that point, as the major elements of social-economic policy' (Modzelewski, 1993, p. 10).

18 'I know by name politicians in Warsaw whose incomes from corrupt practices are many times higher than [their] legal earnings. They are household names. I know a lot about some transactions. Once I even tried to inform the appropriate people: the appropriate office, and in desperation, public opinion. I always lost ... . The problem is that in Poland no one stands a chance against corruption ... . The state turns a blind eye' (Celiński, 1999).

19 In the early stages Polish capitalism was characterised by the gulf between the technocratic-manager group and those whom the writers on this refer to as the 'politocracy', people who really belonged to different worlds. It concerned, however, the same elite of central power. Paradoxically, businessmen had a role to play in the last communist cabinet led by Mieczysław Rakowski (deputy prime minister, and ministers Sekuła, Wilczek and Olesiak). Henryka Bochniarz, the president of the NIKOM partnership, was minister of industry only briefly in Mrs Suchocka's cabinet. In general, however, neither leading managers nor wealthy entrepreneurs were installed as deputy prime ministers

responsible for economic affairs, or as ministers for finance or industry; instead professors or academics of a lesser stature were appointed.

REFERENCES

Adamski, W. (1998), 'Dynamika interesów: preferencji ustrojowych a zmiany właśnościowe w gospodarce', in *Polacy 95: Aktorzy: klienci transformacji* Warsaw: IFISO.

Bałtowski, M. (1998), *Prywatyzacja przedsiębiorstw państwowych, przebieg i ocen* (Privatisation of state firms, progress and assessment), Warsaw.

Beskid, L. (1998a), *Gospodarstwa domowe w krajach Europy Środkowej* (Domestic budgets in Central European countries), in Milic-Czerniak (1998).

Beskid, L. (1998b), 'Ubóstwo w Polsce' (Poverty in Poland), in RSSG, *Podział dochodu i nierówności dochodowe. Fakty, tendencje, porównani* (Income distribution and inequalities. Facts, trends, comparisons), Raport nr 29, Warsaw.

Bruno, M. and Squire, L. (1996), 'The less equal the asset distribution, the slower the growth.' *Transition*, no. 9–10.

Celiński, A. (1999), 'Korupcja', *Nowe Życie Gospodarcze*, 18 July.

Domański, H. (1996), *Na progu konwergencj* (On the threshold of convergence), Warsaw.

Domański, H. (1997), 'Mobilnośc i hierarchie stratyfikacyjne' (Mobility and hierarchies stratification), in H. Domański and A. Rychard, *Elementy nowego ładu* (Elements of the new order), Warsaw.

Dziewięcka-Bokun, L. (1990), *Tygodnik Solidarność*, no. 27.

Eyal, G., Szelenyi, I. and Townsley, E. (1997), 'The theory of post-communist managerialism', *New Left Review*, no. 222.

Gardawski, J. and Gilejko, L. (1999), 'Zmiany w strukturze społeczeństwa polskiego' (Changes in Polish social structure), in A. Noga (ed.), *Szkoła Główna Handlowa i dziesięc lat transformacji w Polsce* (The Warsaw School of Economics and ten years of Polish transformation), Warsaw: SGH.

Golinowska, S. (1999a), *Instytucjonalny ład w sferze społecznej* (Institutional order in the social sphere), Instytut Nauk Ekonomicznych, mimeo.

Golinowska, S. (1999b), 'Nędza, ubóstwo, niedostatek' (Misery, poverty, shortages), *Rzeczpospolita,* September 9, 1999.

Hirsch, F. (ed.) (1977), *Social Limits of Growth*, London.

Jacukiewicz, Z. (1997), 'Płace w Polsce a wynagrodzenia w krajach Unii Europejskiej' (Wages in Poland and the EU), *Polityka Społeczna*, no. 11–12, 1997, s. 21.

Kochanowicz, J. (1999), 'Co pozostało z państwa opiekuńczego (po komunizmie)' (What remains of the welfare state after communism), Szkoła Nauk Społecznych, *Indywidualizm a kolektywizm*, Warsaw.

Komołowski, L. (1999), 'Bezrobocie' (Unemployment), *Wprost*, 5 March.

Korpi, W. and Palme, J. (1997), 'The paradox of redistribution and strategies of equality: welfare state institutions, inequality and poverty in the Western Countries', Stockholm

Kowalik, A. (1999), 'Mieszkania: miastach brakuje 730 tysięcy mieszkań' (Housing: Towns have a 730,000 shortfall), *Rzeczpospolita*, 12 September.

Kowalik, T. (1994), 'A reply to M. Glasman', *New Left Review*, no. 205.

Kowalik, T. (1995), 'From "self-governing republic" to capitalism, the workers and the intellectuals', in K. Nielsen and M. Mendell (eds), *Europe Central and East*, Montreal, New York and London.

Krajewska, A. (1994), 'Opodatkowanie sektora publicznego i prywatnego w Polsce' (Taxing the public and private sectors in Poland), *Gospodarka Narodowa,* no. 7–8.

Krzemiński, I. (1999), 'Strategia rządzenia' (Strategy of government), *Rzeczpospolita*, 31 July/1 August.

Kurczewski, J. (1995), 'Taka młoda a taka brzydka' (So young and so ugly), Gazeta Wyboroza, no. 3,

Kuroń, J. (1991), *Moja zupa* (My soup), Polska Oficyna Wydawnicza 'BGW', Warsaw.

Kuroń, J. (1994), 'Rzeczpospolita dla każdego' (A republic for all), *Życie Gospodarcze*, no. 21.

Kuroń, J (1997a), 'Wykluczeni, wyróznieni, niewidzialni' (The marginalised, the discriminated, the invisible), *Magazyn Gazety Wyborczej*, 22 August.

Kuroń, J. (1997b), *Siedmiolatka czyli kto ukradł Polske?,* Wrocław.

Luxmoore, J. (1999), 'Polish women demand equal rights commission', *Guardian*, 23 July.

Milanovic, B. (1995), 'Poverty, inequality, and social policy in transition, economies', *World Bank Policy Research Working Paper*, Washington DC.

Milic-Czerniak, R. (ed.) (1998), *Gospodarstwa domowe w krajach Europy Środkowej*, Instytut Spraw Społecznych, Warsaw.

Modzelewski, K. (1993), *Dokąd od komunizmu* (Where after communism?), Polska Oficyna Wydawnicza 'BGW', Warsaw.

Państwowa Inspekcja Pracy (1998, 1997), *Sprawozdanie Glównego Inspektora Prac* (Reports of the Labour Inspectorate), Warsaw.

Stiglitz, J. (1998), *More Instruments and Broader Goals: Moving Towards the Post-Washington Consensus*, Helsinki.

Topińska, I. (1998), *Dochody i poziom życia w transformacji* (Incomes and living standards in transformation), (mimeo).

Wesołowski, W. (1993), 'Nowe spojrzenie na interesy' (New views on business), in *Przegląd Społeczny*, no. 11–12.

Winiecki, J. (1994), 'Zródła ekonomicznego sukcesu: eliminacja barier dla ludzkiej przedsiębiorczości' (Sources of economic success: eliminating barriers to enterprise), in Centrum im. Adama Smitha, *Pięc lat po czerwcu* (Five years after June),Warsw.

Wróblewski, A.K. and Nowakowska, E. (1998), 'Parada kieszeni. Raport "Polityki"', *Polityka,* no. 20.

Wyżnikiewicz, B. (1997), 'Zarabiają coraz lepiej' (They earn even more), *Gazeta Bankowa – Magazyn*, May, p. 62.

Żienkowski, L. (1998), *Dochody gospodarstw domowych w okresie transformacji. 1990–1996* (próba syntezy) (Household incomes in transformation 1990–1996), Warsaw.

Żienkowski, L. (1997), 'Rozpiętości społeczne' (Social differentiation), *Nowe Życie Gospodarcze,* 10 October.

4. How has Polish society changed since 1989? Implications for the new decade

Edmund Wnuk-Lipiński

INTRODUCTION

It is impossible to answer the question 'How has Polish society changed since 1989?' without taking into account social processes from the earlier period, well before 1989. We need also to define what kind of social change we have in mind since some of its characteristic features are stable in the sense that they determine the identity of a given society and, at the same time, differentiate it from others. These stable features (for example, language, customs, history) do not change dramatically even in the case of a very stormy revolution.

Of course, dramatic change is always the result of people's action, a collective activity that changes the 'rules of the game' of public life, altering the ways in which position is achieved in authority structures and the institutions that make up the pillars of the social system. Convulsive upheaval is close to the classical concept of revolution in that it also changes the normative basis of order, that is to say, it changes the set of basic values legitimising the new system alongside its internal rules.

This collective activity, and the upheaval that goes with it, does not happen accidentally. The causes may be deeply rooted in society, in social processes that are not necessarily noticeable in public life (especially if that life is controlled in an authoritative way by an undemocratic state). They are in inherent in the basic social tissue, in its microstructures. On the other hand, radical change also generates new social processes, which in turn determine further changes in attitudes and social behaviour. Thus we have to deal here with multiple feedbacks: collective action brings about radical change, releasing certain more general social processes which also shape social behaviour. Self-evidently, Polish society was an instrument of change but also a subject of changes.

In this view the evolution of social attitudes and behaviour in the last decade is, on the one hand, the *outcome*, a dependent variable, while it is also an independent variable, an *input*, continuing to shape a new order. This essay is built on these assumptions: it starts by describing the social processes that led to the 'Round Table', those famous March 1989 negotiations between communist authorities and Solidarity opposition, and very shortly after to the collapse of communism; it then goes on to identify the new social processes which were set in motion by the 1989 breakthrough. Finally, there is an attempt to look ahead and to identify forces that most likely will shape society in the next decade.

1989: CULMINATION OF RADICAL SOCIAL CHANGE

When the Round Table talks started none of the participants supposed that what was beginning was a meeting of 'the commission for the liquidation of communism in Poland', nor that its result would become the model for changes that would take place later in some other Soviet block countries (for example in Hungary, and to certain extent in Bulgaria). The initial demands of one side, as it was called then the 'Solidarity opposition', were modest: legalisation of the trade union NSZZ 'Solidarity' (an absolute minimum demand), and beyond that, to liberate from the tutelage of the state as many aspects of public life as possible, creating the basis for 'civic society'. On the other side, the 'party-government' wanted to draw the opposition into co-responsibility for a fast approaching economic catastrophe without at that time genuinely sharing power. What eventually did transpire, later in 1989, went completely beyond the wildest imagination of the sides sitting down at the March Round Table. Analyses of those events should not overlook their historical context. It is worthwhile therefore to recall briefly that context, both its internal and external aspects.

The most important environmental feature was that, in the first half of 1989, Poland was surrounded by rigid communist regimes: in the east the Soviet Union with its nuclear capability, in the south in Czechoslovakia, Husak's hard-line regime, in the west Honecker's apparently immovable German Democratic Republic (GDR). The actual status of the Brezhnev doctrine was in some doubt (some faint hopes were generated by Gorbachev's enigmatic declarations that 'each country is entitled to its own road to development'). Moreover, the Red Army groups based within Poland were ready to act if called upon. Meanwhile, the Polish armed forces were part of the Warsaw Pact structure and incapable (even if they had wanted to) of surprising strategists in Moscow.

On the internal stage, apart from military structures, two powerful, hierarchically organised forces existed, ready at a moment's notice to mobilise their strength to support the crumbling edifice of state communism: the Polish United Workers' Party (*Polska Zjednoczona Partia Robotnicza – PZPR*) and the Security Service (*Służba Bezpieczeństwa – SB*). Although not strong in number the PZPR had a visible and politically influential 'liberal' wing but alongside this also a numerically strong conservative tendency, the 'hardheads' (*twardogłowi*) which, with the traditionalists and the conformist mass of members, could (and did) determine a real alternative to reformist trends in the party. When in January 1990 the Polish United Workers Party went into voluntary liquidation most of the liberals formed a new social-democratic party, the Alliance of the Democratic Left (*Sojusz Lewicy Demokratycznej – SLD*), which in 1993 won a general election and although once again opposition after 1997, had in 1999 and into 2000, the strongest support in opinion polls. Some other liberals joined the Solidarity-based Labour Union (*Unia Pracy – UP*), the left-wing party that in the 1997 elections failed to cross the 5% threshold needed to get into parliament, or moved to a life outside politics in business; on the other hand the 'hardliners' – in political terms – simply became, like the dinosaurs, extinct and retired from public life. In the critical phase of transformation (1989) they were still a potential alternative to the evolutionary process of dismantling the communist system. In any possible conflict of loyalty the SB would without any doubt have supported the conservative and not the reforming trend in PZPR politics.

These generally well-known facts place in context the *socially visible point* of radical system change. This phase of radical change was something that was felt throughout society. It was not just something for the elite but palpable in everyday social consciousness, here was the feeling that something was going on that could change the course of Polish history. It was of course the culmination of very long-standing social processes that had developed under the surface of daily life since the late 1970s but which were barely visible socially because of the almost complete control of public life by the authorities.

However to get to the Round Table negotiations a range of internal and external condition had to be satisfied. No ruling elite volunteers to give up power and none will risk changes to the system that gives it privileges if there is a chance that it can continue to govern alone. But the communists knew that the 1980s model of authoritarian rule (with its ideological base steadily eroding) had produced economic chaos and was incapable of lifting the economy from crisis. It generated in addition political fiasco since it had no base of social support. Any renewed attempt to re-invigorate the ideology underpinning the communist system and so inject it with new life had not the slightest chance of success given society's experience of its first (August 1980) free association in Solidarity. At the end of the 1980s the Soviet Union had also changed substantially and Gorbachev's reluctance to embrace the Brezhnev doctrine deprived local communists of the iron argument, previously a workable substitute for legitimisation, that 'if it's not us it's invasion'. It also opened the way and gave a wide room for manoeuvre to the reformist, liberal wing of the PZPR. Moreover, despite 1980s repression, the Solidarity 'alternative-elite' maintained itself thanks to support not only from society but also, solidly, from the Church. This generated a 1980s chess game between the 'party-government elite' and the

'Solidarity elite' that was immensely important for the peaceful breaking-up of communism. It could have turned out quite differently. Without the experience of 1980–81 communism's collapse would most probably have been prolonged with the danger of violent upheaval and of bloodshed. In this context it is worth briefly reviewing the visible and hidden processes which led, on the one hand, to the Round Table itself and on the other hand it is worth considering processes (often unexpected or unintended) that were activated by discussants.

This does not mean downplaying the importance of events occurring around Poland, especially the erosion of the Brezhnev doctrine and the greater Soviet flexibility in its reaction to Polish developments. In this study we also overlook the role of the Western (mainly US) factor in encouraging a more 'elastic' Soviet response to Polish events. This external factor certainly created extremely important synergies in relation to processes already underway in the country but to delve into these issues would take us beyond the bounds of the present study. We also avoid the detail of Round Table discussions because on that a considerable literature already exists (see Majcherek, 1999; Skórzyński, 1995; *Ostatni rok władzy*, 1994; Paczkowski, 1995) and this is more the subject of history than sociology. Instead we concentrate on the 'process' aspect of radical system change.

THE PROCESSES LEADING TO 1989

The most important processes which led to the 1989 transformation were set in motion at least a decade earlier. Some were the result of the conscious activity of outstanding historical personalities or social groups others were the unintended side-effects of actions of the communist authorities. We consider the most important below:

- the 'de-ideologisation' of communism in the Gierek period (in the 1970s), stimulating a 'consumerism' alongside an economic policy that ended in chaos;
- the emergence of a Polish Pope and his impact during his first pilgrimage to Poland in 1979 in weakening the social atomisation that had previously existed;
- the emergence in the second half of the 1970s of the first germs of a 'counter-elite' in the dissident movement (led by the Workers' Defence Committee, *Komitet Obrony Robotników – KOR*);
- the beginning of thinking, on a mass scale, of alternatives to the communist system and the establishment of a strong social mandate for the 'counter-elite', as occurred in August 1980 when Solidarity was born;

- the declaration of martial law on 13 December 1981 marking the end of the process of 'de-ideologisation' of communism and the start of the process where the 'counter-elite' could think in terms of alternatives to the existing system.

Each of these processes deserves a few words. The 1970s was characterised, in social terms, by at least by two phenomena, which accelerated the erosion of communist ideology on a mass scale. First, consumers' expectations were raised generating high hopes for improved living standards. Such expectations were fired further by Gierek's 'propaganda of success', which claimed Poland to be the tenth industrial power in world terms. Astronomic foreign exchange borrowings were pumped into a defectively operating economic system. They certainly improved the consumer market situation as, for the first time, Western consumption goods appeared to be in *steady* supply. They were also used to shower domestic industry with licences to produce Western goods. All this created the public impression that even a Poland under communist rule could extract itself from the curse of the 'shortage economy' (using Janos Kornai's term) and become the most Western country in the Soviet block. A few specialists realised that the economic revival was about as beautiful as a bunch of cut flowers; it had neither structural or institutional roots nor any permanent foundations. Meanwhile, ideological communist dogmas (the leading role of the communist party, the centrally planned economy, the superiority of state over private ownership, the alliance with the Soviet Union) lost their magnetic power and became merely a ritual way of public life. This was helped along by a massive recruitment of new members for whom the party was a route to a career rather than a political choice. By the end of the 1970s the emerging spectre of economic catastrophe led to social frustration and to the development of what many theorists called a 'pre-revolutionary situation', a sudden collapse of stability and in society's hopes for a speedy improvement in material conditions. Solidarity represented, according to some sociologists who borrowed the classical idea of Alexis de Tocqueville (see Adamski, 1982), a 'revolution of dashed hopes'.

Pope John Paul's first Polish pilgrimage in 1979 had two far-reaching effects. Firstly, the visit upset one basic pillar of the system, namely its social atomisation. Secondly, it was an opportunity for effective social self-organisation outside the obligatory rules of the state. Social isolation, as is well known, is one of the characteristic features of authoritarian systems and in its totalitarian variant that isolation is almost complete. State control of social life is ubiquitous, the only uncontrolled enclaves remaining at the microstructure level, as sociologists refer to them, primary groups (the family, most close and trusted friends). However these enclaves are also mutually isolated and can communicate with each other only through intermediate institutions where control of the authoritarian state is much more meticulous and effective. In principle, horizontal linkages among these groups does not exist. The social world is sharply divided into two spheres: public and private, a situation described elsewhere as 'social dimorphism' (see Wnuk-Lipiński, 1987). Roles performed in public life (controlled by the state) significantly contrast with roles in private life (and sometimes they are in mutual opposition). This situation allows an authoritarian system to maintain and reproduce itself but as long as effective social isolation persists it generates a mass perception of the ubiquitous state. Alongside this there is a sense of the uniqueness of a small group ethos, where opinions and attitudes are revealed in one's own small group. Moreover there is also a conviction that this 'social dimorphism' is the experience only of each small group alone and none other. Dispersed and mutually isolated microstructures cannot consolidate themselves nor can they exist on the public stage and this explains why they cannot be a factor in transformation.

Apart from all its others aspects, the first visit of Pope John Paul II broke down, at least for a time, the barriers between particular small groups: it lifted social isolation. There appeared on the public scene not only (still unstructured) crowds but also a new language of communication, consonant with the language used by small groups. Moreover, participation in these congregations crossed confessional frameworks and became a safe way to demonstrate 'a way out from the system'. At that moment not only was the effective control of public life by the communist state seriously impaired but it upset something even more important for system stability and maintenance, namely it undermined the, until then, widespread conviction that there was no alternative to the system. This experience multiplied in collective consciousness. A process was therefore set in motion which, one year later, in 1980, led to an open crisis of legitimation (see Pańków, 1982). A side effect of this experience, which also permeated social consciousness and a year later became a model of behaviour, was the self-organisation, outside state structures, of public order and discipline as occurred during Pope John Paul's public meetings.

The emergence in the second half of the 1970s of a semi-open dissident movement meant, from a functional viewpoint, a qualitatively new situation in public life. To be sure these movements were too flimsy to become at that time a real transformational force but they were a base for the crystalisation of social dissatisfaction and, aside from the Catholic Church, and sometimes with it, they created autonomous enclaves (not controlled by the communist state) of civil initiative. The appearance of these movements had still one other significant qualitative feature, namely they created the basic conditions from which a 'counter-elite' could later emerge. It was of course only the beginning, at that time the transformation value of these activities was not strong, they had rather a symbolic function, and the motivation of dissident organisations was mainly moral rather than political.

The birth in 1980 of the mass movement called 'Solidarity' generated at least two crucial processes important for our considerations. First, not only in a narrow elite but also in wider social strata, it generalised popular thinking on the reality of social structures that could serve as alternatives to the communist system. Visions of that social order were rather foggy and eclectic (see for example *Rozmowy z rządem PRL*, 1998). That however was less important than the fact that what was being questioned was not just the governing team, but the entire social system, including its normative basis (the party's leading role, the predominance of public ownership and the inviolability of close relations with the Soviet Union). A process of delegitimisation (albeit passive) of the communist system had clearly started. Second, Solidarity's 'counter-elite', emerged for the first time as a second, alongside the Church, autonomous subject of public life. That 'counter-elite' had massive social support and therefore huge transformational strength giving further impetus to the continuing process of system delegitimisation. Indeed it was so strong that it was (correctly) viewed by the authorities in Warsaw and Moscow, as a real threat to the system.

Against the impossibility of restraining all these processes the authorities decided to throw events into reverse by force by introducing martial law on 13 December 1981. However this dramatic event did not have the effect that the Jaruzelski team expected. On the contrary it intensified and accelerated processes already moving in Polish society. Most important, the unintentional (as far as its authors were concerned) side-effect of martial law was to lead the process of 'de-ideologisation' of the communist system to its conclusion. It killed off any remaining system validity drawing on Marxist-Leninist ideology and which survived the first phase of Solidarity. Second, the Communist Party ceased to fulfil the function of system pillar and foundation stone; the centre of gravity was transferred to military structures. Third, both among counter-elite and masses it strengthened radical thinking in terms of system alternatives. Admittedly, martial law reduced in the short term the transformation strength of the Solidarity leadership, cutting it off from a public life over which the communist authorities again seized control. However, more significantly, Solidarity developed a more radical character, moving from simply being 'outside-system' to being 'anti-system'. The fact that the military formula for lifting the country from its economic and civilisational collapse could not succeed and that this became as evident to the authorities of the day was of course also immensely significant.

Waves of social unrest sweeping across the country in 1988 were for the authorities another clear sign of an impending collapse. The political cost of maintaining the monopoly of power and responsibility was increasing. The 'liberal' wing of the ruling group became increasingly tempted by the perspective of incorporating even a part of the counter-elite so, on one hand, reducing the painful legitimisation deficit and, on the other, weakening the anti-system transformation potential of that elite. The constant appeals of the Church for dialogue and reconciliation could be a suitable bridge in achieving this.

For its part the Solidarity elite, after 1988 strikes, which had only limited impact, became conscious of a weakening social support, alongside a continuing potential for conflict that threatened an uncontrolled explosion and even bloodshed. The strikes, on one hand, did not produce such a mass social movement as in 1980 (in fact, the social support for the strikes was dramatically lower than in 1980), and on the other hand, they were organised by a new generation of Solidarity activists, young workers who were ready to abandon the idea of non-violence and to clash with riot police. That awareness created a climate favouring dialogue with the authorities, but only cautiously and only if an initial condition was granted: Solidarity had to re-legalised. For the Solidarity elite the role of the Church was important. Its presence gave some guarantee that a real breakthrough might be reached. It was also a potential mediator in case of a breakdown in dialogue. It also reduced the uncertainty and risk in making any pact with the communist authorities. Simplifying somewhat one might say that at that moment the road to the Round Table was open.

PROCESSES ACTIVATED BY THE 1989 BREAKTHROUGH

The Round Table negotiations have, as noted earlier, generated their own extensive literature. The talks undoubtedly marked a turning point for processes that were already started but, at the same time, in both intended and unintended ways, they set in motion at least three new processes: first came fundamental political change; second, political change activated radical economic change, largely initiated and controlled from above but also with spontaneous elements (an effect of all this was soon felt in the political sphere where the most spectacular illustration was the clear decline in support for the counter-elite); and third, society had to cope with (and still does) very deep social processes partly to do with politics and economics and partly simply autonomous. We can distinguish at least three processes: (1) adaptation to the new rules of the game (democracy) in the political sphere and in the economy (market principles), (2) reshaping social identity under new circumstances, (3) reconsideration of life strategies (on individual and group levels) that would be more compatible with the new rules of the game (some social groups – farmers, coal miners for example – failed to adjust their individual and group strategies to the logic of the new system).

The 'contract' reached at the Round Table led to the memorable elections of 4 June 1989. As is well known, those elections were not fully democratic. A major element of the 'contract' was that general Jaruzelski would become state president. The election was so designed that that the PZPR and its allies (two other small political parties that had existed throughout the communist period) were guaranteed the majority (65%) of parliamentary seats.[1] Despite this the election produced results unexpected by both sides. Communists believed that they would get more than the guaranteed 65%; Solidarity believed that it would form only a small caucus in the sejm and would play the role of political opposition, with Solidarity MPs gaining valuable experience in a new political role, perhaps also slowly learning how to run the state. However, the victory of 'Solidarity-opposition' was so overwhelming that it pushed on to the agenda not only the question of the validity of communist rule but also the validity of the entire system. The legitimation crisis moved into its final and fiercest phase. Society had, in the elections, chosen the alternative to the PRL (*PRL – Polska Rzeczpospolita Ludowa*, Polish Peoples' Republic) system. Thus emerged the strong political base on which could be constructed Poland's first non-communist government in the post Second World War period, that led by Tadeusz Mazowiecki. The road to the Third Polish Republic was open.

THE CONSTRUCTION OF THE NEW ORDER

This radical turn of events posed the question: what should the Third Republic be like, how to shape it? It quickly became clear that while negation and protest tended to bring people together, building a positive programme was a quite different experience, tending to push people apart. The real perspective of radically breaking with the past set in motion new processes of differentiation (mainly political) among the previously united counter-elite. When the Mazowiecki government was formed those processes were at an early stage. Such differences as were about to appear had no fundamental effect, however, on the introduction in 1990 of radical political and economic reforms. All appeared to agree that success in implementing the first stage of economic reform and in particular the bundle of policies wrapped up in the Balcerowicz plan was crucial. The introduction of new rules of the economic game as well as institutional transformation activated spontaneous adaptive processes, the most spectacular effect of which was the exceptional dynamic of private sector developments, between the twilight and legal spheres. Privatisation of the command economy inherited from the former system is a difficult political process that by the end of the 1990s was not yet complete. On the other hand, market rules opened up room for the emergence and development of new, private economic initiatives that were free from political interference. This process shaped Polish society in the 1990s, but also created structural foundations for the future consolidation of a democratic politics and free market system. In fact, all these developments strongly contributed to the creation of new social strata and structures, signalling the emergence of a nascent middle class. However, these creative processes, beginning in 1990, were by no means complete after a decade. In 1999–2000 privatisation and re-privatisation were still under way, and some interest groups, the legacy of the command economy (above all employees of heavy industry but also private farmers trapped in a Polish agricultural structure 'frozen' under the former system – see Jerzy Wilken, chapter 12 in this volume), vigorously struggled for survival. Nonetheless, the development of social structures typical in a market economy was advanced (see Domański, 1996; Mokrzycki, 1994) although tensions due to the co-existence of 'old' and 'new' elements of social structure will also be visible in the years ahead.

Nor, by the end of the 1990s, was institutional rebuilding (partly steered from above) complete. Most institutional solutions inherited from the old system proved to be incompatible with the *modus operandi* of the new system. The health care system based on direct government subsidies regardless of quality of service and number of patients, the social security system (including pensions which were covered from the state budget) and centralised structures of public administration needed a deep reform much earlier than when it was actually implemented in 1999. Politicians, however, were reluctant to act because such deep institutional reform would inevitably undermine existing group interests formed around old institutional arrangements and produce feelings of instability and uncertainty among those accustomed to the older arrangements. Such profound reform always has a political cost and can initially generate chaos and even social unrest. That was exactly what happened to the reforms introduced in 1998 (decentralisation of public administration) and in 1999 (health care and pensions reform, reforms of heavy industry aimed at restructuring, downsizing or shutting down inefficient coal mines and steel mills, and finally, educational reform aimed at opening wider access to secondary and higher education). The social outcomes of those deep reforms will emerge in the first years of the new millennium. The long-term social response to radical institutional change was, in 1999, unclear although the first symptoms looked rather unfavourable as support for the reformist AWS-UW government drastically declined. However we are discussing long-term, and to a significant degree spontaneous processes. 'Control from above' can at most fix their general course.

SOCIAL REACTION TO CHANGE

A radical change of political system of the type experienced in Poland (even if it is peaceful and evolutionary) can stimulate immensely high social expectations where people look forward to speedily improved material conditions. But hopes can also be dashed and popular support can readily switch even to support forces that were in some way linked with the older order. This, at any rate, is what happened in Poland where radical change took place first in the context of a conflict of values. But the final defeat of the old system and the launch of the new social order occurred as a gradual movement where social perceptions drifted away from their values base to become more strongly anchored to group interests or individual needs. Individuals observe and experience political breakthrough at three levels: concerning *values*, *interests* and *needs*. Of course subjective factors influence all three.[2]

System transformation can objectively expand the scope of achieving some values. Transformation is also experienced and judged in terms of *group interests*. Once again, objective circumstances shift the pattern of group interests. It is worth recalling that the realisation of group interest is connected with a given social and institutional structure while the very definition of group interest emerges from the functioning of the social and institutional structure. The way in which a given structure functions determines the scope for the realisation of diverse group interests and dictates the manner of rational behaviour of group members leading to protection of group interest.

Experiences in achieving interest group objectives and even in defining 'interests' at a time of system upheaval are of limited (or even no) use as the old social and institutional structures disintegrate (along with their behavioural norms) and new structures emerge in their place, operating according to a different logic and new rules of game. This was the transformational situation that Polish society had to cope with after the collapse of communism. Social and institutional structures shaped by, and for, central planning mechanisms gradually yielded to structures emerging from the free market (for example, in the institutional sphere: a central bank independent of current political decisions of the government, a stock exchange, legal protection of free enterprise and private property; in the social sphere the rapid growth of private business). However, these market-orientated structures alone were too weak to overcome the burden of communist system legacy even if there was strong back up in the political class. In fact the problem to be solved was the following: how to build capitalism without capital. Not only in Poland, but also for most Central and East European countries emerging from comunism, capitalism seemed to be the only alternative to the command economy. However, contrary to the Western world, where capitalism gradually emerged from a long-lasting social and technological process, here capitalism was perceived as an ideological project. It had to be constructed on the ruins of the former system. Therefore, some theoreticians labelled this phenomenon as 'political capitalism' (see Offe, 1992; Staniszkis, 1991). This process continues as group interests formed by the previous system meet growing barriers in new conditions. This also shapes political behaviour, especially in elections, with pressure to slow reforms and minimise their social costs. Since transformation takes place in conditions of democracy, social expectations have a critical significance since they can be transformed into collective political action forcing, at central level, decisions compatible with those expectation. Perhaps we can roughly distinguish two diverse and fundamental trends in terms of the social and political implication of economic changes: first, those which strengthen the social base of reform, and second, trends that weaken this base.[3]

Let us first consider positive trends. In the course of the last 10 years the inflation rate was gradually reduced (from 251% in 1989 and 586% in 1990 to less than 10% in 1999), industrial productivity has increased while GDP quickly rose again after an initial sharp decline. Among negative trends the leading place is occupied by unemployment whose rate by the end of the 1990s seemed stuck at 12% to 13%, among the highest in Europe. The level of consumption is, according to many specialists, the most sensitive of the indicators that underpin the abstract category, the 'social costs of transformation' (see Przeworski, 1991). In Poland it systematically declined between 1989 and 1992, following an even more dramatic fall over 1989 and 1990. After 1992 it started to rise gradually, however the pace of that growth was strongly differentiated across particular social-professional groups. If the trend of declining consumption was halted inequalities of life in Polish society increased. Poles generally accept income inequalities so long as they are not too great (see Kolarska-Bobińska, 1998). According to a popular definition of social justice the range of lowest to highest average incomes should not exceed 1:10, whereas the popular *perception* of this proportion is 1:18; in fact it is, according to Roguska (1996), lower at 1:11. However from the point of view of social stability what people believe to be true is more important. The discrepancy between income inequalities that are *defined* as fair and inequalities that are *perceived* leads to considerable dissatisfaction over existing living standards. This is accompanied by a growing feeling of relative deprivation, particularly among the lowest income strata (see Białecki and Zaborowski, 1998). We can expect that the tension produced by widely spread relative deprivation will shape the attitudes of Poles in the next decade.

The most spectacular victims of economic reform are the unemployed, a social category which did not exist in the old system where full employment was a major policy objective. Farmers form another important 'victim' group: they have serious problems with the declining profitability of production and simply in selling their goods in the presence of strong competition on the market. The third group includes public sector workers, both those in state-provided services and in state-owned industry. Across all these categories people find economic reform threatening. They do not feel, following the collapse of communism, compensated by political freedom nor by the clearly visible improvement in macroeconomic indicators.

Nevertheless, public opinion surveys show that positive opinions decidedly predominate. To the question, 'Given the perspective of time can you say whether it was worthwhile or not to have changed the political system in 1989?'

some 60% answered yes in 1994, 75% in 1995, 70% in 1997 and 63% in 1999 (CBOS, 1999a). Since 1995 the trend has pointed down, this however may be explained by the growing feeling of relative deprivation, mentioned above. One can only speculate how the trend will look like in the future. Providing that Poland will not experience an economic crisis over the next decade it seems to be more likely that firm support for 1989 radical change will continue to be expressed by majority of the population. Democracy is also deeply rooted. In answer to the question, 'Do you agree or disagree with the statement – "democracy has advantages over all other systems?"' 52% in 1992 said 'yes', 62% in 1993, 67% in 1995, 63% in 1997, and 64% in 1999 (number of those who disagree varies from 11% in 1993 to 19% in 1999, the rest has no opinion). There is however less satisfaction with the Polish version of democracy. Responding to the question, 'Generally speaking are you satisfied or dissatisfied with the way democracy functions in our country?' some 36% answered 'yes' in 1993, 30% in 1995, 44% in 1996, 41% in 1998 but only 28% in 1999.

The decisive decline of trust in the Polish version of democracy observed in 1999 was connected (directly and indirectly) with the reforms introduced by the AWS-UW coalition government. These were, as noted above: decentralisation of public administration with its new regional administrative structure; health service reform, replacing a budget subsidised system with an insurance system; pensions reform with the introduction of new pension funds; and education reform. These complete the radical phase of institutional rebuilding changing fundamentally the existing procedures and systems. They also have a direct bearing on daily life. Their introduction was however badly managed and the timing was, in a sense, contrary to a general social trend that gathered strength from 1993, opposing further radical change. The reforms caused discontent and even anxiety in some sections of society. As we noted earlier, every deep reform must upset the existing structure of group interests. It was no different in this case. Reform of the health service, for instance, hit those group interests that were rooted in the logic of the former health care system. It also introduced uncertainty among patients, especially older patients, those more familiar with the previous system. Some aspects of this reform certainly made matters worse for some groups (see Cichocka, 1999).

Reforms unavoidably destabilise, even if only for a short time, and in democratic conditions groups under threat defend themselves, playing on and stimulating social dissatisfaction (through confrontation including street riots, road blockades and so on). At the end of 1998 surveys showed that knowledge of the reforms was poor, exacerbating uncertainties and worries. More than half of those polled declared that they knew that reforms of the health service, pensions and education would be introduced in 1999, *but* they admitted that they did not know what the point of the reforms was. One in four were seriously worried about the reforms with one-third expressing hopes in them and a further third concerns (CBOS, 1998). In March 1999 a large majority (69%) of those surveyed thought that simultaneously introducing the reforms was a mistake. Moreover, public support for each reform decreased dramatically after their launch which can only mean that their introduction completely missed the target (CBOS, 1999c). This seems to be a clear indicator that the government badly managed the reforms. However this factor alone is probably not fully responsible for the extent of the sceptical reception they met. If we look at general trends in the last decade we may say that the revolutionary euphoria – related to 1989 – expired roughly around 1993. Since then the majority of Polish society was preoccupied with finding how best to satisfy interests under the new rules of the game. Perhaps the simultaneous start of four key reforms in such a short period of time conflicted with a general hope for stability, for a pause that would allow people to develop life strategies compatible with the logic of the new system.

CONCLUSIONS AND PERSPECTIVES FOR THE FUTURE

In Poland the 'social geography' of initial support for Solidarity and a complete reform package (economic and political) did not neatly map onto the 'social geography' of winners and losers. Many who were initially against reform gained whereas many who promoted reform lost. There was a widespread feeling of relative deprivation among those threatened by market rules and this gave rise to two exceptionally important phenomena:

- *the speedy erosion of the common belief in a better future*, a belief related to a package of radical reforms and linked to a political elite of 'Solidarity' provenance, an elite whose political profile was inextricably tied to those reforms. Victory in 1989 led to a split in the, as it was then, Solidarity 'counter-elite' and the emergence of Solidarity-rooted political parties that started to struggle for power on the ruins of former system. A part of the early counter-elite did not survive this struggle but there were newcomers predominantly recruited from trade-union activists;
- *a narrowing of perspectives*, instead of defining group interests according to the category of long-term benefits for all society this became very much curtailed. This process was accelerated by the fact that the free-market economy was a threat not only to certain defined group interests, but to the very existence of some groups. Among interests defined in relation to economic institutions it concerned (and still does) some enterprises inherited from the communist economy (chiefly in mining and heavy industry), created according to the 'command-rationing' logic and with huge trouble in adapting to free-market rules. On the other hand among social groups, private farmers felt threatened. They realised very quickly that they could

> satisfy their interests better in the 'shortage economy' with its extended 'second economy' and had to struggle to survive in a market system with its limited demand for food and its strong international competition.

The social expectations released by the fall of communism considerably exceeded the possibilities of a weak economy. This led to a significant growth of social pessimism, disappointment and frustration. The widening scissors of social inequality, unavoidable given the starting point of 'equality in poverty', only deepened this gloomy mood. However, groups which reorientated themselves finding their way in the market economy began to emerge comparatively quickly (private business and especially in the service sector). Meanwhile, among the structural 'victims' of transformation hopes revived of a return to a greater state presence in the economy, a return to some aspects of social provision (for example free vacations) or to full employment (even at the cost of economic efficiency). The echo of those earlier times is however weak, with appeals to the regulation of the old system having a very limited reach and a tendency to diminish (CBOS, 1999e).

The market economy and democracy, despite the disappointments of a significant part of society, is accepted by the majority and the new system is moving into a phase of consolidation. Poland enters the twenty-first century as a free democratic state with an economy that is developing fast based on healthy foundations. Of course Poland, as any other medium-sized economy, will also be vulnerable to international economic shocks as well as to the cyclical recessions of the world economy. In the next decade Poland will certainly be more open to the global market; it is obvious that the more it is a part of the world economy the more it is vulnerable to international economic turbulence. We can also expect that the coming years will not be free of internal social conflict. There will be a continuation of conflicts over the further privatisation of the economy, as well as over restructuring agriculture and heavy industry. Another important issue that may produce serious internal conflict is the process of European integration. Poland was perceived by the European Commission as likely to be one of the first candidates to accede to the EU in the early years of the new millennium. The Polish political class is unanimous in its support for the integration of Poland into the political and economic structures of Europe. However as negotiation on accession goes on, the general idea of integration becomes translated into concrete measures (legal and political) that are and will continue to be the subject of intense political debate. As in the case of all other EU members we may expect also in Poland the emergence of *eurosceptics* and *euroenthusiasts*. This difference will most probably shape Polish public debate in the next few years. Some political groups (of nationalist or agrarian orientation) are already developing eurosceptic positions and arguments. The conflict over accession will go on alongside other disputes that seem to be typical of a society undergoing a deep systemic transformation.

Arguments will sometimes be stormy but they will have two key features worth noting. First, they will be conflicts with a much more decentralised character: they will not develop along an 'authorities–society' axis. Second, they will have a 'within-' and not 'anti-system' aspect. That is why it is reasonable to expect that social legitimisation of the new order will continue and will strengthen democratic and free market institutions so reinforcing the process of consolidation.

NOTES

1 During the communist period while the PZPR dominated formal political life two smaller parties were also permitted a parliamentary presence, ZSL (the peasants' party) and SD (the democratic party).

2 To avoid misunderstanding it is necessary to clarify the meaning of the terms: *values, interests* and *needs*. These analytical concepts are variously defined in a rich literature (for example: Joubert, 1992; Rychard, 1999; Adamski, 1999, Ziółkowski, 1993; Wnuk-Lipiński, 1998) but here we limit ourselves to definitions used in the present study. *Values* are considered as established in the cultural tradition, desired by individuals, groups and societies. For example, values like freedom, equality, independence, dignity, tolerance, honesty and so on. Such values perform normative functions which can regulate macro-social rather than micro-social relations and they perform functions in the sphere of national culture rather than at the level of particular structures. *Interests* are understood here, as the revealed preferences or more explicit aims of a group enabling its members to satisfy individual and family needs more effectively. When interests are expressed in terms of group aims they usually produce collective action. Most often, interests are defined in economic terms but one can easily point to some interests that have no direct economic features (for example those connected with the maintenance of the social status quo or linked with public order). If interests refer to social groups (particularly to classes) then *needs* are related mainly to individuals and households.

3 The macroeconomic tendencies which should naturally help build the social base of reforms do not necessarily immediately extend political support to reforming groups since their transmission to the micro level (fundamental for households) requires time and is often not a simple function of general tendencies in the economy and tendencies to resist do not immediately increase support for the reform opposition and inertia causes delays here too. It is worth however noting that 'positive' macro-tendencies (growth of

national income, inflation reduction, decline in unemployment and so on) seem to affect political attitudes more slowly and weakly than 'negative' macroeconomic tendencies (decline of national income, unemployment growth, rise of inflation and cuts in social services).

REFERENCES

Adamski, W.W. (1982), 'Structural and Generation Aspects of a Social Conflict', in *Sisyphus Sociological Studies*, vol. III, Warsaw: PWN.

Adamski, W. (1999), 'The Evolution of Acquisitive and Threatened Interests in the Process of Ownership Transformation', in *System Change and Modernization*, ed. W.A. Adamski, J. Buncak, P. Machonin and Dominique Martin, Warsaw: IFiS PAN.

Białecki, I. and Zaborowski, W. (1998), 'Poczucie deprywacji potrzeb materialnych a cele życiowe jednostek' (The feeling of material needs deprivation and life goals of individuals), in *Polacy '95. Aktorzy i klienci transformacji,* Warsaw: IFiS PAN.

CBOS (1998), *Stosunek do reform systemowych: Komunikat z badań* (The attitude to system reforms: Research communication), Warsaw.

CBOS (1999a), *Oceny zmian po roku '89: Komunikat z badań* (Assessments of changes after 1989: Research communication), Warsaw.

CBOS (1999b), *Społeczna ocena demokracji i instytucji politycznych: Komunikat z badań* (Social assessment of democracy and political institutions: Research communication), Warsaw.

CBOS (1999c), *Krajobraz po wprowadzeniu reform: Komunikat z badań* (Post reform landscape: Research communication), Warsaw.

CBOS (1999d), *Nadzieje i obawy Polaków: Komunikat z badań* (Poles' expectations and anxieties), Warsaw.

CBOS (1999e), *Pełne półki i poczucie wolności – bilans zmian w ostatnim dziesięcioleciu: komunikat z badań* (Full shelves and a sense of freedom – balance of changes over the last decade: research communication), Warsaw.

Cichocka, E. (1999), 'Leczą nas jak wściekli' (They cure us as crazy), *Gazeta Wyborcza*, no. 220, 20 September.

Domański, H. (1996), *Na progu konwergencji. Stratyfikacja społeczna w krajach Europy Środkowo–Wschodniej* (On the verge of convergence. Social stratification in Central and East European countries),Warsaw: IFiS PAN.

Joubert, D. (1992), *Reflections on Social Values*, Pretoria: Human Science Research Council.

Kolarska-Bobińska, L. (1998), 'Postawy egalitarne i interesy w procesie zmian ustrojowych' (Egalitarian attitudes and interests in the process of systemic transformation), in *Polacy '95. Aktorzy i klienci transformacji*, Warsaw: IFiS PAN.

Majcherek, J.A. (1999), *Pierwsza dekada III Rzeczypospolitej 1989–1999* (The first decade of III Republic 1989–1999), Warsaw: Presspublica.

Mokrzycki, E. (1994), 'Nowa klasa średnia?' (A New middle class?), *Studia Socjologiczne*, no. 1.

Offe, C. (1992), 'Kapitalizm jako projekt demokratyczny?' (Capitalism as a democratic project?), *Studia Socjologiczne*, no. 3–4.

Ostatni rok władzy 1988–1989. Tajne dokumenty Biura Politycznego i Sekretariatu KC (The last year of power. Secret documents of Politbureau and Secretariat of Central Committee) (1994), ed. Stanisław Perzkowski, London: Aneks.

Paczkowski, A. (1995), *Półwieku dziejów Polski 1939–1989* (Half a Century of Polish History 1939–1989), Warsaw: PWN.

Pańków, W. (1982), 'The Roots of the Polish Summer; A crisis of the System of Power', in *Sisyphus. Sociological Studies*, vol. III, Warsaw: PWN.

Przeworski, A. (1991), *Political Dynamics of Economic Reforms: East and South, Democracy and Political Transitions*, ed. G. Soboszlai, Budapest: Hungarian Political Science Association.

Roguska, B. (1996), 'Prestiż zawodów a struktura zarobków' (Prestige of occupations and earnings' structure), *Serwis informacyjny CBOS*, no. 10, October.

Rozmowy z rządem PRL (Talks with the Government of the Polish People's Republic) (1998), Warsaw: Niezależna Oficyna Wydawnicza.

Rychard, A. (1999), 'Social Actors and Institutions: Strategies of Adaptation', in, *System Change and Modernization*, ed. W.A. Adamski, J. Buncak, P. Machonin and Dominique Martin, Warsaw: IFiS PAN.

Skórzyński, J. (1995), *Ugoda i rewolucja. Władza i opozycja 1985–1989* (Agreement and revolution. Power and opposition 1985–1989), Warsaw: Presspublica.

Staniszkis, J. (1991), 'Political capitalism in Poland', *Eastern European Politics and Society*, no. 1.

Wnuk-Lipiński, E. (1987), 'Social Dimorphism and Its Implications', in *Crisis and Transition. Polish Society in the 1980s*, (ed.) Jadwiga Koralewicz, Ireneusz Bialecki and Margaret Watson, Oxford-New York-Hamburg: Berg.

Wnuk-Lipiński, E. (ed.) (1998), *Values and Radical Social Change*, Warsaw: ISP PAN.

Ziólkowski, M. (ed.) (1993), *Polacy wobec ladu postmonocentrycznego* (Poles in the presence of post-monocentric order), Warsaw: ISP PAN.

5. Industrial relations in Poland: from social partnership to enlightened paternalism?

Włodzimierz Pańków and Barbara Gąciarz

INTRODUCTION

Our aim in this chapter is to describe and interpret industrial relations developments in Poland in the 1990s and to look ahead to the factors shaping them in the new millennium. We examine the nature of trade unions in Poland, how representative of workers they are and how they function in the enterprise. In this chapter we look at industrial relations largely from a micro perspective (our research is based on what happens in the firm). We describe how the social climate in the enterprise is perceived in the view of the three major groups, or social actors, at firm level – workers, trade union activists and management. However we also consider the wider influence of trade unions and make some suggestions on the evolution of industrial relations and collective bargaining in Poland.

In Poland, the term 'collective bargaining' or 'industrial relations' (*zbiorowe stosunki pracy*) refers to a legally structured activity, based on legislation regulating relations between employers and employees (the legislation dates from May 1991 and applies mainly to state-owned enterprises). *Employers* take on an institutional form in trade associations and as the management of individual businesses. *Employees* emerge institutionally in the shape of national, regional and enterprise trade unions. In Poland, at the micro level that concerns us, industrial relations are shaped in a tripartite framework involving three key social actors: enterprise management, trades unions and workers. We say little about other levels since they did not form part of the specific research reported here and the highest level, the so-called 'tripartite commission (*Komisja Trójstronna*), has not functioned for two years because of a boycott on the part of the OPZZ (*Ogólno-Polskie Porozumienie Związków Zawodowych*).

THE TRADE UNION SCENE IN POLAND

The representativeness of trade unions is a major concern in industrial relations. How representative are Polish trade unions? We try to answer this by drawing a picture of the most important features of trade unions in the enterprise, their evolution and how they behave. Our research builds on the views expressed by people in the workplace and is based on a 1998 survey of 202 state and private firms and institutions across seven areas: (1) food industry, (2) wood and paper, (3) chemicals, (4) cars, (5) construction, (6) education, and (7) health. Our observations, based on the views of the key players, are that:

- first, in the late 1990s industrial relations was almost completely dominated by the Solidarity union (we touch on its competitor, the OPZZ, later). Workers, directors and union activists alike saw Solidarity as the employers' main partner in collective bargaining;
- second, at that time a clear trade union 'conservatism' still existed where some of the 'old', traditional union structures figured prominently. The Polish teachers' union, viewed by many as a 'natural' partner of educational institutions' management, is one such example;
- third, new union structures were also emerging largely based on professional connections (for example, doctors, anaesthetists, or various highly-skilled groups in the mining sector). However those new structures remained, in the late 1990s, rather scattered and constituted only a small part of the industrial relations scene. They were too weak to play a fundamental role and found it hard to develop further because of workers' conservatism and the (for the new unions) uncomfortable institutional structure favouring either a sector-wide approach or else highly atomised local and separate negotiations at the level of the individual enterprise. So, while new union structures can sometimes make much noise in the struggle over working conditions (because of the strategic position of the professional groups they represent, as in the case of the anaesthetists' strike in 1999) it is much harder to secure a permanent position in national negotiating structures. Decentralisation of public administration from 1999 and continuing economic deregulation is not, in our view, likely to make matters any easier for new trade union structures.

Other social survey data provide a useful background and help complete the picture. The CBOS polling organisation found in 1999 a surprisingly low level of unionisation in the Polish labour force (see CBOS, 1999). Only one in five of the economically active population claimed to belong to trade unions (24% of men and 14% of women). In the adult population as a whole only slightly more than one in ten (11%) said they were members of a trade union; middle-aged respondents were the most likely to be involved while the youngest and the oldest were least likely to be in unions.[1] Officially reported data suggest that in Poland there are were around 6 million trade union members in the early 1990s and our estimate is that by the end of the decade that number had fallen to 3 or 3.5 million of which *Solidarność* had around 1 million.

In the light of such statistics, the view that Poland's so-called 'union base' is rapidly contracting seems well substantiated. In most sectors trade unions cannot be described as representative in terms of having a majority of employees although they do continue to constitute the largest workers' organisations. Nevertheless their shallow base is becoming increasingly apparent both in their own activity and in the attitude towards them of other potential industrial relations partners. In more and more industrial relations conflicts where workers' interests are threatened unions react by building superstructures (broader based committees of support and the like), a sure sign of awareness of their own limitations.

There are many different levels of 'unionisation' across socio-professional groups and business ownership structures (public/private sectors). Trade union members, it turns out, are mainly skilled workers (28% of our sample), middle managers and professionals (25%) and lower level white-collar workers (23%). On the other hand, only 5% of farmers and 1% of the self-employed reported any trade union affiliation. Some 40% of state sector industrial workers, nearly 33% of those in the public sector and 17% of those employed in mixed public–private companies are trade union members. In private farming, 6% declared trade union affiliation but a mere 3% of private sector workers (excluding farming) did so.

WHO DO TRADE UNIONS SERVE? PERCEPTIONS IN THE FIRM

It is interesting to ask in this context what workers themselves think of the representativeness (and general usefulness) of their trade unions. In our research only 7% of workers were convinced that Solidarity, which dominates the industrial relations scene in the workplace and in the country as a whole, '*clearly* serves the country's economic interests'. An even smaller proportion (6%) believed that Solidarity 'serves the interests of *all* workers'. The percentage of workers prepared to say that the Solidarity served the country and workers '*fairly* well' was much greater (35% and 29% respectively). But negative views were also strong. As many as 40% of workers thought that Solidarity did '*not* serve the interests of *all* workers', while around 33% believe that the union did '*not* serve the country's economic interests'. The 'don't knows' (around 25% in each case) who found it difficult to evaluate who and what interests Solidarity serves was surprisingly high and was probably due to the fact that a very large proportion of workers, and this may surprise readers in the West, *fail* to notice Solidarity's existence or activity in any form whatsoever.

Solidarity's OPZZ competitor comes off no better. Only around 33% of workers we questioned thought that the OPZZ served the country's economic interests and workers' interests, whilst only 4% believed that it 'served them well'; the remainder however thought that it served them 'fairly well'. Some 27% of workers thought that OPZZ did '*not* serve the interests of all workers', while around 31% believed that the union did '*not* serve the country's economic interests'. A very high proportion of 'don't knows' (around 40%) means that the OPZZ's economic and social activity is even less perceptible than Solidarity's.

It is revealing but perhaps not surprising that management takes a dim view of unions' activity in the sense that a very high proportion of directors (72%) believe that no union or other institution adequately represents workers' interests. This suggests that there is some basis for what Gardawski has called the 'abandoned society syndrome'. Less than 4% of directors believed that workers' interests were well represented nationally by any institution, although 8% pointed to Solidarity as fulfilling this role. Solidarity's involvement as a partner in government after 1997 has probably helped diminish its rating still further.

Table 5.1. Workers' views on Solidarity and OPZZ (% of workers in sample with each view)

	Solidarity	OPZZ
Clearly serves the country 'well'	7	4
Clearly serves the workers 'well'	6	4
Serves the country 'fairly well'	35	33
Serves the workers 'fairly well'	29	33
Does not serve the country 'well'	33	27
Does not serve the workers 'well'	40	31
'Don't know' if it serves the country	25	40
'Don't know' if it serves the workers	25	40

Note: Some may have chosen more than one category so that sub-totals may not add to 100.

Source: Own research, based on a survey of 202 state and private businesses in 1998.

To what extent do institutions in Poland articulate and defend workers' interests? It turns out that nearly 60% of our respondents believed that no institution does this adequately. We have noted that over 70% of directors and chairmen of firms expressed a similar opinion. CBOS has found too that only

16% of the population believe that trade unions represent, in a national sense, the interests of rank and file workers. Another 8% believe that the state President represents those interests. It is striking that institutions that were by the late 1990s 'saturated' with former unionists or their advisers are not held in high regard: some 5% believe that the government defends workers' interests and 2% believe the Sejm does. The Sejm's poor standing is especially noticeable, given that at least one-quarter of deputies are trade union sponsored MPs. Finally, some 3% of workers believe that the Church represents the interests of rank and file workers.

In response to the question: which trade union best represents the interests of 'people such as themselves'? as many as 43% said 'none' and an additional 16% opted for 'hard to say'. This means, in all, that nearly 60% of respondents failed to perceive any representation of workers' interests in Polish public life. Only 14% believed that Solidarity represented working people, 11% that the OPZZ did, while 'Farmers' Self-defence' (*Samoobronna*) got around 9% (but farmers, not surprisingly, opted for it strongly – 47% of them). It is worth noting that during the 1990s the proportion of people regarding Solidarity as the best representative of working peoples' interests fell by one-third (from 21% to 14%), the percentage choosing *Samoobronna* almost doubled (from 5% to 9%) and the percentage preferring the OPZZ remained practically unchanged.

Table 5.2. Popular support for various trade unions (% of respondents agreeing that the 'the union represents 'people like me')

	Late 1990s
Solidarity	14
OPZZ	11
Samoobronna	9
None	43
Hard to say	16

Source: Own research, as in text.

More important, during the 1990s, those who believe that *no* trade union represents the interests of 'people such as themselves' rose by over one-third. As noted above, Solidarity's decline may be explained by its role in government and the implementation (in 1999) of costly social reforms described in some detail in other chapters of this book (see, in particular, Belka, chapter 2, Wnuk-Lipiński, chapter 4). *Samoobrona*'s rise undoubtedly stems from the role it played in farmers' protests against the government's economic policy in the winter of 1999.

All this suggests that in the political and institutional system in Poland at the start of the new millennium trade unions are not in a good position to defend workers' interests effectively. The view that trade unions do not effectively defend workers' interests was held by 63% of our respondents and a further 14% thought it was 'hard to say'. Less than 25% took the opposite view. Moreover, almost half of our sample thought that trade unions had too little influence in public life in Poland (on major decision making), 14% reckoned their influence was 'just right', only 20% believed it was too great, and 16% simply 'did not know'.

As far as the microcosm of the workplace is concerned we wanted to know if, in the case of any employment or work-based difficulty, workers had anyone to turn to. There was a certain amount of enterprise level optimism in this regard – although *not* necessarily in relation to the firms' union organisations. As many as 86% of workers and 77% of trade union activists declared that there was someone at work to turn to if problems arose. Management was even more optimistic, 90% thought that this was so. The striking thing however is that workers would rarely turn to a trade union (see Table 5.3). Workers are, it seems, more likely to turn to immediate superiors than to trade unions for help in dealing with workplace problems. It is stunning that only 2% (one in fifty workers) would turn to their enterprise trade unions. Managers were a little more generous: 7% thought that the trade union was a place for workers to go in this regard. Nevertheless the figure was far from impressive. Trade union activists, as was to be expected, had the most positive outlook but even so only one in ten thought that the union was the best 'guardian'. Even the activists were more likely to turn to immediate superiors or work colleagues for help.

Table 5.3. Workers' views on inter-personal relationships in the workplace

Do you have someone to whom to turn in the event of difficulties?	Responses (%)
Yes	86
My immediate superiors	59
The management of my department	14
Colleagues at work	9
Trade unions	2
Workers' self-management bodies	0
Someone else	1
No	8
Hard to say	6

Source: Own research.

To sum up, many daily events as well as press, radio and television accounts, constantly give the impression that trade unions are powerful and relish their strong following in society. However, somewhat unnoticed, the situation has changed fundamentally with a serious atrophying of confidence in trade unions and much weaker expectations linked to their activity. It seems that trade unions' position and significance in the late 1990s and early years of the new decade stem more from their particular role in the political system than from support and influence in the workplace. Trade unions, particularly Solidarity and OPZZ (supplemented in the late 1990s by farmers' trade unions), do have considerable influence (often through simple lobbying), since they possess a priceless instrument of political campaigning: a national network with full-time staff and organisational apparatus. By contrast, political parties continue to look organisationally like 'popular movements', which is why they try to build their influence through, or alongside, trade union structures, using unions' organisational apparatus as they need. Naturally, these relations rest on reciprocity and politicians must repay unions by acquiescing to at least some of their demands. This is however a situation that is not foreign to European or American traditions (in the UK the Labour Party with the TUC; in Germany the SPD with the BVD; and in the USA the Democrats with the AFL-CIO). The fundamental difference between Poland and the West is that the majority of Polish workers, by the late 1990s, did not see any benefit for themselves in these arrangements. They tended to believe that unions used such links exclusively to serve the particular interests of the trade union apparatus and certain narrow social or political interest groups.

It is particularly interesting that the role of trade unions, traditionally expressed in the idea of solidarity between people, has been dissolving day by day. In times of trouble and difficulties at work a clear majority of workers will tend to turn to superiors at various levels of seniority for help. The decline in union authority in the workplace also seems to suggest that Polish workers are more *inclined* to a corporatist, rather than a class-based perception of the firms in which they work. Perhaps this is partly the result of the ideas, vigorously pushed in the late 1980s and early 1990s, of the virtues of enterpreneurialism and economic success. Maybe this has encouraged workers to be increasingly individualistic in adapting to economic and social problems. Moreover, workers seem to link solutions to their immediate problems more with improvement of the situation in their firm rather than with any struggle over macroeconomic interests on a national level. Apart from a sense of corporatism, identifying rather strongly with the enterprise, this also suggests a preponderance of pragmatism over ideology and of micro-social concerns over those of a macro-social nature.

TRADE UNION ACTIVITY AND INFLUENCE IN THE WORKPLACE

Our research also tried to show how trade union activity was perceived by those who ought to be most interested in it, the workers themselves. Our surveys suggest that in the late 1990s only around one-half of workers were aware of any trade union activity in their own workplaces. One in five workers said they knew nothing about trade unions' work, and almost as many said they were 'not very familiar' with it. In view of the general attitudes towards trade unions noted above this should not be surprising. It is the result of mutually reinforcing factors. In particular, trade unions' activity is most probably mainly directed at existing members. Meanwhile increasingly individualistic workers lack interest in unions and look elsewhere for solutions to their most pressing problems. Looking more closely at unions' activity we found that very few workers saw unions as fighting for better working conditions (only 6% in our sample) or resisting lay-offs (4% in our survey). Trade unions are rarely perceived, at least by workers, as a defence against redundancy. Some other negative perceptions also exist even if they are less frequently put including, for example, the opinion of some workers that unions 'just carry out orders from headquarters; they look out for themselves; they don't do anything', or, very rarely expressed neutrally, the view that they attempt to play the role of firms' joint-owners.

To sum up, trade unions' activity looked, in the late 1990s, none too impressive in the eyes of workers. There is no basis here for the popular view that trade unions are trying to broaden their activities to spheres traditionally reserved for enterprise management. If some trace of union activity in these areas exists, there is not the slightest indication that unions have pretensions to be joint-owners or joint-managers of Polish firms. Our research rather permits the charge that trade unions do *not* make their presence felt in businesses and state enterprises. This has been in one sense the natural consequence of the first 10 years of economic transformation.

When we try to probe the real rather than the supposed influence of trade unions in the workplace through the views of the three key social actors on the intra-firm stage (directors, union activists and workers) we find a richer and more complicated picture although it supports the general tendencies outlined above. *Union activists* are on one hand too optimistic as to the real ability of trade unions to influence matters in the firm and on the other they have by far the strongest aspirations regarding the desirable influence of trade unions in various areas of institutional life. It is the *workers* who have the most pessimistic view of the scope and structure of unions' influence. Workers' views are interestingly close to those of *managers*. If we assume that workers and managers are likely to report the most realistic views as to what goes on in the firm (whereas trade union activists may be more prone to exaggeration) then we can say that trade unions' real influence is limited to areas like allocation of welfare benefits, dispensing allowances and loans, health and safety and so on. Trade unions have barely any impact on firms' development strategies, modernisation and/or restructuring plans, management and administrative appointments and the like. Trade unions have hardly any influence on purely economic matters. If such influence exists, the most the unions have is an input and certainly not any decisive voice. As already noted, in the enterprises we researched, the scope and structure of trade union influence is, as *trade union activists* see it, significantly greater than in the opinion of *management* or *workers*. The activists often believe that trade unions' influence over many areas of working life is great, even decisive. It seems, however, that the activists' optimism as to their influence over decisions in the workplace has no foundation in reality.

TRADE UNIONS AND FIRMS' ECONOMIC HEALTH

What is the connection, as workers see it, between firms' economic health and the presence of trade unions? We examined the attitudes of two of our three key groups within the enterprise, directors and workers, asking how they viewed changes in the economic situation of the firm over a two-year period. We deliberately left out union activists because their views tend to the 'extremes' – either excessively optimistic or pessimistic. It should be remembered too that the views expressed could be the result of 'third factors' such as firms' size, sector, ownership status, all of which have an impact on whether trade unions exist in the workplace.

Starting with management and its views on links between trade union presence and economic condition, it appears that there is no clear connection between the two. Directors believe that the economic situation of firms in which trade unions were active improved or worsened just as frequently, or as infrequently, as in those with no trade unions. A different view comes from workers. Workers in *non-unionised* firms were more likely to report that they observed an improvement in their firm's economic condition. Meanwhile workers in *unionised* firms were much more likely than their non-unionised colleagues to report a worsening in their firm's economic condition.

A different picture emerges if we consider links between trade union presence and pay. As might be expected, management tends towards 'optimism': almost 90% of the directors we questioned thought that pay rates had not worsened; almost half believed that pay had increased and only 10% admitted they thought that pay had fallen. Workers' interpretation of the pay dynamic is less optimistic, although well over half confirmed that their pay had not decreased in the two years prior to the survey date. While there is no clear statistical link between trade union presence and pay as management sees it, workers, if they believe in such a link, also believe it to be negative. Only 25% of workers in unionised firms declared that pay had increased whereas 40% of those in non-unionised firms admitted to pay increases. Pay cuts were reported by almost twice as many workers in unionised firms than in non-unionised.

Turning to the link between status, pay and trade union presence, dissatisfaction comes across more strongly. Some 56% of workers were dissatisfied with their status and 64% with their pay. Moreover there appears to be a rather strong and negative link between status and pay on one hand and trade union presence on the other. This is reflected in the following features:

- many more workers in non-unionised firms (one and a half times as many) appear satisfied with their status as compared to unionised enterprises;
- the proportion of workers *not* satisfied with their position in 'unionised' firms is also nearly 1.5 times greater than in the non-unionised sector;
- workers in non-unionised companies are much more satisfied with their wages than those in companies with trade unions;
- workers in unionised firms are much more dissatisfied with their wages (one and half times as many) as compared to those in non-unionised businesses.

Various explanations for these associations exist. The lowest pay and the slowest growth in pay occurs in the public sphere (health service and education), precisely where trade union presence is strong. The same is true in most publicly owned manufacturing enterprises. In those sectors high pay and large pay increases seldom occur. But high and fast-growing pay (alongside strong profits performance) is, however, a stronger feature of private and privatised firms, where union activity is rare.[2] All of this seems to show that there is no base in reality for the charge of some politicians and journalists that the presence of a trade union is synonymous with aggressive wage-bargaining. Our results suggest that where trade unions are active wages grow more slowly than in companies with no trade union. It is, after all, highly likely that trade unions persist and appear in these firms precisely as a reaction to low pay and once in place it seems they are unable to do much about it.

Is there any connection between the presence/absence of a trade union in a firm and employment – dismissals and redundancies in particular? Few directors (less than 10%) in the enterprises we studied admitted to having overseen redundancy. Nor was there any marked difference in managers' views across the unionised/non-unionised divide (11% and 8% respectively). Trade union presence seems not be important in this respect and workers seem, more or less, to go along with that view. Less than half of workers (44%) said they had witnessed dismissals in the six-year period preceding the research, with a small majority (56%) saying they had seen none. There seems to be no clear statistical link between the presence/absence of a trade union and perceptions on redundancy and lay-off although our data show that slightly fewer interviewees in unionised firms claimed to have experience of redundancies as compared to those in 'non-unionised' businesses. Trade union presence seems also to have no statistical connection with respect to workers' fears of dismissal. Of all workers questioned slightly less than half (44%) were afraid of redundancy. Interestingly, and perhaps surprisingly, in unionised workplaces such fears were more common (47%) than in workplaces with no trade union (41%). Fear of lay-off is probably linked much more strongly to an impression of a firm's economic health rather than to anything else. Workers and managers seem to share the view that there is little connection between trade union presence and employment growth or decline. Of course this also implies that existing forms of trade union representation do not constitute an effective barrier against a management intent on reducing its workforce.

TRADE UNIONS AND WORKING CONDITIONS

Trade unions have an obvious association with matters regarding social activity and working conditions. One aim of our research was to describe how management and workers view the extent to which the firm offers benefits such as housing, medical and recreational facilities, holiday camps for workers' children and subsidised canteens. Our results suggest that a strong, positive correlation exists between the presence of a trade union in a place of work and the existence of the majority of these benefits. However workers suggest too that while social provision may *exist* it is frequently not much *used* because of the high cost involved (especially since state businesses have been 'commercialised' and have hived off many such activities as a prelude to privatisation). Of course, this is not to imply any causal link between trade unions' presence and social benefits. Taken together, trade unions and social benefits constitute the strongest feature of the post-socialist legacy, one that appears to have survived privatisation and restructuring. We can say two things about employees' views of working conditions. First, the vast majority of workers (more than 80%) claim to be satisfied with such elements of working conditions as production organisation, health and safety and the knowledge and qualifications of direct superiors and management. But, second, workers are much less satisfied with certain aspects of working conditions including their own status, the possibility of promotion and wages. There seems to be some evidence suggesting that trade union presence is associated with a more positive view on working conditions.

THE DYNAMICS OF INDUSTRIAL RELATIONS IN THE ENTERPRISE

Industrial relations are highly ambiguous in Poland. How they are viewed depends to a great degree on the social position, interests and ideology of the subject. The adversarial view that industrial relations is an area of severe and perpetual crisis, where the interests of both sides suffer, frequently dominates, especially in public discourse. It is a view that has been reinforced by the process of moving from 'real socialism' to a (some would say extremely) liberal market model although remnants of the old system remain. On the basis of our research we can, however, suggest two themes that seem to characterise the essence of the process that is taking place.

First, co-operation between social partners at enterprise level seems to be becoming stronger. For industrial relations the atmosphere in which they are conducted is of the utmost importance. Our research shows clearly that co-operation and joint activity is perceived by the social actors in the enterprise to be a dominant feature (so thought 79% of workers and 88% of union activists) and conflict is considered to be distinctly marginal (only 3% of workers and 4% of union activists thought it to be a defining characteristic).

Second, collective bargaining suffers from weak institutionalisation in Poland, so limiting its potential. An important aspect here is the state of the relationship between enterprise trade unions. Our research on mutual relations between trade unions shows clearly that at the enterprise level these relations are generally constructive and dominated by co-operation. The perception of co-operation is emphasised particularly strongly by management (81% of directors, 70% of workers and 63% of union activists indicated co-operation to be the norm). Even if trade union activists are least convinced on co-operation the overtones are unambiguous: there is in the enterprise an atmosphere of amicable co-existence. The first sphere where co-operation was thought to be especially strong was in solving wage disputes. The second was in dealing with workers' social problems using resources allocated to the enterprise social fund on the basis of collective bargaining agreements. The third was in dealing with working conditions.

All key players note union collaboration in such matters as setting the rules for working arrangements and bonus allocation. But other areas exist where co-operation is less strongly perceived. These include resolving conflicts between workers and management, dealing with dismissal and redundancy as well as other limitations on workers' rights. Moreover co-operation on matters related to the functioning of businesses such as their transformation (reorganisation, restructuring or privatisation) appears even weaker.

Since co-operation is the dominant aspect of relations between the unions in the workplace it is no surprise that conflicts between unions are rare and concern only minor matters. In many cases conflicts between unions within enterprises are more a matter of symbolic declarations of ideological attachments rather than a reflection of the real day-to-day style of trade union behaviour. There are of course exceptions, and genuine disagreements or old grudges sometimes do appear. But the character of conflicts is closely linked to real problems in the firm, as can be seen from the fact that the most frequent cause of internal disputes is related to pay, bonuses and use of the social fund. Bearing in mind that this is also the area of the most intensive collaboration between unions, the view that trade union activity is sharply focused on strictly defined, narrow and local workers' social interests seems well founded.

CONFLICTS WITHIN THE ENTERPRISE: THEIR FORM AND DYNAMIC

The firms we researched had little experience of industrial action in the 1990s and when asked about the protests that had taken place both trade unionists and directors noted that the 'strike threat' (hardly the strongest pressure) was the most common form of action. Even so, taking together the responses of management and trade unionists it turns out that no more than one-third of the firms in our sample were affected by strike threats in the 1990s. Strikes were even less evident. Trade union activists reported strikes in only 20% of the businesses in the sample.

A gulf between the perceptions of directors and unionists is another interesting feature which could indicate that a great deal of industrial action has a local character, is short-lived and is not regarded as of great significance from the perspective of the entire firm. Management, in other words, tends to ignore incidents which do not involve the entire firm, while trade unionists overestimate the significance of various (often minor) incidents. It seems that organising a strike is not at all easy in Poland. Our sample of enterprises faced greatest strike activity in 1993 when 10 strikes were called and in 1998 when a total of 28 protest incidents took place.

As to the reasons given for protest, it seems that problems over pay figure prominently. Directors are particularly keen to point to unions' aggressive wage demands. Union activists, on the other hand, are more likely to point to non-pay -related reasons such as problems in restructuring and privatisation. Among non-wage-related disputes many involve participation in national demonstrations, a mobilisation to protest that emerges from a 'macro-social' level of organisation, and this is a large part of trade union activity. If we were to eliminate this macro factor it is likely that we would notice that unions' capacity for organising protests and bringing them to a successful conclusion would be significantly less impressive.

INSTITUTIONALISING AND FORMALISING INDUSTRIAL RELATIONS IN THE WORKPLACE

Institutionalisation is becoming a critical feature of industrial relations since this process can generate stability and help guarantee the interests of participants. Institutionalisation limits the scope for arbitrary behaviour on the part of key players on the industrial relations scene. 'Formalisation' is also of great significance since it encourages a more objective approach with greater transparency as to the group interests being expressed. This is leading to a situation where it is becoming possible for industrial relations to rely on a collective bargaining which reduces the level of uncertainty at the individual level. In Polish industrial relations collective contracts take two forms in particular: collective agreements at enterprise level and social contracts (linked to privatisation or restructuring).

Enterprise level collective agreements have a general status and can be utilised or implemented in any business. Their general applicability means that they should be the basic and general form of institutionalisation and formalisation of collective industrial relations. Our research however did not confirm that this was happening (at least at the end of the 1990s) when large discrepancies existed between social actors as to whether such agreements were being, in their perception, applied. Only 18% of workers thought this was so, 34% of managers and 43% of union activists. This suggests that the enterprise level collective contract is not something that figures prominently in the daily thoughts of industrial relations decision makers. It seemed to work and be functional in perhaps one-third of Polish enterprises. But relatively few people seemed well informed on the content of such collective agreements. Only a small proportion of workers, and indeed of union activists, knew for certain whether such collective agreements existed, suggesting something of a communications breakdown between union elites, management and workers. This has various consequences. One of the most important is that social control over the implementation of collective agreements must necessarily be limited. Our and others' research suggests that in Polish industrial relations the fundamental reason for the poor operation of collective bargaining is workers' low awareness of their rights alongside weak institutionalisation of industrial relations. This low awareness means that both workers and lower-ranking union officials react painfully slowly to socio-economic developments that threaten trouble.

Institutionalisation of industrial relations seems also to proceed along different lines according to ownership form and firm size. This is clearly illustrated by enterprise level contracts which exist primarily in large and medium-sized publicly owned firms, often also associated with regulations inherited from the previous system, or rules of employer–employee relations shaped by custom and practice. Such agreements are rare in privately owned firms. Effective collective agreements emerge where workers have access to organised representation prepared for negotiation and determined to see it through. Due to the weakness or lack of organised trade union structures in private or privatised firms (as well as in small or medium-sized firms) collective agreements are something of a rarity in those enterprises. Institutionalising and formalising collective bargaining in Poland demands social activity within a legal framework. But until the end of the 1990s (and into the new decade) Polish industrial relations was rather characterised by a limited sphere for trade union activity, limited use of legal forms of social contract, narrow social participation and lack of awareness on the part of the main social actors of legal possibilities. The disturbing consequence of all of this is that it brings social conflict much closer than it need be. The issue confronting workers, unions and management in the new millennium is how to work out a formula for organising their activity and creating a lasting form for regulating group interests.

THE INDUSTRIAL RELATIONS CLIMATE

Our research leads us to conclude that the industrial relations climate at the firm level is generally good and it is this feature that accounts for the low intensity of industrial conflict as well as the limited pressure to create and develop union structures. Most workers seem satisfied with their working conditions both materially and organisationally. An essential factor in the social set-up in the firm is high regard for managers' professionalism and this appears to bestow on management an authentic social authority. Workers also tend to have a great deal of trust in management. Direct superiors and foremen (rather than trade unions) are most frequently identified by workers as those to whom they would turn with employment problems. As far as people–people relations go, it seems that there is a great deal of solidarity in the enterprise. Most workers feel they can find support in the workplace in the event of problems. Management structures seem to provide the dominant support in inter-personal contacts. In this context trade unions pale. They are perceived as the place to turn by a very small percentage of respondents. Authority and trust in the workplace appears to be established and evaluated on the basis of some notion of professionalism. The poor position of trade unions is very much connected with the weak institutionalisation of industrial relations. Workers seem not to recognise this problem as particularly important as they attach little importance to trade unions and more weight to management structures. Although trade unions are usually viewed as representative of workers in a general sense, workers seem to prefer individual strategies and personal contact with the management structures in resolving problems. If we look at other aspects of the social climate in businesses we notice several characteristic features. First, people–people relations are considered to be much better than those concerning financial or legal matters. Second, satisfaction is clearly higher in non-unionised firms (mainly small and private firms). This is undoubtedly explained by the fact that private firms are newer, so they are in general more modern and better equipped; they are managed in a different way; they offer higher wages. Third, there is a relatively high degree of management's openness to criticism of various aspects of business operations, indicating perhaps an evolution of management methods towards greater participation.

CONCLUSIONS

Our research supports the suggestion that Polish industrial relations is dominated by co-operation, yet alongside a low level of institutionalisation. This tendency has been observed for a number of years and seems to be pretty firm. However some more specific matters are worth considering.

First, weak institutionalisation is apparent both in the lack of organised workers' representation and in the limited application of collective agreements in regulating employer–employee relations. It is especially noticeable in the private sector (new and newly privatised businesses) and in small and medium-sized firms. A 'new' economy is also apparent where industrial relations are based on individual negotiations and contracts between employers and individual ('atomised') workers. On the other hand an 'old' economy exists too where a collective bargaining model holds.

Second, the disposition to co-operate and be conciliatory in industrial relations which is evident is, we believe, the only way to ease social tensions in Polish business and favour the firm's strategic interests. Of course we should not overlook the fact that weak institutionalisation to some extent *forces* workers to be more conciliatory, so we can speak of a co-operation which is partially forced.

Third, in enterprises, wage problems dominate negotiations and conflicts, partly due to the weak institutionalisation noted above, but open conflict has a high eruption threshold so occurs relatively rarely. On the other hand disputes can become significantly dramatised because they take place in an atmosphere of cumulating tensions and threats. This means that collective bargaining fulfils only to a small degree the function of an early warning system for all sides.

Finally, in this industrial relations set-up workers are, in the majority of cases, reduced to the role of passive observers of developments without wider participation in the shaping of its important elements, especially in collective bargaining. An elitist approach to collective bargaining is developing in the workplace.

Our research points to certain ambiguities on the industrial relations scene in Poland and forecasts of likely developments are by no means straightforward. Nevertheless it seems that the transformations taking place in Polish collective bargaining is best interpreted in terms of notions of Offe's (1985) 'disorganised capitalism' or the end of 'organised capitalism' (see Lash and Urry, 1987). Both these concepts emphasise that in the latest phase of capitalist development processes are released that disturb the functioning of those institutions which previously helped (or were thought to help) bring about some balance between the interests of capital and labour (see Hirszowicz, 1998, pp. 85ff). The crux of the matter in the Polish context is that Polish capitalism is new and in its initial phase of development as the country joins the international economic system. However Poland also has a wide sphere of 'disorganised capitalism', devoid of institutions regulating the relationship between capital and labour. This is the result mainly of a fast and dynamic process of *ab initio* privatisation and new business development, a process that brought into life several million small businesses in the 1990s.[3] It is also true that the disappearance of firms' trade unions is in part connected to privatisation.

It is however by no means clear that all Western concepts are relevant to Polish conditions. Take for example the idea that, from the perspective of industrial relations, the capitalist economy has passed through three basic phases, with a first phase of *liberal capitalism* ('wild capitalism'), a second phase of *organised capitalism* based on widely interpreted social contracts between capital and labour (the interventionist phase) and a third phase, *the end of organised capitalism*. The authors of this view (see ibid., pp. 85–86) believe that 'economic disorganisation brings with it disorganisation in civil society expressed in fragmentation and multiplication of interest groups, which go hand in hand with institutional and cultural disorganisation'. These stages may apply only to a limited extent to Poland, where we should rather speak of the co-existence of various distinct forms of industrial relations. No doubt there are enclaves of *wild capitalism* on which there has been little research but at the same time there exists a fairly broad sphere of institutionalised relations between employers and employees, the main inheritance from *real socialism*, especially its final phase. It is also true that the sphere of disorganised capitalism has expanded, and it is possible that, as small firms grow and become middle-sized, trade unions or other forms of workers' representation *may* appear within them. In addition to workers' talent for self-organisation, existing trade unions may play a role, as can the legislation it will be necessary to adopt in the immediate future in line with obligations attached to EU accession. For the time being, however, the tendency seems to be for the scope of *disorganised capitalism* to expand.

Moving away from theoretical frameworks we can risk stating that industrial relations in Poland will develop in such a manner as to incorporate many of the traits of earlier stages associated with building the free market and private economy. In the late 1990s and into the years ahead relations between workers and their bosses are increasingly taking a form that can be described as *enlightened and humanitarian paternalism*. It leads to relatively harmonious and conflict-free relations between 'labour and capital' where 'Polish bosses' are, on the one hand, rather highly regarded for their qualifications and behaviour towards their subordinates, while on the other, they are regarded by most workers as the 'patron' to whom they can turn in the event of troubles or difficulties. This relationship between subordinates and superiors is a little reminiscent of military units, with all their negative consequences (for those taking orders). On the other hand, it suggests the onset of more civilised relations in hundreds of thousands of small and middle-sized Polish firms, which must head towards maximum competitiveness and flexibility in confrontations with a permanent and growing 'economic aggression' of foreign firms. It is hard to say for certain whether this model of industrial relations will prove durable and provide the dominant formula for social co-operation in a Poland entering Europe.

NOTES

1 Other features worth noting are that among trade union members 19% had higher education, 15% basic technical education. Most trade union members live in medium-sized and small towns *rather than the city*. The least unionised group in society is also the least well educated stratum: of those with basic education only 4% belong to unions.

2 One possible explanation for this pattern of opinion, which, unfortunately cannot be verified on the basis of our data, is that satisfaction with wages in firms where trade unions are rare results from the fact that these are, by and large, private businesses, where (according to our general understanding) longer hours of work are expected than in state–owned firms. Staff simply work more hours per day, week and month, resulting in more satisfactory pay.

3 A recent publication documenting these processes gives a figure close to 2.4 million such people. See *Stan i Rozwój Sektora Małych i Średnich Przedsiębiorstw w Latach 1994–96,* ed. L. Żienkowski, (Polska Fundacja Promocji i Rozwoju Małych i Średnich Przedsiębiorstw, Warsaw, 1998). One should bear in mind that such firms are constantly appearing and disappearing, so their exact number lies in a 'grey zone'. See also chapter 8 in this volume by Macieja and the comments of Rapacki (chapter 7) on private sector developments.

REFERENCES

CBOS (1999), *Opinie o związkach zawodowych. Komunikat z badań* (Opinions on trades unions: research note), Warsaw, April.

Gardawski, J. (1996), *Polish Workers*, Warsaw: F. Ebert Foundation (1996).

Hirszowicz, M. (1998) *Spory o Przyszłości,* Warsaw: IFiS PAN.

Offe, C. (1985), *Disorganized Capitalism*, Cambridge: Polity Press.

Lash, S. and Urry, J. (1987), *The End of Organized Capitalism*, Oxford: Polity Press.

Żienkowski, L. (ed.) (1998), *Stan i Rozwój Sektora Małych i Średnich Przedsiębiorstw w Latach 1994–96,* Warsaw: Polska Fundacja Promocji i Rozwoju Małych i Średnich Przedsiębiorstw.

6. Polish politics in the new millennium

Aleks Szczerbiak

INTRODUCTION

While the Polish political scene has many superficial similarities to more established Western democracies it also has a number of distinctive features. This chapter attempts to provide a basic introduction to help the reader make sense of the contemporary Polish political system. Post-1989 developments are summarised and consideration is given to how stable and consolidated the current Polish party system is as the country enters the new millennium. The most significant parties and political groups and their bases of support are described and examined and some of the special features of Polish politics identified. The chapter concludes by speculating on the possible future shape of the Polish political scene and the likelihood of realignments within the party system. It should be stressed that this is a brief introduction to much broader developments and provides only the most basic outline of the key issues.

POLITICAL DEVELOPMENTS AFTER 1989

Political developments in post-communist Poland can be divided into four broad historical phases. The first phase (1989–93) dates from September 1989 when Solidarity adviser Tadeusz Mazowiecki became Poland's first non-communist prime minister. It was a period characterised by political instability as Solidarity gradual decomposed.[1] Table 6.1 lists Poland's post-1989 prime ministers. After the initial euphoria of sloughing off communist rule, divisions quickly emerged within Solidarity. They tended at first to focus on the consequences of the 'shock therapy' programme of economic liberalisation introduced by the then finance minister, Leszek Balcerowicz. Policy divisions soon became exacerbated by personality differences, particularly as Solidarity's legendary leader Lech Wałęsa, began to show resentment at being marginalised by the government that he helped to broker and install. Decomposition was accelerated by the bitterly contested presidential election of 1990 where Wałęsa defeated

Mazowiecki, who promptly resigned as prime minister to be replaced by Jan Krzysztof Bielecki, a leader of the so-called 'Gdańsk liberals', the 'post-Solidarity' Liberal Democratic Congress party (*Kongres Liberalno-Demokratyczne – KLD*).

Table 6.1. Polish prime ministers, 1989–2000

Name	**Term of office**
Tadeusz Mazowiecki (Solidarity)	September 1989–December 1990
Jan Krzysztof Bielecki (Solidarity–KLD)	January 1991–December 1991
Jan Olszewski (PC)	December 1991–June 1992
Waldemar Pawlak (PSL)	June–July 1992
Hanna Suchocka (UD)	July 1992–September 1993
Waldemar Pawlak (PSL)	October 1993–March 1995
Józef Olesky (SdRP–SLD)	March 1995–February 1996
Włodzimierz Cimoszewicz (SLD)	February 1996–November 1997
Jerzy Buzek (Solidarity–AWS)	November 1997

Post-communist Poland's first fully free parliamentary elections were held in October 1991 and marked a further stage in the break-up of Solidarity. A society that was increasingly divided reacted with a highly proportional election law to produce an even more fragmented and polarised parliament than had been feared. No political organisation won more than 12.3% of the vote and 10 parties and groupings obtained 16 or more seats in the 460-member Sejm, the more powerful lower house of the Polish parliament. The range of parties represented in and the extensive fragmentation of the 1991–93 parliament led to a series of unstable coalition governments.

Government followed government in quick succession. After Bielecki came Jan Olszewski with his radically anti-communist but fissiparous minority government, a government built on the main parties of the post-Solidarity right: the Christian National Union (*Zjednoczenie Chrześcijańsko-Narodowe – ZChN*), the Centre Agreement (*Porozumienie Centrum – PC*) and the agrarian-populist Peasant Agreement (*Porozumienie Ludowe – PL*). Olszewski's government lasted until June 1992 and was followed by an unsuccessful attempt to form a new administration around Waldemar Pawlak, leader of the Polish Peasant Party (*Polskie Stronnictwo Ludowe – PSL*), the successor to the former communist satellite *ZSL* party. In July 1992 Hanna Suchocka took over as head of a broad seven-party coalition of post-Solidarity groupings involving the two liberal centrist parties, Mazowiecki's Democratic Union (*Unia Demokratyczna – UD*, of which Suchocka was also a member) and the KLD as well as the ZChN and the post-Solidarity peasant and Christian Democratic parties. The coalition also enjoyed the backing of the Solidarity trade union's parliamentary caucus.

Suchocka's unstable and ideologically heterogeneous government survived 10 months until it fell on a motion of no confidence in May 1993 (passed by just one vote and, ironically, initiated by the Solidarity trade union).

The second phase of post-communist politics (1993–95) began with the September 1993 parliamentary election. This saw a substantial victory for the two 'successor' formations: the former communists in the Democratic Left Alliance (*Sojusz Lewicy Demokratycznej – SLD*) that won 20.4% of the votes and 171 seats and their erstwhile agrarian allies in the PSL (15.4% and 132 seats).[2] The SLD was an electoral coalition of 30 parties and groupings clustered around the Social Democracy of the Polish Republic (*Socjaldemokracja Rzeczpospolitej Polski – SdRP*), the direct organisational successor to the communist PZPR that had successfully refashioned itself as a Western social democratic party and harnessed discontent with the post-Solidarity governments' economic and social policies. It included the OPZZ trade union federation that had also been closely linked to the previous communist regime. Similarly, although it was the organisational successor to the ZSL, the PSL also attempted to draw on the traditions of the pre-war (anti-communist) peasant movement.[3]

The only post-Solidarity party to win significant parliamentary representation in 1993 was the UD, finishing third with 10.6% of the vote and 74 seats. Political restructuring soon followed and in April 1994 the UD merged with the KLD to form the Freedom Union (*Unia Wolności – UW*). The Labour Union (*Unia Pracy – UP*), a social democratic party of both former communists and Solidarity activists, also performed well and came fourth with 7.3% of the vote and 41 parliamentary seats. A new electoral law, designed explicitly to favour larger parties and avoid the fragmentation of the 1991–93 Sejm by introducing a 5% threshold for parliamentary representation (7% for coalitions), considerably exaggerated the scale of the 'post-communist' parties' victory, giving them just short of a two-thirds majority in parliament. This also meant that virtually all of the highly fragmented Polish right, including the ZChN, PC, PL and Solidarity trade union with a combined 30% plus of the Polish electorate, was excluded from parliament.

The new SLD–PSL coalition government that emerged with PSL leader Pawlak at its head was the first in post-communist Poland to enjoy a stable parliamentary majority. Even if the turnover of prime ministers would be high (from Pawlak to the SLD's Józef Oleksy in February 1995 then to the non-party SLD nominee Włodzimierz Cimoszewicz in January 1996) the coalition served its full four-year term. Indeed, the SLD's grip on power was strengthened when its leader, Aleksander Kwaśniewski, narrowly defeated Lech Wałęsa by 52% to 48% in the November 1995 presidential election.

The run up to the 1995 election marked the beginning of the third phase of post–1989 politics, characterised by the increasing polarisation of the Polish political scene between the former communist left and post-Solidarity right. The latter slowly began drawing the lessons of its successive electoral defeats and united its disparate forces. Initially, sections of the right rallied around Jan Olszewski's Movement for Poland's Reconstruction (*Ruch Odbudowy Polski – ROP*) after Olszewski's respectable performance in the presidential elections on a radical anti-communist platform. However, the more significant development proved to be the formation in June 1996 of Solidarity Electoral Action *(Akcja Wyborcza Solidarności – AWS*). AWS was a broad coalition of the main parties and groupings of the post-Solidarity right including the ZChN, PC and various Christian democratic, liberal conservative, nationalist and agrarian parties. It was, however, firmly under the control of the Solidarity trade union and its leader Marian Krzaklewski, whose hegemony provided AWS with an organisational cohesion that had evaded previous attempts to unite the post-Solidarity right. Although, as Table 6.2 shows, the SLD increased its vote significantly in the September 1997 parliamentary election to just over 27%, its parliamentary representation was reduced to 164 seats and the grouping was clearly defeated by AWS (34% of the vote and 201 seats).[4] In the autumn of 1997 the AWS reached agreement with the UW, led by Leszek Balcerowicz (with its 13% of the vote and 60 seats in the Sejm), to form a coalition government. The 1997 election was disastrous for the PSL peasants' party. It came fourth, its share of the vote halved to just over 7% and its parliamentary representation slashed to only 27 seats. Meanwhile Olszewski's ROP just managed to jump the 5% threshold (5.56%) to get six parliamentary seats and the UP fell just below (4.74%) ending up without any parliamentary representation.

The formation of the AWS–UW government in November 1997 under Solidarity premier Jerzy Buzek marked the beginning of the fourth phase of post-1989 politics. The new government developed some momentum by introducing a 'second wave' of reforms in local government, health, pensions and education. However many of the reforms (especially in health) were badly prepared and badly managed. The government also mishandled a wave of protests and labour disputes at the beginning of 1999 and began rapidly to lose support. To make matters worse the disparate nature of the internal structure of the AWS meant that it could not always rely on its MPs to support government sponsored legislation.

Prime minister Buzek's tendency to compromise and avoid confrontation also created the impression of dithering and contributed to a general image of incompetence. All this exacerbated tensions within the government and between the coalition parties, particularly over the economic policy pursued by Balcerowicz (who was back as economics supremo running the finance ministry but also with the rank of deputy premier), until the coalition finally collapsed in June 2000, leaving Buzek at the head of an AWS minority government. At the same time the SLD emerged as a highly disciplined opposition led by the effective and pragmatic former communist official Leszek Miller and appeared well placed to return to power after the next parliamentary elections scheduled to take place before September 2001.

Table 6.2. September 1997 parliamentary election: winners and losers

	Votes	%	Seats
Above the threshold:			
Solidarity Electoral Action (AWS)	4,427,373	33.83	201
Democratic Left Alliance (SLD)	3,551,224	27.13	164
Freedom Union (UW)	1,749,518	13.37	60
Polish Peasant Party (PSL)	956,184	7.31	27
Movement for Poland's Reconstruction (ROP)	727,072	5.56	6
Below the threshold:			
Labour Union (UP)	620,611	4.74	0
National Party of Retirees and Pensioners (KPEiR)	284,826	2.18	0
Union of the Republic Right (UPR)	266,317	2.03	0
National Agreement of Retirees and Pensioners (KPEiRRP)	212,826	1.63	0
Christian Democratic-Bloc for Poland (ChD-BdP)	178,395	1.36	0

Source: *Rzeczpospolita*, 2 October 1997.

A PARTIALLY CONSOLIDATED PARTY SYSTEM

After 10 years of pluralist, multiparty politics Polish voters appear to have developed clearer and more stable political preferences, with a previously fragmented and unstable party system slowly giving way to a relatively consolidated one. This can be seen in the reduction in the number of parties and groupings entering parliament after successive elections: 29 in 1991, six in 1993 and only five in 1997.[5] The Polish political scene is dominated by two larger electoral blocs, a centre-right emerging from the Solidarity camp (AWS) and a centre-left based on the heirs of their communist opponents (SLD), while two-medium sized parties, the liberal UW and agrarian-populist PSL, dominate the political 'centre' and are roughly equal contenders for the mantle of 'third force'.

Although numerous smaller parties still operate on the political scene, unless one of the main groupings splits (the prospects of which are discussed below), only a couple of potential challengers can threaten an emerging four-party cartel. First, given that its opinion poll ratings since September 1997 have hovered consistently around the 5% threshold, the UP remains at least a potential challenger. However, it is also a party that seems to find it extremely difficult to translate generalised expressions of support into actual votes at election time. Second, and perhaps more significantly, AWS remains potentially vulnerable to an electoral challenge from the radical right. With Olszewski's ROP increasingly marginalised following successive splits, the most serious threat could emerge from the 'religious right' clustered around the fundamentalist Catholic-nationalist broadcaster *Radio Maryja,* a specifically Polish phenomenon that has struck a deep chord with the most traditional elements of Polish society. While it has yet to translate this into a coherent political movement it is possible that one could develop around the *Radio Maryja*-aligned Polish Agreement party (*Porozumienie Polskie – PP*) which broke away from AWS in 1998 and is attempting to use opposition to EU membership as a rallying point.

Although a relatively stable configuration of political actors appears to exist and there are superficial similarities with more established Western party systems, at this stage it is only really possible to talk about the *partial* consolidation of the Polish party system.

First, question marks remain over the future shape of the Polish right. While at one stage after the 1997 elections it seemed that AWS had established itself as a more or less permanent feature of the Polish political landscape, its long-term organisational cohesion (or even survival) is in some doubt. Unlike the SLD, which transformed itself into a single, unitary political party with a clearer decision making structure in 1999, AWS faces continued conflict over its internal organisation and, even in mid 2000, chose to remain a political conglomerate, with all the disadvantages that entails. The AWS has partially consolidated around its five largest constituents. Trade union Solidarity retains a key role but has devolved greater power to four political parties: the union-based Solidarity Electoral Action Social Movement (*Ruch Społeczny Akcji Wyborczej Solidarności – RS AWS*) led by Jerzy Buzek and established gradually to take over all of Solidarity's political functions within AWS; the ZChN; the liberal conservative Conservative People's Party (*Stronnictwo Konserwatywno Ludowe – SKL*) and the Polish Agreement of Christian Democrats (*Polskie Porozumienie Chrześcijańskich Demokratów – PPChD*). However, by placing the political parties on a more equal footing with the previously hegemonic trade union, this has only succeeded in making an already fractious political grouping even more organisationally unstable.[6]

Second, the links between Polish parties and their electorates is shallow. While they are fairly strong at the level of state institutions, capable of structuring elections and recruiting political elites, Polish parties are also developing as remote and somewhat distant institutions. With low levels of party membership and social implantation, they are, with the partial exceptions of the SLD and PSL, extremely weak at the societal level. This is important because the stabilisation of West European party systems was based, at least in part, on parties' ability organisationally to encapsulate their supporters in relatively stable and cohesive partisan blocs.[7] Consequently, the lack of parties with any significant societal roots will mean that levels of party identification remain low and the Polish electorate is much more available (and, therefore, potentially more volatile) than in established Western democracies. This is part of a more

Table 6.3. September 1997 parliamentary election: voting patterns (% of total polled)

	AWS	SLD	UW	PSL	ROP	UP
Voting by sex						
Men	31.8	27.5	13.0	7.8	5.9	4.3
Women	36.0	25.6	14.3	5.8	4.7	5.2
Voting by age						
18–29	32.3	22.4	18.6	6.3	5.6	5.1
30–39	35.6	20.8	15.9	8.8	5.9	5.2
40–49	32.4	29.2	13.1	7.3	5.5	5.5
50–59	31.9	32.9	9.4	6.2	5.1	4.0
60+	36.4	30.3	8.2	5.4	4.5	3.1
Voting by place of residence						
Villages	35.2	20.3	6.7	17.0	5.9	4.2
Towns	32.0	30.5	14.4	4.0	5.1	4.9
Cities	33.6	29.0	18.4	0.9	5.1	4.9
Voting by education						
Primary	37.9	21.3	4.4	12.9	4.6	4.2
Vocational	38.1	24.2	7.2	10.1	6.0	4.9
Secondary	33.1	29.5	13.4	5.8	5.5	5.0
Higher	27.7	27.2	25.1	2.8	4.8	4.4
Voting by occupation						
Managers	26.9	33.8	21.2	4.3	3.5	4.4
Specialists	32.7	21.4	24.8	2.9	5.4	4.9
Businessmen	34.2	22.0	19.2	4.0	6.9	4.5
Farmers	30.4	12.7	2.5	37.9	5.7	2.5
Workers	40.3	26.0	7.6	6.5	6.3	5.5
Office workers	32.7	31.0	14.5	4.5	5.1	6.2
Service workers	36.8	26.7	14.3	4.9	5.8	4.2
Retired	34.2	32.2	7.5	4.5	4.7	3.6
Housewives	39.6	21.0	12.3	7.0	4.3	3.9
Students	29.7	23.9	22.3	3.7	5.3	5.5
Unemployed	36.8	25.4	8.1	7.0	6.0	7.7
Average	*33.83*	*27.13*	*13.37*	*7.31*	*5.56*	*4.74*

Source: Exit poll figures supplied to the author by the Institute for Public Opinion Research (OBOP).

generalised pattern of weak links between state institutions and the citizenry in Poland, exemplified by the extremely low turnout in successive parliamentary elections that fell to only 47.9% in September 1997.

Third, and perhaps most significantly, the Polish party system remains potentially unstable because of the nature of the divisions within the Polish electorate. In most Western democracies parties have traditionally defined themselves as 'left' or 'right' primarily according to their attitudes towards socio-economic issues such as the level of taxation, public expenditure and welfare benefits; and support or opposition to state intervention in the economy and economic redistribution – with various parties representing different socio-economic interests. In Poland, however, the key divisions between left and right continue to be defined primarily on the basis of attitudes towards the communist past and different approaches to moral-cultural issues, particularly the role of the Catholic Church in politics and public life. On the other hand, the differences between the two main blocs on socio-economic issues are, in practice, minimal. This is reflected in their bases of support and socio-economic profile. As Table 6.3 shows, in 1997 the AWS and SLD electoral profiles were fairly heterogeneous with only minimal variations of support between various socio-economic and occupational groups. In other words, their bases of support did not appear to be rooted in any particular, subjectively felt socio-economic interests. Other survey evidence has indicated that the AWS and SLD electorates could be distinguished primarily by their ideological self-placement on the 'left–right' spectrum. This was, in turn, generally understood to refer more to different assessments of the communist past and attitudes towards moral-cultural rather than towards socio-economic issues.[8]

It seems paradoxical that religion plays such a key role in shaping political attitudes and voting preferences in an overwhelmingly Catholic country like Poland. However, although 90% of Poles profess to be 'believers', they are much more divided on what role the Church should play in public life. While the Church was a universally acknowledged and relatively unquestioned moral authority during the communist period it has found it much more difficult to adapt to the different challenges of the post-communist era. Its position on changes to the abortion law, religious education in state schools and the promotion of Christian values in public life were not universally welcomed. Arguably, the way that the Church over played its hand the early 1990s created a backlash that contributed significantly to mobilising the anti-clerical electorate that was critical to the SLD's consolidation and broadened appeal in the 1993 and 1995 elections.[9] The best simple indicator of a voter's attitudes towards the Church's role in politics and public life is probably her or his level of participation in religious services. This is, in turn, the single most important indicator of whether a Pole locates on the left or right of the political spectrum.[10] Indeed, the degree of 'religiosity' was a key characteristic of the 1997 AWS and SLD electorates and they were almost mirror images of each other in this respect.[11]

Divisions stemming from voters' positions on socio-economic issues or class are secondary in defining left and right in Polish politics and structuring the party system. They do, however, play a more significant role in determining the bases of electoral support for the two medium-sized parties: the PSL and UW.[12] As Table 6.3 shows, the PSL drew most of its support from rural areas and particularly the large proportion (nearly one-quarter) of the Polish population employed in the agricultural sector most of whom worked in peasant small-holdings (and discussed more fully by Wilkin in chapter 12 of this collection). This large private peasantry survived the communist era with both a reasonably well-defined collective identity and a subjectively felt set of clear socio-economic interests. As such, it provided the PSL with a 'natural' socio-economic base around which it could mobilise support. Although not quite as socially homogeneous, the UW's electorate was also relatively concentrated. However, the UW tended to draw its support disproportionately from the actual or potential beneficiaries (or supporters) of economic reform: younger voters, residents of larger towns and cities, the better educated, students and the more financially secure occupational groups such as specialists, managers and businessmen.

PROSPECTS FOR REALIGNMENT

How sustainable is a party system where key divisions are based on attitudes towards a communist past and moral-cultural issues? Taking a long-term perspective, some Western scholars have predicted that, given the likelihood of Polish economic reforms succeeding, party competition will eventually be structured on the basis of socio-economic cleavages that emerge from the new interests created by the economic transition.[13] In a similar vein, some Polish commentators have argued that the prospect of EU membership could act as the catalyst for bringing these new divisions between transition 'winners' and 'losers' (and new party configurations based upon them) to the fore.[14]

The EU membership issue has certainly acquired a much greater salience in political debates since Poland formally submitted its membership application in 1994 and accession negotiations began in March 1998. Although the figures vary somewhat across polling companies there has been a significant drop in Polish support for EU membership in the last couple of years and the emergence for the first time of a significant current of eurosceptic opinion representing about 20% to 25% of the population.[15] Given that small farmers, who constitute the PSL's core electorate, feel particularly threatened by the prospect of accession, this party is likely to develop a more critical tone towards the EU, as are the Catholic-nationalist elements of the AWS coalition, such as the ZChN. A number of fringe and protest parties, such as the *Radio Maryja*-aligned Polish Agreement and Andrzej Lepper's radical Self-defence (*Samoobrona*) farmers, union, may also try to use the issue strategically as a way of differentiating themselves from the political mainstream. However, EU membership is unlikely to provide the basis for a major political realignment in Poland. The consensus among Polish political elites is likely to remain broadly pro-EU and it is unlikely that any major party or grouping will adopt an overtly anti-EU position and, thereby, risk being seen to place themselves outside the political mainstream.

Nevertheless, it seems logical that Polish politics could realign around a new set of divisions and issues as memories of the communist period become more distant. But there are also reasons to expect any such realignment to be slow with Polish politics organised around 'historic' divisions for some time.

First, the new socio-economic interests emerging as a result of the post-1989 economic transformation have not yet firmed sufficiently to act as a major influence on voting behaviour. Moreover, any emerging socio-economic interests and identities will be extremely fluid, amorphous and uncrystallised for some time before they can provide a clear basis for party alignments. With the process of socio-economic interest formation still very much in flux 'ideological' issues are likely to remain the clearest points of reference for most Poles in the immediate future at least.

Second, as noted above, it is not simply attitudes towards the past that form the main line of division within the Polish party system. These are reinforced by a moral–cultural cleavage so that, in practice, they do not correspond simply to a sympathetic or critical attitude towards the communist period but also appear to be emblematic of two separate, distinct and deeply rooted value systems. While the salience of attitudes towards the past may recede as memories of the communist past fade, these moral–cultural divisions are more fundamental and could outlast the 'historic' divide as a means of structuring party competition in the future.

Third, as the continuing divisions within the Irish party system illustrate, party alignments can outlast the reasons why they originally came into being for several generations. Indeed, the longer that Polish elections are dominated by the two 'historic' blocs the more likely it is that their voters will develop long-term attachment to or partisan identification with them and that they will continue to form the building blocks of the party system.

Fourth, voting patterns among young people should provide some crude indicators of how future party alignments are likely to develop. Moreover, given that we might expect young people to be the most 'future-orientated' segment of the electorate with the least interest in 'historic' divisions, if a political realignment is to occur in Poland then we should expect to see some evidence of this in the voting behaviour of the young. As Table 6.3 shows, there is some evidence of this in the above-average levels of support among young people for the 'future-orientated' UW. However, most 18–29 year old voters actually supported AWS and the SLD, the two groupings whose electoral base was determined primarily by its supporters' attitudes towards the past.

This does not, of course, rule out a political realignment taking place at some point in the future. It is simply to stress that there is nothing *inevitable* about such a process taking place, at least not imminently. The presidential election scheduled for October 2000 and the 2001 parliamentary election are likely to provide a number of clues as to whether or not this bipolarity based on attitudes towards the communist past is still the most salient issue dividing Polish voters. The parliamentary elections will be particularly significant if they produce substantial evidence of large numbers of voters crossing the 'historic' and 'moral–cultural' divide by switching directly from the AWS to the SLD.[16] Indeed, even if the elections failed to produce evidence of a stronger correlation between party support and socio-economic class, this pattern of vote switching could still suggest the emergence of voting patterns based on 'valence' issues – such as the assessment of party leaders' competence to govern (which a number of commentators have identified as an increasingly significant feature of electoral politics in Western democracies) – rather than 'ideological' issues such as attitudes towards the communist past or moral–cultural questions. Similarly, although taking place at the level of political elites rather than mass politics, the emergence of a coalition government based on the SLD and a post-Solidarity party, such as the UW, would also provide a further indicator of the declining salience of this 'historic' divide.

CONCLUSIONS

After 10 years of pluralist, multiparty politics Polish voters appear to be developing clearer and more stable political preferences and a previously highly fragmented and often confusing Polish system seem to have been replaced by a relatively consolidated one. However, although the Polish party system appears to have become much tidier and there are many superficial similarities with more established Western systems, there is still considerable scope for reshaping as Poland enters a new millennium. Polish parties are weak as institutions, levels of party identification are low and Polish voters are much more 'available' than in established Western democracies. Significant question marks remain over the future of the Polish right, particularly over AWS's long-term organisational cohesion and survival. Above all, the Polish party system remains potentially unstable because the main issue dividing the left and right wing blocs, attitudes towards the communist past, is likely to become less salient as memories of the pre-1989 period recede. At this stage, therefore, it is only really possible to talk about a *partially* consolidated party system.

None the less, although some of the key political actors are unstable and the Polish electorate remains potentially volatile, there are also a number of reasons why we might not expect any fundamental realignment in the major lines of division within Polish politics to occur imminently. With the process of socio-economic interest formation still very much in flux, 'ideological' issues are likely to remain the clearest points of alignment and reference for most Polish voters, for the immediate future at least. Party alignments can outlast the reasons why they originally came into being, while younger voters, whose electoral behaviour provides a rough indicator of future trends and whom we might expect to be more 'future-orientated', have also tended to support the two 'historic' blocs. Moreover, although the importance of attitudes towards the communist past as a defining issue may recede with the passage of time, it is overlaid and re -inforced by moral–cultural issues that are more timeless and could outlast the 'historic' divisions as a means of structuring party competition. However, it should be stressed that all such considerations are highly speculative and require more research before any firmer conclusions about the future shape of Polish politics can be reached.

NOTES

1 For a good analysis of the first period of post-communist Polish politics see Millard (1994a).
2 For more on the September 1993 parliamentary election see, Millard (1994b).
3 Indeed, it was the peasant movement led by Stanisław Mikołajczyk that formed the main opposition to the communists in the immediate post-war years.
4 See Szczerbiak (1998).
5 This does not include parties representing the German minority, for whom the 5% threshold does not apply.
6 By June 2000 AWS had lost 15 of its 201 Sejm deputies as a result of defections and a further 15–20 frequently voted against the parliamentary caucus or AWS-led government position in parliament.
7 See Lipset and Rokkan (1967).
8 See Szczerbiak (1999) and Szawiel (1999).
9 See, for example, Markowski and Toka (1993). Indeed, disputes over the Concordat negotiated by the outgoing Suchocka administration with the Vatican (which the SLD-led coalition refused to sign) and references to Christian values in the 1997 Constitution played a critical role in the post-1995 polarisation of Polish politics and, as one commentator put it, provided 'a touchstone of party polarisation between the two large blocs.'
10 See Grabowska (1997).
11 See Szczerbiak (1999, pp. 1422–1423).
12 See Centrum Badania Opinii Spoecznej (1999).
13 See Evans and Whitefield (1993).
14 See Kolarska-Bobińska (1998) and Bachman (2000). Cf. Grabowskia, (1999).

15 See Szczerbiak (2000).
16 One commentator claims to have already detected some evidence of this in opinion polls showing that 10% of AWS defectors from September 1997 were planning to switch directly to the SLD. See Kublik (2000).

REFERENCES

Bachman, K. (2000) 'Historyczny kompromis inaczej' (A different kind of historical compromise), *Rzeczpospolita,* 9 June.

Centrum Badania Opinii Społecznej (Centre for Public Opinion Research), *Opinie o istotnych kwestiach społeczno-politycznych w elektoratach partyjnych* (Opinions on key socio-political questions among party electorates), Warsaw: CBOS.

Evans, G. and Whitefield, S. (1993) 'Identifying the bases of party competition in Eastern Europe', *British Journal of Political Science,* 23 (4), pp. 521–548.

Grabowska, M. (1997), 'Partie polityczne: reprezentant społeczeństwa czy twórca nowego ładu' (Political parties: representatives of society or creators of a new order) in M. Grabowska and S. Mocka. (eds), *Pierwsza Sześciolatka 1989–1995: Próba Bilansu Polityki* (The first six years 1989–1995: an attempt at a political balance sheet), Warsaw: Instytut Studiów Politycznych PAN, pp. 29–52.

Grabowska, M. (1999), 'Przyszłość polskiej sceny politycznej – stabilność i zmiana' (The future of the Polish political scene – stability and change), in Instytut Spraw Publicznych (Institute of Public Affairs), *Przyszłość polskiej sceny politycznej* (The future of the Polish political scene), Warsaw: ISP, pp. 39–66.

Kolarska-Bobińska, L. (1998), 'Co innego będzie dzielić Polaków' (What else will divide Poles?), *Rzeczpospolita,* 26 November.

Kublik, A. (2000), 'Obroty Elektoratów: Rozmowa z politologiem dr Radosławem Markowskim' (Turnover of the electorates: interview with political scientist Dr Radosław Markowski), *Gazeta Wyborcza,* 7 February.

Lipset, S.M. and Rokkan, S. (1967), 'Cleavage Structures, party systems and voter alignments: an introduction', in S.M. Lipset and S. Rokkan, (eds), *Party Systems and Voter Alignments: Cross-national Perspectives,* New York: Free Press, pp. 1–64.

Markowski, R. and Toka, G. (1993), 'Left turn in Poland and Hungary five years after the collapse of communism', in *Sisyphus. Social Studies* 1 (IX), pp. 75–99.

Millard, F. (1994a), 'The shaping of the Polish party system, 1989–93', *East European Politics and Societies*, 8 (3), pp. 467–494.

Millard, F. (1994b), 'The Polish parliamentary election of September, 1993', *Communist and Post-Communist Studies,* 27 (3), pp. 295–313.

Millard, F. (1999), *Polish Politics and Society,* London: Routledge.

Szawiel, T. (1999), 'Zróżnicowanie lewicowo prawicowe j jego korelaty' (Left–right differentiation and its correlates), in R. Markowski (ed.), *Wybory Parlamentarne 1997* (The 1997 Parliamentary Elections), Warsaw: Instytut Studiów Politycznych PAN.

Szczerbiak, A. (1998), 'Electoral politics in Poland: the parliamentary elections of 1997', *Journal of Communist Studies and Transition Politics,* 14 (3), pp. 58–83.

Szczerbiak, A. (1999), 'Interests and values: the new Polish parties and their electorates', *Europe-Asia Studies,* 51 (8), pp. 1401–1432.

Szczerbiak, A. (2000), *Public Opinion and Eastward Enlargement: Explaining Declining Support for EU Membership in Poland*, Sussex European Institute Working Papers in Contemporary European Studies no. 34, Brighton: SEI.

PART II

Economic Performance, Institutional and Sectoral Transformations

7. Economic performance 1989–99 and prospects for the future

Ryszard Rapacki

INTRODUCTION

At the turn of the twentieth and twenty-first centuries, 10 years after its dramatic departure from central planning and 'socialist democracy', Poland was regarded by most observers as the most successful transition economy in Eastern and Central Europe.

Our aim in this contribution is to shed some light on major development trends in the Polish economy during the past 10 years. Simultaneously, an attempt will be made to sketch out longer-term prospects and to discuss the major problems that may hinder sustainable development in the years ahead. Our discussion focuses on the growth path of the Polish economy, including a review of both demand- and supply-side factors as well as efficiency changes. It also covers the most important dimensions of macroeconomic performance such as internal and external equilibrium, and the behaviour of factor markets.

ECONOMIC GROWTH IN THE 1990s

The second half of the 1980s witnessed a deceleration of the growth dynamic of the Polish economy coupled with mounting macroeconomic imbalances. These negative trends culminated in 1989 when GDP growth stagnated (allowing for a possible statistical error) and both internal and external disequilibria dramatically widened. With accelerated inflation a sort of 'socialist' stagflation resulted. Consumer prices growth for the year reached 264.3% and in the autumn of 1989 the country was on the brink of hyperinflation (in October the annualised inflation rate reached 3200%). According to some estimates, the central budget deficit had reached some 8% of GDP (see Blazyca and Rapacki, 1991).

The scale and depth of macro- and microeconomic imbalances (for example, mounting difficulties in the inter-firm supply system, growing payment arrears, and the mismatch between the commodity composition of demand and output) that characterised the Polish economy exerted a decisive impact on the choice of 'shock therapy' by the Mazowiecki–Balcerowicz government when, in 1989, it aimed to stabilise the economy and restore basic macroeconomic equilibria.

As an immediate consequence of the stabilisation package applied from January 1990 and the simultaneous liberalisation of the key areas of economic activity (including foreign trade), the Polish economy experienced a deep slump or, using Kornai's phrase, a 'transformation recession'. The cumulative decline in GDP amounted to 17.8% in 1990–91 – nevertheless recovery, beginning in 1992, soon became a fast and self-sustained economic growth (see Figure 7.1). The highest growth rates were recorded between 1995 and 1997 (6.0% to 7.0%) then growth slowed to 4.8% in 1998 and to 4.1% in 1999.

Figure 7.1. GDP growth in Poland, 1989–98 (annual average % growth)

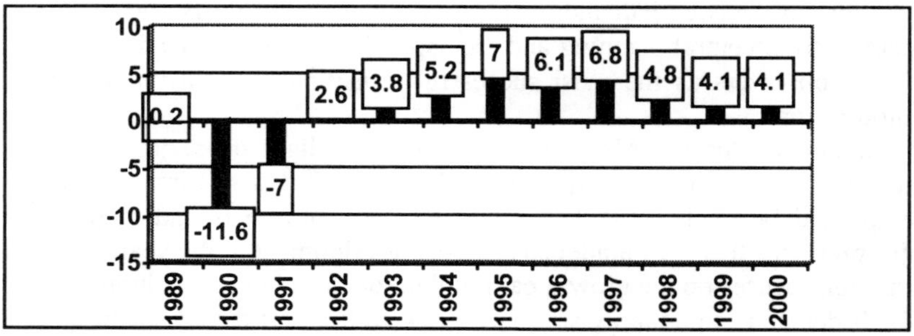

The data in Table 7.1 reveal several key features of Poland's economic growth path during the 1990s in a comparative perspective. First, they clearly demonstrate that the 'transformation recession' was the shallowest of all the transition economies (only Hungary experienced a similar output decline). Second, the recession lasted only two years, the shortest in the group of post-communist countries. Finally, Poland was the first economy to regain (in 1996) and then considerably exceed its pre-transformation development level.[1] By end-1999 the only other transition economies that succeeded in slightly exceeding their 1989 GDP levels were Slovakia and Slovenia. It is perhaps worth noting that in 1999 the Czech Republic and Hungary, that is, the two countries often perceived as the top reformers in the region, still fell short of their pre-transition GDP levels and in the former case the gap was some 14 percentage points. Poland's better performance may be viewed as a pay-off to the 1989 decision to embark on radical systemic reforms and a vindication of the 'shock therapy' approach. It also contributed to narrowing the development gap with the European Union. While in 1992 Poland's GDP per capita (in PPP terms) was 31% of the EU average, six years later it was 41%.[2]

Table 7.1. Economic growth in selected transition economies, 1990–99

Country		GDP per capita in 1998 $ ('000)			Economic growth (1) GDP growth rate on previous year, (2) 1989 GDP = 100									
		GDP[a]	GDP[b]	EU =100	1990	1991	1992	1993	1994	1995	1996	1997	1998	1999[c]
Central Europe:														
Czech Rep.	(1)	5.3	13.1	63	-1.2	-14.2	-6.5	-0.9	2.6	4.8	3.9	1.0	-2.3	-0.5
	(2)	-	-		98.8	84.8	79.3	78.5	80.6	84.4	87.8	88.6	86.5	86.1
Hungary	(1)	4.7	10.8	51	-3.9	-10.5	-3.0	-.08	2.9	1.5	1.3	4.6	5.1	4.2
	(2)	-	-		96.1	85.0	82.4	81.9	84.4	85.6	86.8	90.7	95.3	99.2
Poland	(1)	*4.1*	*8.5*	*41*	*-11.6*	*-7.0*	*2.6*	*3.8*	*5.2*	*7.0*	*6.0*	*6.8*	*4.8*	*4.1*
	(2)	-	-	-	*88.4*	*82.2*	*84.3*	*87.5*	*92.1*	*98.5*	*104.5*	*111.6*	*117.1*	*121.8*
Slovakia	(1)	3.8	10.2	49	-2.6	-8.1	-7.0	-4.1	4.9	6.9	6.6	6.5	4.4	2.4
	(2)	-	-	-	97.4	83.3	77.9	75.1	78.8	84.2	89.2	89.8	95.6	102.2
Slovenia	(1)	9.9	14.9	72	-8.1	-8.1	-5.4	1.3	5.5	4.1	3.1	4.0	3.9	3.5
	(2)	-	-	-	91.9	84.4	79.9	80.9	85.4	88.9	91.6	95.3	99.0	102.5
Eastern Europe:														
Bulgaria	(1)	1.6	5.4	26	-9.1	-11.7	-7.3	-1.5	1.8	2.1	-10.9	-6.9	3.5	1.5
	(2)	-	-	-	90.9	80.3	74.4	73.3	74.6	76.2	67.9	63.2	65.4	66.2
Romania	(1)	1.8	6.1	29	-5.6	-12.9	-8.2	1.5	3.9	7.1	4.1	-6.6	-7.3	-4.8
	(2)	-	-	-	94.4	82.2	75.0	76.2	79.1	84.8	88.2	82.1	76.1	72.4

Table 7.1 continued

Country		GDP per capita in 1998 $ ('000)			Economic growth (1) GDP growth rate on previous year, (2) 1989 GDP = 100									
		a	b	EU =100	1990	1991	1992	1993	1994	1995	1996	1997	1998	1999
Baltic States:														
Estonia	(1)	3.0[d]	4.4[d]		-8.1	-10.0	-14.2	-8.2	-1.8	4.3	3.9	10.6	4.0	-
	(2)	-	-	-	91.9	82.7	71.0	65.0	63.7	66.4	69.0	76.3	79.4	79.4
Latvia	(1)	2.0[d]	3.5[d]		2.7	-10.4	-34.9	-14.9	0.6	-0.8	3.3	8.6	3.6	0.5
	(2)	-	-	-	102.7	92.2	60.1	51.1	51.5	51.0	52.7	57.2	59.3	59.5
Lithuania	(1)	2.1	6.2	30	-3.3	-13.1	-39.6	-30.4	1.0	3.3	4.7	7.3	5.1	-1.0
	(2)	-	-	-	96.7	84.0	50.7	35.3	35.7	36.8	38.6	41.4	43.5	43.1
CIS Countries:														
Belarus	(1)	1.3	5.3	25	-2.0	-1.2	-9.6	-10.6	-12.6	-10.2	2.8	11.4	8.3	4.0
	(2)	-	-	-	98.0	96.8	87.5	78.2	68.3	61.5	63.2	70.4	76.3	79.3
Russia	(1)	1.9	6.1	29	-3.0	-9.1	-19.4	-12.0	-12.7	-4.1	-3.5	0.8	-4.6	1.0
	(2)	-	-	-	97.0	92.2	78.8	71.9	62.8	60.2	58.1	58.6	55.9	56.5
Ukraine	(1)	0.8	3.3	16	-3.6	-11.0	-13.7	-14.1	-23.0	-12.2	-10.0	-3.2	-1.7	-1
	(2)	-	-	-	96.4	88.0	79.2	68.0	52.4	46.0	41.4	40.1	39.4	39.0

Notes:
[a] official exchange rates;
[b] in purchasing power parity;
[c] preliminary;
[d] 1996.

Sources: Rapacki (1998); UNECE (1999), Poeschl et al. (1999).

The demand side

The contribution of different demand components to economic growth has varied throughout the review period (see Table 7.2).[3] However a closer look at the relevant data from the demand side reveals a number of peculiarities in the Polish economy's growth path.

The final year of the command economy, 1989, witnessed a decline in gross fixed investment accompanied by shrinking government spending on goods and services. The impact on GDP growth was offset by two other demand components, net exports (an improved trade balance) and private consumption. As a result GDP increased by a token 0.2% which, combined with high inflation, meant stagflation.

In 1990, the first year of the Balcerowicz Plan, a sharp GDP contraction was due in the first place to a 15% decline in personal consumption and to a lesser extent to shrinking investment. The former was triggered by a dramatic fall in household real incomes, down by 25% compared to 1989. This was due to the combined effect of liberalisation of markets and 'corrective' inflation, as well as the incomes policy component of the stabilisation package. The steep decline in consumption, much deeper than for GDP, was an unexpected feature of transformation recession in 1990. The transformation shock of 1990 was partly cushioned by a slight rise in government spending and an improvement in the current account. The impact of the latter factor on economic growth, despite its small weight in aggregate demand (1%), was significant. In the absence of any trade improvement the GDP decline would have amounted to some 14.3% rather than 11.6% (see Table 7.2).

The second year of recession, 1991, brought a complete reversal within demand components. Investment and net exports fell but private consumption and government spending rebounded, thus partly offsetting the adverse impact of the former. As can be inferred from the data in Table 7.2, the major single factor responsible for negative economic growth in 1991 was a dramatic fall in inventories. Recovery soon followed and became firmer from 1992 until 1998. It was a recovery fuelled by private consumption (up by 6.3% in 1991). Of particular interest is the role of government spending as a growth factor. It seemed to contrast sharply with the orthodox liberal and free-market economic philosophy of the first Solidarity governments.

Another peculiarity of Polish growth was that the role of investment in pulling the country out of 'transformation recession' was negligible; investment was not a growth engine in the early stages of economic recovery (1992–93). One possible explanation may have been low capacity utilisation (especially in industry) due to transformation shock and the resulting demand constraint. The growth paths followed in other transition economies indicate, however, that nowhere did investment become a catalyst of economic recovery. However from 1994 investment demand triggered a marked acceleration of Poland's economic

Table 7.2. Polish GDP and its demand components, 1989–99 (% growth rates, unless otherwise stated)

Item	1989	1990	1991	1992	1993	1994	1995	1996	1997	1998	1999
Real GDP	0.2	-11.6	-7.0	2.6	3.8	5.2	7.0	6.0	6.8	4.8	4.1
Personal consumption	0.4	-15.3	6.3	2.3	5.2	4.3	3.6	8.3	6.8	4.7	5.0
Gross capital formation			-4.1	0.4	2.3	8.1	17.1	19.5	20.8	13.8	6.8
Gross fixed investment	-2.1	-10.6	-4.4	2.3	2.4	8.2	17.5	19.7	21.7	14.2	6.9
Government spending	-4.6	0.5	10.2	5.9	3.2	2.2	2.9	3.4	3.2	1.6	1.0
Current account balance – contribution to GDP growth (% points)	-	2.7	-3.5	-	-2.3	1.6	-1.6	-2.2	-2.2	-1.7	-1.0

Sources: GUS (1998); UNECE (1999).

growth. During 1995–98 gross fixed investment grew two to three times faster than GDP. In the short run this led to a decreasing marginal productivity of investment but it also helped create the basis for a sustainable development of the Polish economy in the medium and long run (supply-side effects).

The largest component of aggregate demand, private consumption, tracked the growth path of national income very closely. The only divergence from this general pattern occurred in 1991 when, despite a substantial rebound in consumer spending, Polish GDP contracted for the second consecutive year. Otherwise private consumption growth rates either followed, or slightly exceeded, GDP growth throughout the 1990s.

The role of government spending as a factor contributing to overall economic growth after 1992 fell substantially. Its pace of growth in 1993–97 stabilised in the range 2.8% to 3.8% per annum and never again exceeded that of GDP. In 1998–99 it decelerated further, to 1.6% and 1.0%, respectively, as a derivative of a more general trend diminishing the role of government in Poland.

The growth contribution of net exports after 1991 was negative, except in 1992 and 1994. As the current account deficit widened (although not in 1994), even taking into account so-called unclassified current account transactions, the Polish economy met mounting problems with external equilibrium.[4] The current account deficit increased from 1.0% of GDP in 1996 to 3.1% in 1997, 4.4% in 1998 and 7.6% in 1999.

Two further points are worth making on the demand side of Polish growth. First, Poland, unlike Hungary in 1995 and the Czech Republic in 1997, succeeded (at least in the 1990s) in avoiding serious financial and economic crises caused by imprudent macroeconomic policy or by any incomplete and incoherent transformation strategy.[5] However, it did not avoid a period of unbalanced growth that threatened serious economic overheating. As a consequence of the fast increase of consumer spending in 1996–97, accompanied by even faster investment growth, the gap between domestic absorption and GDP growth opened up with a rising mismatch between domestic demand and supply. In 1996 that gap amounted to 3.5 percentage points and in 1997 it narrowed to 2.4 points. The boom in consumer spending in the household sector, which was increasingly financed through bank credits (in 1996 alone consumer credit more than doubled in nominal terms), generated a surge in import demand. This in turn led to a widening trade deficit and aggravated the current account situation. In 1998–99, because of external shocks and some tightening of macroeconomic policy, the overheating danger seemed to be dispelled. The divergence between the growth rates of domestic absorption and GDP diminished to 1.8 percentage points in 1998 and further narrowed to 0.8 points in 1999. Nevertheless, the current account disequilibrium in Poland continued to deepen even as economic growth slowed.

The second point concerns the reasons for the growth slow down in Poland in 1998–99. Until 1998 it appeared that the country was resilient to international crises and its growth was robust enough to cope with negative external shocks. However, the adverse impact of the Russian crisis of August 1998 turned out to be much stronger than anticipated. Based on available data it may be estimated that 'the Russian factor' (lost exports and negative multiplier effects on domestic output) may be held responsible for up to 1 or 1.5 percentage points (that is 50% to 66%) of the growth rate loss Poland suffered in 1998 (a deceleration of the GDP growth from 6.8% in 1997 to 4.8% in 1998; see Rapacki, 1999a).

These findings hardly seem consistent with the claims of some Polish economists and vociferous politicians (for example minister Kropiwnicki) who tended to blame domestic economic policy for the slowdown in 1998–99.[6] In their view, policy was excessively restrictive and overshot in its attempts to 'cool' the Polish economy in the earlier period. These claims are not hard to discard. The monetary aggregates into 1997 and through 1998 clearly indicate that the prevailing tendency was to make monetary policy more expansionary rather than restrictive.[7]

The supply side

A closer look at growth across major economic sectors sheds some new light on the economy's growth path from the supply-side (see Table 7.3).

Three findings are worth highlighting. First, it was industry (both in terms of output sold and value added) that displayed the closest pro-cyclical relationship with the general growth pattern in Poland throughout the period 1989–99. Industrial growth rates have also fluctuated widely (from –24.2% to +12.1%). Second, agricultural growth tended to be the most anti-cyclical in relation to GDP. At the same time agricultural output and value added exhibited the highest volatility among all economic sectors. Third, other sectors can be placed between these two extremes. For example, whereas growth in construction followed a path similar to industry, performance in trade and repair, as well as in exports, was closer to the agricultural growth pattern.

Output contraction in industry and construction preceded the implementation of the Balcerowicz Plan's shock therapy. Value added produced in these sectors shrank in 1989, that is even before the transformation shock took its toll and the general economic recession in Poland began. From the point of view of GDP the adverse supply shock in 1989 was offset by a considerable growth in trade and repair and, to a lesser extent, in agriculture and exports.

From the supply side the 'transformation recession' of 1990–91 was triggered mostly by a deep slump in industry (value added fell by 22.0% and 17.1% respectively) and construction (only in 1990) followed by a fall of export revenues in 1991. Sectors with the relatively strongest cushions against recession included financial services, trade and repair, construction (only in 1991), agriculture (1991) and exports (1990).

The supply-side sources of economic recovery from 1992 are not quite clear. The recovery started in industry and construction but the growth of value added in these two sectors either matched or only slightly exceeded that of GDP. Simultaneously, agricultural output suffered a deep contraction, paralleled by a decline of value added in trade and repair and shrinking export revenues. This may suggest that the strongest growth stimulus came from the service sectors and activities not shown in the table, such as transport, storage and communication, hotels and restaurants, real estate and business services.

From 1993 industry entered a fast and sustainable growth path since when both production sold and value added growth rates consistently exceeded the pace of GDP growth.

The service sector also became a major growth engine. In 1993–96 financial services grew fast and in 1996–98 so did trade and repair, hotels and restaurants. The contribution of agriculture to growth was most significant in 1993, 1995 and in 1998, otherwise it tended to be either negative (as in 1992, 1994 and 1999) or negligible. The role of construction in supporting growth was mostly supplementary except for 1997 and 1998, when its growth rate considerably exceeded GDP growth.

Polish exports tended to under-perform, although not in 1994–95, and their contribution to economic growth was lower than expected. The export growth rate also tended to be below that for imports, putting strong pressure on the external balance (see Blazyca, chapter 13 in this book, for a fuller discussion).

Divergent growth rate on the supply side generated substantial shifts in Poland's economic structure in the 1990s. Agriculture's share in gross value added fell from 6.7% in 1992 to 4.7% in 1998, while industry's share fell from 34.0% to 27.7%.[8] On the other hand, the trade and repair share went up from 13.1% to 20.3% and that of real estate and business services from 7.5% to 13.0%, respectively (GUS, 1999b).[9] As a general trend, the service sector share in the economy substantially increased. Nevertheless comparable international statistics suggests that structural change in Poland has been smaller than in other transition economies (see UNECE, 1998).

PRODUCTIVE FACTORS: UTILISATION AND PRODUCTIVITY

Systemic transformation in Poland also led to important changes in the stock and flows of productive factors, in their utilisation, and in allocative efficiency. The relevant data are shown in Table 7.4.

Table 7.3. Growth across major sectors in Poland, 1989–99 (% growth rates)

	1989	1990	1991	1992	1993	1994	1995	1996	1997	1998	1999
Real GDP	0.2	-11.6	-7.0	2.6	3.8	5.2	7.0	6.0	6.8	4.8	4.1
Industry (production sold)	-0.5	-24.2	-8.0	2.8	6.4	12.1	9.7	8.3	11.5	3.5	4.8
Industry (value added)	-2.1	-22.0	-17.1	2.6	8.6	10.3	10.4	7.6	10.3	4.3	3.0
Agriculture (total output)	1.5	-2.2	-1.6	-12.7	6.8	-9.3	10.7	0.7	-0.2	5.9	-5.6
Agriculture (value added)	1.0	-0.3	6.8	-12.3	7.0	-15.1	10.4	2.4	1.1	5.9	-1.7
Construction (value added)	-0.3	-14.5	6.7	3.8	1.1	2.7	5.8	2.8	13.6	9.3	3.5
Trade and repair (value added)	4.7	0.7	7.9	-0.2	5.8	-1.5	5.0	6.1	8.1	5.0	7.3
Exports of goods and services	2.6	15.1	-1.7	10.8	3.2	13.1	22.8	12.0	12.2	14.3	-2.6
Imports of goods and services	4.3	-10.2	29.6	1.7	13.2	11.3	24.3	28.0	21.4	18.5	1.0

Sources: As for Table 7.2.

The transition period to 1999 witnessed a steady increase in the stock of productive factors (labour and capital) in Poland. Simultaneously, the early years of systemic transformation brought a dramatic decline in the utilisation of resources. This process tended to be particularly pronounced in the case of capital: at its lowest level, in 1991, capacity utilisation in manufacturing was only 61% while for labour this ratio reached a minimum of 83.6% in 1993.

In the 'transformation recession' period (1990–91), as capacity utilisation fell so too did factor productivity.

The main factors responsible for low capacity utilisation were a dramatic fall of real incomes in 1990 (by some 25%), the emergence of a strong demand constraint, the structural mismatch between supply of goods and new patterns of demand, liberalisation with resulting competition from imported and higher quality products, as well as the collapse of the Soviet market forcing Polish producers to switch their exports to more demanding Western markets. This 'structural shock', coupled with the parallel transformation of a seller's market, typical for a command economy, into a buyer's market resulted in a significant change to the role of investment in the growth process. A part (although it is hard to determine its size precisely) of the existing capital stock inherited from the centrally planned economy had become a redundant 'dead-weight', useless in the new competitive market environment.

One of the challenges of transformation policy has been to get rid of the excessive and poor investment inheritance from the command economy. This could be done through injecting new technologies into old plants and/or through scrapping the latter and putting in place new capacities. These measures do not directly translate into an increase in capital stock. Instead, they raise its technological level, increasing its productivity, and give rise to new output, reducing the structural mismatch between supply and demand; and last but not least, they enhance the quality and international competitiveness of new or improved products. But a side-effect is that the link between investment and economic growth becomes temporarily loose. At the same time, an unequivocal interpretation of statistical data on factors' productivity becomes quite difficult.

Returning to the data in Table 7.4 it is worth stressing that the process of overcoming the transformation recession and the subsequent recovery took place while unemployment increased. In 1992, when positive GDP growth was recorded for the first time since the start of systemic reforms, the level of total employment fell by more than 4% and in industry alone by almost 9%. Capacity utilisation in manufacturing amounted to 62%, unchanged in 1991. The 1993 experience was similar, employment both in the economy and in industry fell further while capacity utilisation in manufacturing was virtually unchanged (63%).

Table 7.4. Utilisation and productivity of labour and capital in Poland, 1989–99 (annual change %, unless otherwise stated)

	1989	1990	1991	1992	1993	1994	1995	1996	1997	1998	1999
Real GDP	0.2	-11.6	-7.0	2.6	3.8	5.2	7.0	6.0	6.8	4.8	4.1
Total employment	-0.8	-6.2	-5.9	-4.2	-1.6	1.1	1.8	1.9	2.3	-0.3	-2.6
in industry	0.0	-5.6	-8.0	-8.7	-3.0	-0.8	3.2	-0.7	0.8	-1.0	-6.1
Unemployment rate (%)	0.1	6.5	12.2	14.3	16.4	16.0	14.9	13.6	10.3	10.4	13.1
Productive fixed assets	3.4	1.1	1.2	1.3	1.9	2.6	2.1	4.8	3.5	3.9	3.9
in industry	3.2	2.4	0.9	1.2	1.7	2.8	0.3	6.1	3.6	3.2	3.6
Capacity utilisation in manufacturing (%)	88.0	74.0	61.0	62.0	63.0	66.0	71.0	73.0	77.0	77.0	78.0
Productivity of labour	1.0	-5.8	-1.2	7.1	5.8	4.3	5.1	3.6	4.3	5.1	6.9
in industry	0.3	-19.7	-4.2	12.6	9.7	13.0	6.3	9.3	10.6	4.5	11.6
Productivity of fixed capital	-3.1	-12.6	-8.1	1.3	1.9	2.5	4.8	2.0	3.2	0.9	0.2
in industry	-3.6	-26.0	-12.7	1.6	4.6	9.0	9.4	2.3	7.6	1.5	1.2
Incremental capital–output ratio (ICOR)	-2.3	1.1	2.8	-0.3	-1.3	2.9	9.8	12.9	13.9	9.0	2.7

Sources: GUS (1999b); UNIDO (1997); own calculations and estimates.

Large-scale labour shedding in the early stages of systemic transformation meant that the rate of registered (or open) unemployment rose very fast and ranked initially among the highest of all transition economies, reaching a peak in 1993 (16.4%), falling to 1997 (10.3%) but rising in 1998. This labour market behaviour reflects the 'shock therapy' approach to systemic reforms and is in sharp contrast with the experience of Russia and the CIS countries as well as the Czech Republic, where unemployment growth tended to be restrained by the government for most of the 1990s. It is perhaps worth pointing out that by 1998 the unemployment rate in Poland (10.4%) was at the average EU level and was below Slovakia (15.6%), Slovenia (14.6%), Russia (12.4%) and Bulgaria (12.2%) (see UNECE, 1999).

A reversal of the earlier downward trend on the Polish labour market occurred over 1998–2000. In 1998 the unemployment rate rose slightly (from 10.3% in 1997) and in 1999 it further increased, to 13.1%.[10] Six factors seem to be responsible. The first was due to stronger demographic pressure from new entrants on the labour market (a rising number of school leavers). The second stems from long-delayed and much-needed structural reforms launched by the Buzek government in 1998 and aimed at restructuring a number of 'sunset' sectors (coal mining and metallurgy) to make them viable in the medium and long run. Third, institutional reforms in health and education had labour market effects. A fourth, one-off, factor contributed to a sharp rise of unemployment in the first months of 1999. It was linked to the health care reform of January 1999: to become eligible for medical coverage some people, previously making a living in the 'shadow economy', registered as unemployed for the first time. Fifth, many privatisation deals with foreign investors involved job protection provisions for a specified period (usually 2–5 years). It is claimed that – as a large proportion of these provisions expired in 1999–2000 – new owners made a part of their manpower redundant. Finally, the general slow down of economic activity combined with the second wave of restructuring efforts of Polish firms facing growing competitive pressure may have also significantly contributed to the rise in unemployment. According to some estimates, in order to create net new job opportunities the Polish economy should grow at a rate of at least 5–6% per annum.

A different category of factors are to be blamed for the worsening state of the labour market in Poland is embedded in institutional and political set up. They included a sort of a 'corporatist capture' of the government, that is the excessive political clue of trade unions (both Solidarity and OPZZ) who have strongly defended the status quo on the labour market and opposed changes aimed at irs deregulation and increase of its flexibility. They tended to be strongly biased towards the interests of jobholders (the 'insider–outsider' problem) and maximisation of their wages, in particular those employed in the public sector and sunset industries. As a matter of example, two implications of this policy for the labour market and unemployment are worth highlighting. First, it is coincidence that – despite a generally lower GDP per capita – the level of wages and salaries in Poland has been above those of Hungary of the Czech Republic. The average gross monthly wage amounted in mid-2000 to US$358 (Business Central Europe, November 2000). Second, compared to these two countries, the Polish labour market exhibited a higher rigidity in terms of minimum wage legislation. While in Poland the minimum wage amounted to 40% of the average was and has tended to stay at this level since 1993, the same indices in Hungary and the Czech Republic amounted to 35% and 20% respecively and displayed a downward trend.

Labour and capital productivity rebounded after 1992, providing an important stimulus to economic growth. Labour productivity gains were especially strong in industry where they were accompanied (until 1996) by labour shedding.

One of the distinctive features of Polish growth (Hungary is similar) in comparison to other Central and Eastern European countries was a combination of fast growth of labour productivity with a simultaneous decline in real unit labour costs (Table 7.5). This was due to the fact that despite the strength of Polish trade unions labour productivity tended to grow faster than real wages (with the exception of 1996 and 1998). This trend, if it continues, should lead to improved price competitiveness in the global market place. Polish and Hungarian experience sharply contrasts with the labour market policy pursued in the Czech Republic until 1997 (with its concealed unemployment, artificially low figures for registered unemployment, low labour productivity growth and a steady rise in real unit labour costs). The latter sheds an interesting light on some of the possible structural and microeconomic roots of the 1997 Czech economic crisis.

Interpretation of the data in Table 7.4 with respect to the efficiency of capital use is much more difficult than for labour. Whereas changes in labour productivity relate to the actual number of persons employed (rather than to the total registered workforce), the average and marginal productivity of capital is a function of total fixed assets. This implies, among others, that part of the incremental product of these assets is in fact due to a gradual decrease of idle capacity. Under these circumstances it seems advisable to resort to another yardstick that (albeit also subject to some drawbacks) better measures changes in the efficiency of capital – the incremental capital–output ratio (or ICOR), a ratio of the gross fixed investment to GDP growth rates (Table 7.4).[11] Changes in the ICOR measure not so much the current productivity of capital (as today's investment brings about increases in the stock of capital with a time lag) but rather the potential or future effects of today's investment effort. The ICOR should be seen, therefore, as a kind of leading indicator providing a basis for predictions on future economic growth. Positive ICORs from 1994 can be interpreted, first, as a symptom of the rising role of investment as a demand factor fuelling economic growth and, second, as indicating the ever-increasing potential supply-side effects of today's investment.

Poland succeeded in attaining in the 1990s the fastest, yet most stable GDP growth performance in East–Central Europe, while having one of the lowest investment to GDP ratios and an even lower domestic savings to GDP ratio (see Table 7.6). The investment–domestic savings gap, the result of the low propensity to save and the persistent budget deficit, was filled by international savings and in particular by a growing current account deficit and ever-greater inflow of foreign direct investment. If Poland aims to sustain growth in the longer run, at 6% to 7% per annum, this will require, as some authors have suggested (for example Gomułka, 1998), a much higher investment ratio, say in the range of 30% to 35%. Accordingly, the ratio of domestic savings to GDP must also be raised substantially. This may not be easy since the late 1990s' growth pattern shows the domestic savings gap to have widened. While the savings to GDP ratio grew slowly after 1996, reaching some 21% in 1998, the investment ratio tended to increase much faster to 25.9% in 1998 and 26.5% in 1999.

The propensity of households to save is not easily described in Poland. On one hand, after a one-off increase in 1997, the ratio of households' savings to gross disposable income declined in 1998 (from 10.5% to 9.0%) to its lowest level since the start of transformation (see *Poland*, 1999). On the other hand, the share of domestic currency and foreign exchange bank deposits to GDP increased from 19% to 21% in 1991–96, to 25% in 1997 and reached 24.3% in 1998. Meanwhile the ratio of incremental deposits to GDP (a more accurate measure of the propensity to save) rose sharply from 1% to 2% in 1991–96, to 6.4% in 1997 and 5.1% in 1998. One explanation is that the savings pattern is due to fast-rising real interest rates (a feature of 1997 and 1998), coupled with a substantial increase of real incomes.

A key determinant of the likely future supply-side effects of investment is linked to its composition. Two unfavourable trends prevailing in the mid to late 1990s in Poland are worth highlighting in this context. First, investment tended to be biased towards sectors and industries that could hardly be termed research- or technology-intensive. To give one example, in 1995 65% of investment outlays in the public sector (responsible for 56% of total investment) were channelled to coal mining, power generation, gas provision and metallurgy (see *Poland,* 1996). Second, the first half of the 1990s witnessed a steep decline in the high-tech share in total manufacturing investment (see Table 7.7). Moreover, although this share was higher in 1994 as compared to 1990, it was the lowest among the reformers, usually considered to be most advanced (Hungary, Czech Republic, Slovenia).

Table 7.5. Labour productivity[a] and real unit labour costs[b] in industry in selected transition economies, 1991–98 (annual average percentage changes)

	1991	1992	1993	1994	1995	1996	1997	1998	1999
Bulgaria									
Labour productivity	-5.2	-3.1	-2.8	12.6	6.6	5.2	-6.4	9.0	-4.8
Real unit labour costs	-28.8	33.8	24.7	-14.0	0.7	-15.7	16.9	7.8	12.5
Czech Republic									
Labour productivity	-21.4	-0.2	-0.5	7.9	8.6	7.2	5.6	2.2	-2.0
Real unit labour costs	-13.9	11.6	11.8	1.8	0.9	4.7	1.3	2.7	7.9
Hungary									
Labour productivity	-7.2	-0.2	16.3	14.7	10.5	4.3	9.3	7.5	7.3
Real unit labour costs	8.1	7.5	-9.3	-7.7	-14.6	-4.8	-7.9	-2.7	1.7
Poland									
Labour productivity	-4.2	12.6	9.7	13.0	6.3	9.3	11.2	4.6	5.9
Real unit labour costs	22.7	-7.2	-5.7	-3.0	-1.5	1.8	-3.8	2.5	-2.2

Table 7.5 continued

	1991	1992	1993	1994	1995	1996	1997	1998	1999
Romania									
Labour productivity	-18.7	-10.0	10.4	8.6	16.2	13.3	-4.9	-12.0	-2.8
Real unit labour costs	-11.8	7.0	10.0	-11.6	-1.8	- 6.7	-16.0	32.1	7.2
Slovakia									
Labour productivity	-10.7	-3.6	-5.0	8.0	8.3	2.5	3.7	8.2	-1.8
Real unit labour costs	-24.3	18.8	-	-1.1	-2.6	7.6	0.7	-1.8	7.0
Slovenia									
Labour productivity	-2.3	-3.2	6.8	11.2	5.8	2.1	5.5	4.8	-0.4
Real unit labour costs	-16.7	-2.3	17.0	-1.9	-1.7	4.7	-	-0.3	6.6

Notes:
[a] gross industrial output/employed person;
[b] real wages deflated by labour productivity;

Sources: *Transition Report* (1996, p. 118); *World Economic Outlook,* May (1997, p. 100); UNECE (1997b, p. 93); UNECE (1999, no. 1, p. 121); and UNECE (1997a, p. 31).

Table 7.6. Investment and savings in selected transition economies, 1980–96 (% of GDP)

Country	Gross domestic investment							Domestic savings			
	1980	1989	1990	1991	1994	1995	1996	1980	1994	1995	1996
Bulgaria	34.0	32.9	25.6	22.6	20.8	14.4	9.3[a]	39	21	-	-
Czech Rep.	-	26.8	28.6	29.9	20.4	27.8	34.2[b]	-	20	-	-
Hungary	30.7	26.1	25.4	20.8	21.5	22.8	-	29	15	-	-
Poland	*26.4*	*28.7*	*25.6*	*19.9*	*15.9*	*18.3*	*20.8*	*23*	*17*	*19*	*18*
Romania	39.8	25.8	30.2	28.0	26.9	24.3	25.4	35	25	-	-
Slovakia	37.3		33.5	-	23.3	28.5	38.2	31	23	-	-
Slovenia	-	-	16.9	-	20.8	23.2	24.9	-	25	-	-
Estonia	28.5	-	30.2	-	28.6	26.9	27.6[a]	25	28	-	-
Latvia	25.7	-	40.1	-	19.1	19.7	28.4	32	25	-	-
Lithuania	31.2	-	34.3	-	15.4	22.6	16.3[c]	16	11	-	-

Notes:

[a] January–June;

[b] January–September;

[c] January–March.

Source: World Bank, (1996, pp. 173, 212 and 1998); UNECE (1997b, p. 100); UNIDO, (1997, p. 43)

HUMAN CAPITAL AND INNOVATIVE CAPABILITY

One of the most crucial dimensions of macroeconomic performance, especially from the view point of the technological level of the Polish economy and its international competitiveness, lies in the activities contributing to human capital formation enhancing innovative capacity. Our discussion of these issues relies on rather scarce and incomplete data and has therefore a very modest scope: it aims only to sketch the most salient trends and inter-relationships with a view to providing some rough yardsticks for assessment.

From this perspective, transformation in Poland has some important drawbacks, particularly regarding the domestic R&D effort and innovative capacity but also (perhaps to a lesser) degree regarding human capital.

With regard to the latter, the 1990s witnessed a dramatic growth in demand for higher education as well as for upgrading existing and acquiring new skills. Between 1990 and 1999 the number of enrolled students more than tripled: from 404,000 to 1.4 million (GUS, 1998; see also *Rzeczpospolita,* 1999). The ratio of students per 100,000 inhabitants increased from 12 in 1990 to 35 in 1999 but it still lagged behind many countries.[12] Notwithstanding the fast expansion of higher education and training during the 1990s the educational and human capital gap (at least in quantitative terms) with most of the advanced market economies remained remarkably wide. By way of example, in 1998 higher education graduates made up some 7% of the total population in Poland as compared to 18% in Spain (*Gazeta Wyborcza,* 1998).

Polish long-term growth prospects may also be adversely affected by worrisome developments in research and development and innovative capability. The data suggest that unfavourable tendencies dominated in these fields after 1989, embracing both the inputs to and outputs of the R&D effort. Throughout the 1990s government expenditures on research and development tended to grow more slowly than GDP and, as a result, their share in GDP systematically fell to reach in 1998 the lowest level (0.42%) since the end of World War II. If corporate sector funding of R&D were also included, the ratio would rise to 0.72%, still well below the EU average (1.85% in 1996) and the mean for 29 OECD countries (2.15%). The Czech Republic ratio was 1.15% in 1996 while Hungary reached 0.75%. Among OECD countries only Mexico (0.31%), Turkey (0.38%), Greece (0.48%) and Portugal (0.61) had lower figures than Poland. In 17 OECD countries it exceeded 1.5% of GDP and in 10 of them it was above 2% (OECD, 1997).

During the 1990s the innovative capability of the economy also declined. Data on inventive and patent activities both domestically and abroad are shown in Table 7.8.

To complete the picture it should be added that while in 1990 Poland filed 154 patent *applications* abroad this increased to 851 in 1994 and to 903 in 1995 before falling in 1996 to 635. The number of patents *granted*, however, moved in

Table 7.7. Investment composition in selected transition economies, 1970–94 (% share in manufacturing investment)

Country	Type of industry	1970	1980	1990	1994
Former Czecho-slovakia[a]	Low-technology	62.3	59.0	52.6	46.5
	Medium-technology	21.3	19.3	22.3	34.4
	High-technology	15.2	20.8	23.3	17.0
Hungary	Low-technology	59.5	61.6	62.3	61.8
	Medium-technology	23.5	19.5	24.9	23.6
	High-technology	15.0	16.7	11.7	14.0
Poland	*Low-technology*	*58.4*	*53.0*	*58.7*	*66.9*
	Medium-technology	*24.0*	*20.7*	*29.3*	*19.9*
	High-technology	*17.3*	*25.8*	*11.3*	*12.2*
Romania	Low-technology	56.7	50.0	61.7	68.1
	Medium-technology	20.7	26.1	17.6	14.4
	High-technology	19.6	21.8	17.3	5.6

Table 7.7 continued

Country	Type of industry	1970	1980	1990	1994
Slovenia	Low-technology	99.3	86.3	55.3	46.6
	Medium-technology	0.2	4.0	28.1	39.3
	High-technology	0.4	8.8	16.5	13.7
Former Soviet Union[b]	Low-technology	53.9	48.1	49.4	61.4
	Medium-technology	17.7	17.6	12.3	5.9
	High-technology	21.1	26.8	29.0	21.6

Notes:
[a] data for the Czech Republic and Slovakia are combined in the totals for 1994;
[b] CIS countries since 1992.

Source: UNIDO (1997, p. 44).

the opposite direction falling from 146 in 1990 to 119 in 1994, 65 in 1995 and only 43 in 1996. The ratio of patents registered in Poland per 100,000 inhabitants was 9 in 1995 whereas in the Czech Republic it was 16, in Hungary 50, in Spain 31, in the USA 371 and in Japan 389. It is also worth noting that non-residents owned 88.2% of all patents registered in Poland, as compared to 96.9% in the Czech Republic and 94.7% in Hungary (all data from GUS, 1999, and OECD, 1997).

Table 7.8. Inventive activity in Poland, 1980–98

	1980	1990	1995	1997	1998	1999
Domestic inventions						
Patent applications	6,198	4,105	2,595	2,399	2,407	2,285
Patents granted	5,736	3,242	1,619	1,179	1,174	1,022
Domestic industrial patterns						
Applications	2,523	2,578	2,119	1,589	1,525	1,290
Protection rights granted	1,680	1,694	992	885	976	778
Non-resident inventions in Poland						
Patent applications	1,644	1,316	2,874	3,948	4,128	4,571
Patents granted	1,962	405	989	1,151	1.242	1,214

Sources: GUS (1998 p. 225) and (1998, p. 303).

These indicators of inventive and patent activities in Poland were consistent with developments in trade of licences. In 1998 Polish firms exploited 213 imported licences (175 in 1997); at the same time Poland exported only nine licences (23 in 1997). Revenues from exports of disembodied technology totalled some US$21 million while payments for its import were almost seven-fold greater, that is US$137 million. Compared to earlier years the deficit in Poland's technology trade rose substantially.

The low innovative capability of the Polish economy was also reflected in the declining share of new and improved products in industrial sales. While during 1995–97 their average share was 20.1% in 1998 it was only 8.2%.

These data suggest that major threats exist to sustainable long-term growth in Poland. They are the limited ability of the Polish economy to encourage the indigenous R&D effort, to develop its science and technology base and to generate new knowledge and technological innovations. This may impede the further growth of productive and allocative efficiency and by the same token adversely affect the future competitive position of Polish firms in the global environment.

PRIVATISATION AND PRIVATE SECTOR DEVELOPMENT

Poland embarked on the road to capitalism with the largest private sector of any former socialist country. In 1989 the private sector share in GDP was 19%, compared to 15% in Hungary and 2% to 4% in other East–Central European economies (see Milanovic, 1989; Rapacki and Linz, 1992). One of Poland's peculiarities was its predominantly private agriculture (with 80% of land in private hands) which contributed some 11% of GDP in 1989. This was initially thought to be a favourable starting condition for systemic transformation. However, with the benefit of hindsight we can say that the asset was more apparent than real.

Privatisation proper began in early 1990 based on a multi-track approach with three major privatisation methods: (i) the 'capital' (or indirect) track, later to include also the Polish version of 'mass privatisation' via National Investment Funds (NFI); (ii) the direct path (liquidation of viable state-owned enterprises – SOEs); and (iii) liquidation of insolvent SOEs. Table 7.9 shows privatisation outcomes.

By end-1999, of the initial number of 8872 SOEs some 6438, that is 72.6%, were privatised. At that point of time 2599 state-owned firms still existed (29.3% of the 1990 number). Privatisation was completed in 55% of all non-agricultural SOEs (2646 from 4784).

The overall economic impact of government-led or 'top-down' privatisation turned out to be smaller than initially expected. In the entire 1990–97 period 496,000 jobs were transferred from the public to the private sector as a result of completed privatisations (GUS, 1998). Even adding the expected impact of the mass privatisation programme will make little difference, taking, in all, a further 309,000 jobs to the private sector. This should be compared with the 3 million new jobs created in 1990–97 in the private sector as a whole. The effects of 'top-down' ownership changes on economic growth and efficiency were also below expectations. It was the 'grass-roots' or 'bottom-up' privatisation (including both the expansion of existing firms and new starts) that, according to many authors (see, for example, World Bank, 1996), may have fuelled fast private sector growth in Poland. This is illustrated by the increase in the number of sole-proprietor firms from 350,000 in 1989 to some 2.1 million in 1998. Perhaps one reason for this was that since 1956 Poland had enjoyed the highest relative openness in the Soviet bloc in terms of both the flow of ideas and, after 1971, people. Soon after the Gierek group came to power in December 1970 Poles were allowed, with some restrictions, to travel to the West. For more than 10 years several millions used this new window of opportunity to find seasonal or temporary jobs in Western countries. New skills and work habits were acquired, some acquaintance was made with key market institutions and, of utmost importance, some capital was accumulated that could be invested in business start-ups in the late 1980s and early 1990s (see Rapacki, 1999b).

As a result of both 'top-down' privatisation and 'grass-roots' developments the share of the private sector in Poland's GDP increased from 19% in 1989 to over 70% in 1999. Similarly, by end-1999 the private sector provided some 70% of total employment. Private firms tended also to grow faster and to perform better than the state sector.

MACROECONOMIC EQUILIBRIUM

The transformation process also brought important changes in terms of macroeconomic equilibrium. Economic performance, however, displayed strongly diverging trends as between internal and external balance. Whereas the situation on domestic markets tended almost consistently to improve over the 1990–99 period Poland's trade and current account position, especially after 1995, deteriorated.

On the other hand, despite a growing trade and current account imbalance the central bank's international reserves increased from 1993 to reach US$27.4 billion in 1998, the equivalent of seven months' imports. Their growth stemmed from a surplus on the capital account and, in particular, from the net inflow of short- and long-term capital that, for many years, more than offset the deficit in current transactions. As can be seen from Table 7.10, capital inflow came mostly from foreign direct investment. For example, in 1998 the FDI stream alone (cash basis) nearly matched the current account deficit. According to a broader definition of FDI used by the State Agency for Foreign Investment (PAIZ), including also in-land contributions and reinvested profits, the FDI inflow in 1998 exceeded US$10 billion; their cumulative stock over the whole transformation period amounted to US$30 billion, the largest of all transition economies, although very modest on a per capita basis.

The accelerated inflow of foreign direct investment reflects growing investor confidence. For as long as it lasts this is a strong advantage, providing a cushion against international financial crises. Long-term investment has predominated in foreign capital inflow to Poland in contrast with the experience of the Czech Republic and South-East Asia where short-term speculative capital created a particular vulnerability to external shocks and eventually triggered a financial crunch.

One other positive development in Poland's foreign financial position was the simultaneous increase of official reserves and the considerable fall of external debt: from US$44 billion in 1995 to US$38 billion in 1999. Again, at least until 1999, compared to other transition countries, Poland seemed to be relatively robust and immune to external shocks, even allowing for a worsening current account situation (see Table 7.13).

Table 7.9. Privatisation of state-owned enterprises in Poland, 1990–99 (numbers of firms)

	1990–99	1990[a]	1991	1992	1993	1994	1995	1996	1997	1998	1999
SOEs subject to privatisation	*6,438*	*130*	*1,128*	*1,401*	*1,271*	*791*	*485*	*385*	*288*	*289*	*270*
Transformed into Treasury corporations	1,419	58	250	172	156	209	230	154	40	112	38
Privatised under the capital (indirect) track	256	6	24	22	46	36	25	24	41	16	16
Direct track privatisation	1,710	44	372	246	203	120	113	146	185	134	147
Actually privatised	1,641	15	228	305	216	159	127	184	158	127	122
Insolvency track	1,655	28	506	263	294	155	133	85	63	43	85
Actually liquidated	749	3	30	90	103	92	108	110	102	70	41
Treasury Agricultural Property Agency	1,654	-	-	720	618	307	9	-	-	-	-
Total number of SOEs Actually privatised	**2,646**	**24**	**282**	**417**	**365**	**287**	**260**	**318**	**301**	**213**	**179**

Note: [a] since 1 August 1990.

Source: GUS (1998); *Dynamics...* (1998); Ministry of Treasury data.

Table 7.10. Poland's external financial position, 1989–99 (US$bn, unless otherwise stated)

	1989	1990	1991	1992	1993	1994	1995	1996	1997	1998	1999
Merchandise exports	14.7	18.3	14.9	13.2	14.1	17.2	22.9	24.4	25.8	28.2	27.3
Merchandise imports	12.9	12.6	15.5	15.9	18.8	21.6	29.0	37.1	42.3	46.6	44.9
Trade balance	1.7	5.7	-0.6	-2.7	-4.7	-4.3	-6.1	-12.7	-16.6	-18.4	-17.6
Current account[a]	-1.8	0.7	-1.4	-0.3	-2.3	-0.9	5.4 *-2.3*[b]	-1.4	-4.3	-6.8	-11.7
Current account (% of GDP)	-2.7	1.2	-1.8	0.3	-2.7	-1.0	4.3 *-1.8*[b]	-1.0	-3.0	-4.3	-7.6
FDI inflow	-	0.1	0.1	0.3	0.6	0.5	1.1	2.8	3.1	5.2	6.6
Official reserves	2.5	4.5	3.6	4.3	4.3	6.0	15.0	18.0	20.7	27.4	25.5
Gross external debt	43.3	48.7	48.4	47.1	46.8	42.2	44.0	40.6	38.5	33.0	32.0

Notes:

[a] since 1995 including 'non-classified' current account transactions, that is, informal, or 'cross-border' trade;
[b] excluding non-classified transactions.

Sources: GUS (various); World Bank (1991); Poeschl et al. (1999); UNECE (1999), own estimates.

Table 7.11. Selected indicators of internal equilibrium, 1989–99 (annual % change, unless otherwise stated)

	1989	1990	1991	1992	1993	1994	1995	1996	1997	1998	1999
GDP deflator	298.5	480.1	55.3	38.5	30.5	28.4	27.9	18.7	14.0	12.5	8.1
CPI inflation	264.3	585.8	70.3	45.3	36.9	33.2	27.1	19.8	14.9	11.8	7.3
PPI inflation	212.8	622.4	40.9	28.0	32.6	31.0	26.0	12.4	12.2	7.3	5.6
Budget deficit (% GDP)	-8.0	0.7	-3.8	-6.0	-2.8	-2.7	-2.4	-2.4	-1.3	-2.4	-2.1
Public debt (% GDP)	-	90.0	80.0	86.0	86.0	69.0	55.0	48.0	46.0	43.0	43.0

Source: GUS (various years); author's calculations.

PROSPECTS AND CHALLENGES AHEAD

It seems safe to conclude that, in a comparative perspective, Poland entered the new millennium as one of the best performing transition economies, albeit not free from problems that may potentially endanger development prospects. We turn now to the short- and long-term prospects of the Polish economy with special emphasis on major threats and challenges.

Despite the fact that Poland tended to be partly cushioned against international financial crises (a low share of short-term capital in total inflows) the events of late-1998 and 1999 showed that it was not immune to external shocks. During the fourth quarter of 1998 and the first half of 1999 the Polish economy struggled to overcome the consequences of the August 1998 Russian crisis. At the most aggregate level GDP growth (annualised) slowed to 2.9% in the last quarter of 1998, 1.6% in the first before rising to 3.0% in the second quarter of 1999. The hardest hit sector was industry – its output fell in absolute terms in the first half of 1999 but picked up after August, underpinning (with services) acceleration in GDP growth to 5.0% in the third and 6.2% in the fourth quarter of 1999. Most observers expected the Polish economy to overcome the adverse effects of the Russian crisis and to return to a sustainable growth path. Table 7.12 summarises the key indicators of macroeconomic performance as projected by the government in late 1999. They were compatible with (May 2000) projections by the European Commission for 10 candidate countries for the years 2000–2001 (see Table 7.14).

Table 7.12. Main macroeconomic indicators in Poland, 1999 and 2000 (percentage changes, unless otherwise stated)

Item	1999 (actual)	2000[a]
GDP	4.1	5.2
Personal consumption	5.0	4.4
Gross fixed investment	6.9	13.0
Industrial output	4.3	5.7
Merchandise exports[b]	2.0	14.0
Trade deficit (US$ bn)[b]	-18.5	-14.0
Current account (US$ bn)	-11.6	-10.5
CPI inflation	7.3	5.7
Budget deficit (percentage of GDP)	-2.0	-1.9
Unemployment rate (end year rate)	13.1	11.5

Notes: [a] government forecast; [b] customs data.

Source: Government blueprint of the 2000 budget (*Rzeczpospolita*, October 1999, 2–3); *Biuletyn Statystyczny,* 12, 2001; press reports.

Among the major threats to macroeconomic goals three deserve a special mention:

- the current account deficit may grow too fast, bringing external imbalance to unmanageable levels, triggering capital flight and loss of investors' confidence;
- higher than expected costs of the four institutional reforms of 1999 (decentralisation of public administration, health care, pensions and education) may increase the burden on the central budget leading to stronger inflationary pressure through extra government expenditures and a higher budget deficit;
- the effective loosening of the budget constraint may force the central bank to tighten the monetary policy (higher interest rates). This move may in turn be conducive to growth slown down and rising unemployment.

Even if the Polish government meets its macroeconomic targets in 2000, the sustainability of long-run economic growth will crucially depend on its ability to solve major structural problems persisting after 10 years of transformation as well as to overcome existing and new development barriers, in particular:

- low competitiveness in the global marketplace adversely affecting export performance;
- low innovative capability due to insufficient government funding of domestic R&D and limited private sector innovation;
- persistence of monopolies in many key sectors and industries (for example telecommunications, power generation, air and rail transport);
- delayed privatisation of several sectors including network industries, as well as delayed and too slow restructuring of many 'sunset' industries and 'problem' sectors aimed to make them economically viable and responsive to market signals (coal mining, metallurgy, arms industry, sugar processing, spirits);
- lack of any clear and cohesive strategy towards agriculture in view of European Union accession;
- poor shape of a number of key segments of physical infrastructure (in particular roads) and insufficient progress in upgrading to European standards;
- possible slowdown in 'grass-roots' privatisation as a powerful source of Polish growth. In particular, sole-trading and small firms may face a capital barrier as many will lack the funds necessary to upgrade their product mix and to introduce technological innovations;

Table 7.13. Foreign financial position in selected transition economies (US$ billion)

	Gross external debt		Official reserves				Current account in % of GDP		
	1997	1998	1997		1998		1997	1998	1999
			[a]	[b]	[a]	[b]			
Poland	38.5	33.0	20.7	5.8	27.4	6.9	-3.0	-4.3	-7.6
Czech Republic	21.6	24.4	9.7	4.2	12.6	5.2	-6.1	-2.4	-2.0
Hungary	23.7	26.7	8.4	4.7	9.3	4.3	-2.1	-4.9	-4.3
Slovakia	9.9	12.2	3.3	3.3	2.9	2.7	-10.0	-10.1	-5.7
Slovenia	4.2	4.9	3.2	4.2	3.6	4.3	0.2	0.2	-3.0

Notes:
[a] in US$ billion;
[b] in months of import coverage.

Sources: UNECE (1999, pp. 163 and 177); Poeschl et al. (1999, p. 5); author's estimates.

Table 7.14. Economic projections for 10 EU candidate countries, 2000–01

	GDP growth (%)		Average CPI inflation (%)		Current account in % of GDP	
	2000	2001	2000	2001	2000	2001
Poland	5.1	5.5	9.2	5.3	-6.8	-6.2
Bulgaria	4.5	4.9	7.9	4.8	-4.1	-3.1
Czech Rep.	1.8	3.1	3.0	3.3	-1.7	-1.0
Estonia	4.0	5.5	3.5	2.4	-6.1	-6.1
Hungary	4.7	5.1	8.0	5.8	-4.5	-4.4
Latvia	2.5	3.9	3.5	3.5	-9.6	-9.1
Lithuania	2.2	3.4	1.8	2.5	-10.9	-9.0
Romania	-0.6	2.8	39.0	25.0	-4.1	-4.9
Slovakia	2.2	3.3	13.2	7.5	-4.9	-3.8
Slovenia	4.1	4.1	5.0	4.5	-3.1	-3.1
Average	3.7	4.6	10.4	6.6	-5.3	-4.9

Source: European Commission, Brussels, 2000.

- Poland's accession to the European Union will entail large-scale transfers of EU funds and development aid to facilitate integration. The main challenge for Poland is to follow the example of Spain and Portugal rather than that of Greece in effectively absorbing and using EU funds (see Orłowski, chapter 14 in this volume);

The large inflow of EU funds will most likely lead to the real appreciation of the domestic currency in the long run, which may additionally depress the (price) competitiveness of Polish exports.

The very fact of Poland–EU accession negotiations and forthcoming EU membership may partly mitigate the seriousness of some of these threats. The need to meet EU convergence criteria in a growing number of areas will bring greater external pressure (and a handy argument for the Polish government) on much needed structural reforms, tackling at least some of the hurdles to sustainable growth. This seems likely even under the scenario of the (post-communist) SLD winning the next parliamentary elections in 2001. Their clear political commitment to Poland's integration with Western Europe and the sense of realism in macroeconomic policy as shown during 1993–97 (see Blazyca and Rapacki, 1996) appear to suggest continuity rather than any dramatic change on the Polish road to Europe.

NOTES

1 If unregistered activities in the 'shadow economy' are taken into account the actual decline of Polish GDP during the transformation recession of 1990–91 was substantially smaller than suggested by official statistics. Consequently in reality, Poland regained its pre-transformation development level before 1996. According to some estimates GDP in 1998 exceeded its 1989 level by 29% rather than 17% (see Table 7.1). For more detail on this, see Orłowski, chapter 11, in this volume.

2 The real appreciation of Polish currency also helped.

3 Table 7.2 enables us to see the data on gross capital formation and gross fixed investment (the difference being inventories). High volatility of inventories over 1989–98 may be 'blamed' for substantial discrepancies between the dynamics of gross fixed investment and gross capital formation in particular years.

4 These included mostly unregistered trade transactions along Polish borders as well as the inflow of foreign exchange to the banking sector. Poland enjoyed a substantial surplus in these transactions. In 1995 it amounted to some US$ 7.8 billion.

5 An interesting discussion on the sources of the Czech crisis can be found in Myant (1999).

6 Jerzy Kropiwnicki was minister head of the centre for strategic studies (RCSS) in the AWS-UN government in 1997–2000. During this period he was at times strongly critical of polices followed the finance minister.
7 To give one example, the real money supply (M2) grew in 1998 by 15.1% (CPI as deflator) compared to 14.0% in 1997. Similarly, the supply of credit for the household and corporate sectors increased in real terms by 21.8% (PPI as deflator) and 19.7%, respectively. A more detailed discussion can be found in (Rapacki, 1999a).
8 This may be due in part to the fact that PPI inflation has been for the last several years consistently lower than the price indices in the service sector and below the GDP deflator.
9 In terms of gross domestic product, the respective shares in 1998 were: 4.2% for agriculture, 24.4% for industry, and 18.3% for trade and repair (GUS, 1999a).
10 In 2000 the unemployment rate grew even more – to 15.0% (GUS, 2000).
11 It is fair to note, however that – notwithstanding its shortcomings – even this former measure of capital productivity has displayed steady growth since 1992 both in the economy and in industry. Moreover, the marginal product of capital tended to rise at an accelerated pace since 1996, which may prove the emergence of the supply-side effects of fast-growing investment outlays (since 1994).
12 For example in 1994–95 Canada had 69, USA 55, France 40 Spain 39 while Poland had 20, the Czech Republic 17, and in Hungary 15 (GUS, 1998).

REFERENCES

Blazyca, George and R. Rapacki (eds) (1991), *Poland into the 1990s: Economy and Society in Transition,* London: Pinter.

Blazyca, George and R. Rapacki (1996), 'Continuity and change in Polish economic policy: the impact of the 1993 election', *Europe-Asia Studies,* 48 (1).

Business Central Europe (2000), November

De Melo, Martha and A. Gelb (1996), 'A comparative analysis of twenty-eight transition economies in Europe and Asia', *Post-Soviet Geography and Economics*, 37 (5).

Dynamics of Ownership Transformations (1998), no. 39; Warsaw: Ministry of Treasury, December (in Polish).

Gazeta Wyborcza (1998), no. 244, 17–18 October.

Gomułka, Stanisław (1997), 'Higher interest rates encourage', *Gazeta Bankowa,* no. 47, 27 November (in Polish).

Gomułka, Stanisław (1998), 'Short-term cautionary forecast', *Gazeta Bankowa,* no. 11 (490), 15 March (in Polish).

GUS (1998), *Statistical Yearbook 1998,* Warsaw: Central Statistical Office.

GUS (1999a), *Concise Statistical Yearbook 1999,* Warsaw: Central Statistical Office.

GUS (1999b), *Statistical Yearbook 1999,* Warsaw: Central Statistical Office.

Milanovic, Branko (1989), *Liberalization and Entrepreneurship: Dynamics of Reform in Socialism and Capitalism*, Armonk, NY: M.E. Sharp.

Myant, Martin (1999), *The International Financial Crisis and the Czech Republic,* paper presented at the annual BASEES Annual Conference, Cambridge, 27–29 March.

OECD (1997), *OECD Indicators 1997,* Paris.

Poeschl, J., et al. (1999), *Transition Countries in 1998/99: Widespread Economic Slowdown with Escalating Structural problems,* Vienna: WIIW.

Poland. International Economic Report 1995/96 (1996), Warsaw: Warsaw School of Economics.

Poland. International Economic Report 1998/99 (1999), Warsaw: Warsaw School of Economics. Warsaw.

Rapacki, Ryszard (1998), *Industrial Policy Concerns of Economies in Transition*, WERI Working Paper no. 182, Warsaw School of Economics, Warsaw.

Rapacki, Ryszard (1999a), 'Macroeconomic performance', in *Poland. International Economic Report 1998/99,* Warsaw: Warsaw School of Economics.

Rapacki, Ryszard (1999b), *Privatization in Poland: Major Issues, Trends and Policy Concerns,* paper presented at the UN Expert Group Meeting on Privatization and Regulation, New York, 16–18 February.

Rapacki, Ryszard and S.J. Linz (1992), *Privatization in Transition Economies: Case Study of Poland,* Econometrics and Economic Theory Paper no. 9011, Michigan State University, East Lansing.

Rzeczpospolita (1999), 6 October.

Rzeczpospolita (2000), 4 January.

Transition Report (1996), EBRD, London.

UNECE (1997a), *Economic Bulletin for Europe,* vol. 49, New York, Geneva: Economic Commission for Europe.

UNECE (1997b), *Economic Survey of Europe in 1996–1997*, Geneva: Economic Commission for Europe.

UNECE (1998), *Economic Survey of Europe,* 1998, no. 2, Geneva: Economic Commission for Europe.

UNECE (1999), *Economic Survey of Europe,* 1999, no. 1, Geneva: Economic Commission for Europe.

UNCEC (2000), *Economic Survey of Europe,* 2000, no. 1, Geneva: Economic Commission for Europe.

UNIDO (1997), *Industrial Development. Global Report 1997*, Vienna.

World Bank (1991), *World Development Report 1991,* Washington, DC.

World Bank (1996), *World Development Report 1996*, Washington, DC.
World Bank (1998), *World Development Indicators 1998 CD-ROM* (Internet: http://www.worldbank.org).
World Economic Outlook (1997), Washington, DC: IMF.

8. Private and public sector: new and old patterns of entrepreneurship

Jan Macieja

THE ORIGINS OF POLAND'S STATE ENTERPRISE SECTOR

Poland's public enterprise sector dates back to the first half of the nineteenth century when Stanisław Staszic began to establish state-run mines and steel mills. Before 1913 the state owned no more than 10% of productive assets in areas controlled by Austria and Russia and about 11.5% in areas controlled by Prussia. After World War I nationalisation had a huge impact on the economy. The government of the Second Republic of Poland either confiscated or took over state assets abandoned by the former partitioning powers. Nationalisation after the Great War was not the result of any 'statism' aimed at overcoming the imperfections of the market but was imposed by circumstances: there were no private buyers able to put abandoned assets to proper use. In the mid-1920s the public sector's share in the Polish economy was lower than in Germany and Austria but higher than in Britain and France. The situation changed after 1929, when as a result of the Great Crash and depression, the state took over private businesses indebted to state-owned banks. After 1935, as governments became more consciously 'statist', the importance of the state sector grew considerably. In 1938 state enterprises were responsible for 25% of chemical industry production, 55% in steel, 85% in gas, 96% in rail transport and 97% in inland navigation (see Gołębiowski, 1985).

After World War II mass nationalisation took place with little regard for legalities. In so far as a rationale existed it was based on three premises. First, the assumption that state ownership was more effective than private ownership. Second, nationalisation was a precondition of the political system securing 'the dictatorship of the proletariat'. As Lange (1959) wrote, the idea was to 'remove the economic base of the former ruling classes'. Third, nationalisation was indispensable in a central planning system with a huge scope for the redistributive role of the state. Central planning plus state ownership also made it easier for the communist authorities to subordinate the Polish economy to the needs of the Soviet Union.

THE STATE SECTOR IN 1989–98

At the start of transition in 1989 the public sector dominated the Polish economy. In many branches of industry, the financial sector and transportation, the private sector was non-existent. The public sector (including state-owned and municipal enterprises) accounted, according to official data, for 70% of the country's GDP in 1989. Together with the co-operative sector, which until 1990 did not differ from state ownership in any major way, the public sector share was just over 80%. In 1989 employment in the public sector, including co-operatives, accounted for 70.4% of the national labour force. In industry the share was 83.4%, in construction 66.7%, forestry 100%, transportation 93.6%, communications 100%, and trade 90.7%. Agriculture was the only sphere where private sector employment (81.6%) was greater than public sector. In the first 10 years of transition the situation changed considerably.

Agriculture

In 1989 the state sector had 18.8% of all farmland compared to 3.8% for co-operative farms and 77.4% for private farms.[1] By 1998 the share of private farms in land ownership had increased to 83.4% with the remaining 16.6% held by the State Agricultural Property Agency. The state share in total agricultural production was lower at 10.5%.

Industry

In industry few state firms exist (2% of the total number in 1993 and 1.3% in 1998) but they still had a substantial share of sales (65.4% in 1993 and 31% in 1998), employment (66.2% and 33.1% in each year respectively) and investment spending (70% and 40.9% respectively). As might be expected these proportions varied considerably across industry sectors. In mining and quarrying, where no substantial privatisation has taken place (this sector, like the utilities, has a strong trade union presence with excellently organised interest groups who easily delay privatisation); state firms even increased their share in investment spending (from 83.2% in 1993 to 88.4% in 1998). The opposite was the case in manufacturing where in 1993 state enterprises accounted for 48.7% of total investment as compared to 20% in 1998. In electricity, gas and water supply public enterprise accounted for about 92% of total investment spending in 1993–98. More than two-thirds of industry fixed assets were in state hands in 1998: 96.4% in mining and quarrying and 38.4% in manufacturing. On the other hand, in many other industries the role of the state sector has been reduced to a minimum. In 1998 there was virtually no state presence in the dairy industry (0.3% of net sales), motor vehicles (0.7%), consumer electronics (3.7%), the chemical industry (3%), man-made fibres (4%), fish processing (5%), the clothing industry (5.2%) and paper and cardboard (5%). Privatisation in these sectors can be considered largely completed.

Table 8.1. Polish industry ownership structure, 1993–98 (% shares)

	1993	1998
Active business units		
Public sector	2.0	1.3
Private sector	98.0	98.7
Net sales (current prices)		
Public	65.4	31.0
Private	34.6	69.0
Average mployment		
Public	66.2	33.1
Private	33.8	66.9
Investment spending		
Public	67.9	40.9
Private	32.1	59.1
Gross value of fixed assets (current prices)		
Public	87.2	68,2
Private	12.8	31.8

Source: 'Zmiany w strukturze własnościowej przedsiębiorstw i produkcji przemysłowej w latach...', GUS, *Studia i Analizy Statystyczne*, Warsaw, relevant years.

Retail and wholesale trade

Privatisation in trade (retail and wholesale) was practically completed in 1992. In 2000 the state still owned most filling stations and controlled coal, electricity and gas sales, also grain and cattle feed. Though there is little left to sell off, various group interests are blocking further privatisation and it is difficult to predict when the assets still held by the state will be disposed of. In the mid

1990s foreign capital began flowing to retail trade with the construction of supermarket and hypermarket chains with great benefits to consumers.

Construction

The construction sector is another that is now almost entirely in private hands, in this case privatised through domestic capital.

Transport

The railway system is wholly owned by the state and services are provided by *Polskie Koleje Państwowe* (PKP). Passenger road transport is also predominantly in the state's hands. The state-owned *Państwowa Komunikacja Samochodowa* (PKS), which includes 174 enterprises, is the largest carrier in Poland. It competes mainly with small private companies which lack infrastructure (bus stations, stops, communications systems) and do not have equal chances in competition with their state-owned counterparts. The privately owned *National Express Polski* is an exception here.

Table 8.2. The ownership structure of the commercial banking sector (in % of total share capital, 31 December unless otherwise stated)

Share capital owned by	1996	1997	1998	1999	2000[a]
State treasury	30.6	22.0	18.8	13.5	12.9
The National Bank of Poland (NBP)	7.9	2.9	0.1	0.1	0.1
Other state entities	10.9	5.6	4.5	3.3	3.2
Private domestic entities	8.8	9.9	9.6	11.3	15.8
Foreign capital	29.8	41.5	49.6	53.2	51.6
Individual shareholders	12.0	18.0	17.3	13.7	11.5
Cooperative banks	-	-	-	4.9	4.9
Total capital (million złoty)	4,465.0	5,930.1	7,172.8	7,698.1	8,028.2

Notes: [a] 31 March

Source: General Inspectorate of Banking Supervision

Banking

The banking sector has seen major changes in its ownership structure. As the figures in Table 8.2 show, the state treasury, central bank and other bodies had

16.2% of Polish banking share capital in March 2000. Private Polish shareholders had 27.3% with over half in foreign hands, a dramatic increase from just under 30% in 1996, to over half (53.2%) by the end of 1999. It is worth stressing that Poland, similar to Hungary and the UK, has a very high share of foreign capital in the domestic banking system. The share of foreign capital (wholly or majority-owned) in the *assets* of the Polish banking sector was increased from 17% in 1998 to 47% in 1999.

THE RETURN OF THE ENTREPRENEUR

Small business growth

Leszek Balcerowicz's 1990 reform programme stimulated unprecedented entrepreneurial activity among the Polish population. Small business, both registered and unregistered, suddenly mushroomed.

Table 8.3. Private business 1989–99

Year	1989	1990	1998	1999
Small foreign manufacturing companies	841	862	549[a]	-
Co-operatives	16,691	18,575	19,638	19,328
Individual partnerships	813,485	1,135,492	2,014,000[a]	-
Domestic companies	15,252	33,239	91,903	98,365
Foreign companies	429	1645	36,850	40,142
Total	846,698	1,189,813	2,132,756	-

Notes:
[a] J. Mujżel, 'Przedsiębiorstwo w procesie transformacji ustrojowej – synteza wyników badań', in J. Mujżel (ed.), *Przedsiębiorstwa w procesie transformacji*, Warsaw: PAN Institute of Economic Sciences, Poltex, (1997).
[b] preliminary.

Sources: Data from *Rocznik Statystyczny* (various years); also *Informacja o sytuacji społeczno-gospodarczej r. 1999.*

Over 1989–98 the number of private businesses increased from 846,700 to 2.1 million, or 2.5-fold. The increase varied considerably across business types. For example, the number of small foreign manufacturing companies fell from 841 to 549 while the number of companies with foreign capital participation, most of them large businesses, increased 56-fold. The number of registered domestic companies increased five-fold, while the number of co-operatives increased by only 18%. In quantitative terms the greatest increase was in individual partnerships: in 1998 more than 2 million were registered in Poland, 2.5 times more than at the start of transition. The rapid growth of private businesses led to a major change in the share of the private sector in the Polish economy which is illustrated in Table 8.4. To supplement the figures it is worth adding that the estimated share of private businesses in GDP and industry's net sales exceeded 70% in 1999.

Table 8.4. The private sector's share in the economy, 1990–98 (including agriculture, %)

Year	1989	1995	1998
Employment	47.2	62.6	70.7
GDP	23.1	58.0	69.4
Industry[a]	16.2	44.0	69.1
Construction[a]	25.5	87.2	93.7
Retail–Trade	27.4	92.3	95.0
Exports	4.8[b]	56.8	78.8
Imports	14.4[b]	69.7	86.5

Notes:
[a] sales;
[b] 1990.

Source: *Rocznik Statystyczny,* various years.

To sum up, after 10 years of transition, private businesses employed more than twice as many people as state businesses and accounted for almost three-quarters of the country's GDP. Private enterprise played an especially strong role in both domestic and foreign trade in addition to the construction and assembly sector and many types of market services. Nevertheless at the end of the 1990s public enterprises continued to dominate in manufacturing, defence industry, steel and infrastructure (energy generation) as well as in communications and transportation (especially rail and air transport). Thus, the need to press ahead with privatisation is one of the main challenges facing the Polish economy in the coming years.

The private sector and the 1990–91 recession

The rapid growth of the private sector helped Poland weather the storm of the deep recession of 1990–91. It also explains why the Polish economy overcame the crisis so quickly. The data in Table 8.5 show that the economic crisis lasted two years (1990–91). Even in 1990 when GDP fell by 11.6%, pulled down by a 20.1% decline in public sector value added, the private sector began to make headway, its value-added up by 8.5%. In 1991 private sector value added increased by 33% while the public sector recorded a 26% decline with GDP falling by 7%. One can argue that when the Polish economy overcame the crisis (in 1992 when GDP increased by 2.6%) it was thanks to the private sector. The crisis in the public sector deepened until 1995 then bottomed out before a new slump in 1998.

Table 8.5. The private sector's role in overcoming the early 1990s' 'transition recession' (% change)

	1990	1991	1992
GDP	-11.6	-7.0	2.6
Public sector	- 20.1	-26.0	-7.0
Private sector	8.5	33.0	11.0
Industry net sales			
Public sector	-28.0	-19.5	-3.3
Private sector	22.0	25.4	23.4
Construction and assembly sector sales			
Public sector	-17.6	-30.0	-38.1
Private sector	-18.8	63.2	32.0
Exports			
Public sector	-	14.7	-30.0
Private sector	-	368.9	54.9
Imports:			
Public sector	-	-4.8	-6.5
Private sector	-	466.6	11.6

Sources: as for Table 8.3.

The importance of the private sector, and especially small businesses, was greater however than suggested by the official data. This is because many new businesses operated in the unregistered segment of the economy, 'the grey zone'. Until the mid 1990s the informal sector accounted for about a third of Poland's GDP. From 1996 it began to shrink and at the end of the 1990s its share stood at something in the range 15% to 25% of GDP.[2] The early explosion of entrepreneurship in Poland is likely to attract researchers for many years to come. The social consequences of this trend are not known, and its influence on the future shape of Polish capitalism is difficult to predict. Overall, without privatisation and the expansion of private entrepreneurship Poland would probably have failed to overcome the crisis of the early 1990s and would then have followed instead in the footsteps of most former Soviet republics as well as Bulgaria and Romania.

The adaptability of state and private enterprise

During the 1990s Polish business faced at least two periods of extremely difficult market conditions. The first was in the second half of 1990 and through all of 1991, and the second was in 1998 and the first half 1999. In 1990–91 the principal reasons behind the difficult situation were the loss of Soviet markets, the imposition of an embargo on arms deliveries to Iraq and Libya, and the loss of the domestic market to imports. At the very start of transition the private sector practically did not exist outside agriculture and even rapid growth from 1990–91 could not compensate for the difficulties in the state sector. State-owned enterprises were unable to adapt to new conditions even though they did have some successes (blown out of proportion by the World Bank in my opinion). In particular, state-owned enterprises failed to reorientate their exports quickly from the former Comecon markets in favour of other markets. They also failed effectively to challenge foreign producers on the domestic market. Difficulties in the first half of 1998 and in 1999 were caused by a slowdown in world economic growth (from 4.2% in 1997 to 2.5% in 1998) and, of course, by the August 1998 Russian crisis. The available statistical data suggest that as a result of the first factor the GDP growth rate in Poland fell by around 0.7 percentage points while the Russian crisis shaved a further 0.4 percentage points off the growth rate. If external conditions had not deteriorated and the share of the private sector had not changed, Poland's 1998 GDP growth rate would have been 5.9% instead of the 4.8% actually recorded. The key question is why global economic deterioration so strongly affected economic growth in Poland, or, in other words, why the Polish economy failed to display sufficient adaptiveness to prevent slower growth. In my view the state sector again clearly failed to cope in a situation more difficult than in previous years and *it* was responsible for slower economic growth.[3]

The informal economy

One important factor that made it possible to overcome the 1990–91 crisis was the emergence of a strong unregistered segment of the economy, 'the grey zone'. This was the result, mainly, of the desire to evade taxes, social insurance contributions, import duties and border taxes, as well as regulation (especially on the labour market on working hours and minimum pay) and problems linked with the registration of business activity (the proliferation of the need for permits). However, all Polish governments in the 1990s continued the policy initiated by

Balcerowicz whereby the grey zone was tolerated and this produced many benefits for Polish society:

- *Job creation.*
  The informal economy evaded steep labour-related costs, generated jobs and played a greater role in overcoming unemployment than suggested by its GDP share. Thanks to this, high registered unemployment was less socially painful than suggested by official statistics. According to GUS some 2,034,000 people worked without legal contracts in Poland in 1995. The grey economy provided jobs primarily to unskilled young people and people with low qualifications. It is estimated that for at least 880,000 employees this informal work was their *only* source of income. The true figure may be higher since in 1995 as many as 900,000 private businesses are reported to have taken on informal employees (see Kałaska and Witkowski, 1996).
- *Mobilisation of savings and investment.*
  The grey economy depleted government revenue but increased opportunities for investment. Informal activity was an important source of capital accumulation in the first stage of transition. Unregistered investment in 1990–93 became a factor behind accelerated economic growth in 1994–97.[4]
- *Competitive advantage on cross-border markets.*
  Thanks to lower costs and low taxes Polish companies attained a competitive advantage on cross-border markets, an important informal contribution to the current account as well as a source of substantial benefits to local economies. Total revenue from unregistered exports and spending by foreigners to cover the costs of their stay in Poland approached \$2.7 billion in 1994, accounting for 16% of Poland's total exports and 33% of exports to neighbouring countries. Revenue from unregistered exports peaked in 1995 at about \$4.3 billion. In the following years, the figure began to shrink as Polish goods lost competitiveness on the German market due to tax and price equalisation. The introduction of visas for Russian and Belarussian citizens did not help matters and the rouble crisis of August 1998 had a profound effect on trade in 1998. In 1996 revenue from cross-border exports totalled \$3.8 billion (see Macieja, 1997). According to unpublished research it dropped to about \$3 billion in 1997 and in 1998 it shrunk further to \$2.5 billion. But over the longer transition period, 1991–98, revenue from unregistered trade approached \$25 billion.

To sum up, informal business activity and unregistered exports played a major role in Poland's economic transformation. Around 2.1 million jobs, including about 1 million permanent positions, were created by this activity. This clearly helped avoid social tensions. Second, over 1991–98, unregistered exports brought a net inflow of foreign currency of around \$25 billion. The informal economy was also a large incubator of free enterprise. After a time some enterprises left the grey zone and began to compete effectively with state-owned fims. Private companies eased the pain of Poland's deep 1990–91 slump and the crisis of 1998–99. The country's successful transition is largely due to the unprecedented (at least for Poland) explosion of entrepreneurship, both registered and unregistered, a surge of private business activity that had enormous influence in shaping Polish capitalism.

THE POLITICAL ECONOMY OF PRIVATISATION

When economic reform was discussed in Poland under communism the proposals that emerged did not go beyond 'marketisation' and decentralisation. In the past Polish economists have wasted much time in a search for a 'third way', the favourite goal of intellectuals. Some Western economists agree that Poland could or should have explored such a 'third way' (Blazyca, 2000). On the other hand Janos Kornai (1988) called the search of the communist economic reformers 'naïve' because it disregarded the fundamental aspect of a market economy by avoiding the matter of privatisation (the first such proposals were made only in 1987).

In practice Polish privatisation was not the result of an economic debate or measures instituted by any economic reform committee. Nor did it result from the decisions made during the Round Table talks of 1989. The origins of privatisation can instead be traced to the emergence of 'nomenklatura-controlled' companies in 1988 when, in one of its periodic reform attempts, the communist government permitted the transfer of state enterprise assets to private companies. It also established the right of individuals to lease those assets. This made it possible for the nomenklatura to appropriate many attractive assets. But privatisation was also given a further fillip by a law (December 1988) on business activity, establishing the principle of economic freedom and equality, regardless of ownership type, in access to the market. Those measures, despite the absence of any full-fledged privatisation act, helped create a situation where at the end of 1989 in the manufacturing sector alone 500 large nomenklatura-controlled companies were in operation. In the period that followed (1991–95) ex-communist management boards expanded their activity via employee-owned companies and share purchases. Grass-roots, *ab initio* or *de novo* privatisation also developed on a mass scale. It is worth noting that those taking control over state assets did not have to have any capital: assets were bought with the use of loans (some never repaid) from nomenklatura-controlled banks. The nomenklatura companies, together with other private concerns, generated a huge demand for the assets of state-owned enterprises that, from 1991, were either collapsing or trying to save themselves by selling off property of various types.

Whatever the 'rights and wrongs' it has to be said that without either nomenklatura-controlled companies or the informal private sector Poland would most probably not have experienced the economic boom of 1993–97.

The Balcerowicz programme of October 1989 did not focus on privatisation. This was probably because, as its author explains (see Balcerowicz, 1994), the main problems at the time were the budget deficit, inflation and foreign debt. These had to be dealt with through 'shock therapy'; privatisation, on the other hand, was seen as a gradual process. Practice confirmed the wisdom of this approach. Moreover, as Bałtowski rightly points out (1998), the Balcerowicz Plan introduced tough budgetary limitations for enterprises and, by exposing them to external competition, forced them into a pro-efficiency behaviour that preceded privatisation, and this, in my opinion, was the main reason behind its success.[5]

Another important source of Polish success was so-called 'small privatisation' (practically completed by 1992), the sale, or lease, of state assets to individuals. This triggered privatisation in the retail and food service sectors, changing the face of the Polish economy. Small privatisation served another useful function in creating a 'school' for new private entrepreneurship, something that was virtually unknown after 1947.

It was also possible for large-scale privatisation to start on the basis of earlier legislation (the 1981 act on state enterprises) rather than on the basis of separate privatisation laws.[6] The first post-transformation privatisation law was passed in July 1990 but it had no immediate practical impact because of lack of clarity over the ownership status of land used by state-owned enterprises. That act became important only after the passage (in December 1990) of a law permitting the conveyance of legal title to land.

Poland's first privatisation programme was approved in November 1990 but was not fully implemented. It called for the privatisation of 50% of state assets over three years: after five years the ownership structure of the Polish economy was to be similar to that in the EU. The data (see Table 8.4 and Rapacki in this volume) show that this did not happen and the reason was the obstruction of groups and political interests that benefited from blocking privatisation. Privatisation usually leads to greater transparency, and 'insiders' (trade unions, workers' self-management councils and management boards) find it much more difficult to obtain subsidies or debt forgiveness. Moreover, the owners of a privatised enterprise feel responsible for its financial performance because of the personal risks they carry. The 'insiders', however, often tried to avoid privatisation. This appears to have been most effective in heavy industry where, as a result of political and group pressure, sectors with strong trade union presence like mining, the defence industry and energy (under a February 1993 law) were excluded from the general rules of privatisation. Moreover, until the late 1990s it was easy for some highly politicised enterprises to fight off privatisation. Politicians can offer their services to such enterprises in exchange for political and even financial benefits.

Unfortunately privatisation delays mean tangible economic losses. They include the opportunity cost of continued lower-than-average efficiency in the use of resources. Private firms (especially those involving foreign capital) quickly out-performed state enterprises in productivity, growth and exports. My research on Poland's 500 largest enterprises in various ownership sectors shows that in the mid 1990s private businesses operating on competitive markets began to out-perform their state-owned counterparts functioning on similar markets. Only a handful of market-dominant state enterprises had better economic results than private enterprises. Some of the best state enterprises prior to 1989 such as Cegielski (turbines), Ursus (tractors), Bumar Łabędy (construction equipment), and Huta Stalowa Wola (defence equipment) have not been able to cope well on the market and many state firms collapsed. Private enterprises' superiority stems from lower costs of obtaining funds and technology in addition to the incomparably easier access to international distribution channels. Moreover, private owners have greater possibilities for disciplining management. The most important factor, however, is that investment by private businesses is motivated by a desire to maximise profit in the long term while public funds are invested to fulfil a specific mission of the enterprise. In state enterprises development decisions are burdened by group interests or politics. Moreover, only the threat of losing one's property, coupled with the natural desire to increase one's possessions, guarantees rational decisions. It is worth noting here that the evidence on economic growth in the 1990s shows that the Japanese alternative has lost much of its attractiveness in the era of globalisation. The same is largely true of the German alternative. Throughout the world in the 1990s companies established for reasons other than profit found it increasingly difficult to stay competitive.

PRIVATE SECTOR DEVELOPMENT: TENDENCIES AND BARRIERS

Polish private sector development is undoubtedly assisted by access to the large EU market, the relatively well-developed domestic financial and capital markets, the substantial reserves that guarantee productivity growth with small investment, as well as a relatively cheap although a rather poorly educated labour force. The state's still excessive presence in the economy, a state that over-regulates business activity, represents the major threat to the private sector. Moreover Poland is not competitive in terms of (too great) taxes on small family businesses. The labour market (modelled on markets such as Germany) is also over-regulated. It is not easy to hire workers for a short period and 'on-costs' are high. Underdeveloped infrastructure is another acute problem: rail transport is very expensive; trucks have to wait many hours and even days at border crossings for clearance; international telephone connections are among the most expensive in the world and the same goes for the costs of accessing the Internet. Those barriers substantially reduce the ability of Polish businesses to compete not only on foreign markets but also on the domestic market.

Corruption is another problem. The still great role of the public sector in the life of individuals, coupled with the huge range of both old and new regulations and the wide scope of state redistribution, create a climate favourable to the spread of corruption. Removing the sources of corruption by reducing the role of the public sector in the economy and reducing regulation and redistribution will be difficult since these measures undermine the interests of the largest political parties and well-organised social groups. With weak standards of law enforcement corruption will continue to bear down on business conditions in Poland in the years to come. Corruption discourages foreign direct investment and, as a result of highly uncertain returns, it limits domestic investment.

Finally, much research on transition economies (see for example, Fischer, 1999) shows that growth has been faster in countries where macroeconomic stabilisation and structural reforms were introduced early on. The condition of the economy at the starting point had no influence on future growth rates; instead the faster reform and the shorter the time needed to suppress inflation tended to produce faster economic growth. These observations mean that Poland's economic policy makers have some difficult challenges before them. In the late 1990s Poland still faced the problems of how to bring inflation down further, how to implement structural reforms and privatisation of key infrastructure sectors. However weaknesses in the political system exist: the two main political forces, Solidarity Election Action (AWS) and the Democratic Left Alliance (SLD) both have a trade union base and enlist voters by the use of populist slogans. This will make it difficult to reduce the budget deficit, overcome inflation and complete privatisation.

On the other hand EU membership will improve growth conditions. First, the EU will impose deregulation on key infrastructure services and will encourage further privatisation. The situation on border crossings and roads should get better and the financial market will become even more competitive. But there are also fears that EU accession will mean import of institutions and approaches (excessive labour market regulation, the introduction of elements of a welfare state) that will reduce the international competitiveness of the Polish economy, bringing down its long-term sustainable growth.

POLISH CAPITALISM: WHAT TYPE?

Private sector development in Poland is responsible fundamentally for shaping the new system. In this respect *ab initio* privatisation, registered and informal, was immensely important. It offered particular opportunities for young, hard-working, ambitious and generally well-educated people. Older and less qualified workers on the other hand have fared less well and have faced problems despite significant social support. Turning to the other aspect of private sector development, privatisation in a strict sense, the disposal of state-owned assets, the Polish approach and the legal basis it rested upon meant that 'insider' approval had to be won before much could happen. While this arrangement slowed the process of ownership changes it also protected public assets from being misappropriated. Few flagrant privatisation abuses were recorded in Poland and only a handful of privatisations have failed outright.

However, perhaps the most disturbing feature of Polish capitalism is the corruption-generating linkage between political parties, politicians and trade unions. Ruling parties tend to wield power in their own narrow interests using, for example, appointments to firms' and public agency supervisory boards as a form of patronage. Some enterprises and sectors are supported from public funds and find it easy to win state help of various forms.

It is easy to see how in this context privatisation is a major tonic for Polish capitalism. It removes politics from the economy, reduces the scope for regulation and redistribution, stimulates entrepreneurialism and the inflow of capital. It encourages an upgrading of labour skills, leads to greater competitiveness and the creation of new jobs. Privatisation, in short, improves the quality of the economic mechanism. Most probably, Polish capitalism will evolve towards a 'competitive managerial model' (following Dallago, 1999) but with much greater state regulation. This applies especially to labour regulation because, in part, of the proximity of the German market. Time will tell if such a system will meet the test of globalisation.

The re-emergence of the private sector saved Poland from a deep crisis in the early 1990s making it possible for the economy to embark, as early as 1992, on a rapid growth path. At the time about 2 million new businesses were officially established creating 2.5 million new jobs. The informal economy employed another 2 million people including some 880,000 for whom informal work was their only source of income. Most probably, only about 450,000 of the nearly 2.5 million registered unemployed did *not* work in the grey economy. Thanks to this, unemployment was less painful socially than suggested by official statistics. The dynamic private sector also increased the resistance of the Polish economy in face of the Russian crisis in 1998 – it was better equipped to adapt and quickly overcame negative external shocks. At the threshold of the twenty-first century the private sector accounts for almost 75% of Poland's GDP, about three-quarters of the labour force and a comparable share of total revenue and investment spending. Nevertheless at the end of the 1990s state ownership continued to dominate in utilities like electricity, gas and water as well as in coal, steel, chemicals and defence where even after 10 years of transformation state enterprises still accounted for about 90% of output.

With globalisation, deepening economic integration, technological advance, a new system of global security and new methods of regulating infrastructure sectors, the economic, social and defence-related rationale behind public enterprise has disappeared regardless of whether nationalisation was rational in the past or not. Today it is difficult to find business sectors in which state ownership should be maintained for any economic or social reasons. Social needs in education, health care and social insurance, even though they must be taken into account and funded by the state, do not mean that a state enterprise sector must exist. Public ownership no longer furthers the implementation of general social goals and is not needed for purposes such as the fight against unemployment or the creation of conditions supporting the effective functioning of private business (such as through infrastructure developments). When it comes to social justice and the creation of opportunities for individual institutions such as the family, churches, social organisations, clubs and charity institutions are usually more successful than state sector initiative. This, among other factors, explains the ongoing disassembly of welfare state systems in many countries in Europe, taking place under the catchy name of 'third way'.

FUTURE CHALLENGES

The medium- and long-term prospects for economic growth in Poland seem to be promising. Most enterprises have already been privatised and restructured and thus made more competitive. All the structural reforms designed to adapt the economy to a capitalist system have been either completed or initiated. A spirit of private entrepreneurship has developed. The country's geopolitical situation is stable and favourable. Poland's membership of various international organisations reduces investor risk. Further advantages should be expected after Poland joins the EU. Accession is expected to aid economic restructuring. It is also helping Poland to upgrade its education system and its scientific research base. At last Poland stands a realistic opportunity to overcome centuries-old lags and reunite with 'Europe' as an equal partner.

Many opportunities will however be difficult to grasp. Globalisation and integration mean difficult challenges for Poland. First, achieving international competitiveness demands that Polish business undergoes a still deep restructuring with significant labour-shedding. This at a time when the labour market has to accommodate around an additional 1.5 million new entrants over a few years as a result of the early 1980s' demographic boom. The creation of so many new jobs will be exceptionally difficult and there is no certainty that the country will meet this challenge. If not, one should be prepared for the emergence of destructive social movements impeding economic growth. Another alarming fact is that policies orientated towards growth and the creation of new jobs do *not* find the required degree of political support. Polish voters (like many others) are still susceptible to populism and often see more redistribution as the best method for solving social problems. In fact, it is difficult to explain why populism has not exerted a more destructive influence on economic policy so far! Second, Poland is experiencing enormous problems in its balance of payments where the current account deficit in the late 1990s was 7% to 8% of GDP. This large deficit means increased risk of a financial crisis that could ruin many of the positive effects of transition. In the years ahead debt service payments are also scheduled to grow, placing the external account under still greater pressure.[7] The basic problem is the low level of exports and this, in turn, stems from unfavourable microeconomic conditions.

One great failure of Polish transformation is the poor state of the engineering industry where too slow privatisation has deprived enterprises of capital inflow, modern technology and access to international distribution channels, making too many firms incapable of competing, not only on foreign markets, but also at home. In 1999 the share of machine and motor industry products (the SITC-7 group) in Poland's total exports stood at about 30%, half the level noted in countries such as Mexico, Finland, Germany and Japan, and much less than in Hungary (55%) and the Czech Republic (46%) (see Blazyca, chapter 13 of this volume, for a fuller account). Unfavourable microeconomic conditions will not be easy to overcome, creating a strong barrier to economic growth. Moreover, on the macro scene, increasing exports requires the limiting of domestic demand. Needless to say that is not easy to achieve. This is partly because of weaknesses in the tools of demand management (higher interest rates hit investment more strongly than domestic demand) and partly due to the lack of political support for a tight fiscal policy. In addition, the main political parties (AWS and SLD) both depend on an electorate calling for even more redistribution, the implementation of which in a country like Poland would undermine the foundations of long-term sustainable growth.

It is not easy to predict, from a year 2000 vantage point, if Poland will manage to take advantage of its historic opportunity to bridge the gap separating it from the West. Several scenarios, each with its own logic, seem almost equally probable. It is worth noting however that some logically improbable scenarios have also appeared in Poland recently.

NOTES

1 The data are from *Rocznik Statystyczny 1991, 1999.*
2 Ministry of Finance, White Paper on Taxes, 1998.
3 My own research, carried out in 1999 on a sample of 57,000 businesses submitting reports to GUS for 1998, shows that if state-owned enterprises and joint-stock companies wholly owned by the Treasury had grown at the same rate as private businesses and partially privatised businesses, the country's GDP would have increased by 26.9% nominally and 15.3% in real terms. However such rapid growth was obviously impossible. First, there was a shortage of qualified labour. Furthermore, such fast growth, given the poor competitiveness of the Polish economy, would have produced a huge current-account deficit that would have pulled down GDP growth. A structural effect would most probably also have occurred: while a state-run coal industry would have improved its effectiveness after privatisation, its growth would, inevitably, have been slower than the industry average. According to recent research more committed privatisation could have led to a situation (Belka and Macieja, 2000) where GDP growth in 1998 could have been comparable to 1996–97, reaching about 6.3%. Private business has, it seems, better adaptability than state business and this stems from better management, more modern technology, easier access to loans, the possibility of raising funds through bond issues and easier access to global distribution channels.
4 Interestingly, Western economists often fail to understand the difference between the propensity to invest in small businesses in Poland and, for example, Britain. In Poland many small enterprises were established after 1989, with a view to later expansion. They helped create fortunes, including fortunes based on assets purchased from state-owned enterprises. In Britain, on the other hand, small businesses are rarely set up with expansion in mind but usually because their owner wants to be self-employed.
5 The so-called 'Beksiak Group' (a group of economists around Janusz Beksiak in Warsaw) was influential in setting the scene for Polish privatisation. Their 'plan' called for a transition to a market economy instead of any further attempts to 'upgrade' the communist economy. Earlier works by Lewandowski and Szomburg (1989) as well as Kawalec (1989) also played a positive role in this area.
6 The best example of privatisation based on the old legal regulations was the establishment of the Zamech ABB company through the contribution of the assets of the state-owned Zamech enterprise to a company established jointly with the ABB corporation.
7 Poland is also particularly susceptible to the problem of the weak euro since the EU accounts for about 70% of Poland's exports but the country still has

substantial dollar liabilities. Eventually, accession to the EU and the ERM will remove this problem but that is still some way off.

REFERENCES

Balcerowicz, L. (1994), 'Przekształcenia gospodarcze w Europie Śródkowej i Wschodniej – próba bilansu', in *Społeczne konsekwencje transformacji ustrojowej* (Social consequences of system transformation), Warsaw: ISP PAN, pp. 31–33.

Bałtowski, M. (1998), *Prywatyzacja przedsiębiorstw państwowych. Przebieg i ocena* (Privatizing state firms: progress and assessment), Warsaw: PWN, p. 144.

Belka, M. and J. Macieja (2000), 'Jaki gospodarz, taka efektywność', *Rzeczpospolita*, Special Supplement '500 największych przedsiębiorstw' (The Top 500 Businesses), 17 April.

Blazyca, G. (2000), 'Uwagi na temat polskich przemian – czy naprawdę nie ma "trzeciej drogi"?, in *Polscy ekonomiści w Świecie* (Polish economists in the world), eds T. Kowalik and J. Hausner, Warsaw: PWN.

Connolly, S. and A. Murno (1999), *Economics of the Public Sector,* London: Prentice-Hall Europe.

Dallago, B. (1999), 'Privatisation: the teaching of Western experiences', in Ivan Major (ed.), *Privatisation and Economic Performance in Central and Eastern Europe. Lessons to be Learnt From Western Europe*, Cheltenham, UK and Northampton, MA, USA: Edward Elgar.

Fischer, S. (1999), 'The transition economies after ten years', in *Ten Years After,* CASE, Warsaw, International Conference.

Gołębiowski, J. (1985), *Sektor państwowy w gospodarce Polski międzywojennej*, (The state sector in Poland between the wars), Warsaw, pp. 208–281.

Kałaska, M. and J. Witkowski (1996), 'Praca w szarej strefie w Polsce w 1995 r', *Gospodarka Narodowa*, no. 1–2, pp. 33–39.

Kawalec, S. (1989), 'Zarys programu prywatyzacji gospodarki polskiej', in *Propozycje przekształceń polskiej gospodarki* (Proposals for transforming the Polish economy), Warsaw: PTE.

Kornai, J. (1988), 'Reformatorzy naiwni i radykalni', *Wektory Gospodarki*, no. 6, p. 13.

Lange, O. (1959), 'Podstawowe zagadnienia okresu budowy socjalizmu', in *Zagadnienia ekonomii politycznej socjalizmu* (Problems in the political economy of socialism), 2nd edition, Warsaw: Książka i Wiedza, p. 38.

Lewandowski, J. and J. Szomburg (1989), 'Uwłaszczenie jako fundament reformy społeczno-gospodarczej. Zarys programu', in *Propozycje przekształceń polskiej gospodarki* (Proposal for transforming the Polish economy), Warsaw: PTEO.

Macieja, J. (1997), *Rozwój przygranicznej współpracy gospodarczej w latach 1994–1995* (Cross border economic co-operation, 1994–1995), Zeszyty Centrum im. Adama Smitha (Adam Smith Center publications), no. 17, Warsaw.

9. The new banking and financial sector: its role, potential and weaknesses

Marian Górski

INTRODUCTION

This chapter aims to review and assess Polish financial system transformation. We examine in turn each of its four principal elements: central banking, commercial banking, the financial markets and the development of non-depository financial intermediary institutions. We must however bear in mind the overall context in which each part of the financial sub-system developed from the early 1990s. The following features are particularly important:

- a new financial infrastructure (with its law and institutions) was being built as an integral element of a market-based economy;
- the financial sector had to play from the start a key role in overcoming the transformation recession of the early 1990s;
- this was happening alongside privatisation of the financial sector itself not to mention its part in more general privatisation processes in the economy.

Meanwhile, financial regulations and the sector's style of operations had to be adjusted, initially to OECD requirements, and then to those of the European Union as the accession process developed.

Polish financial sector transformation was built on legislation dating back to the late 1980s: the National Bank of Poland Act and the Banking Act, passed by parliament in January 1989. These Acts created the legal framework for the operation of a two-tier banking system, that is, one that clearly distinguished central banking from commercial banking. They also permitted, for the first time in 40 years, the introduction of market forces into banking and finance. The fact that those acts were implemented from 1989, and predated by one year, the most important political and systemic changes in Poland was undoubtedly a very positive aspect of the overall transformation process.[1]

An assessment of any system has to be made in relative terms. On one hand, at the beginning of the 1990s, the banking sector in Poland was, by the standards of contemporary market economies, underdeveloped. On the other hand it turned out to be the best prepared for systemic transformations when compared to other formerly planned economies. This is particularly true when Russia and other former Soviet republics are chosen as reference points. In those countries the banking system had to be developed virtually from scratch and banking laws and other regulations were adopted only later after a period when banks and quasi-banking institutions arose spontaneously.

CENTRAL BANKING

Laws and institutions

Until 1988 the National Bank of Poland, the central bank and also the main (indeed the only) depository institution, was a key element of the central planning system. Then in the 1990s it became a fully autonomous entity starting to fulfil the role of a modern central bank as in any market economy. The systemic changes that were launched in 1989 in central banking reached a conclusion in the National Bank of Poland Act 1997. That Act guaranteed the NBP independence as the body responsible for conducting the government's monetary policy. Simultaneously, to a large extent it also brought the bank's structure and operations closer to EU standards. Under the 1989 law the NBP (and in particular its president) was responsible for monetary policy and banking supervision. The 1997 law introduced two new institutions in these areas. One was the Monetary Policy Committee (*Rada Polityki Pieniężnej – RPP*) with nine members in all, three appointed by the state President and six by both houses of parliament, and chaired by the NBP president. The other was the Banking Supervision Commission (*Komisja Nadzoru Bankowego – KNB*) with members appointed by the state President, the minister of finance, the securities and stock exchanges commission, and banking guarantee fund, again, chaired by the NBP president. These autonomous central banking agencies were set up in line with what might be called 'best 1990s' practice' and conformed also to the demands underpinning the EU's Economic and Monetary Union (EMU).

The Banking Guarantee Fund (BGF), established at the beginning of 1995, has become an important element of the Polish banking system. Apart from guaranteeing deposits (in 1999 100% of those with a value of up to the equivalent of E 1000, and 90% of those up to E 7000), the fund helps in restructuring banks on the verge of bankruptcy where it had considerable success. It is worth recalling that before the BGF was established only the deposits of private citizens held in state-owned banks were guaranteed by the government. As deposit safeguards are further adjusted to EU standards there will be a gradual increase of the guaranteed ceiling (up to E 20,000 as the ultimate target). The fund will also give up its support role which, because of the levy on all Polish banks, has in practice, reduced the competitiveness of those banks vis-à-vis foreign institutions.

With regard to the central bank's currency issuing function, the successful re-denomination of the złoty in 1995 is worth special emphasis. The choice of the right moment for this currency reform (after a period of exceptionally high inflation), its scale (1 new Polish złoty (PLN) for 10,000 old Polish złoty) and the technical problems in introducing new notes and coins (with the danger of forgery) were all handled exceptionally smoothly by the Bank.

Monetary policy: objectives and instruments

In what follows our aim is not to evaluate the central bank's monetary policy in the transformation period but rather we try to show that the NBP has in the 1990s become a central bank in the sense of a modern market economy.

Since the outset of the transformation process, the prime objective of monetary policy was to curb inflation. While this objective was given a high priority, as reflected for example in its inclusion in the 1997state constitution, reducing inflation was especially difficult in a transforming economy where inflation was not determined mainly by the money supply. From 1998 the NBP (together with the RPP) conducted monetary policy using traditional central banking tools including:

- manipulation of obligatory reserve requirements;
- setting interest rates;
- open market operations;
- exchange rate policy.

Obligatory reserves can be fixed at anything up to 30% of banks' demand deposits and up to 20% of term deposits. Throughout the 1990s the NBP was particularly active in using this instrument. In 1989 the ratio was set at its maximum (30%) level. Over 1992–96 it was reduced (to as low as 17% for demand deposits). In 1997 however it was raised again and then maintained at the following levels until mid-1999: 20%, for złoty demand deposits; 11%, for złoty term deposits; 5%, for all foreign currency deposits. The central bank's policy on obligatory reserves intended to increase the security of bank deposits but the high levels chosen also reflected the NBP's view that the banking sector had, throughout this period, excess liquidity. High levels of obligatory reserves deposited in non-interest bearing accounts with the central bank impose significant costs on the commercial banks. In Poland this became particularly evident as bank margins fell, the result also of growing domestic competition between banks, as well as foreign competition as the Polish banking system became ever more open. In 1999, responding in part to pressure from the banks, reserve ratio requirements were cut substantially: from that October they were set at 5% for all types of deposits. This *could* immediately have given the banks extra liquidity but they agreed to invest the resources released only in non-marketable inflation-linked treasury bonds. It seems likely that in the future the obligatory reserves instrument will be used much less actively, in line again with the EU style. It can be expected that in due course a further reduction in reserve ratios will take place and that the reserves will become interest-bearing in line with EU practice. One should also expect that an obligatory reserve requirement may be extended to other near-bank depository institutions (credit unions, co-operative savings and loans associations).

Due to the excess liquidity of the banking sector the scale of refinancing commercial banks by the NBP, particularly in the second half of the decade, was modest.[2] This meant in turn that the direct impact of central bank base rates on lending rates was also marginal. From the late 1990s the most important rates were the Lombard and reference rates which set the upper and the lower level of interest rates on the inter-bank market. The rate on a Lombard loan, backed with securities, sets the upper limit of WIBOR (the Warsaw Inter-Bank Offered Rate) while the reference rate, at which the NBP undertakes to sell its 28-day bills, sets the lower limit of the one-month WIBID (the Warsaw Inter-Bank Bid Rate).

Since the outset of transformation the central bank repeatedly declared that it aimed to maintain positive real interest rates as a means of reaching (dis)inflationary objectives. This was not fully achieved in the first half of the decade but from 1996 real interest rates were consistently positive and in 1999, depending on the type of deposit or loan, they ranged from 3% to 12%.[3] Interest rates policy did succeed in weakening excessive demand for money. At the same time, however, it contributed to real złoty appreciation (and to a loss of international competitiveness) as high real interest rates were among the most important factors triggering foreign capital inflow, growth of international reserves imposing high sterilisation costs on the central bank. In the mid 1990s disagreements between the finance ministry and central bank over the conduct of monetary policy were particularly acute. The ministry at that time felt very strongly that interest rates should have been eased down, in part to dent speculative inflows. The bank meanwhile believed that its anti-inflationary policy called for higher interest rates (see, for example Nuti, 1996, for the finance ministry case and Gomułka, 1998, for the central bank's viewpoint). The choice of the most appropriate real interest and exchange rates remains the most important question facing monetary policy in Poland at the beginning of the twenty-first century, at least until the moment of entry to EMU.

By the late 1990s open market operations (which were only started 1993) became the basic tool of central bank intervention. The medium-term monetary strategy for 1999–2003 reaffirmed that they would remain important also in the future. Nevertheless selection of the most appropriate policy tools to meet inflationary targets depends on specific market conditions. The RPP's intention is to let the market determine long-term interest rates with the central bank focusing essentially on short-term operations (see *Średniookresowa strategia polityki pieniężnej*, p. 10).

These developments in central banking and monetary policy activity derived also from the central bank's changing role in financing the government. At the beginning of the 1990s the NBP frequently extended direct loans to cover government budget needs. Securitisation of the public debt, however, was progressing very fast as the government began to finance its needs by means of issuing T-bonds and T-bills. In 1994 36% of the total public debt was financed by the NBP, whereas in 1998 this ratio had declined to only 9%. Commercial banks remain the main source of financing the domestic part of public debt and their share in 1997–99 amounted to some 60%, while treasury paper accounted for around 30% of banking sector assets. However treasury securities were being shifted from the NBP portfolio mainly to the non-banking financial sector which financed 25% of domestic public debt at the end of 1998 and to foreign investors whose share rose to 7%. Growth in the share of the foreign sector in financing the domestic public debt and the inflow of foreign direct investments created a substantial increase in international reserves in central bank assets. At the end of 1998 they reached $27.5 billion, equivalent to approximately 65% of the NBP's assets.

Exchange rate policy

The exchange rate regime has gone through considerable evolution in the post-communist period. In the early stages of transformation a fixed exchange rate, was used as a nominal anchor for anti-inflation policy and played a key role in macroeconomic stabilisation. Its stability in 1990–91 was not only important from a strictly economic point of view but was intended to signal the determination of government to continue the transformation process. In the second half of the 1990s a crawling peg mechanism was substituted for the fixed rate. This permitted the currency to depreciate in nominal terms at a pre-announced and steadily falling monthly rate. The crawling peg regime later evolved into a semi-free mechanism with ever wider margins: in mid 1999 the złoty's central rate was determined against a foreign currency basket (in which the $ had a 55% weight and the Euro 45%) in which the market rate could depart from central parity by as much as +/-15%. Then in April 2000 the authorties took the plunge to an exchange rate that was entirely market determined.

Real appreciation continued throughout most of the 1990s as the currency was pulled upwards by strongly positive real interest rates. At the end of 1998 as compared to end 1994 this appreciation was substantial and amounted to almost 20% against the US dollar and 25% against the DM. It is worth noting however that the main reason for currency appreciation was not the overvalued central rate but upward pressure on the market rate, the result of foreign investors' demand for domestic currency (long-term and speculative). NBP data permit breaking down foreign investment in Poland into flows and stocks of FDI and portfolio investment respectively. The latter may be of a more speculative nature. Foreign investment inflow to Poland in 1995–98 amounted to $17 billion with FDI making up some 70% of the total and portfolio investment the remaining 30%.

The basic dilemmas facing monetary policy in Poland at the turn of the century are well rehearsed by Polański (See Polański, 1999, pp. 29–44), who describes the situation as 'a dilemma of the incoherent quadrangle of systemic solutions in a small open economy'. His concept is built on an observation that in the second half of the 1990s the Polish economy was becoming more and more open but because of its small share in the global economy it was receiving impulses from the world economy but not exerting any impact on it. 'In such a situation', he argued 'economic policy must respect parameters set by the international economy (world levels of inflation and interest rates, foreign exchange rates and changes in the real economy, which are eventually also reflected in financial streams).' The essence of 'incoherence' here stems from the fact that in the long run the following four features cannot coexist:

- free trade
- full freedom of capital flows
- fixed exchange rates
- autonomous national monetary policy.

Polański's suggestion has to be accepted that macroeconomic management in a small open economy is based mainly on meeting the so-called interest rates parity condition. The balance of capital flows between the domestic economy and the rest of the world will only be maintained if the possible disparities in interest rates levels (on assets in a similar risk class) are offset by expected changes in the exchange rates.

Before Poland joins the EMU system it will most likely move into the Exchange Rate Mechanism (ERM2). One of the difficult choices that lies ahead will be the selection of a good moment to join ERM2. In early 2000 the first step towards ERM2 was taken when the złoty was allowed to float freely. But the tricky issue for the future will be deciding how to deal with moving to a currency fix in an atmosphere where many investors may expect a once-for-all depreciation prior to that fix.

It seems to us that, despite the criticisms sometimes voiced, the NBP in the 1990s has successfully exerted a stabilising impact in the process of system transformation both due to its own institutional transformation and to the monetary policy it pursued. A relatively high stability among the bank's top management has also helped. Mrs Hanna Gronkiewicz-Waltz has been president of the NBP since 1992. In 1998 she was reappointed for a second, six-year term of office. This stability is worth stressing, particularly in view of frequent changes in government (Poland had eight prime ministers in the 1990s).

Comparing the experience of Poland with that of other countries going through a similar process of transformation it seems that the achievements of the central bank policy are by no means bad. In macro terms inflation fell by 1998 to less than 10% and the annual rate of GDP growth exceeded 5% over 1994–98. In Hungary the inflation rate fluctuated from 1994 at around 20% per annum and in the Czech case at around 10% while the annual rate of GDP growth in these countries was also lower. Monetary policy undoubtedly had a positive impact on maintaining external equilibrium, permitting, at least until 1998, a relatively calm movement through some stormy weather on world financial markets, especially following the Russian crisis.

COMMERCIAL BANKING

Corporatisation and privatisation

Corporatisation (also called commercialisation) of the Polish banking system was first permitted by the 1988 banking law. This set in motion the following major processes in the 1989–92 period:

- the state-owned banks (*Powszechna Kasa Oszczędności – PKO BP, Bank Handlowy SA, PEKAO SA*) became independent entities, clearly separated from the NBP;
- the regional branches of the NBP were given independence, establishing nine new state-owned regional banks which were then transformed into joint stock companies wholly owned by the Treasury;
- new state-owned banks were set up (*Bank Rozwoju Eksportu SA – BRE* in 1988, *Bank Inicjatyw Gospodarczych – BIG SA* in 1988; *Polski Bank Rozwoju – PBR S.A.* in 1990) which were owned by the Treasury, state-owned enterprises (SOEs) and government agencies;
- liberalisation of entry regulations to the banking industry led to the emergence of several hundred small private banks.

Changes in the ownership structure of the banking sector over the 1993–98 period are shown in Table 9.1

Polish banking law permits banks to take on three legal forms: state banks, co-operative banks and joint stock companies. In 1999 only two state banks had not been transformed into joint stock companies: *Powszechna Kasa Oszczędności Bank Państwowy (PKO BP)* and *Bank Gospodarstwa Krajowego*

(BGK). Most banks (by number) take the form of co-operatives despite the fact that their market share (4.3% of total sector net assets) is tiny. Most of these are local institutions serving mainly their members, in general farmers and tradespeople. The most important institutions within the banking sector are joint stock companies, with a state, foreign and domestic private capital share.

Table 9.1. The Polish banking scene, 1993–98

Types of banks	End 1993		End 1996		June1998	
	No. of banks	Total net assets (%)	No. of banks	Total net assets (%)	No. of banks	Total net assets (%)
All banks, of which:	1,740	100.0	1,475	100.0	1,329	100.0
Commercial banks	87	93.4	81	95.4	84	95.7
Banks with majority state ownership	29	80.4	24	66.5	15	48.3
directly owned by the Treasury	16	76.1	8	51.1	6	37.5
indirectly owned by the Treasury	11	-	11	-	8	-
owned by the NBP	2	-	3	-	1	-
Private banks	58	13.0	57	28.9	69	47.4
majority-owned by Polish capital	48	10.4	32	15.1	38	30.9
majority-owned by foreign capital	10	2.6	25	13.7	31	16.5
Co-operative banks	1,653	6.6	1,394	4.6	1,245	4.3

Source: Hajkiewicz-Górecka (1999, p. 97).

Bank privatisation started in 1991 but, as the data show, it was not until 1998 that the sector could be formally considered privatised, with the share of private and co-operative banks in total assets of the banking sector exceeding 50%. Privatisation was achieved in two ways. Numerous new private banks, including those with foreign capital, were set up alongside a process of privatisation of state banks. By the late 1990s the view was that the central bank's licence granting policy with regard to small private banks in the early years of transformation had been too liberal: by mid decade a large number of those banks faced bankruptcy. Restoring their economic viability became one of the elements of banking sector consolidation after 1996.

The privatisation of state-owned banks started in 1991–93 when such institutions as the *BIG Bank, BRE, Wielkopolski Bank Kredytowy* (WBK) and *Bank Śląski* (BSK) were disposed of. At that time the privatisation approach aimed at selling a block of shares (50% to 60%) in a public offering (IPO) to domestic and foreign investors, giving some shares away to bank employees (5% to 7%) and retaining a controlling stake (20% to 30%).

Privatisation was also supported by the European Bank for Reconstruction and Development (EBRD) which bought into the process. This sell-off strategy was thought necessary because of the poor standing of banks due to a high share of bad loans in their portfolios. As a consequence the IPO sales of privatised banks' shares with a pre-set price used to end up with high reductions in the number of shares eventually sold to investors as compared to the numbers ordered. The Treasury was not achieving the optimum prices and investors could cash their purchases quickly with hefty profits on the Warsaw Stock Exchange. An atmosphere of 'economic racketeering' surrounded, in particular, the privatisation of *Bank Śląski* in October 1993 with consequences for the entire banking privatisation strategy.

The biggest problem over 1992–93 however was not privatisation but a rapid growth of bad loans in banks' assets. In 1991 doubtful and lost loans accounted for 7% of the sector's loan portfolio. In 1992 it increased to 21% and in 1993 it rose further to 24%. This can be explained by several factors. First, the banks had inherited doubtful credit portfolios from the command economy. Second, the transformation shock experienced in the early 1990s led to a dramatic deterioration in borrowers' standing. Third, a serious shortage of experienced professionals existed (despite various transfers of 'know-how' including 'bank twinning' schemes). This was combined with a lack of appropriate procedures, indispensable for weighing risks and for prudent lending, something true both of large state-owned and small private entities (although a more acute problem in the latter sector).

This situation required special solutions which were eventually introduced via the 1993 law on financial restructuring of firms and banks. It is worth adding that this was one of those situations where, through good luck, Polish solutions were distinctive and perhaps, time shows, better than in other transforming economies. The Act devised new instruments for restructuring bad loans, in particular a bank 'reconciliatory settlement' and public sale of bank debt. 'Reconciliatory settlements' (between bad debtors and creditors, available only for state-owned firms) required agreement on a restructuring programme for the debtor firm including its transformation into a joint stock company in order to facilitate a potential debt/equity swap or privatisation.

Because of the scale of the problem bad loan portfolios could not be restructured at the expense of the banks alone. State-owned banks and banks in which the Treasury was a majority shareholder were recapitalised with so-called restructuring bonds issued for 15 years, non-transferable and with interest, at the rediscount rate level, for the most part compounded. The bonds were to be serviced by the central budget until the banks involved were privatised, at which point they would be repurchased using the resources of a special 'Bank Privatisation Fund', established with foreign support. Crucially it was a precondition for disbursing those funds that bank privatisation would be fairly speedily completed. This restructuring process over 1993–95 had several important effects. First, banks could write off or, through debt/equity swaps, recover some of their bad debts so reducing the share of bad loans in their portfolios. By 1996 the bad debt share had fallen to 9.5% and it continued to decline in the years that followed. Second, many companies regained economic viability and creditworthiness. Third, the requirement that firms undergoing restructuring also be commercialised (as a first step towards privatisation) accelerated the privatisation process. Fourth, the possibility of an earlier repurchase, with foreign financial assistance, of restructuring bonds when bank privatisation took place encouraged both the management boards of banks (who felt that it would improve the portfolio of assets) and the Treasury (as a means to reduce the burden on the budget) to move faster on banks' privatisation.

Meanwhile, as noted above, the early experience of bank disposal up to 1993 stimulated subsequent changes in both the strategy and techniques of their privatisation. Share offer prices were set by tender or at a special stock exchange session rather than the previous system where sales were conducted at a pre-set price. Foreign interests were encouraged to get involved in banks' privatisation through the issue of Global Depository Receipts (GDRs) and American Depository Receipts (ADRs) offered on foreign stock exchanges.[4] Public flotations began to take place alongside a simultaneous search for strategic investors as well as invitations to tender for blocks of shares still held by the Treasury even in banks previously part privatised.

In the second half of the 1990s the privatisation process was accompanied and, in a sense, strengthened and guided, by a new feature of policy towards banks – 'consolidation'. In practical terms this involved a number of measures, of which the following were the most important. Three remaining (of the nine original) regional state-owned banks were incorporated into the structure of the nation-wide *Pekao SA Bank*. An incentive scheme was developed by the central bank and the Banking Guarantee Fund to encourage healthy banks to take over banks on the verge of bankruptcy by offering, among other factors, partial or complete exemption from obligatory reserve requirements. The NBP favoured in its licences policy those foreign banks directly investing in the Polish banking sector, especially those pledging help in restructuring local non-viable banks, so creating a tieing-in policy. The central bank also encouraged domestic concerns to purchase remaining Treasury shares in banks, as for example when *BIG SA* was encouraged to buy into *Bank Gdański* or when *Kredyt Bank SA* was encouraged to buy into *Polski Bank Inwestycyjny* Finally, the national bank also prompted voluntary mergers and hostile take-overs of domestic private banks, for example, acquisition of *Polski Bank Rozwoju SA* (a small listed bank) by the larger *Bank Rozwoju Eksportu SA (BRE)*, followed later in mid 1999 by a merger of the latter with *Bank Handlowy (BHW)*. Consolidation in the Polish banking sector, as elsewhere, at the end of the 1990s, was not complete. The process continues especially as foreign capital becomes more involved.

Foreign capital in Polish banking

One of the most contentious issues of the 1990s, in academic debate as well as among politicians and the general public, is the role of foreign investors in the Polish banking sector. Following the controversial sale, in mid 1999, of 53% of the shares of *PeKaO SA* (the second largest bank in Poland in terms of assets) to *UniCredito Italiano*, and 80% of the equity of *Bank Zachodni* (the tenth largest bank in Poland) to the Irish AIB plc, foreign capital accounted for more than 50% of shareholders' funds of banks operating in Poland. The role of foreign capital in the banking sector is frequently discussed from three different perspectives: the political, the economic and the social. Views from each vary substantially and often conflict.

From the political angle, foreign capital is claimed by its opponents to be responsible for the loss of the 'national character' of Polish banks. This, the argument continues, is unhealthy because it may lead the country to lose 'economic independence'. On the other hand, the advocates assert that in the absence of foreign investors, the banks would be taken over by 'former nomenklatura capital' leading to a strengthening of 'post-communist' interests. The proponents of foreign investment argue that the autonomy of the domestic banking system does not depend on the country of origin of the capital invested in banks but rather on host country monetary authorities who can influence *all* banks operating domestically.

From the economic perspective the opponents of foreign capital emphasise that privatised banks are sold for too little (loss of the 'family silver'), which means that the national wealth is being transferred abroad both currently and in the future through transfers of profit. Supporters, on the other hand, suggest that deterring foreign capital would only push down the prices of banks being divested. Domestic capital is insufficient for banks to be sold at reasonable prices. One can add here that over 1993–94, in selling banks the state could achieve a price/book value (P/BV) ratio of 1.2 to 2.0 while selling a large packet of shares to foreign investors brought a P/BV ratio of 3 to 4. More important, the advocates of banking FDI argue that this is an effective way of quickly gaining foreign capital, modern technologies and know-how, all of which enhance competitiveness. They add that lack of foreign capital would condemn the banks and the enterprises they serve to growing inefficiency.

As far as the wider social aspects are concerned opponents sometimes argue that the banking sector has a 'special significance' in any economy, it is a 'strategic' sector that underpins all commercial and economic activity and a foreign-owned banking sector will be less sensitive to domestic needs. Further social arguments are sometimes advanced, for example that foreign capital impedes career opportunities for Polish managers, particularly for top executives. But this argument is readily countered by those who believe that foreign capital opens professional career paths in parent multinational financial institutions.

It is worth recounting how foreign capital actually did enter Polish banking. Over 1993–99 this occurred via:

- opening directly owned branches (Societe Generale, ING Bank, American Express);
- affiliations of banks in the form of joint-stock companies owned by foreign investors both banking and non-banking (Citibank, Creditanstalt, Opel Bank, and others);
- purchasing majority stakes of Polish banks through privatisation;
- taking up new rights issues in private banks;
- repurchasing strategic blocks of shares from original domestic investors who bought into banking in earlier stages of privatisation;
- purchasing banks' shares on the Warsaw Stock Exchange;
- purchasing GDRs on foreign stock exchanges and converting them into banks' shares;
- purchasing convertible bonds of banks issued abroad.

The above list is most likely not complete. It indicates, however, that by the end of the decade foreign investors were certainly interested in gaining access to the Polish banking services market. At the end of 1997 there were in Poland 31 banks predominantly in foreign ownership, of this three were wholly owned branches, 18 were domestic affiliates of foreign banks and 10 were banks with foreign capital accounting for more than 50% (but less than 100%) of shares (Kosiński, 1999, p. 147). The situation is very fluid especially for the latter two groups. Purchasing shares of Polish banks directly from the state Treasury is only one of a number of ways into the Polish market. Many foreign investors have tried to enter the market by using a number of entry routes simultaneously. The market is fundamentally attractive because of its size and underdevelopment and foreign investors are purchasing a stake in a potentially lucrative and fast expanding banking services market rather than 'Polish banks'. In these circumstances, erecting political and administration hurdles to foreign investors would most probably be counterproductive and self-defeating. It would only hinder capital inflow temporarily or force it to look for ways to detour a maze of restrictions.

The main factor influencing foreign investors' decisions to enter Polish banking is not the standing of a given domestic bank. It is not even the general appraisal of the Polish banking sector (paradoxically an underdeveloped branch network, and high costs of operations may be treated as an asset). The key determinant is definitely a positive assessment of progress achieved in economic transformation as well as of development prospects, including Poland's anticipated EU accession.

The market for banking services

Changes in the ownership and organisational structure of the banking sector have been accompanied by deep transformations in the organisation of money circulation and banking technologies. At the beginning of the 1990s the only non-cash settlements that were carried out regularly were mainly those between business entities. The population would normally settle its affairs in cash. Even by mid decade, in 1995, cash accounted for 25% of the domestic money supply. But by 1998 its share had fallen to 16%. In the first half of the decade the main retail bank providing retail services was the state-owned PKO BP with over 6000 outlets. The remaining commercial banks were mostly focused on corporate business. Typically they had at most only several dozens of branches and mainly, or even exclusively, served the needs of business customers. By the end of the decade, however, fierce competition existed between all commercial banks on the retail market. Competition was conducted via the opening of new branches and sub-branches and ATM sites, for example *Millennium Bank*, the retail wing of *BIG SA* and the Portuguese bank BCP, *Handlobank*, the retail operation of *Bank Handlowy* SA were both set up to exploit and develop the retail side of the market.

Yet despite the expansion of all commercial banks into retail services, by mid 1999 only half of the population had bank accounts, which means that the banking services market in Poland has the largest development potential in Central Europe. Its additional advantage is the possibility of joining, in 3–5 years, the single European financial market.

The technological gap which widened in Polish banking for over 40 years had to be, in the first place, narrowed by developing the necessary technical and institutional infrastructure facilitating the proper operation of a non-cash settlements system, including inter-bank settlements.[5] Computerisation arrived in Polish banking very late as compared to Western Europe. But this had some advantages, for example, in making information systems 'year 2000 compliant' at less expense than in other European countries. Modern, telecommunications-based settlements systems led, at the end of the decade, to banking products seen for the first time in Poland: charge and credit cards, the ATM network, electronic and home banking, and so on.

After a decade of adjustment and systemic transformation the banking sector at the end of the century had a well-established legal, institutional and technological infrastructure, facilitating its further expansion. Nevertheless, the industry (and particularly retail banking) is still at an early stage of development. Consider the following (Jaromin, 1999, p. 165):

- in 1997 the banking sector's assets to GDP ratio amounted to 53% while in France it was 204% and in Germany 168%;
- in Poland there are 270 bank outlets per million residents while in Germany or France this ratio approaches 900;
- only some 50% of Poles are bank customers and, on average, each customer has used 1.8 banking products.

The new decade is bound to witness an intensification of competition as banks already operating in Poland meet growing rivalry from foreign banks entering the retail market. This will be an environment of shrinking bank margins, innovations in banking products and technologies, as well as cost cutting, particularly with regard to labour. Moreover in the struggle for customers banks will not only compete with one another but also with other non-banking financial institutions such as pension funds, investment funds, leasing companies, hire purchase providers and others. In response to that competition, banks are establishing groups (holdings) in which banks, as parent companies, establish offshoots to offer their clients a comprehensive range of financial services. The market shares of the main Polish players in banking services at the end of the 1990s are shown in Table 9.2.

Clearly the market in Poland for banking services remains open and ripe for development. As it does develop further it will do so much more in line with general tendencies where the major features are globalisation, unification and consolidation. The flow of foreign inward investment is also far from complete. It seems likely that there will be more banking acquisitions within the country and further redistribution between foreign owners. From the year 2000 foreign banks will face a dilemma stemming from further market liberalisation when they will have to decide whether to service customers in Poland through branches/subsidiaries operating in the Polish market *or* directly through their existing national branches providing over-the-border services. This type of competition will create a new and serious challenge for government regulatory agencies (as well as for the tax authorities). This is because the outflow of Polish customers abroad is potentially much more damaging for the economy than the inflow of foreign capital to the Polish banking sector. In the late 1990s it was estimated that the short-term foreign debt of the non-household sector could be even as high as $12 billion.

Table 9.2. Leading banks' market shares for various services (end 1998)

	Form of ownership	Deposits (%)	Loans (%)	Personal accounts (%)	Payment cards (%)
Banking sector		100.0	100.0	100.0	100.0
PKO BP	State-owned bank, privatisation scheduled for 2000	26.3	12.7	45.0	3.9
PEKAO S.A.	Public company, strategic investor – UniCredito Italiano (53%)	17.3	14.2	20.9	55.4
BGŻ S.A.	Company owned jointly by state and some co-operative banks, privatisation planned in 2000	5.4	5.7	2.0	0.9
Bank Handlowy S.A.	Public company with several foreign investors	3.5	6.8	n.a.	n.a.
BRE S.A.	Public company, strategic investor – Commerzbank (41%)	2.5	4.4	n.a.	n.a.
Bank Handlowy and BRE jointly – merger planed in the end of 1999	Public company	6.0	11.2	n.a.	n.a.
WBK S.A[a]	Public company, strategic investor – Allied Irish Banks (61%)	3.2	2.9	4.9	9.6
Bank Zachodni S.A.[a]	Private bank, strategic investor – Allied Irish Banks (80%)	2.8	3.4	3.3	3.5
WBK S.A. and Bank Zachodni (jointly) the group does not formally exist	Strategic investor – Allied Irish Banks	6.0	6.3	8.2	13.1
Bank Śląski S.A.[a]	Public company, Strategic investor – ING Bank (55%)	4.3	4.8	7.8	19.3

Table 9.2. continued

	Form of ownership	Deposits (%)	Loans (%)	Personal accounts (%)	Payment cards (%)
Banking sector		100.0	100.0	100.0	100.0
BPH S.A.[a]	Public company, Strategic investor – BHW AG (50%)	4.3	4.4	5.8	2.6
BIG Bank (group)	Public company with several foreign investors	4.2	3.5	4.9	0.5
PBK S.A.[a]	Public company, strategic investor – Bank Austria-Creditanstalt (44%)	4.1	4.6	4.2	1.5
Kredyt Bank PBI S.A.	Public company, Strategic investor – KBC Bank NV (33%)	2.9	3.8	1.4	3.1

Notes: [a] Regional banks with nation-wide branches: in local market places their market share in individual types of products can reach up to 50%.

Source: Author's estimates based on internal materials of WBK Bank S.A.

THE CAPITAL MARKETS

Laws and institutions

Despite its weaknesses it would be hard to claim that banking was a completely new feature of the Polish economy in the early 1990s. The situation was quite different however with regard to non-depository financial intermediaries and the capital markets. Before 1990 insurance firms (mainly property insurance) and a pensions institution (*Zaklad Ubezpieczeń Społecznych – ZUS*) did exist in Poland but they were organisations that survived largely on state subsidy and had no capital basis. To set up capital markets a sound legal framework had to be created although the pre-war (1934) commercial code was immensely useful. In the 1990s two legal Acts were crucial in setting the scene for capital markets developments. These were the 1991 Acts on the commercialisation and privatisation of state-owned companies and the law on public trading in securities and in trust funds. The second law, in particular, permitted the establishment of institutions needed for the operations of a Polish capital market based on western patterns. These include:

- the Securities and Stock Exchanges Commission (*Komisja Papierów Wartościowych i Giełd – KPWiG*), the agency that decides on whether securities can be publicly trading, including admission procedures to the Stock Exchange, granting brokerage and investment adviser licences, supervising the market, protecting investors' interests and ensuring fair competition;
- the Warsaw Stock Exchange, WSE (*Warszawska Giełda Papierów Wartościowych, WGPW*) is the only centralised stock exchange in Poland, on which are traded, shares, pre-emption rights, bonds (treasury and corporate), foreign exchange and stock exchange index derivatives;
- brokerage houses at end 1997 47 operated in Poland, of which 16 were owned by banks. The commercial banks played an important part in establishing financial intermediary institutions but they could only enter the market by setting up distinct companies or brokerage offices quite separate from the parent banks;
- OTC market (Centralna Tabela Ofert – CeTO) established in 1996 as an organised public over-the-counter trading market, a public market separate from the stock exchange.

In assessing the development, performance and significance of the Polish capital market we can take two approaches, one based on legalities and frameworks the other on economic developments.

The legal framework appears to have passed the tests of the 1990s in that most investors believe that clear rules co-exist with effective supervision and management. As a 'late developer', Poland capitalised on others' experiences, permitting the creation from scratch of a modern legal and institutional infrastructure compatible with the best European standards.

The stock exchange and the economy

The second approach is to consider wider economy issues such as the impact on the efficiency of the investment process and on system transformation and economic growth. Capital market trends, particularly on the stock exchange, depend on the supply of securities derived from economic agents' needs for funds and on investors' search for profitable business opportunities. Privatised companies' shares were the securities initially traded on the exchange. Later, other listed firms raised capital through new share issues. This was particularly popular between 1993 and 1994 when the Polish securities market experienced its first boom. From a quantitative point of view the period 1995–98 saw further important developments as 'mass privatisation' (the National Investment Funds

– NIF – programme) vouchers were traded on the exchange, subsequently followed by the shares of 15 National Investment Funds themselves, and then by the shares of the companies owned by NIFs and figuring in their portfolios.[6] By mid-1999 the shares of 212 companies (as well as shares of 15 NIFs) were quoted on the Warsaw Stock Exchange, of which 119 were on the main floor, 58 on the parallel floor, and 20 on the OTC market. As compared to the end of 1995 the number of quoted companies had more than tripled.

The development level of a stock exchange can be measured through the market value of quoted companies. At the end of 1998 the WSE capitalisation exceeded zł 72 billion ($20.5 billion), around 14% of Poland's GDP. It is worth stressing that the period 1997–98 was particularly successful for its quantitative growth since in 1997 its capitalisation reached only 5–6% of GDP. One of the reasons behind this was privatisation policy. It tended to combine the sale of majority stakes to strategic investors with the public flotation of minority blocks of shares; as a result, the increase in stock market capitalisation was not accompanied by a proportional growth in turnover. In the opinion of many experts a stock exchange begins to play an important role in an economy once its capitalisation is 20–25% of the country's GDP. In Poland this level may have been reached by the year 2000. If so it will have been brought about mainly by the privatisation of large companies including *Telekomunikacja Polska* (Polish Telecom), the PKO BP Bank, PZU (the insurer), Polish Airlines LOT and the Polish Oil Holding Company.

At the end of the century the European capital market witnessed strong competition between traditional and previously isolated (partly due to quotations in different currencies) national stock exchanges. While it was developing at a fast pace the Warsaw exchange was also losing to that competition in the sense that Poland saw privatisation issues 'drift out' to the well-established European stock markets. In 1999 for example the shares of six Polish companies, as GDRs, were traded in London. Moreover in anticipation of EU accession competition has already started between Central European exchanges (Vienna, Prague, Budapest, Warsaw) to be the regional leader in the capital market. It is likely even in the near future that alliances will emerge between these centres. The Warsaw exchange is also preparing for greater competition, for example by considering trading in shares of companies from some other Eastern European countries (Lithuania, Latvia, Ukraine). The Polish stock market has sufficient potential to become one of the strong regional European capital markets in the first half of the next decade.

The state Treasury is the second major supplier of tradable securities to the stock exchange. In 1997 the Treasury bonds trade represented almost 20% of the entire value of turnover on the exchange. Investor interest in the bonds has grown alongside their development over longer maturity periods (from 1 to 10 years) and in variety (for example, variable and fixed yield bonds). If the bond sector was entirely dominated by state treasury instruments in the early 1990s corporate bonds also started to appear from 1996. In 1994–97 the short-term debt securities market performed the corporate bond market. The issuers tended to be 'blue-chip' companies, some multinational corporations, with banks acting as intermediaries. Pioneers included a Polish computer company, *Optimus SA* (convertible bonds), and a major brewery, *Elbrewery* (ordinary bonds). The relatively late introduction of corporate bonds on the Polish capital market was the result partly of the lack of appropriate legal regulations (only enacted in 1995) and partly the persistently high inflation which made it difficult to calculate future returns. Given the perception of high risk issuers preferred to raise capital through stocks rather than bonds because the former allows much more risk to be passed on to the buyers (shareholders) than is the case with bonds. This explained the popularity of convertible bonds in the initial period. By the end of the 1990s the bond market had become an attractive source of capital for many companies.

Another group of issuers has also appeared on the bond market, the municipal sector. But by the end of the decade only a few municipalities had decided to dip into the market. Situated at the lowest level of the local authority structure in Poland they are not usually strong entities and the value of bonds issued by them has not been high (the highest issues ran at the level of around zł20 million to zł25 million ($5 million to $5.25 million), and the bonds issued have not been traded publicly. Significant changes in the municipal bond market might be expected after the year 2000 stemming from decentralising administrative reforms of 1999. The larger regional local authority units that emerge should find it easier to finance infrastructure-related investments via bond issues.

Summing up our description of the Polish capital market from the angle of supply of financial instruments, it should be stressed that, by the end of the decade, this market was dominated by Treasury paper and by shares, mainly through privatisation and to a lesser degree through new rights issues. It was only at the end of the 1990s that appropriate conditions existed for other instruments to emerge: corporate bonds, municipal bonds and derivatives. Further expansion of this market at the beginning of the twenty-first century will depend mainly on the overall economic situation in Poland and its major trading partners.

Let us now look at the capital market from the demand perspective. At the initial stage of development there were, apart from the banking sector, which (jointly with the NBP) was investing mainly in Treasury paper, no other institutional investors. Slowly however investing in shares became more and more popular among some groups of the general public. It is worth mentioning that, in this respect, the stock exchange played not only the role of an institution facilitating privatisation but it simultaneously performed an important educational function. As they invested on the stock exchange or just tracked the changes in stock exchange indices some people internalised the principles of a market economy. The mass privatisation programme contributed to this. After the stock exchange debut of the 15 NIFs the number of investment accounts in brokerage houses and offices grew to reach some 1.2 million in 1998. Nevertheless, the Polish stock market remained relatively shallow, making it vulnerable to speculative movements. According to one author (see Frąckowiak, 1996, p. 17) in the mid 1990s some 60% to 70% of turnover on the WSE was dominated by speculative investors, particularly individuals. The Polish capital market still faces a clear imbalance between speculative and long-term capital and the reason, in the 1990s, was the absence of large institutional investors.

Non-depository financial intermediaries

The first group of non-banking institutional investors to enter the Polish capital market were trust funds. Until 1997 the operations of trust funds were regulated by a 1991 law according to which only open-ended trust funds could operate in Poland. From 1997 a new law on investment funds also allowed the establishing of closed-end and mixed funds.[7] However by the end of the decade no such funds had been established. The open-ended trust funds are managed by investment fund corporations (or fund managers) organised as joint stock companies. The first trust fund corporation *Pioneer* was established in Poland in 1992. By the end of 1998 the units of five trust funds, managed by seven fund companies, were available on the capital market. Although the number of funds has increased, their role in the capital market and in personal savings remained insignificant. At the end of 1997 trust funds' net assets accounted for 4.8% of stock exchange capitalisation and represented only 1.7% of the value of households' savings deposits. During 1995–97 investment funds' share in stock exchange capitalisation actually decreased (from 6.5% in 1995), the result of higher demand for less risky securities (mainly T-bills). By the end of 1998 Polish investment funds managed assets worth over zł2 billion, equivalent to an average investment of $14 dollars per capita. In the Czech Republic the comparable figure was $44, in Hungary $127, and in France $10,300. Clearly, the long-term prospects of the investment funds market in Poland looks, from this angle, promising. Nevertheless in sheer quantity terms investment funds will most likely not play a major part on the Polish market, serving rather as a supplementary source of funds flowing into the capital and money markets especially as the wealth and investment awareness of Polish society increases.

Insurance companies, including life assurance firms, have become one of the major institutional investors on the financial market. At the end of 1998, 55 companies conducted insurance business in Poland, of which 24 operated in the life market. The capital raised by insurance companies has been systematically growing. Over 1996–98 the annual growth in the life assurance sector reached 25–30%. Over that same period insurance companies managed to raise almost three times more capital than the investment trust funds discussed earlier and they have become the largest non-banking financial intermediary in Poland.

In spite of the presence of a large number of companies the insurance market in Poland is highly concentrated. The dominant players are *Rzeczpospolita* (no. 81, 1999) *Powszechny Zakład Ubezpieczeń* (PZU), a state-owned firm (privatisation was slated for the year 2000) and *Warta SA*, a private concern with a significant shareholding held by the Treasury. Life business at the end of 1998 was dominated by four companies, with a total market share of 96%. *PZU Życie* had 66%, *Commercial Union Poland* 18%, *AIG Poland* 9% and *Nationale Nederlanden* 7%. The rapid late 1990s expansion of the market was the result mainly of the new entry of top-class international players: *Commercial Union, AIG, Allianz* and *Nationale Nederlanden.*

The investment portfolios of insurance firms in Poland most resemble German insurance companies in that the bulk of their portfolios is composed of safe investments. At the end of 1997 investments in T-bonds and T-bills accounted for 88% of their assets, and the value of shares they held did not exceed 6% (yet the regulations allow for up to 30% of assets to be held in shares). Such a composition derived from the high yield and safety of Treasury securities as well as the lack of alternatives on the market, the lack of mortgage loans, mortgage bonds, corporate bonds, and so on. The development of the life insurance market will continue to be dynamic, as a result of pensions reform (the shift to a capital based pension system from 1999), and insurance companies will remain the second most important group of financial intermediaries after the pension funds.

As far as other financial intermediaries are concerned, domestic investment banks have never been established in Poland. Investment banking services are partially offered by domestic commercial banks. They mainly consist of brokerage services provided by banks' brokerage divisions (which, however, enjoy organisational and financial autonomy). Banking law sets limits on the investment activities of commercial banks, constraining for instance their investments in shares to 25% of shareholders' funds. The banks do get involved in rights issues and in underwriting such issues for clients on the domestic capital market. Among those most active in this field are *BRE SA* and *Bank Handlowy SA*. It is possible that these banks will set up, individually or jointly with other entities, new companies specialising in investment banking services which will not be constrained by the provisions of the banking law since the law refers to deposit-taking institutions. The basic reason for the absence of domestic investment banks is, most definitely, the lack of concentrated domestic private capital willing to get involved in higher risk operations, as well as the lack of highly qualified and experienced staff. This gap, however, has been filled by the largest European and American investment banks which entered the Polish market in the 1990s. They have been involved, for example, in the largest privatisation projects as well as in domestic and foreign issues of shares, and the bonds issues of large Polish firms.[8]

The major financial intermediaries in the market economy, pension funds, began to be established in Poland only in 1999. The pension system reform is of key importance for further development of the financial sector and capital markets in Poland as well as, of course, for the country's social safety net. This new pension system assumes that employees can be insured under three pillars: Pillar I, an obligatory insurance in the state *Zakład Ubezpieczeń Społecznych, ZUS*, to which 15% of pension premiums go; Pillar II, an obligatory insurance in open pension funds, managed by the *Powszechne Towarzystwo Emerytalne* SA (PTE) and which gets 9% of premiums; Pillar III, voluntary private employee pension plans.

In the first half of 1999 21 PTE companies were granted licenses from the Pension Funds Supervision Office. It is worth noting that almost all of the financial intermediaries operating on the Polish market became involved: banks (domestic and foreign), insurance companies, investment funds, but also the Polish Post Office, a TV station, and even the Church.[9] An unprecedented race took place between pension funds, which attempted to attract as many clients as possible and as much premium income as possible. The market is large and it is estimated that 5–6 million people (in an economically active population of 9 million) will be looking for pensions products. By mid-1999 the market leaders, with a combined market share of 70%, included four pension funds established by *Commercial Union*, the banks *BPH SA* and *WBK SA*; *PZU Życie; Nationale Nederlanden*; and *Norwich Union*. Polish law imposes certain constraints on the free movement of members between funds, and those who might wish to switch funds in the first two years will have to pay a penalty fee. In these circumstances it may be expected that we will witness, in the near future, many mergers and acquisitions of pension funds in the consolidation process of the social insurance system.

Estimates suggest that in the year 2000 pension funds will have generated around zł13 billion (approximately $3.3 billion) in premium income, a sum that will be twice as much as the capital of all life assurance companies, and six times more than that of all the investment funds active in Poland. At the start of the twenty–first century the pension funds will become the most important non-banking financial institution with a huge growth potential. It is estimated that the capital raised by the funds by the end of the first decade of the twenty–first century will total over zł160 billion (around $40 billion). Existing laws impose no limits on pension funds' investments in Treasury paper and securities. The funds can invest up to 40% of their assets in publicly traded shares and corporate bonds and up to 5% in foreign securities. Assuming that the funds invest 20% of their assets in private securities these investments will total some zł4 billion (around $1 billion) by the end of the year 2000, accounting for 5% of the present capitalisation of the Warsaw Stock Exchange. In the middle of the coming decade they will account for 50% of its capitalisation. Pension funds will undoubtedly exert a strong impact on the performance of the capital market in

Poland. The volume and liquidity growth of that market will also enhance its efficiency. The development of the capital markets may then be conducive to a more rational allocation of resources in the most profitable investments and start to play a more effective role in promoting economic growth and development.

CONCLUSION

In conclusion, it is worth emphasising that in the last decade of the twentieth century the Polish financial sector established an infrastructure indispensable for its smooth future operation. It is also one that is compatible with the needs of a market economy in terms of law, institutions and markets. However, so far, the influence of financial markets on the real economy has been marginal because of the shallowness of the capital market and the lack of large domestic institutional investors with sufficient funds. Of particular importance for the further development of this sector are long-delayed reforms in three key areas, reforms eventually launched in early 1999 in public administration, pensions and health. These reforms created institutions and conditions indispensable for the accumulation of domestic capital. Meanwhile the most active players on the emerging capital market were the banks, both the domestic commercial banks as well as foreign banks seeking new markets. They have vigorously promoted new institutions as well as the expansion of Polish capital markets. These activities are partly a symptom of intensifying competition in the banking industry.

The effects of changes in the financial sector can be observed at both the macro- and microeconomic levels. The former undoubtedly includes the success of anti-inflationary policy (touched on earlier in our discussion of central banking), the relatively fast pace of economic growth, and the inflow, in comparison with other transforming economies, of stable foreign capital. With regard to microeconomic effects it is worth emphasising that the market-orientated development of the financial sector has stimulated ever fiercer competition between banks and other financial intermediaries, leading not only to a much wider range of savings opportunities but also to substantial improvements in the quality of customer services for both the household and business sectors.

Rebuilding the banking sector at the beginning of the decade as well as the longer-term process of creating from scratch a financial sector provided a solid basis for the further development of the economy. The success of the entire economy and its financial sector in particular was undoubtedly one reason why Poland was able to negotiate an association agreement (alongside Hungary and the Czech Republic) with the EU. The perspective of Polish EU accession is one of the factors encouraging the stable inflow of long-term capital to the economy. EU accession and EMU membership, whenever it takes place, determine the direction of the financial sector's systemic transformation. Harmonisation with

EU norms is one of the most important features of the new system solutions (endorsed by both Sejm and government) being adopted and at the same time creates a barrier to any experiments in searching for other unproven solutions.

NOTES

1 The major acts that established the new banking-financial system in Poland are shown below:

a. Ustawa z dnia 31 stycznia 1989 r. Prawo bankowe Dz. U. 1989 nr 4 poz. 22 (The 1989 Banking Law);
b. Ustawa z dnia 31 stycznia 1989 r. O Narodowym Banku Polskim Dz. U. 1989 nr 4 poz. 22 (The National Bank of Poland Act 1989);
c. Ustawa z dnia 15 lutego 1989 r. Prawo dewizowe Dz. U. 1989 nr 6 poz. 33 (Foreign Exchange Law 1989);
d. Ustawa z dnia 13 lipca 1990 r. O prywatyzacji przedsiębiorstw państwowych. Dz. U. 1990 nr 51 poz. 298 (Privatisation of the State-Owned Enterprises);
e. Ustawa z dnia 22 marca 1991 r. Prawo o publicznym obrocie papierami wartościowymi i funduszach powierniczych. Dz. U. 1991 nr 35 poz. 155 (Law on Public Trading of Securities and the Mutual Funds);
f. Ustawa z dnia 3 lutego 1993 r. O restrukturyzacji finansowej przedsiębiorstw i banków oraz o zmianie niektórych ustaw. Dz. U. 1993 nr 18 poz. 82 (Financial Restructuring of Enterprises and Banks);
g. Ustawa z dnia 30 kwietnia 1993 r. O narodowych funduszach inwestycyjnych i ich prywatyzacji. Dz. U. 1993 nr 44 poz. 202 (National Investment Funds and their Privatisation);
h. Ustawa z dnia 2 grudnia 1994 r. Prawo dewizowe Dz. U. 1994 nr 136 poz. 703 (The Foreign Exchange Law, 1994);
i. Ustawa z dnia 14 grudnia 1994 r. O Bankowym Funduszu Gwarancyjnym Dz. U. 1995 nr 4 poz. 18 (Banking Deposits' Insurance Fund);
j. Ustawa z dnia 30 sierpnia 1996 r. O komercalizacji i prywatyzacji przedsiębiorstw państwowych Dz. U. 1997 nr 118 poz. 754 (Commercialisation and Privatisation of State-Owned Enterprises);
k. Ustawa z dnia 21 sierpnia 1997 r. Prawo o publicznym obrocie papierami wartościowymi Dz. U. 1997 nr 118 poz. 754 (Public Trading of Securities);
l. Ustawa z dnia 28 sierpnia 1997 r. O funduszach inwestycyjnych Dz. U. 1997 nr 139 poz. 934 (Investment Funds);
m. Ustawa z dnia 28 sierpnia 1997 o organizacji i funkcjonowaniu funduszy emerytalnych Dz. U. 1997 nr 139 poz. 934 (Organisation and Functioning of the Pension Funds);

n. Ustawa z dnia 29 sierpnia 1997 r. O Narodowym Banku Polskim Dz. U. 1997 nr 140 poz. 940 (The National Bank of Poland Act 1997);
o. Ustawa z dnia 29 sierpnia 1997 Prawo bankowe Dz. U. 1997 nr 140 poz. 941 (The Banking Law 1997);
p. Ustawa z dnia 13 października 1998 r. O systemie ubezpieczeń społecznych Dz. U. 1998 nr 137 poz. 887 (Social Insurance System);
q. Ustawa z dnia 26 listopada 1998 r. O finansach publicznych Dz. U. 1998 nr 155 poz. 1014 (Public Finances).

2 The excess liquidity of the banking sector is expressed in the level of net central bank debt in this sector. 'The level of such NBP debt, a measure of minimum excess liquidity, reached zł50 billion ($3.8 billion), which is over 20% of banking sector net assets value at the end of 1998. One should remember that in a normal situation the central bank is the last resort of liquidity for the banking sector and not its creditor' (Grabowski, 1999, p. 20).

3 In the third quarter of 1999 real interest rates on 1-year deposits were 3–4%, business loans 5–7%, and consumer credit 10–12%

4 American Depositary Receipts (ADRs) and Global Depositary Receipts (GDRs) are dollar denominated certificates that represent shares of non-US companies but are traded, cleared and settled in the same way as US securities. Shares are held in trust by a trust bank, which in turn issues receipts to investors.

5 An important and expensive change took place as recently as 1997–99 when the old settlement system based on the circulation of paper documents (SYBIR) was replaced with a new telecommunication-based network (ELIXIR).

6 Based on the Act passed by the Sejm in 1993, 15 National Investment Funds (*Narodowych Funduszy Inwestycyjnych – NFI*) were set up. Their assets were made up of the equity (shares) of 512 eligible portfolio companies contributed by the state Treasury. All adult Polish citizens could acquire, a token fee, one Universal Share Certificate (*Powszechne Świadectwo Udziałowe– PŚU*), a coupon to be subsequently exchanged – free of charge – for fifteen shares of the National Investment Funds (one share of each). From the angle of the capital market the NIF scheme contributed to the expansion of trading volume on the Warsaw stock Exchange – first through floating the Universal Share Certificates (PŚU) and then through the listing of shares in the NIFs themselves and finally through the flotation of some of the participating portfolio companies. (For further reading see, for example, Rapacki, 1999.)

7 Open-ended investment funds issue investment units through a public offering; they may be subject to redemption by the fund at the request of the investor (or fund member). Closed-ended funds issue investment certificates without any obligation to redeem them; they are traded on a secondary

market. Mixed investment funds issue investment certificates which are redeemable at the request of the investor but at dates fixed by the fund (at least once a year). Between these fixed maturity dates certificates are traded on secondary markets.

8 Among others, Deutsche Bank, JP Morgan, Merrill Lynch, Credit Suisse First Boston, Schroders, have been very active on Polish financial markets – especially in the second half of the 1990s.

9 The open-ended pension fund *Polsat* was set up by a private TV station of this name, with a minority foreign investor stake (PAI Media, 36%), a small Polish bank (Invest-Bank, 21%), and the state lottery monopolist (Totalizator Sportowy, 3%). Yet another fund – *Arka Invesco – was* established by the pension fund, Powszechne Towarzystwo Emerytalne, in which shareholders are a foreign investor (Amvescap, 80%) and the Polish Catholic Church (20%).

REFERENCES

Frąckowiak, W. (ed.) (1996), *Rozwój rynku kapitałowego w Polsce a restrukturyzacja i prywatyzacja przedsiębiorstw* (Development of the capital market in Poland and the restructuring and privatisation of firms), Poznan: Akademia Ekonomiczna.

Gomułka, S. (1998), 'Managing capital flows in Poland 1995–98', *Economics of Transition*, 6 (2).

Grabowski, B. (1999), 'Fundamentalne problemy polityki pieniężnej NBP' (The fundamental problems of NBP's monetary policy), *Bank i Kredyt,* no. 7–8.

Hajkiewicz-Góecka, M. (1999), 'Sytuacja finansowa banków', (The finanancial condition of the banks) in *Banki polskie u progu XXI wieku* (Polish banks at the turn of the 20th century), Warsaw: Poltext.

Instytucje rynku kapitalowego 1999 (1999), (Capital market institutions in 1999), *Parkiet*, Warsaw: Warsaw Stock Exchange.

Jaromin, J. (1999), 'Kierunki zmian w polskim sektorze bankowym', in *Banki polskie* ..., op. cit.

Jaworski, W.L. (1999), Kierunki reform sektora bankowego w Polsce', in *Banki polskie* ..., ibid.

Kosiński, B. (1999), Banki zagraniczne w Polsce jako przejaw konkurencji w sektorze bankowym', in *Banki polskie* ... , ibid.

Lutkowski, K. (1999), 'Unifikacja walutowa Europy a przyszłość złotego', (Currency unification in Europe and the future of the Polish złoty), *Bank i Kredyt*, nr 7–8.

Nuti, D.M. (1996), 'Inflation interest and exchange rates in the transition', *Economics of Transition*, 4 (1).

Polański, Z. (1999), 'Polityka pieniężna w Polsce na przełomie dekad: strategiczne wyzwania', in *Banki polskie* ... , op. cit.

Puławski, M. (ed.) (1999), *Rynek kapitalowy w Polsce. Raport 1998* (The capital market in Poland. Report 1998), Warsaw: PWE.

Rapacki, R. (1999), 'Privatization in Poland: major issues, trends and policy concerns' paper presented at the UN Expert Group Meeting on Privatization and Regulation, New York 16–18 February.

Studium Bankowości (A study of banking) (1998), Warsaw: Warszawski Instytut Bankowości.

'Średniookresowa strategia polityki pieniężnej na lata 1999–2003' (A medium term monetary strategy for 1999–2003) (1998), Monetary Policy Committee, *Bank i Kredyt*, no. 10.

10. Going beyond transition: pension reform in Poland

Marek Góra

INTRODUCTION

Pension systems throughout the world face financial difficulties. The traditional ways of raising funds for pensions, especially through Pay-As-You-Go (PAYG) systems, have, for many reasons, become ineffective. Among these the most important factors are demographic change (ageing), pension systems' (over) generosity and low retirement ages, and they affect countries irrespective of their specific economic situation. Pension reform therefore has a more universal character, one that goes well beyond the problems of economic transformation in Poland and other Central and Eastern European economies. Three main responses to pensions problems seem to exist: governments may choose simple *subsidisation*, allocating a part of general government revenue to make up for financing gaps in pension provision; they may on the other hand try *rationalisation*, which really means playing with various coefficients determining pension revenue and expenditure; and finally, they may opt for *reform*, a fundamental change in the system.

The most affluent countries, especially many European Union members, use the easiest and the least socially painful method – *subsidisation*. These countries can afford, at least for the time being, the huge cost of such a policy. It is likely, however, that even the rich countries will eventually need to *rationalise* their systems by cutting pension expenditure, the policy option widely used in less affluent countries. Although both subsidisation, if affordable, and rationalisation can help in solving short-run financing problems, they cannot solve pension problems in the long run.

There is a growing conviction in many countries that pension reform is needed and is in fact inevitable.[1] Moreover, the earlier reform is implemented the cheaper it will be. Prevarication is, in most of cases, the worst policy, especially in countries running expensive public pension systems. Poland, with almost 15% of GDP spent on pensions, is undoubtedly at the top of the list and a Polish pension reform was desperately needed. Luckily a new system was introduced in January 1999. In what follows we review the pre-reform situation, the new system's key characteristics and its expected outcomes.

THE POLISH CASE

Although the need for pension reform is a worldwide phenomenon it was particularly pressing in Poland because the system was, relatively speaking, exceptionally generous and was weighed down by heavy use of very costly early retirement schemes. The so-called 'replacement ratio', a ratio of average pension to average wage before retirement, rose in Poland in the 1990s to more than 60% (see Table 10.1) while in most countries of the region 40% to 50% was the norm (see Pallacios and Pallare-Mirrales, 2000). Easily available early retirement schemes embraced around 20% to 25% of Polish workers with huge additional pensions cost.[2] If the extra pension expenditure and the contribution loss due to early retirement are taken into account, the cost of early retirement is estimated at around 25% to 30% of total pension expenditure in Poland (see Chlon et al., 1999). Paradoxically, the demographic situation itself, although worsening, is actually better in Poland than in other countries in the region.

Table 10.1. The replacement ratio in Poland from the 1960s to the 1990s

Year	1960	1970	1980	1990	after 1990
Replacement ratio (%)[a]	43	54	48	56	over 60

Note: [a] Average pension to average remuneration ratio. Average pension in the table refers to both old-age and disability pensions. Old-age pensions are higher, so if disability pensions were excluded, the replacement ratio would be even greater.

Source: Department of Statistics, Analysis and Forecasting, Social Security Institution (ZUS).

The particularly high costs of running the Polish pension system were to a large extent due to past policy decisions, an additional and much overlooked legacy of the 1980s. Most of today's pension privileges (principally early retirement schemes) were established in 1981 and 1982 just after martial law was declared (on 13 December 1981). Providing large groups of workers with pension privileges was a way of buying social peace. At the time it cost almost nothing. The bill came in the 1990s and was to increase rapidly since early retirement options remained open and were widely taken up in the first half of the 1990s. This meant that policy in the early 1990s created an additional burden on the pension system. Of course softening social problems at an early stage of transition was necessary but it would have been much better for the pension system if that policy had been implemented more cautiously. Both policy decisions and demographic developments generated high pension costs requiring equally high revenue, or large subsidies, or both. The fast-growing social security contribution rate gives a clear picture of the scale of the problem (see Table 10.2).

Table 10.2. Social security contributions in Poland, 1981–98

	1981	1982	1986	1987	1990	1992	1998
Contribution ratio[a] (%)	15.5	25	33	43	38	43	45

Note: [a] The contribution ratio is calculated as contribution divided by remuneration net of the contribution, following Polish convention. If gross remuneration is used instead in the denominator then the 45% figure reported for 1998 would fall to 31%.

Source: ZUS.

Just as in most European countries, the demographic situation in Poland is expected to worsen. This implies additional expenditure on pensions at the same time as contributions decline. However, according to demographic projections, Poland expects a different trend in the first decade of the twenty–first century with a temporal stabilisation or even an improvement of demographic coefficients (see Table 10.3). This comes about due to the coincidence of the post-war 'baby boomers' (early 1950s) still being in employment while the second wave of 'baby boomers' (from the early 1980s) will move into the labour market. The second baby boom was caused by a complex of social phenomena. Fertility rates in the early 1980s were very high and an expected 'second wave' of the original post-war baby boom had superimposed on it another baby boom.[3] However the high fertility effect will soon be offset by large-scale labour market outflow as the original 'baby boomers' of the 1950s reach retirement age. The latter effect will be much stronger and demographic coefficients will quickly worsen. Table 10.3 illustrates the tendency clearly and projections going beyond 2020 have the same tendency (see Chlon and Tidner, 2000).

To sum up, the pension system in Poland prior to the 1999 reform was in bad shape. Its traditional PAYG structure was running into deep financial trouble, made worse by demography and extensively applied schemes for early retirement. Each year it consumed around 15% of GDP and needed a budget subsidy equivalent to around 2% of GDP. Contribution rates were high, reducing the competitiveness of Polish firms as well as stimulating a large informal sector. Moreover, actuarial projections clearly cast a very gloomy shadow on the future.

Table 10.3. Demographic estimates and projections, 1985–2020 (population, millions)

	1985	1990	1995	2000	2005	2010	2015	2020
Pension age	4.5	4.9	5.3	5.6	5.7	6.1	7.0	7.9
Working age	21.8	22.0	22.6	23.6	24.7	24.8	24.0	23.3
Ratio (%)	20.6	22.3	23.5	23.8	23.1	24.6	29.0	33.9

Source: Unpublished GUS (Central Statistical Office) projections.

THE STRUGGLE FOR PENSION REFORM

From the mid 1980s Polish demographers and economists became alarmed that a social security crisis looked inevitable. But this was difficult for the general public and for the politicians to understand since they observed only the year-by-year revenues and expenditures and the balance did not look so bad. High (in comparison to wages) pensions were paid in due time and pensioners were the most protected members of society. This meant that the need for reform was not obvious either to the people or to the politicians. At the same time, however, the old pension system, being dependent on both demographic and policy driven factors, was actuarially bankrupt. From the early 1990s the need for a reform became more and more obvious to pension system experts and eventually also to politicians and the general public. The coincidence of that growing awareness with the economic transformation of the 1990s made the situation both more, but also less, difficult. It was more difficult since other reforms seemed to be more urgent and their implementation did not leave much room for other major undertakings. It was less difficult since the time, and the mood, was ripe for change. Indeed in comparison to the rich and stable societies of Western Europe, Poland was both more open and more ready for radical change of its pension sysstem. As far as pensions reform is concerned four important 1990s' sub-periods, very different from each other, can be identified:

- losing control over the pension system (1990–92);
- implementing measures to rationalise the system (1992–96);
- designing the new system (1996–98);

- implementing the new system (1999 onwards).

The first three periods are described in detail in Góra and Rutkowski (1998). Here we stress only two issues. The first is the importance of switching from wage indexation to price indexation in early 1996. That was the crucial precondition for the reform itself. The second is the clear distinction between the period before and after 1996. In the latter period as opposed to the earlier one an internally consistent concept of reform received strong political support. Both the SLD-PSL and AWS-UW governments accepted the entire concept and took part in consecutive stages of turning it into reality. It is worth mentioning that the parliamentary elections and change of government did not affect either the concept or its implementation.

The 1999 reform is radical and gets to the heart of the old system's problems rather than trying to soften poor outcomes due to the malfunctioning of that system. On the other hand the reform was relatively narrow and focused on the old-age system alone, leaving other (badly needed) aspects of social security reform for the future. For example, in Poland expenditures on disability pensions are extremely high, accounting for around 13% of payroll, some two to three times greater than the average in other countries. Even minor inroads into that 13% will have a tremendous effect on the economy. Another reason for disability system reform is that the old-age and the disability parts of the social security system, while different, are related to each other and must be made consistent or problems may quickly appear. Nevertheless choosing the pensions part of social security as the priority for reform was no accident. The decision was taken for two reasons. First, pensions are the most expensive element in the social security system so pension reform brings the greatest benefits. Second, the pension system needs a long time before its effect becomes significant.

Radical pensions reform needed strong social and political support – normally difficult to assemble. The turning point of the reform struggle in Poland came in autumn 1996 when a government 'Office for Social Security Reform' was set up, bringing together a team of Polish and foreign pensions experts. In 1997 the Office published its reform blueprint, *Security through Diversity*. It is important to note that the reform was designed by experts independent from the day-to-day political struggle: they were not bureaucrats, nor politicians, although politicians facilitated and protected reform efforts. The latter aspect was a unique feature and it left the experts free to design the new system unconstrained by politicians and bureaucrats. The clear support from ministries of both labour and finance was also of immense importance. These ministries (and not only in Poland) usually have strongly differing views but fortunately not in Poland, at least with respect to pensions. The pension reform was also strongly supported by the media, the trade unions and the general public. Indeed the Solidarity trade union had prepared its own reform proposals that were very similar to those in *Security through Diversity*. That support was another uniquely helpful feature. In general it seems that society by the late 1990s was convinced by the argument for reform, that basically the old pension system was bankrupt and created an unacceptably insecure situation for workers. Although they paid high contributions to the existing PAYG scheme there was less and less certainty over their *own* future pensions provision. The state guarantee was a guarantee to be financed by the workers themselves, but in Poland in the late 1990s it was clear (and clearly accepted) that the long-term sustainability of their pensions was at risk. It is interesting to note in passing that this is exactly what is being suggested in the contemporary EU discussion on pensions. Of course, thinking in terms of decades is not easy for most people. Today matters more than tomorrow. This is why it is so difficult to avoid the trap many pension systems are in. Moreover, younger people do not think about their old age. Older people do, but for them it is too late to be won over by the (distant) benefits of reform and so the old are normally against reform unless it boils down to a pensions increase. While the young do not normally care too much about a distant future, what does matter to them, however, are their contributions.

At the very beginning of work on the reform (1996) it was clearly announced and frequently repeated that the reform would not change anything for current pensioners and people aged over 50 years. In that way those who would normally be against change were won over, so creating space for a radical reform for people below 50 years of age. Of course, not changing the system for older people meant giving up short-term fiscal benefits but that was a kind of investment in long-term effects which were expected to be much larger. Younger people (below 50 years) were won over by focusing on contributions. One of the key targets of the reform was to reduce contributions in the future as well as change their nature since the central element of the new old-age system was to be an individual account. Contributions moved from being a tax to quasi-savings. Contributions paid to the new system would no longer 'vanish' as in the extremely unpopular old pension system. Promoting all of this was important, with, from the very beginning, much media attention. Nothing was hidden, much publicity material was prepared and study tours were organised to help opinion makers grasp the idea of the reform.

Once prepared, the reform had to get the backing of parliament, and although that took some time eventually a majority of MPs voted for the package in more or less its initial design. The only substantial change was on retirement ages for men and women where the reform project equalised the age at 62 years but parliament opted for 65 years for men and 60 years for women.[4]

THE NEW SYSTEM: KEY FEATURES

Poland is not the first country to implement pensions reform. Much worldwide experience exists to draw on. The Polish reform owes much to that experience and the new pension system capitalises in particular on reforms in Sweden, Latin American countries (Argentina, Chile, Mexico), Singapore, and also Anglo-Saxon countries (UK, USA). Nevertheless the new Polish system significantly differs from many others, even from those it builds on. Although in general terms the system in Poland is in line with what is known as the 'World Bank three pillar approach' it also significantly differs from that pattern (see World Bank, 1944, or Holzmann, 2000).

The three pillar system is a concept in which elements of the pension system have a different function and structure. The first or basic pillar is commonly financed on a PAYG basis, is always mandatory and run by a government institution and its purpose is to provide full career workers with at least a basic level of retirement income protection. The second pillar is mandated by law or by collective agreements, is usually run on a defined contribution basis and is usually fully or partially funded, run by the private sector or by a government institution. The third pillar is a range of voluntary additional arrangements designed to supplement a worker's retirement income.

Differences between the Polish and other approaches can be summarised as follows. First, market-based, entirely voluntary options for pension contributions, the so-called 'third pillar', although badly needed, do not really contribute to solving the problems of mandatory pension systems, the heart of the Polish problem. Second, the Polish pension reform contains a much deeper reform of the mandatory part of the system. The first pillar design builds on Swedish experience and is based on the so-called 'notional defined contribution' (NDC). It is not a continuation of the old system. The new system is based on individual accounts, the so-called 'defined contribution' (DC) scheme. This is an unusual design.[5] It is much more common to turn only the second pillar into a DC system leaving the first pillar in a quasi-tax system, the so-called 'defined benefit' (DB) scheme. In the new scheme 50% of pension contributions are paid by employees and 50% by workers.

The different methods of determining benefits can be summarised as follows:

- in *defined benefit* (DB) systems pensions are determined by a formula, a wide range of which are used in traditional pension systems;
- in *defined contribution* (DC) systems pensions are determined by the amount of contributions paid throughout working careers plus interest due;
- a notional defined contribution (NDC) system is a kind of DC in which contributions are not spent on regular financial instruments. The nature of NDC claims is similar to purchasing government bonds; however, 'bonds'

are not traded and returns are not determined by financial markets' performance but by the overall performance of the economy (GDP growth).

The design of the new system has serious implications. Among them probably the most important is elimination of redistribution among pensioners in the old-age part of the system although redistribution from men to women remains due to differences in life expectancy. A simple rule is applied in the new system: on the day of retirement a person receives (in the form of an annuity) whatever he or she has paid into the system plus interest earned on that money. It also withdraws pension privileges, but the fact that the pension system is not used for redistribution does not mean elimination of redistribution in society: the reform relocated redistribution from the pension system to the state budget, a more efficient and fairer solution. The old system tried to compensate people for many things, creating inefficiency and much undesirable cross-subsidisation. Essential workers *should* be compensated but this should be through the remuneration they receive and not through the pension system. The elimination of privileges will dramatically reduce pension costs so creating room for lower contributions in the future. The sole goal of the new Polish pension system is to provide people with a secure, efficient and transparent way of allocating income over the life cycle.[6]

Key features of the new Polish old-age pension system
• Separation of the old-age pension system from social security provisions. • Both first and second pillars are newly designed (the first pillar is not a continuation of the old system). • Individual accounts are created throughout the system. • The first and second pillars play equivalent roles. • Risk diversification achieved by splitting contributions between two individual accounts run in different ways. • Annuitisation of accounts at day of retirement. • Minimum guarantee on top of the sum of first and second pillar pensions (financed by the state budget).

The system was phased in with three different approaches for three age groups. The over-50s remained in the old system. The under-50s, those people born after December 1948, moved into the new system. Their entire pension contributions, 19.52% of wages, are paid to their own individual accounts and their future pensions will be solely determined by the amount accumulated in those accounts and their retirement age. A simple yet crucial formula is used to calculate pension, where the annual pension is derived by dividing the capital accumulated in an individual account by life expectancy at retirement. As opposed to many other pension reforms there is no option of remaining in the old system. Within the under-50s, those under 30 years must divide their pension contributions between first and second pillars (12.22 percentage points and 7.3 percentage points respectively). Those aged between 30 and 50 (born between 1 January 1949 and 31 December 1968) had the option of dividing contributions between two accounts (pillars 1 and 2) or paying contributions entirely to the first pillar individual account.

EXPECTED REFORM EFFECTS

The Polish reform's individual accounts make it self-sustainable and predictable. A model prepared for the Polish pension reform and illustrated below in Figure 10.1 (see Chlon and Tidner, 2000) permits us to examine likely developments. Panel (a) indicates expenditure and revenues in a notional defined contribution (NDC) system. One can see that this creates a large surplus in the system but shifting a part of old-age contribution to the second pillar will reduce that surplus, as panel (b) shows. In this way that surplus, will be saved instead of being used for unpredictable expenditure not necessarily related to pensions. Panel (b) demonstrates that the introduction of the second pillar will not be difficult to finance.

Figure 10.1. Revenue, expenditure and balance in the new (NDC) first pillar pension system, 1997–2052 (with and without introduction of the second pillar (% GDP))

(a) Without introduction of the second pillar

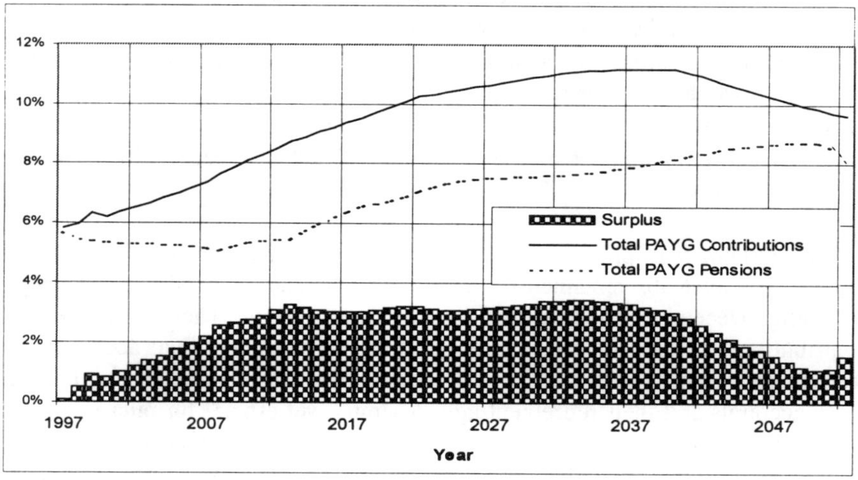

(b) With introduction of the second pillar

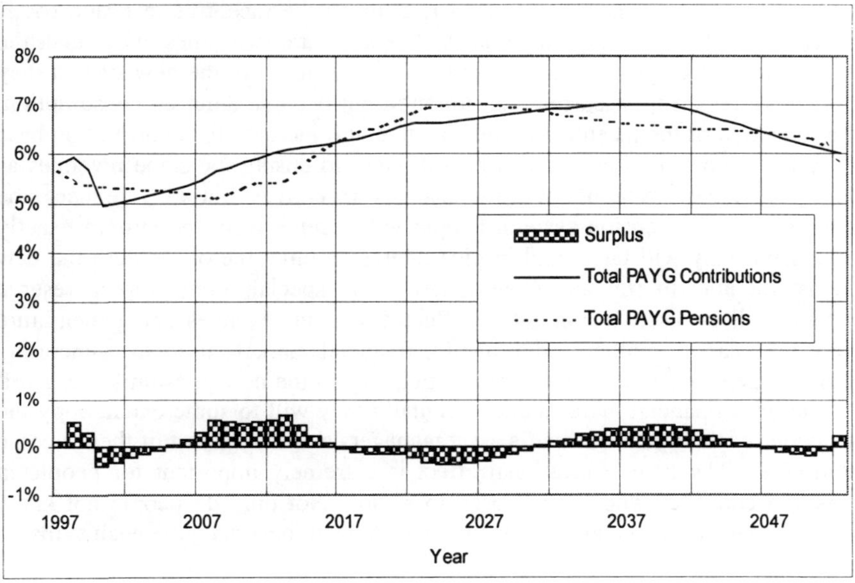

Notes: Assumes GDP growth of over 5% per annum to 2006, then 4% to 2020 and 3% thereafter. Also real wages assumed to grow by 1 point above the GDP growth rate to 2040.

Source: Chlon and Tidner (2000).

As stated above, the reform was implemented with a view to providing people with a secure and efficient method of income allocation over the life cycle. The new system will simultaneously create desirable side-effects, reducing the costs of production factors, labour and capital, so contributing to long-term economic growth. Under the new system savings should increase (see Figure 10.2) and even if they did not their structure would change in favour of longer-term savings.

In the old system contributions were increasing very quickly and if the reform had not been implemented they would have kept increasing. The new system creates the possibility for contributions to decline but this will need some time to reach any significant scale. Individual accounts and the manner of calculating pensions generates 'neutrality' in retirement decisions. In the old system people were strongly motivated to retire as early as possible since there was very little adjustment in benefits levels from postponing the retirement decision. Retiring early was rational at the micro but not at the macro level. The elimination of incentives to retire early which were built into the old system will lead to postponement of retirement decisions.

Paying contributions to individual accounts also reduces the incentive to hide income. The grey economy in Poland is built on the incentive to evade social security contributions rather than taxes. The latter are two times lower than the former. In the old system contributions paid were 'lost'. In the new system they still cannot be spent on current consumption but become deferred consumption. The reduction of the incentive to hide income will increase the contribution base and a lower contribution rate will be sufficient to ensure the same revenues as before. The new system not only changes incentives but also reduces the generosity of the pension system. People will receive from the system exactly the amount they will have paid in plus interest. Unlike the old system the new one is not able to run an actuarial deficit. A special 'demographic reserve system' will be used for smoothing fluctuations in revenues and expenditure from one year to another. Additionally, financial markets used for generating funds for pensions will grow faster. Participants in the new pension system will also observe financial markets and eventually they will to some extent copy the behaviour of their pension fund's asset managers and save a part of their income themselves. The latter educational effect is extremely important for people in transition countries who are not used to saving. Not only do people not know how to behave in financial markets but they also will never acquire such skills.

FINANCING REFORM

Pension reform transition costs can be analysed from two angles. First there is, in a budgetary perspective, the financial gap caused by the reform. The second, macroeconomic perspective is different. It takes into account the net present value of future revenues and expenditures and acknowledges that the reform shifts revenues and expenditures in time. From the budgetary viewpoint what matters most is that splitting contributions between first and second pillars creates a financial gap in the system. However from the macroeconomic viewpoint the reform just shifts money in time. We can understand the reform as an advanced payment of future pensions. Instead of being paid in the future, they are appropriately discounted and paid now, but not in cash, rather as transfers to pension accounts.

From the budgetary viewpoint there are two ways of financing the gap: (a) from tax revenues, either special contributions (social security) or general taxation; or (b) from debt. If taxes are used, then the second pillar's costs are shifted to current taxpayers, reducing their current consumption. Although sometimes more difficult politically that financing method is used in many countries including Poland. Debt financing is more equitable. Those who will eventually be reform beneficiaries pay for the reform. The triangle represents the gap created by the reform. Financing the gap can be either by tax revenues, or by rationalisation of the old system, or by issuing debt. If the three ways of financing do not cover the entire gap, the scale of shifting contributions to the second pillar has to be reduced

Figure 10.2. Savings in the multi-pillar pension system, 1997–2052

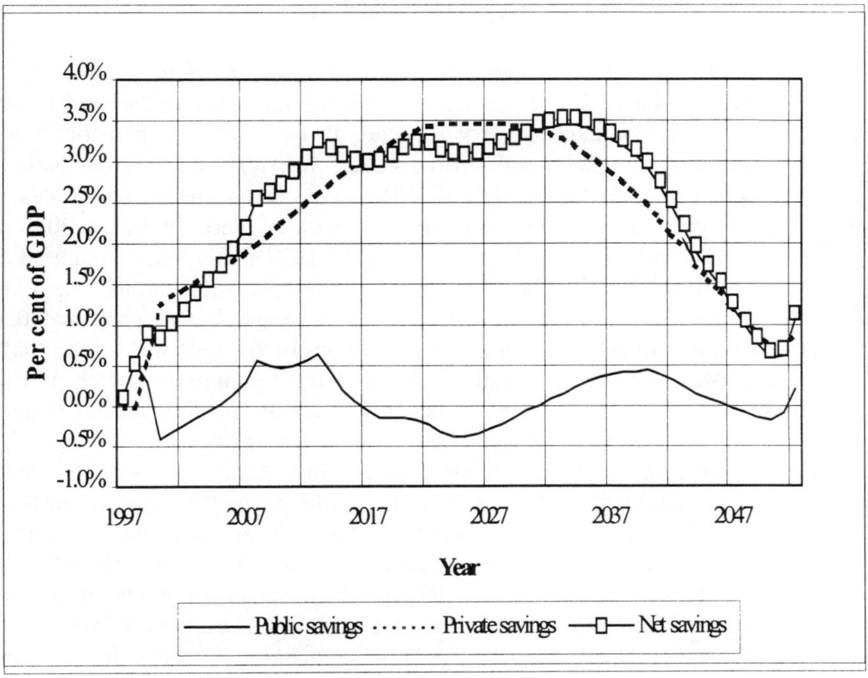

Source: Chlon and Tidner (2000).

Pension reform creates a transition gap in social security that needs to be financed in the short run but it also creates a chance of achieving important longer-run economic goals especially in reducing claims on the state budget in the future and in encouraging savings growth. Budget savings occur because without reform the social security funding gap would have to be financed; for social and political reasons there is no choice, and some other expenditure would be crowded out. But with reform the need for subsidy declines. In terms of its short-run financing the existence of privatisation revenues makes matters easier. Paradoxically Poland's relatively slow (in comparison to most other countries in the region) pace of privatisation helps. It is worth adding that if the pension reform had not been introduced privatisation revenues would have been used to finance other expenditures, probably ending up mainly as current consumption. Savings would also have been lower but the pension reform and the funding gap it creates help turn public savings into private savings. Without reform savings would most probably decrease.

THE NEW PENSIONS FUNDS MARKET

From April 1999 it began to be possible to allocate pensions contributions across two accounts and the option of putting some money into the new 'second pillar' accounts was quickly taken up. By the end of 199 some 21 pension funds operated and had attracted 9 million individual investors with a contributions flow equivalent to 1.5% to 2% of GDP. It turns out that some 60% of Poles in the 31 to 50 years age bracket had joined a pension fund. Of these, 90% of accounts were opened in the 10 largest funds. In 1999 funds asset amounted in all to zł2.5 billion ($600 million) rising to zł5.6 billion ($1.3 billion) by May 2000 with around 30% invested on the stock exchange. It was projected that assets would jump to zł 13 billion (some $3 billion) by the end of the year 2000. This fast growth is because of individual voluntary decisions to switch part of pension contributions to the new 'second pillar' funds. As this special feature works its way out, future growth in contributions will be driven by demography alone. It is also worth noting a peculiar feature of the 'second pillar' funds – they will receive contributions without any need to make payments since, for at least 10 years, nobody will retire within the new system. The accumulation of savings in 'second pillar' pension funds could exceed 30% of GDP by the year 2020. In the race to get into the market in 1999 the insurance based funds (thanks to effective and energetic sales agents) did best while banks and investment funds lost out. While 21 open pension funds were licensed in 1999 it remained possible, although perhaps difficult, to enter the market. Since the number of funds is rather large and the market shares of the smaller are very small indeed consolidation is likely.

What do the second pillar funds do with the money paid as contributions? The prevailing investment pattern, especially in the early stage of pension funds' operations, was to spend the vast majority (even 100%) on government bonds.[7] This is the easiest and safest way (as it is perceived) of managing assets. However, this is little more than rolling-over the public debt and that is what the first pillar pension contributions end up being used for. The second pillar should be more about investment and this may be becoming more important already (see Figure 10.3). The aim of the reform is to invest the bulk of contributions money in financial instruments other than government bonds.

POLAND, PENSIONS AND EU ACCESSION

The 1990s' economic transformation has deeply changed the country and its economy, changes that were essential for many reasons, not least in preparing for EU accession. That process is not easy and there are many areas where much remains to be done. In that context the pension reform is a clear plus. It offers better protection for future pensioners and removes what might have been an impossible strain on the state budget. Unlike Poland, many EU countries have not yet implemented any pensions reform despite a pressing need to do so. This means that their pension systems' debt is high and is likely to keep growing in the future (see Roseveare et al., 1996) suggesting that levels of debt as a proportion of GDP are likely to be, in fact, much greater than the famous Maaastricht criteria permitted in the run up to the single currency launch. Public indebtedness in Poland, after pensions reform, is rather low relative to many EU economies and this should work in favour of the Polish economy in due course. In the meantime it is a point that needs to be promoted in accession negotiations.

Figure10.3. Polish pension funds' investments in 1999 (million złoty)

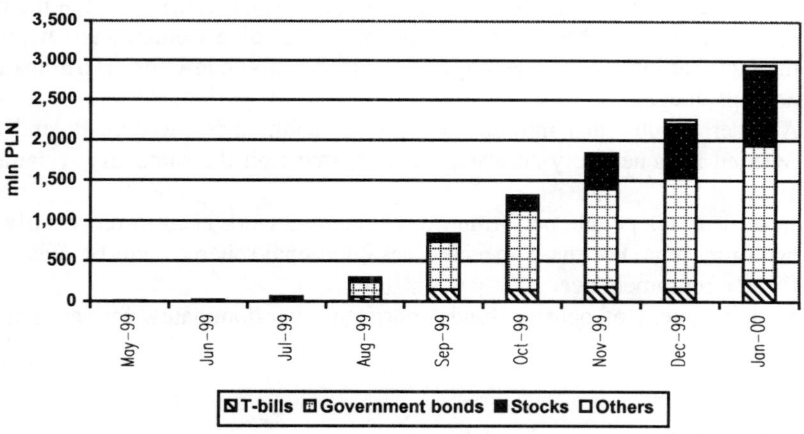

Source: UNFE.

CONCLUSIONS

Pension reform takes the Polish economy into a new stage of development beyond 'transition' and the new system will work in favour of Poland in the decades ahead. The Polish success here was due to the coexistence of a number of helpful factors in the second half of the 1990s. They included, in particular, a still favourable demography, fast economic growth, the availability of privatisation revenues, public support and a political window of opportunity. The chance for reform in this sensitive area was not lost. The experience of many other countries shows that this is not so common. Policy makers are always tempted to postpone reforms but, in the case of pensions, prevarication is the worst possible policy.

NOTES

1 Recently a group of academics and pension system experts urged EU politicians to press ahead with pension reform, see Fondazione Rodolfo Debenedetti (2000).
2 Exact numbers are not known since there was no advance registration of eligibility to early retirement.
3 Fertility rates were above 2 until the end of the 1980s with a maximum of almost 2.5 in 1983. In end-1990s it was below 1.5.
4 This was a clear failure although without any short term destructive effects. These may come when the first people (women) start retiring within the new system from 2009. More and more people – including women – are aware of the fact that lower retirement age for women is a window for discrimination, not a privilege.
5 Another country that introduced the same solution is Sweden. Poland and Sweden launched very similar pension systems on the same day, 1 January 1999.
6 In some cases people performing very onerous work need to retire early for health reasons. For these special cases additional schemes will be created to finance retirement age.
7 Such a pattern of pension funds' portfolio also dominates, for instance, in Hungary.

REFERENCES

Chlon, A., Góra, M. and Rutkowski, M. (1999), 'Shaping pension reform in Poland: security through diversity', *Pension Reform Primer*, SP Discussion Paper no. 9923, Washington, DC: World Bank

Chlon, A. and Tidner, G. (2000), *Polish Pension Model,* mimeo.

Fondazione Rodolfo Debenedetti (2000), *An Appeal to President Prodi 'European citizens should be informed about the long-term sustainability of their pension systems'*, Milan.

Góra, M. (2000), *Polish Approach to Pension System*, Paris: OECD.

Góra, M. and Rutkowski, M. (eds) (1997), *Security through Diversity*, Warsaw: Office of the Government Plenipotentiary for Social Security Reform.

Góra, M. and Rutkowski, M. (1998), 'The quest for pension reform: Poland's security through diversity', *Pension Reform Primer*, SP Discussion Paper no. 9815, Washington, DC: World Bank; extended version with same title, William Davidson Institute, Working Paper no. 286.

Góra, M. and Rutkowski, M. (2000), 'New old-age pension system in Poland', *Spectrum*, no. 2, pp. 11–14.

Holzmann, R. (2000), 'The World Bank approach to pension reform' *International Social Security Review,* 53 (1), pp. 11–34.

Palmer, E. (1998), *The Swedish Pension Reform Model – Framework and Issues,* mimeo.

Palacios, R. and Pallares-Mirrales, M. (2000), *International Patterns of Pension Provisions*, Washington, DC: World Bank.

Roseveare, D., Leibfritz, W., Fore, D. and Wurzel, E. (1996), *Ageing Populations, Pension Systems and Government Budgets: Simulations for 20 OECD Countries*, Economics Department Working Papers no. 168, Paris: OECD.

World Bank (1994), *Averting the Old Age Crisis*, New York: Oxford University Press.

11. Decentralisation, regional development and regional policies

Grzegorz Gorzelak

REGIONAL HISTORICAL HERITAGE AND TRANSFORMATION TRAJECTORIES

The transformation

In the 1960s and 1970s highly developed countries started a process of restructuring, which led to a shift from industrial economic structures to the contemporary post-industrial or information economies. The countries of 'real socialism' were well insulated from these changes. Until the end of the socialist system they pursued the industrial (or Fordist) development path which, in due course, generated economic difficulties that could not be resolved. Those economic systems, unable to restructure themselves, collapsed.

Many analyses of post-socialist transformation exist (see, for example, De Melo et al., 1997; Woo et al., 1998; World Bank 1996). These studies seem, however, to overlook the fact that the post-socialist transformation initiated in 1989 in Poland and in other countries of Central Europe resembles the beginning of structural changes which took place in the more developed economies some 20 years ago. This is both a delayed and an accelerated restructuring and one occurring in different conditions. It is helpful in this context to 'demythologise' the post-socialist transformation, remove it from its ideological underpinnings (although this dimension should not be entirely overlooked), and regard it instead as a normal process of technological and organisational change, albeit one performed later than would have happened if Central Europe (and other socialist countries) had been incorporated earlier into an open global economy (Gorzelak, 1996).

As a result of this process some segments of the Polish economy are beginning to show the characteristics of a new development model, that of knowledge-intensive in lieu of resource-intensive development. Moreover, due to the international opening of the Polish economy the impact of universal phenomena such as globalisation, de-industrialisation changed location criteria and decentralisation, are becoming much more manifest.

The two latter phenomena have a particularly important spatial significance. Contemporary innovations in the information economy are 'light': they do not weigh much but cost a great deal. The location of innovative activity does not depend on the existence of minerals, sea harbours, abundant labour resources; what matters is the quality, efficiency and reliability of production factors. Cities and regions actively shape the conditions of economic activity. They are also becoming entrepreneurial entities competing globally for capital and must provide structures supporting innovation, a superbly qualified workforce as well as the best living conditions.

Along with changes in the broader economy administrative decentralisation is taking place, supported by regionalist movements (very often built on a sense of separate ethnic and cultural identity) and 'localism' is being revived.

The heritage

Spatial processes are a long time in the making. The physical features of any space, its topography, climate, water conditions and so on, change in cycles lasting hundreds of years. Human action may change those features quickly only on a small scale (for example dams on a river, urban structures, new agricultural plantations). The spatial distribution of socio-economic features also has a long heritage (for instance the settlement network of Europe had already been shaped in the Middle Ages) even though socio-economic processes are considerably more flexible than physical and natural phenomena.

Most of the regional studies conducted in Poland identify a strong impact of historical factors on currently observable socio-economic spatial patterns. The contemporary shape of Polish socio-economic space dates back many hundreds of years. Since the very beginning of Poland's history a west-east division determined different development paths for the two parts of the country.

In the most general dimension the Vistula river is the main line of division separating Poland's more developed western territories from the less developed eastern part of the country. Territorial differences in Poland reach back long before the partitions and occupation of the late eighteenth, nineteenth and early twentieth centuries, to the first wave of urban development between the thirteenth and fifteenth centuries. This wave brought from the West to Poland *locatio civitas* under the Magdeburg law and its variants, which determined the spatial pattern of several cities created at that time. In addition, the adoption of a specific agrarian regime gave a specific shape to villages. This urban pattern of

Poland was modified by the nineteenth century industrialisation of Polish cities which was also much more intensive on the territories west of the Vistula.

The nineteenth century deepened already existing divisions not only by uneven industrialisation and infrastructure development but also through the administration of Polish territories by the three states: Russia, Prussia and Austria. Poland lost its independence in the last quarter of the eighteenth century and regained it as late as 1918. Whatever can be said about the hardships suffered by Poles under Prussian rule, it must be admitted that those territories were part of a European state which was undergoing fast modernisation and in which the rule of law was preserved, notwithstanding particular cases of abuse. Consequently, despite their peripheral location in the German state, the regions of *Wielkopolska* (Greater Poland) and *Pomerania* enjoyed rapid modernisation processes, and the Polish population lived under conditions of respect for law, work, thrift and the increase of personal wealth; that is, values facilitating capitalist growth. Paradoxically, it is perhaps the political, cultural and economic pressure exerted by the occupying state which contributed in *Wielkopolska* to an even stronger consolidation of Polish society and Polish economy in that region, which was able to protect itself against the German economy despite the state's strong support of the latter. Those values also resulted in a more orderly spatial planning.

The situation on Polish territories annexed by Russia was substantially different. Those territories were under the strong influence of Asian civilisation and were administered in a way typical of it. The bureaucracy was poorly remunerated, inefficient and operated by often very corrupt czarist officials. Although, at least in some cases, this corruption sometimes softened the Russian occupation, it had a clearly demoralising effect on society. Polish territories situated on the western outskirts of the czarist empire were in a way a bridge between Russia and Europe, and they took a clear advantage of this location rent, enjoying relatively good conditions for economic development. The most spectacular example is Łódź (textiles) but it was also true to a lesser extent for the Dąbrowa coal basin (bordering Upper Silesia, at that time belonging to Prussia), Częstochowa (metallurgy), Żyrardów (textiles, light industries) and Warsaw (diversified industries) – all cities lying west of the Vistula.

The differentiated developmental conditions of the three territories, which in 1918 joined to form the independent Polish state, left behind deep traces in the level of economic development, infrastructure (roads, railways), the degree of urbanisation, the legal system, business – supporting and civil institutions, the education and attitudes of the population and the cultural landscape. The Second Republic managed to integrate the Polish territory composed of the three different parts and to undertake two major investment efforts: constructing a sea harbour in Gdynia (which gave Poland direct access to the sea, since Gdańsk, officially a free city, was in reality dominated by Germany) and launching a major regional development project around the so-called central industrial district. The latter project was based on an approach to regional development which was exceptionally innovative, even until today, involving integrated regional planning, complementarity of industries and other activities, as well as the joint action of state and private investors. World War II disrupted that strategic endeavour, although its first period (1935–39) had an impact that can still be seen on the industrial map of Poland (Mielec – machinery and transport equipment; Stalowa Wola – metallurgy and heavy machines; Dębica – chemical and rubber plants; Świdnik – aviation industry).

After World War II Poland's borders were shifted westwards at the expense of eastern territories absorbed by the former USSR under the terms of the Yalta treaty. The newly acquired territories were much better equipped with technical infrastructure and a dense network of relatively modern towns and villages. Sociological and ethnographic research carried out on those territories immediately after the war and repeated in 1956 revealed a considerable maladjustment of the existing material base – not only in rural areas, but also in urban areas – to the technical attitudes and customs of the population repatriated from the East. For many years the new inhabitants of the western and northern areas of Poland had to adjust to the material environment, as well as to the natural and cultural landscapes. They also had to adjust this environment to themselves and their requirements. This resulted largely in the degradation of the material base but at the same time in the rapid technological and cultural advancement of the new inhabitants of these territories.

In post-war communist Poland the state officially pursued a policy of equalising interregional differences. However in practice a constant concentration of economic development could be observed in the biggest urban and industrial agglomerations, and the western part of the country's investment effort mainly targeted areas which had already started on the road to industrial development as well as newly established centres for natural resources extraction, such as the Legnica–Głogów–Lubin copper basin in the south-west, sulphur extraction and processing near Tarnobrzeg (in the south-east), brown coal mines and electricity plants in Konin (centre), Bełchatów (centre) and Turoszów (south-west). For almost four decades Upper Silesia (the Katowice region) concentrated over 20% of all capital formation outlays and provided a similar share of national GDP. However those processes did not overcome the division of Poland into two parts: western and eastern, the latter continuing to be referred to, somewhat disparagingly, as 'Poland B'.

In summary the historical differentiation of the former and present Polish territories can be described as follows (Gorzelak, 1998):

- territories situated west of the Vistula (basically west of the Gdańsk-Kraków line) developed under a strong Western influence and undoubtedly constituted a part of Western Europe;
- territories situated east of the line between Vilnius and Lwów (the so-called Huntington line, see Huntington, 1995) dividing Slavic Christendom into two parts, the western (Roman–Catholic) and eastern (Orthodox), under the influence of the East;
- 'transitory' territories, those between these two historical borders, in which the influences of Western and Eastern Europe intertwined and jointly shaped social, economic and spatial structures.

Transformation trajectories

The experience of other countries across the world proves that overcoming the entrenched spatial disparities of many centuries, even if possible, can be extremely difficult. Backward regions are capable of making up the distance lost only if they can be perceived to be interesting to those who dispose of capital, particularly for large companies and especially multinational corporations (MNCs). Recent EU experience shows that even considerable public expenditures may not result in any distinct developmental acceleration in those areas that are not sufficiently attractive in terms of location. This is particularly true in the contemporary information-driven globalised economy in which only a limited number of localities may enjoy dynamic development. The most successful localities are those few which attract activities like financial services, head office functions of MNCs, R&D, science-intensive production; in short, types of economic activity that generate a wider control over economic activity. Regions which host labour-intensive branches, the consumers of innovation created in other regions, are becoming more and more dependent on decisions taken elsewhere – in the few cores of the global economy.

A traditional phenomenon of polarisation between regions on grounds of quantitative differences in production factors is thus replaced by a process of segmentation in which spatial differences become more rigid and persistent, since the qualitative differences in innovation potential are more difficult to overcome. In the industrial economy it was easier to overcome historical backwardness especially if regions had natural resources which became, through technological innovation, an economic asset. This seems to be more difficult in the post-industrial economy in which natural resources are less important (if important at all) and in which qualitative features such as those mentioned earlier, which are especially lacking in poor, backward and peripheral regions, replace traditional 'quantitative' factors.

This may sound like a kind of historical determinism and to some extent that may be so: yes, in general terms in the modern information economy history seems to have a stronger impact on the development trajectory of a region than in the former industrial paradigm of economic development. However, there are several examples of countries (for example Ireland) and regions, such as South Carolina in the USA (with its core in the 'research triangle'), Languedoc–Roussillon in France (and especially Toulouse) which were able of overcome traditional backwardness and move on to a fast track of growth and structural change. A closer examination of such cases reveals that they fulfilled two conditions. First, they were embraced by macro-spatial changes, such as US investment in modern branches, accompanied by assistance from the EC and later the EU (Ireland) the North–South ('frost belt'–'sun belt') shift, or the opening of new markets (as in the case of the western regions of Central European countries). Second, such territorial entities prepared themselves well in advance to accommodate externally induced change. If the preparatory stage was missing they were not able to utilise external positive impulses and missed the development chances coming from outside. The last condition is of special importance. Not *all* territorial entities (or economic agents, enterprises and individuals) can take advantage of new conditions. Only those that make some effort to prepare do well. Those regions that are either unable or unwilling to undertake adaptive actions in advance have to go through a restructuring process often referred to as a J-curve trajectory (Bradshaw and Stenning, 1999), which means that there are some indispensable costs of restructuring and adaptation which have to be borne if sound foundations for future development are to be created. Simplifying somewhat, Poland since 1993 was able to reach and sustain a high rate of growth because it went through shock therapy in 1990–91. This was not so in many other post-socialist countries which tried to avoid restructuring costs and have not achieved fast growth or have even found themselves in deep and persistent economic decline.

Four trajectories of regional transformation in post-socialist countries can be identified (Gorzelak, 1998). Regions may be either *leaders*, *winners*, *losers* or *laggards* as follows:

(a) *Leaders* – regions able to proceed along a rather steep J-curve and able to prepare themselves for the new paradigm of the information economy. In Poland these are: Warsaw, Kraków, Poznań, Wrocław, Szczecin and the Tri-City (Gdańsk–Sopot–Gdynia);

(b) *Winners* – regions that took advantage of external macro-spatial change: it may seem that they do not have to sacrifice much but nevertheless they face a 'wider' J-curve. They are the western regions of Poland where entrepreneurs did well out of transborder trade, taking advantage of the German market but rather than invest they turned profits into luxurious consumption;

(c) *Losers* – regions (like Łódź) that have to go through a J-curve, pay the economic and social costs of restructuring and adaptation to new conditions. However, some such regions like Upper Silesia have, due to political pressure exerted by workers, been able to postpone this.

(d) *Laggards* – regions that are to some extent 'sentenced' to backwardness, since they have little to restructure and no impulses may come to them from outside. In Poland they are the eastern regions, where rapid advancement and growth is much more possible on the local than on the regional scale.

Each type can be found in post-socialist countries. Poland, at least in the first part of the 1990s, had the greatest persistence and determination in following the J-curve trajectory. Other papers in this volume describe how it was the first country to fall into recession and the first to achieve positive growth (from 1992). In the later 1990s Poland achieved the highest rate of economic growth among transforming economies. The recent (1998–99) GDP growth slow-down may be attributed to abandoning from 1993–94 the restructuring effort, which paralleled the negative effects of the international situation, such as the collapse of the eastern (post-Soviet) markets and slowdown in Western Europe. Since the 'simple reserves' released by the first wave of systemic reforms and structural changes were used up in the early 1990s and no fresh growth impulses were created by new reforms, the slowdown is not unexpected. Many examples of all four types of transformation trajectory can be found in the 1990s in post-communist economies. We discuss some of them in the next section.

POLISH SPATIAL DEVELOPMENTS IN THE 1990s

Towards an 'open economic space'

The 1989 systemic transformation destroyed the COMECON system and opened Poland to the world. For the national economy this process was evident in a radical geographical restructuring of foreign trade (see Blazyca, chapter 13, in this volume for a fuller account). At a 'micro' regional level within the country this 'opening-up' quickly became evident in transborder co-operation and, later, in a highly uneven spatial distribution of foreign capital inflow. Transborder co-operation had varied forms. Initially, it was restricted to trade, primarily to the unofficial trade that mushroomed in certain areas, the result of individual private initiatives reacting to price differences across frontiers. Owing to the fact that purchases made by Germans were approximately two times greater than the aggregate purchases of all the other neighbours of Poland the influence of informal cross-border trade was in the 1990s much stronger along the western border than along the east or south. Cross-border trade became an important development factor for some towns, creating jobs in retail and wholesale trade and services, providing profits for businesses and contributing through local taxes and fees to municipal budgets. In the late 1990s the role of cross-border trade gradually fell, due in part to the appreciation of the Polish currency, a levelling of prices, disturbances in the economies of Poland's eastern neighbours, growing competition from the German side and administrative restrictions.

More enduring economic ties in exports, economic co-operation, influx of foreign capital and Polish outward investment (until now a minor factor) were markedly stronger features along the western border than the eastern or southern ones. These differences are visible not only in the intensity of normal economic activity but also in the activities of the 12 Euroregions created along Polish borders.[1] All four western Euroregions (Pomerania, Pro Europa Viadrina, Sprewa-Nysa-Bóbr and Nysa, the last comprising also Czech municipalities) have a broader range of activities than those on the eastern and southern borders. To some extent this is due to the greater willingness of German partners to co-operate. Also, as surveys indicate (Gorzelak and Jałowiecki, 1999; Gorzelak et al., 1999), local authorities in the west of Poland are more active and innovative social actors than those in the other parts of the country.

For a few years Polish western regions enjoyed an economic boom from trans-border trade. German 'trade tourists' spent some DM5 billion yearly on products which were much cheaper than in Germany, mostly basic commodities, such as food, cigarettes, simple services (also erotic), cheap textiles, leather, carpets, crystal and plastic goods. But since merchants and commodities came from all parts of Poland this meant that a substantial share of incomes generated was exported to other Polish regions. Even so, local border region economies benefited greatly, especially in employment terms. But by the late 1990s it was clear that the 'golden age' of cross-border trade was coming to an end. Price differences between Poland and Germany were slowly being eroded. Meanwhile profits made in previous years were mostly consumed or invested in new homes rather than in business development. Unemployment began to creep up as cross-border trade was reduced, mostly, to petrol, cigarettes and sex. The chances, small though they were, to reinvest profits to create enterprises that could take advantage of German markets and co-operation with German partners were not fully exploited.

By opening its borders Poland's western regions were offered a great development chance. It was utilised only partially. The effort to turn this temporary advantage into a durable competitive advantage was simply too weak. Polish western territories did not move on to the 'high road' of economic trans-border co-operation and may end up on the 'low road' of dependency on stronger and more technologically advanced German partners and competitors (see Krätke, 1997).

The most important form of new international economic ties comes through capital inflow (see Figure 11.1). By the end of 1999 those inflows had exceeded $40 billion. The inflow is distinctly higher in the western part of the country than in the east. German capital, about 12% of the total, is, much more frequently than capital from other countries, invested in small companies located near the border. Non-German capital has different location preferences. It is concentrated in large cities, predominantly in Warsaw (which has approximately 30% of the total).

The opening of Polish space to international co-operation is by no means complete. One factor delaying the process is stagnation in the construction and modernisation of the transport infrastructure. Poland has only about 200 km of motorways and more than 95% of Polish roads are two-way with one lane in each direction. There is a shortage of city by-passes and double level crossings and road surface quality is poor. The major transit route, from Świecko on the border with Germany to Terespol on the border with Belarus, runs through several important towns and cities, Poznań and Warsaw included, which puts a heavy strain on the agglomerations concerned and, of course, slows traffic flows. The tragic and constantly deteriorating state of Polish roads, in relation to rapidly growing needs, is one of the most serious barriers to the further opening of Polish economic space and to its more effective integration with European space.

The condition of Polish railways is a less severe barrier although problems remain. The rail network density is one of the highest in the world but quality and efficiency is relatively low.

On a local scale Polish cities still lack roads, bridges (Warsaw needs at least three new bridges across the Vistula river), by-passes (in Poznań work on a by-pass started in 1998) and modern public transport (metro systems, fast and silent trams). In all, during the 1990s, there was little improvement in overcoming the deficiencies inherited from the previous epoch of delayed urbanisation when the development of 'consumption space' was strongly subordinated to the requirements of 'production space'.

Towards a clean and aesthetic space

In the 1970s and 1980s, southern Poland, along with the southern part of the former GDR and the western part of the Czech Republic, was Europe's centre of pollution production. The region had the highest concentration in Europe of sulphur dioxide, dust and pollutant emissions. The tragic quality of surface water was a consequence of the lack of facilities for the treatment of municipal and industrial waste.

Figure 11.1. Regional concentration of foreign capital companies, 1997

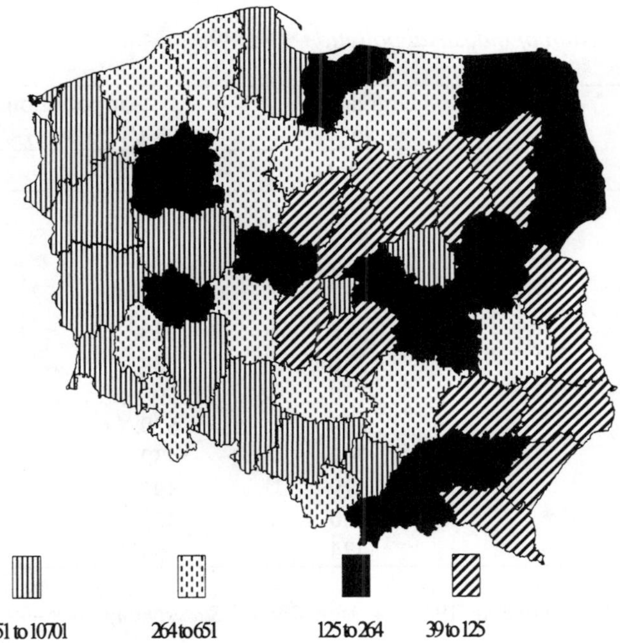

Number of foreign capital companies
1997

The 1990s brought an important, if still greatly inadequate, improvement in the quality of Polish space. This resulted from better environmental policy and changes in the structure and technology of industrial production, to a great extent due to production decline in the most obsolete and usually the most environmentally damaging branches of industry. Some improvement in water purity resulted from agriculture's reduced use of artificial fertilisers and some from local government investment in municipal sewage treatment plants (Warsaw is an infamous exception, the city still lacked appropriate sewage facilities in 1999).

Despite steady improvement the natural environment in many Polish regions remains poor. The most difficult situation is in Upper Silesia, where over 700 dangerous pollutants were still being emitted in the late 1990s (Wódz, 1997). Legally required ecological emission standards are exceeded many times over (ten-fold on average, in some places much more). In Upper Silesia, deaths from cancer are 10% and deaths from heart diseases 20% more frequent than the national average; half of pregnancies are endangered and every tenth birth is premature (Wódz, 1997).

Table 11.1. Emission of industrial pollution, 1985–98

Years	Untreated sewage	Air pollution ('000 tons)	
	(in hm^3)	Dusts	Gases
1985	2,206	1,788	4,933
1988	1,989	1,615	5,193
1989	1,962	1,513	5,113
1990	1,801	1,163	4,115
1991	1,588	923	3,552
1992	1,386	684	3,155
1993	1,170	599	3,001
1994	809	529	2,941
1995	702	432	2,785
1996	619	391	2,672
1997	530	323	2,460
1998	424	255	2,267

Sources: *Roczniki Statystyczne*, 1989–94; *Mały Rocznik Statystyczny*, 1995–99.

The aesthetic value of the landscape, including the man-made landscape, generates a specific form of environmental quality. Poland has experienced some change in this in the 1990s in the emergence of a new utility architecture (modern filling stations, car dealer shops, fast food outlets, shopping malls with huge parking areas) and although they might be considered aesthetically undesirable and unattractive they do change a landscape previously dominated by ugly housing blocks and unattractive industrial plants. Business architecture (office buildings, banks, warehouses) and residential architecture have also changed (luxury apartment blocks are appearing) in addition to high security neighbourhoods of exclusive detached houses. The architecture of large residential developments (housing schemes) has improved. However, even those changes, making the country more similar to the 'West', are still tainted by the patterns of 'real socialism' where greyish colour and rectangular shape dominated the landscape and the devastation caused by the primitive architecture of the previous system has not been overcome.

Transformation processes have not led to sufficiently deep changes in urban planning. Because of the neglected infrastructure the functionality of space in

Polish cities has not improved, many new buildings were chaotically placed in the urban structure, disrupting the local spatial order (a classical example is the chaos of the new business architecture in Warsaw where the availability of land, and not any urban plan, decides on the location of particular buildings). Nevertheless in general and due to the activity of local governments the infrastructure has been considerably enhanced.

Towards a diversified economic space

One of the features of Polish space inherited from 'real socialism' was its uniformity in aesthetic, functional and structural terms. On the one hand, the doctrine of speedy industrialisation produced many inefficient industrial establishments often built in regions with hardly any industrial tradition. Though at one time this was viewed positively in terms of a regional policy that aimed at 'equalising' development and generating employment, raising also the 'civilisational level' of those poorly developed regions, this policy did not bring sound effects: the industrial plants were still less efficient than similar establishments built in more industrially advanced locations and during the first stage of post-socialist restructuring they were usually the first to go bankrupt. On the other hand the underdevelopment of the social and municipal infrastructure made living conditions in even heavily industrialised regions hardly better than in poorer ones.

Poland entered the transformation period in 1989–90 with relatively small interregional disparities – only the Warsaw region had a much higher level of GDP per capita than the national average (as much as two times greater). In the least developed regions GDP per capita was never below two-thirds of the national average and in the highest developed regions GDP per capita exceeded the national average by more than 20%. Transformation generated interesting processes of regional diversification although formally in statistical terms regional disparities have not increased considerably during the 1990s. Generally speaking their dynamics might be summarised as follows:

1. In the period of so-called 'transformation shock' (1989–90):
   - less developed voivodships improved their situation in relative terms, they suffered an economic contraction that was less severe than in the better developed regions. This resulted from a higher share of (individual) farming in the structure of their economies which 'cushioned' them from the recession of the early 1990s brought about mainly by the restructuring of industry;
   - the urbanised and industrialised regions faced a sharp output decline caused by market reorientation and the need to adapt to new conditions.

2. In 1991–92 the first stage transformation tendencies were reinforced:
   - voivodships with a large share of individual farming saw a relatively strong GDP recovery;
   - those with a large share of state-owned agriculture (north-western regions) noted a decline in GDP similar to some underdeveloped regions, for example those with significant tourism (such as north-eastern and south-eastern parts) and in some of those regions acute social problems (mass unemployment) appeared;
   - the majority of the regions with large agglomerations experienced a further decline in GDP caused by industrial recession.

3. In the period of recovery (from 1992–93 through to the late 1990s) the following pattern emerged:
   - less developed voivodships proved to be relatively less capable of dynamising their development;
   - regions with large agglomerations facing restructuring of traditional industries noted relatively slower GDP growth;
   - regions with diversified economies were in a better situation (large agglomerations, efficient farming), as well as those which underwent successful economic restructuring (for example post-state farm regions, which were able to reduce exceptionally high unemployment rates, pushing them down from 30% to over 20% – still high, but considerably lower).

These regional trajectories may perhaps be interpreted within the J-curve framework outlined earlier. Backward, rural regions proceeded along a more shallow ‘J-curve’, and the more industrialised ones a steeper one. The former did not have much to restructure, their agriculture was not (and still is not) orientated towards the market (it is mainly a self-sufficient subsistence agriculture), and therefore market changes did not greatly affect their economies. A ‘restructuring price’ was not paid but a ‘development price’ will be paid since the capacity of these regions to sustain strong growth is rather limited. The steeper J-curve, the trajectory of the industrialised regions, incurred higher restructuring costs (bankruptcies, unemployment, temporary poverty), but enabled those regions to enjoy a ‘development premium’ since restructuring passed a critical point.

Figure 11.2. Regional GDP per capita, 1996

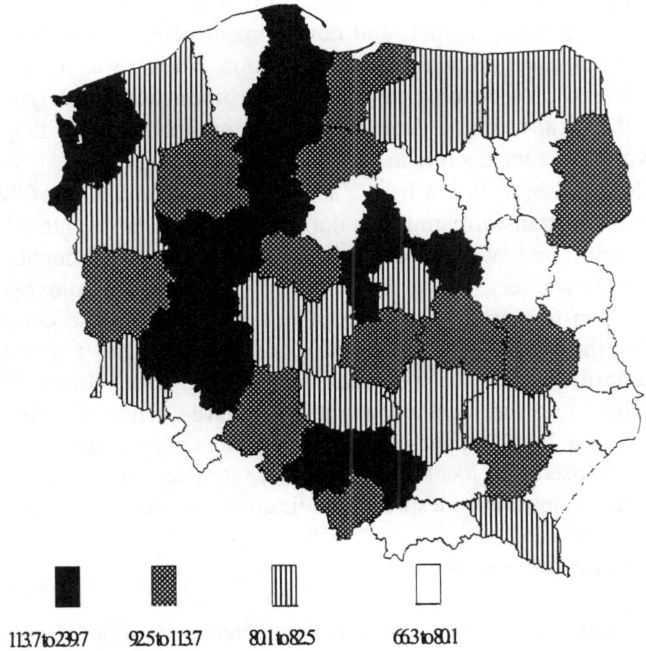

Regional GDP per inhabitant, 1996 (national average = 100)

Case studies. Taking or missing development chances: Żary and Nowa Sól

- Żary (40,000 inhabitants) was a town where economic activity was based on textile and wood industries. In 1990 the major local employers went bankrupt. Unemployment soared to over 20% and the local budget fell into deficit. The local authorities refused to bail out bankrupt firms, favouring instead the creation of opportunities for new start-ups or for fundamental restructuring (with privatisation) of the old enterprises. The first large state-owned industrial enterprise to go through bankruptcy procedures was in Żary, somthing local leaders take some pride in. Since 1992 several new local business-supporting institutions were created: loan funds, a foundation for entrepreneurship, a small business support centre, a business incubator. The town hosts a genuinely local company producing technologically advanced electric equipment, which is listed on the Warsaw stock market, has a daughter company in Mexico and has relocated some of its production to Lithuania (to take advantage of lower labour costs). Unemployment, after reaching a peak of over 20% in 1990 was cut to 8% in 1999. Several small and medium-sized firms prosper, and development perspectives in the late 1990s looked optimistic. Since the transformation in Żary was already to a great extent based on technologically advanced production (largely export-orientated), the local business community looks optimistically to the future with little worry over the decline in cross-border trade.

- Nowa Sól, located some 20 km from Żary and with a population of 42,000, at the beginning of transformation was dominated by two large enterprises: a metals industry plant with a large share of military production and employing 4000 workers, and a textile factory with 8000 employees. The first stage of transformation shook the prosperity of both these companies since they lost their traditional Soviet markets. Their managers together with the city authorities tried to postpone restructuring. Both firms became heavily indebted and the local budget assigned large sums to assist them, guaranteeing their loans (spent mostly on an excessive wages bill). Both firms are now closed, the local unemployment rate exceeded 30% in 1999, social pathologies became widespread and future prospects much darker.

Losing regions: Łódż and Katowice

The development paths of two major regions dominated by traditional industries (Upper Silesia and Łódż) may also be instructive. The Łódż region, a traditional centre of textile and clothing industries from the nineteenth century, seems to provide, at least until the late 1990s, a modestly positive example of industrial restructuring. After lifting restrictions on foreign trade in 1990, the Polish textile and clothing industries became suddenly exposed to vigorous international competition, especially from the Far East and Turkey. Moreover, traditional foreign markets in other former COMECON countries collapsed. As a result those industries, concentrated in the Łódż region, had to cut production. No one came to the defence of the politically weak, mostly female workforce in textiles. In comparison with other branches, those industries were of minor national significance. Łódż was left to itself and this isolation was one of the factors underpinning the mobilisation of regional and local elites. Łódż managed, at least partially, to revitalise its economy although that recovery remained, at the end of the 1990s, still rather shallow, relying on demand for simple and inexpensive textiles and on unskilled labour. The collapse of the Russian market after 1998 was a serious blow.

Łódż region is still dominated by traditional industries, which produce for undemanding markets. This makes it vulnerable to changes in demand and competition from other simple textiles centres. Instead of being satisfied with recent restructuring processes, Łódż should search for chances in more modern and more advanced sectors which would be based on existing potential. Instead of providing simple and cheap garments, Łódż should strive to become the Central European centre for clothing design and fashion. It could also expand its existing potential (there are two medical universities and several other research institutes in medical and biological sciences) to become a centre for medical and pharmaceutical research. This development strategy seems much more promising and durable in the innovation-driven open competitive economy than maintaining the traditional profile of a textile producing region.

Throughout the whole socialist period, and even earlier, Upper Silesia was the main industrial region of Poland. It consumed some 25% of national investment industrial and provided some 22% of national industrial output. 'Black gold' (coal) extraction peaked in 1979, reaching 201 million tons. At the beginning of the 1990s the region accounted for almost 50% of all cars manufactured in Poland, over 56% of steel, 53% of rolled products, 100% of tin and lead, 25% of domestic industrial production and 20% of all Polish goods exported abroad. The region was, and remains, a typical coal-and-steel industrial region, with social and education structures biased towards heavy industry, a heavily polluted environment and an infrastructure that is relatively well developed but badly run down (see Wódz, 1994).

Upper Silesia produces too much coal (117 million tons in 1998) too expensively. Poland consumes less than 80 million tons of coal per annum and demand continues to decline due to rationalisation of energy consumption and a shift to other energy sources (mostly natural gas and oil). Each ton of coal extracted needed in the late 1990s a subsidy of $4. Exports of coal are especially heavily subsidised ($12 per ton). The total accumulated public debt of Silesian coal mines reached $4 billion in 1998 and in 1999 alone mines were expected to generate a loss of almost $1 billion. This is because there is no political power in the country able to close inefficient mines and lay-off thousands of miners who are the only income earners in their families. Employment in coal mines has a 'social' and not an economic character. Efforts to cut coal production and employment have been limited. Recently miners were offered generous redundancy payments (up to $10,000), but since too much money was lost in coal production there is not enough money to satisfy all those who apply for these payments. Employment decline was too slow to return the industry to profitability. Up to the end of the 1990s there was no coal sector privatisation. The slower than economically justified decline of industrial employment in the Katowice region is due to the political power of workers and their trade unions. This is based on at least three elements: the large number of people involved and the electoral consequences that would follow; the concentration of large numbers of workers in a small geographical space which facilitates political mobilisation;

and 'energy blackmail' (more than 50% of energy is generated from black coal), which can become pretty dangerous in the middle of a cold winter. Due to high dependency on coal, even high stocks would be not sufficient if supplies were halted for a long period of time.

All the restructuring programmes for the Katowice region formulated by consecutive governments (for example the so-called Markowski plan prepared during the post-communist–peasant coalition 1993–97 and the programme of the 1997 AWS–UW coalition) have assumed that creating jobs in new enterprises must *precede* the rationalisation of production and employment in declining sectors. This approach appears to be misguided. The example of the Katowice region suggests that activity in declining sectors should be sharply reduced before restructuring processes are started. This is indispensable for reconstructing infrastructure, diminishing ecological hazards (also outside Silesia), diversifying skills and vocational qualifications, restoring and improving the cities and towns of the region. Modern industries would then enter the core of the region and not limit new activity to the fringe of the industrial region (as happens now). Moreover new investment in Upper Silesia, mainly in the automobile industry, does not create a demand for workers made redundant in the traditional sectors. New companies create demand for skilled personnel and drain experienced engineers from coal mines and steel mills, thus making the restructuring process of these traditional industries even more difficult.

The leaders

As in other countries, contemporary Poland is experiencing a new development where cities prosper as centres of academic and scientific life, seats of financial institutions and specialised services, or sites of MNCs' headquarters. The Polish leaders in this respect are Warsaw, Poznań, Wrocław, Gdańsk, Kraków, Łódż and to a lesser degree, Gdańsk–Gdynia–Sopot on the Baltic coast. These regions also constituted the core locations in the previous system. In a natural way, they took advantage of the fact that their features complied with new requirements: economic diversification, a high level of investment, and proximity (by means of modern transport and telecommunications) to sources of capital. The relatively high qualifications and the entrepreneurial spirit of the population coupled with well-developed academic and research structures created the foundations for prosperity (see Table 11.2).

The laggards

As noted in our opening remarks Poland has its very clearly marked periphery – its eastern part, 'Poland B" or the 'Eastern Wall'. They are the least developed, relatively sparsely populated rural areas with a poorly developed urban system and infrastructure. Such areas are crossed by main East–West transportation routes and no major artery exists, nor is any envisaged, which would connect them in a North–South direction. Transformation processes are relatively slow, the level of education low and they do not attract foreign investors.

During the transformation the eastern regions of Poland displayed specific trajectories. In the first period – the overall recession – they improved their position in relative terms (measured by GDP per inhabitant) since they noted smaller losses than the country as a whole and the more developed regions. In the second phase of transition the eastern regions, due to lack of investment, grew much more slowly (see Table 11.3).

This pattern may be easily interpreted in the J-curve approach. The eastern regions had a 'shallow' or 'wide' J-curve, while the urbanised regions had a steep J-curve experience. This shape of the curve induced lower restructuring costs – but did not allow for rapid growth afterwards.

Towards a self-governing space

Poland was the only post-socialist country that by the end of the 1990s had thoroughly reformed its administrative structure and decentralised. The restoration of territorial self-government at the local level, launched as early as 1990, was a momentous systemic change. There is little exaggeration in the statement that local communities and private enterprise were the main actors upon which the success of Polish transformation was built. The establishment of territorial self-government at the *gmina* level (the basic unit of administrative division: around 2500 exist) made it possible for local elites to generate initiatives independent of central government. This created opportunities for the liberation of resourcefulness, energy and enterprise. Local elites of small entrepreneurs, local government officers, managers of local state enterprises could for the first time in the post-war period act independently. Local government became a school for civic education, and social activity, together with local government actions, contributed to laying the foundations of a civic society.

The capacity for local government action is however strongly varied spatially. The legacy of history has had a distinct impact on the income potential of local budgets. Belonging to an opulent region ensures 'immunity from poverty' while, on the other hand, even in a poor region, thanks to activity and efficiency of action, local success is possible, though less frequent and more difficult to achieve.

Table 11.2. The leading centres in Poland's transformation, late 1990s

Features	Warsaw	Poznań	Kraków	Wrocław	Łódż	Gdańsk
Population, city ('000)	1,625	580	741	639	812	756
Population, urban region ('000)[a]	3,266	1,444	1,937	1,546	2,035	1,225
Working people/1000 pop.	429	389	372	327	302	340
University education/1000 pop.	157	117	126	115	84	97
University institutions.	118	30	38	21	24	24
Students/1000 pop.	80	115	110	92	53	51
Scientific degrees granted[b]	21.4	11	14.4	11.3	8.5	4.6
Telephones/1000 pop.	456	312	334	304	339	310
Computer servers (1996)	164	22	58	57	23	-
Average wage, złotys[c]	1,818	1,413	1,337	1,272	1,173	1,319
Housing cost per sq.m	3,700	2,300	2,950	2,500	1,350	2,500
Bank headquarters/1000 pop.	2.83	1.03	0.68	0.47	0.37	0.42
Employment in finance/1000 pop.	2,612	1,680	1,281	1,394	1,143	1,100
Infrastructure outlays/inhabitant	599	334	190	144	263	380
Distance to western border, kms	467	176	390	158	365	330
Distance to international airport, km[e]	0,0	305/264	342	346/328	142	329
Number of foreign investors[f]	255	69	55	51	60	68
Direct foreign investment/inhabitant[g]	5.89	2.58	1.49	2.36	1.17	1.88
Three-star and better hotels/1000 pop.	12	19	0.019	0.027	0	0.011
Number of theatres	29	10	14	16	14	8
Twin cities	6	8	20	3	3	13

Notes: [a]In 30 km radius. [b]As per cent of those granted nationally. [c]In old voivodship. [d]Spent by city authorities. [e]To Warsaw/Berlin. [f]With equity over $1 m. [g] $'000.

Source: Jałowiecki, 1999

Table 11.3. GDP growth in the eastern regions of Poland (1996 constant prices)

Regions	Absolute growth rates (earlier year =100)			Regional and national growth rates compared (Poland = 100)		
	1990/ 1986	1992/ 1990	1996/ 1992	1990/ 1986	1992/ 1990	1996/ 1992
Biała Podlaska	97	124	110	104	130	89
Białystok	82	103	103	87	108	83
Chełm	107	115	91	114	121	73
Krosno	85	98	125	90	103	102
Lublin	93	99	130	99	104	105
Łomża	98	116	113	104	122	91
Olsztyn	106	97	113	113	102	91
Przemyśl	94	105	124	100	111	99
Rzeszów	79	110	113	84	116	91
Siedlce	99	117	112	105	123	90
Suwałki	112	85	119	128	89	96
Zamość	100	108	112	106	114	90
Poland	*94*	*95*	*124*	*100*	*100*	*100*

Source: Czyżewski, 1998.

The activity and efficiency of local governments is strongly varied spatially. research indicates (see Gorzelak and Jałowiecki, 1998; and Gorzelak et al., 1999) that the most efficient are those local governments in the western and northern regions and in Wielkopolska. Northern and southern territories were regained from Germany after World War II and settled by migrants from the eastern territories lost to the Soviet Union as well as the overpopulated central part of the country. It can be argued that this mix of population, younger than in other regions, resulted in more active and dynamic local communities, as opposed to the stagnant, rural communities in the southern and eastern parts of Poland. The western regions demonstrate even better local government performance than the northern ones. This can be explained by a modernisation effect stimulated by the proximity of a richer and better developed neighbour – Germany. Wielkopolska has traditionally been the best organised and most orderly region of Poland, and the dynamism of its local governments is not surprising.

The historical heritage has therefore a clear impact on both the wealth of local communities and also on the ability of local elites to manage local affairs and promote locally stimulated development in an open competitive economy.

Despite deficiencies and shortcomings the administrative decentralisation established from 1 January 1999, for the first time in Poland's history, regional self-government at the level of 16 voivodships and restored over 300 sub-regions (abolished in 1975). This appears to be of great importance. The set up creates:

- new regions (16, voivodships, see Figure 11.5) with strong self-government (the regional council) elected in direct elections, presided over by a political leader elected by the regional council, resourced from Warsaw in the form of shares in state taxes and subsidies. Alongside the self-governmental, directly elected authorities exists a parallel administration headed by a governor *wojewód* nominated by the prime minister and responsible for implementing state policies (maintaining law and order and other general obligations). One consequence of building larger voivodships assuming many of the responsibilities previously discharged by national government is that central government should become smaller but stronger;
- over 300 fully self-governing districts (*powiaty*) which assume some responsibilities previously performed by the old voivodships (such as local roads, education and employment services);
- over 2500 local, self-governmental units (*gminy*), responsible for basic service delivery to the population and the (very) local infrastructure.

The reform will have an important bearing on regional development. First, the regions themselves take on some of the responsibilities previously carried by national government, such as building regional development strategies; implementation of regional labour policy; provision of services of region-wide importance; making international contacts (within the framework set by the foreign ministry). As decentralisation deepens they will also be able to take on new tasks which at present are not carried out at all (for example, creating regional innovation strategies, technology transfer centres, international promotion). However, since the abilities of regional and local political elites are bound to differ, a wider differentiation in the development trajectories of the regions themselves should be expected. The wiser will become more successful and the less able will not cope so well with the challenges of the global competitive economy. This will probably happen in spite of some direct and indirect intervention from the state and the European Union.

Figure 11.3. Regional administative structure from January 1999

REGIONAL POLICIES

For some decades the state's regional policy was more formal than real. Governmental agencies formulated better or worse programmes of regional development but not much was put into practice. In the 1970s, when investment was strong, the arbitrary decisions of central authorities, that is the communist party apparatus, overruled the spatial considerations of planning bodies. A decision of the prime minister or party committee could easily change any regulations in the national spatial plan (the Katowice steel mill, for example, one of the biggest steel mills in Europe, was built in the mid-1970s on the decision of the highest party authorities although it was not mentioned in the spatial plan approved by parliament in 1973). Polish socio-economic space remained under-developed in the 1980s since the collapsing socialist system had a declining ability to foster economic development and therefore once again failed to deal with regional development issues. In the 1990s the liberal approach to economic policy did not leave too much room for regional polices and the weak actions which were undertaken under the rubric 'regional policies' had mainly a reactive and passive character, with interventions only where transformation and industrial decline created grave social problems. Both industrial decline and fast-growing unemployment in several areas (including rural, those dominated by state farms) were dealt with inefficiently.

Since 1990 no single governmental department has been responsible for regional development. The long-term, strategic issues of spatial development were to be dealt with by the central planning office, later (in 1996) transformed into the government's Centre for Strategic Studies (RCSS). Most daily matters related to regional issues, in fact limited to the regions with high unemployment, came to be dealt with by the ministry of labour and social policy which emerged at the beginning of the 1990s as the main governmental agency conducting any explicit regional policy. The Polish agency for regional development (PARR) was created in 1993 and made responsible for managing the part of the Phare-STRUDER programme (see Kozak and Pyszkowski, 1999).

In 1995–98 some progress was made with regard to the state's spatial policy. Major spatial and regional problems were discussed in a 1999 document issued by the RCSS (1999). It stated that during the phase of accelerated growth of the Polish economy, necessary to close the civilisational gap with the Western European countries, interregional differences in Poland would increase. It acknowledged that the few already existing metropolitan centres would become centres of accelerated growth and innovation, becoming the gateways connecting Poland to the global economy. Great stress was put also on environmental issues but within a perspective suggesting that a compromise between economic and environmentalist considerations should be sought and reached, as opposed to 'fundamentalist' standpoints suggesting that Poland should immediately implement a rigorous 'eco-development' strategy.

A similar approach was adopted by the economy ministry which also developed a national strategy for regional development. Taking these two documents together, one may say that in general terms the focus has slowly moved, along with tendencies also evident in the EU (see Bachtler, 1997), from a redistribution-orientated doctrine to an efficiency-orientated one. The national strategy that is emerging will create the foundations for bringing Poland closer to the regional policy requirements of the EU and, in the future, to the EU's rubric for the use of structural funds.

Up to the end of the 1990s no institution responsible for formulating and implementing national regional or spatial policies existed in Poland. Particular departments of central government in fact distribute large public resources among particular regions, but they do this in an unco-ordinated manner. As a result, there is extensive redistribution through the central budget (public revenue accounts for almost 50% of GDP, of which over 60%, that is 30% of GDP, goes through the central budget). In general, richer regions lose and poorer regions gain from this redistribution, but this happens as a result of several sectoral (vertical) policies without much territorial (horizontal) co-ordination (see Owsiak et al., 1998).

New ideas for regional policy began to emerge alongside the decentralisation process at the end of the 1990s. Regional budgets will no doubt be too small to cover all needs and financial flows from the central budget to the regions will be necessary. Strictly speaking the regions do not have their 'own' resources. Their budgets are composed of a share in the national personal income tax collected in a given region, a share of corporate income tax paid by firms located in a given region and a general subsidy, which in practice (in 1999) equalised revenues per capita in all 16 voivodships to a value of around 22 złotys ($5.5). The administrative territorial units at the intermediate level, the districts (*powiaty*), have even less since their incomes are composed of only one stable source, a small share of personal income tax. The communes (*gminy*) are by far the richest units of territorial self-government in Poland since they have their own taxes (the most important ones are on fixed assets, on agricultural land and, in the future, also on property) and they enjoy high shares in state taxes: 27.6% on personal income tax and 5% on corporate income tax. *Gminy* also collect considerable fees and user charges and earn profits on their property.

According to proposals formulated by the government in the future the flows from the central budget to the regions will have two parts: a general subsidy, aimed at levelling total regional differences in revenues per inhabitant and purpose-orientated contracts between regions and the national government. The contracts should permit the co-financing projects of mutual interest between region(s) and the central state (see Gilowska et al., 1999). One can hope that in this way external assistance would fall on fertile socio-economic soil, avoiding the 'external aid dependency syndrome' for long widely observed among the poorer regions of Western Europe and the USA (see also the comments of Orłowski, in chapter 14 of this volume).

The discussion around a model of regional policy adequate for Poland as it approaches EU membership is becoming ever more vivid. Although governmental officials tend to shy away from it, the equity–efficiency dilemma has to be solved albeit in new economic and political conditions. In Poland as elsewhere, politicians prefer not to notice the necessity of efficiency and speak almost entirely about regional equalisation, which is politically less risky (usually, as a result of rapid and deep structural changes, there are more losers than winners since dynamic growth is normally concentrated in the few leading centres that have the highest innovation potential and can be internationally competitive). It appears however that in the new knowledge-driven development paradigm the equity goal is even more difficult to achieve and the efficiency one is becoming more widespread as better responding to contemporary challenges. Furthermore the regional policies of the European Union, which are themselves being reformed, will increasingly influence Polish policies in ways that are difficult to foresee.

PROSPECTS FOR THE FUTURE: TOWARDS A 'COMPETITIVE SPACE'

History, as well as the opening of Poland to global development mechanisms and processes, will jointly shape the future competitiveness of Polish regions. A review of the strengths and weaknesses of regions allows us to anticipate that the main cities, and some areas within their sphere of influence, will be areas of accelerated development. Regions with pronounced tourist assets should also do well. The region in the north-west, around Szczecin, also stands a good development chance since it may become an economic, transport and even recreational support for Berlin (even though earlier hopes that Berlin would promptly gain the status of a global city proved to be unfounded). Gdańsk seems to be in a worse situation (albeit not hopeless) because of its slightly peripheral location in relation to the main European development corridors (see Domański, 1999). The Katowice agglomeration has good development prospects provided that it undertakes large-scale restructuring, which however cannot be confined to reducing the mining and heavy sector's role in the region's economy but must also deal with improving the quality of the natural environment, reclamation of derelict industrial areas and restoration of urban space. Łódź is one of the old industrial districts with all the associated historical burdens: its development chances are linked with its academic and research potential as well as with developments in nearby Warsaw. The remaining Polish regions, particularly the eastern periphery and less developed central areas, will experience a narrow growth that will emerge in localities, those able to initiate indigenous development factors on the local and sub-regional scale.

It should be clearly stated that the competitiveness of individual regional and local structures in Poland depends almost entirely on the regions themselves. No one can expect that the state, in implementing an overall regional policy, will attend to the situation in individual regions. The state's role is to ensure the development of the national economy and to support its global competitiveness. Local government at the appropriate level should act to ensure the development of the regions and local structures. The state may intervene in specific parts of the country's economic space but such intervention ought to be subordinated to the national interest, such as economic growth, national infrastructure, national systems of education, health care and so on. It should be stressed that the growth of regional differences in Poland should be of a temporary character. It can be foreseen that the means which Poland will gain from pre-accession and later from structural the structural funds of the European Union should alleviate this process. It should be also kept in mind that since Poland is a nationally homogeneous country, the danger of growing separatist movements is very small, and regionalism is virtually non-existent (with the two exceptions of Wielkopolska and Upper Silesia, where some regional identity has been preserved). After the phase of accelerated growth and structural change, Poland may well pursue – at that time as a full member of the European Union – policies aiming at closing interregional gaps and increasing interregional equity.

NOTE

1 A map of Polish Euroregions can be found on the web at: www.us.wroc.pl/euroreg/euro2.htm, 5 February 2001.

REFERENCES

Bachtler, J. (1997), 'New dimensions of regional policy in Western Europe', in M. Keating and J. Loughlin (eds), *The Political Economy of Regionalism*, London and Portland, Or: Frank Cass

Bradshaw, M. and A. Stenning (2000), 'The progress of transition in East Central Europe', in J. Bachtler, R. Downes and G. Gorzelak (eds), *Transition, Cohesion and Regional Policy in Central and Eastern Europe,* Aldershot, Hants: Ashgate.

Czyżewski, A.B. (1998), *Regional Development of Poland 1986–1996. Measurement and Analysis,* World Bank Report, Warsaw.

Domański, R. (ed.) (1999), *The Changing Map of Europe: The Trajectory Berlin–Poznań–Warsaw,* Warsaw: Rewasz.

Gilowska, Z., Gorzelak, G. and Jałowiecki, B. (1999), *Założenia kontraktu regionalnego dla Ściany Wschodniej* (Principles of a regional contract for the Eastern Wall), Warsaw: Municipium.

Gorzelak, G. (1996), *The Regional Dimension of Transformation in Central Europe*, London: Jessica Kingsley.

Gorzelak, G. (1998), *The Regional and Local Potential for Transformation in Poland*, Warsaw: EUROREG.

Gorzelak, G. and Jałowiecki, B. (eds) (1999), *Koniunktura gospodarcza i mobilizacja społeczna w gminie* (Economic performance and social mobilisation in municipalities), Warsaw: EUROREG.

Gorzelak, G., Jałowiecki, B., Woodward, R., Dziemianowicz, W., Herbst, M., Roszkowski, W. and Zarycki, T. (1999), *Dynamics and Factors of Local Success in Poland*, Warsaw: CASE.

Huntington, S.P. (1998), *The Clash of Civilisations and the Remaking of World Order*.

Jałowiecki, B. (1999), *Polskie metropolie w średniookresowej strategii rozwoju regionalnego* (Polish metropoles in medium-term regional development strategies), Ministry of the Economy, mimeo.

Kozak, M. and Pyszkowski, A. (eds) (1999), *Phare-STRUDER: Pilot Regional Development Programme. Experiences, Results, Inspirations,* Warsaw: PARR.

Krätke, S. (1997), 'Regional integration or fragmentation? The German–Polish border region in a New Europe', paper presented at the Regional Studies Association Conference, Frankfurt (Oder).

De Melo, M., Denizer, C. and Gelb, A. (eds) (1997), 'Patterns of transition from plan to market', *World Bank Economic Review*, 19 (3).

Owsiak, S., Kurowski, P. and Stepaniuk, K. (1998), 'Finansowe aspekty redystrybucji pieniężnych środków publicznych w przekroju przestrzennym' (Financial aspects of redistribution of monetary resources), in G. Gorzelak (ed.), *Przemiany polskiej przestrzeni* (Changes of Polish space), Warsaw: EUROREG.

RCSS (1999), *Koncepcja polityki przestrzennego zagospodarowania kraju* (A Conception for national spatial policy), Warsaw: Rządowe Centrum Studiów Strategicznych (Government Centre for Strategic Studies.

Wódz, K. (ed.) (1994), *Transformation of Old Industrial Regions as a Sociological problem*, Katowice: Friedrich Ebert Stiftung.

Wódz, J. (ed.) (1997), *The Problems of Ecological Awareness,* Katowice: Silesian University.

Woo, T.W., Parker, S. and Sachs, J. (eds) (1998), *Economies in Transition: Comparing Asia and Europe*, London: MIT Press.

World Bank (1996), *From Plan to Market:, World Development Report*, Oxford: University Press.

12. Polish agriculture, rural areas and EU enlargement

Jerzy Wilkin

POLISH AGRICULTURE AFTER 'SHOCK THERAPY'

The situation of Polish agriculture and rural areas is unusually complicated and rather unclear. As a result, various problems related to the state's economic and social policy have arisen, both practical and theoretical in nature. In describing this complicated reality in a coherent way caution is needed. The problems of the countryside and farming have special significance in Poland for economic, social and political reasons. At the same time, the subject is burdened with an enormous number of stereotypes, emotions, misunderstandings and conflicts.

In the early 1990s interest in these questions increased because Poland began preparations to join the European Union. Polish agriculture and the social and economic situation of the countryside are commonly mentioned as some of the most important and complicated aspects of Polish integration into the EU. Inefficient farming and the 'backwardness' of the countryside are perceived as the most important barriers to be overcome in EU accession. But it is worth asking: is this really the case? The answer is not simple and involves an extremely complicated set of problems where generalisations to all rural areas and the entire farming sector may be inappropriate.

Poland's rural population has not changed significantly since the end of the World War II, from which period the countryside has lost only its natural population growth to the cities. Polish farmers held on to their land notwithstanding the efforts of the communist authorities to persuade them that progress depended on merging small individual farms into larger collective farms, or on migrating from the village to the city in order to take up jobs in socialist industrial workplaces. Polish peasants, however, stubbornly clung to both their villages and their land. In 1949–55 the communist government tried to force agricultural collectivisation. The effort was both much less brutal and much less successful than in other communist countries. Most of the co-operative farms established during this period were dissolved after October 1956 when Władysław Gomułka became communist party leader. When, in 1989, the period of 'real socialism' ended approximately two million small individual farms remained in existence. Poland was the only country in the Soviet bloc whose farmland remained for the most part in private hands. In the post-war years, when Western Europe underwent a rapid concentration of landholding and the number of farms was reduced at a high rate, in Poland the number of farms tended to decline very slowly, at a rate of less than 1% per year. In 1960, there were 2,856,000 individual holdings; in 1989, this number was 2,186,000 (see Frenkel, 1999).

The perseverance of Polish farmers in their resistance against collectivisation was, however, not appreciated in the new reality of the 1990s. The farmers, who considered themselves to be the moral and economic victors of socialism, were quickly made to understand that it was they who were the weak link in Polish capitalism, that they were an anachronism, an unproductive and backward element that was making Poland's entry into the EU difficult. The farmers, who during the communist years had been producing valuable food supplies (notwithstanding system induced shortages), were shown in a rather brutal way that in the competitive market economy it was not easy to sell what they produced, that their products did not meet Western sanitary and marketing norms and that they produced goods inefficiently and expensively. In the past, Polish farmers had been able to adjust even to extremely bad economic and political situations and were capable of producing a relatively large amount of food. But after 1990, in a highly competitive market environment, they began to feel helpless and abandoned. They were still able to produce but they no longer knew for whom, nor did they know how to sell their goods. They also did not understand, in the early 1990s, how to organise to defend their interests, or where to get important information about the market, or how, for example, they should change the structure of their production. More important, they did not understand why change was needed. Farmers' financial situation also reflected the shock of these changes. Their income fell much more than for other large social groups. Various data on income levels during the 1990s attest to this. In 1998 income per person employed in agriculture amounted to only 40% of the national average wage.[1]

Farmers' dramatic financial situation also affected their farms in terms of production and development. Most farmers not only did not invest in their own farms but were also not able even to preserve existing productive assets. A very serious decapitalisation, a shrinking of the production base, occurred. Besides low incomes and uncertain prospects, changes in rural families' consumption patterns also contributed to reduced agricultural investment. The pressures of advertising, the spread of an urban lifestyle and the wide range of attractive products on the market meant that farmers were more likely to buy VCRs, new TV sets, satellite dishes or cars than agricultural production assets.

Table 12.1. Polish agriculture, 1990–98 (% growth rates and shares)

	1990	1991	1992	1993	1994	1995	1996	1997	1998
Growth of gross agricultural output	-0.3	6.8	-12.3	3.0	-9.3	10.7	1.1	0.5	6.6
Agriculture share in GDP	8.4	6.9	6.9	6.8	6.3	6.4	6.0	5.1	4.8
Agriculture share:									
in exports	14.1	16.6	14.6	11.6	12.1	11.0	11.3	12.8	11.2
in imports	8.2	13.5	12.4	12.0	11.2	10.3	10.7	8.9	8.2
Agricultural income per farmer as % of average wage	92	49	49	58	57	69	66	53	40

Source: Own computations based on GUS (Central Statistical Office) data.

The new economic reality demonstrated quite dramatically that only a small number of farms had any chance in the market economy while the rest would have to find new ways to survive. Farmers came to realise this very slowly. In the early 1990s they blamed their difficult financial and production situation entirely on Leszek Balcerowicz and his ‘shock therapy’, which, among other things, opened the Polish economy to agricultural imports. Farmers were also inclined to look to the government to guarantee production levels, prices and a decent standard of living. After a decade of building a market economy as many as 84% of farmers believed that the government should guarantee farm prices and blamed the it for the countryside’s plight

Figure 12.1. Farmers’ earnings compared to overall wages growth

Agricultural income parity 1988–98

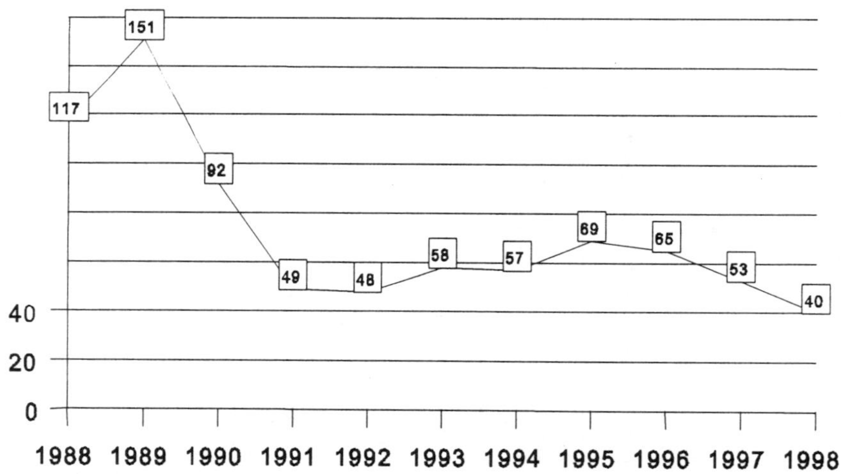

Agricultural income as % of average wage in Poland

Source: Institute of Agricultural Economics and Food Economy, Warsaw, 1999.

THE STRUCTURE OF AGRICULTURE AND THE RURAL ECONOMY

For over 40 years Poland's rural population has hovered around 15 million. Demography suggests that this figure is unlikely to change much and may even slowly increase. At the same time rural areas seem bound to undergo a process of becoming less agriculturally dependent. Rural areas make up 93% of Poland's total land area and two-thirds of rural land is used for agriculture. Approximately 38% of Poland's population live in rural areas, of whom 60% are in some way connected with agriculture although in most cases this involvement is limited and takes the form of part-time farming. Because only a small proportion of the agricultural population depends *solely* on agricultural income (around 20%) Polish agriculture is less sensitive to classic agricultural policy supporting prices and incomes. Polish agriculture has also proved that it is highly resistant to unfavourable economic conditions, and is able to survive for long periods of time.

Estimating the precise share of agriculture in total employment is not easy. Official statistics suggest that it is some 27% (five times the EU average) but quarterly surveys of labour activity put the share at around 20%. Other studies on labour structure and activity (see Frenkel, 1999) based on EU methodology suggest that the figure is even lower at around 12 –13%. Unemployment, both officially registered and concealed, is the most serious socio-economic problem facing Poland's rural areas. At the end of 1998 over 45% of the total number of unemployed were registered in rural areas, where over half were not eligible for unemployment benefits. Moreover, hidden unemployment, estimated to affect approximately 900,000 people at the end of 1998, should be added to the above figures.

Within the rural population we can distinguish three major socio-economic groups with varying abilities to adjust to market conditions and agricultural policies. The first is the group of *commercial farmers*, for whom farming constitutes the main source of income. These farmers produce primarily for the market and their incomes are dependent on market conditions. They are deeply interested in domestic agricultural policy and in the EU's Common Agricultural Policy, from which they hope to benefit after Poland joins the Union. The second group is the *multi-occupational peasant population.* This segment of the rural population depends on two or more sources of income. They farm small-holdings and a high percentage of their output is for own consumption. Incomes and living conditions are modest but relatively stable due to the variety of income sources. This group has a lower sensitivity to market conditions. The third group is the *rural non-agricultural population*, the rural population dependent on non-agricultural incomes. About half of this group relies on wages and salaries and 40% depend on pensions and unemployment benefits. All three groups believe that an effective and comprehensive rural policy that would stimulate job creation and improve living conditions in rural areas is in their best interest. They differ significantly, however, on what the role of agricultural policy should be in terms of determining their incomes. Since most agricultural holdings produce for their own consumption the effects of agricultural policies on their farms and incomes are very limited.

The conditions prevailing in Poland during the communist era did not stimulate modernisation and development of commercial farms. The authorities tolerated only small farms that operated primarily at a subsistence level. That command economy legacy 'froze' the agrarian structure in Poland. Before 1990 big farms (PGRs) existed only in the state farm sector, which utilised 20% of agricultural land in Poland. Later several thousand big private farms were established on the basis of the land formerly in the state farm sector. The command economy also hindered the rural population from a definitive move away from farming and the countryside. Urbanisation did not necessarily follow industrialisation, giving rise instead to a pendulum-like migration between the cities and villages. As a result, there was an 'indefinite' migration, dependent on jobs, rather than a 'spatial' migration that would have meant a permanent change in place of residence. Because the scope of collectivisation and nationalisation of agriculture was limited, the agricultural population did not move away from structures typical of a peasant economy. Quite the opposite happened since the constant threat that farming might be 'socialised' actually made the peasants inclined to defend themselves – to keep their property (especially their land) at any cost. In the end, this was also the basis for maintaining a significant degree of economic independence. In Western countries, it was the market that instigated a kind of 'pull' and made it possible for new non-agricultural sectors (such as industry, construction and services) to absorb population. Under the conditions prevailing in People's Poland, the market mechanism was turned off but the centrally planned economic mechanism was at the same time incoherent and ineffective. Ideological considerations meant that the authorities, who were unable (or unwilling) to eliminate the peasant economy, at the same time did not create conditions that would encourage its development. This made it impossible for peasant farms to go through processes of modernisation, specialisation and concentration. The agrarian structure of Polish farming was frozen for decades, and peasant farming developed in an artificial and autarkic environment. The essence of this environment may be captured in the metaphor of a 'glass lampshade', which protects but also greatly restricts.

Polish society embarked on transformation and preparation for EU accession with around 2 million small, multifunctional and multi-income agricultural units (farms or small agricultural plots) – a reflection of the high percentage of the population living in rural areas, the large number of individual farms, relatively easy access to small pieces of arable land and the strong motivation of having to provide one's own food supply. These small farms provided either a basic income or a supplementary income for about 25% to 30% of all households (mainly in the countryside but also in the cities). In the first years of the 1990s' transformation these trends, far from diminishing, were even strengthened because of the dramatic increase in unemployment and the general impoverishment of the population. Polish society became even more entangled in various forms of agricultural activity on a wide scale and in a complicated way. The socio-economic structures that made it possible for a large part of society to survive state socialism and which comprised an effective means of coping with economic disturbances (a shock absorber) even in that first period of transformation became more of a problem, and even an obstacle, in the EU accession process. If socio-economic structures in Polish agriculture are an obstacle to integration it is nevertheless important to note that they are not insurmountable. The 1996 agricultural census also provided interesting data on farm structure according to yield of marketable agricultural produce (see *Zróżnicowanie produkcji rolnej w gospodarstwach 1996–1997, 1998).* Those farms with production level of over 2500 złoty (1995–96) were categorised as farms producing principally for the market (commercial farms); and using this criterion, a low threshold of 'commercialisation', it is estimated that some 45.9% of individual farms fell into this group. Thus, as we can see, most Polish farms tend to produce exclusively or primarily for their own needs. If the threshold for the yield of marketable agricultural produce were raised to 5000 złoty then the share of farms producing primarily for the market would fall to 33% of the total. This is, in our view, a much better approximation for the number of agricultural units that in Poland's new economic conditions deserve to be called 'farms' (as commercial agricultural households). Another measure of the number of 'real' farms in Poland is given by the number of individuals paying into the farmers' pension fund (KRUS): the figure is around 1.4 million as compared to the 'official' number of individual farms of about 2 million. This is the group of farms that might benefit from the Common Agricultural Policy and its price and income support. Oddly, this is precisely the group of farmers most active in organising protests against the poor financial conditions of Polish farming. In 1998 the 'price scissors' index (the ratio of agricultural to industrial prices) was 77.7, its worst level since 1990–91. In a 1997 survey of the Central Statistical Office (GUS) on the economic situation in agriculture only 17.9% of farmers polled believed that their income allowed them to meet the everyday needs of their families *and* to expand agricultural production. This is similar to the percentage of farmers (17.6%) who in the 1996 agricultural census indicated that their farms had some prospects of further development. As might be expected, the proportion of farms earning enough to meet the needs of their families *and* to develop their farms increases with farm size and reaches 38.2% in the group of farms of 15 hectares and larger.[2]

The scale of the yield of marketable agricultural produce in Poland, and other methods of evaluating farms' relationship to the market indicate that although it is true that there are many productive units in agriculture (so-called farms), most of them are not able to survive independently as agricultural units, much less participate in trading or investment. This situation is illustrated by the fact that only 12% of Polish farms use bank loans as a source of financing operations and that over 80% of the credits taken by farmers are short-term loans. Polish farmers tend to be quite reluctant to borrow from banks, and clearly prefer to finance both everyday expenditures as well as long-term investments with own funds. They had a painful experience in the early 1990s when many fell into a 'debt trap' and were unable to pay even the interest (it was growing rapidly at that time) on loans from the 1980s while at the same time agricultural income fell sharply. In the late 1990s farmers' borrowing increased thanks in part to subsidised interest rates. However the collapse of agricultural profitability in 1998 alongside a budget squeeze on preferential credits seemed certain to reduce borrowing further. For some farmers it seemed likely also to create mounting troubles in repaying older loans.

The rural population's low average educational level also contributes significantly to the weakness of Polish agriculture. Poor education makes it difficult to use the newest technology and biological innovations, adversely affects farmers' ability to adjust to changing economic conditions, and reduces their chances of finding jobs outside agriculture. Often, farmers' low educational level also has an impact on their children, both through lack of emphasis on education within the family and because of difficulties in financing children's education. Even if children do take advantage of free public education, essential expenditures on school-related items rise quickly in Poland. The deteriorating educational situation of children from farming families as well as those from former state farms is not only one of the most painful side-effects of reform but is also an example of a shocking lack of foresight on the part of the leaders of peasants' political parties, other farmers' groups and the government itself. Any plan to develop farming and rural areas in Poland must have as a priority a radical improvement in educational level. This is a precondition for better performance in other spheres of agriculture and the countryside as a whole. Studies have shown how important education is to farming productivity. Marketable output per person fully employed in farming was, according to 1997 studies, six times higher on farms run by individuals with higher or post-secondary education than on farms run by individuals with only elementary school education or with no education at all (19,056 złoty as compared to 3264 złoty). Individuals with higher education more often run larger farms but even if output per hectare is used as a measure of efficiency instead of output per person the results show that productivity is still two times greater than on farms run by individuals with elementary education or none at all (1817 złoty and 943 złoty respectively).[3]

In conclusion we may say that no more than 400,000 farms out of a total of around 2 million that exist in Poland are economically viable, that is, have the ability to survive and expand in a competitive market environment. They will constitute the main CAP 'clients' after Poland joins the EU. This does not mean however that the remaining farms will disappear quickly following EU enlargement. Most of them will continue to operate as subsidiary farms, part-time farms or hobby-farms. Due to demographic conditions in Poland, the number of people involved in agriculture will slowly fall. In 1996–2010, the number of people of employment age will increase in Poland by 1,860,000. Over the same period, in the EU-15 the corresponding increase will be only 253,000. For Poland job creation will be the biggest challenge of the next 15 years. Fast and sustainable economic growth is the most important factor that will determine whether Poland will successfully meet this challenge. Another important factor is an effective and comprehensive rural policy.

Table 12.2. Poland's rural population by socio-economic groups

	Number of persons (million)
Rural population,	14.7
of which:	
living on individual farm holdings	9.7
Major socio-economic groups in rural areas	
Commercial farmers (with families)	1.6
Multi-occupational peasant population	5.9
Non-agricultural rural population	7.2

Source: Own computations based on the agricultural census 1996.

Table 12.3. Major changes in farms' structure and character in Poland and the European Community since World War II

	European Community	Poland
Number of farms	Rapid decline	Stabilisation
Migration from agriculture	High	Low
Concentration of land	Fast	Stagnation
Specialisation in production	High	Low
Commercialisation of production	High	Low

Source: Author's estimates.

In recent decades, conditions in Poland have not been favourable for significant structural change in agriculture. This experience contrasted sharply with the rapid structural changes observed in EU agriculture.

Structural change in Polish agriculture in the 1990s was polarised since the number of small farms (1–5 hectares) was stable while the number of larger farms (over 15 hectares) increased rapidly. However the number of medium-sized farms (5–15 hectares) declined.

A new phenomenon in Polish agriculture in the 1990s was the appearance of a large private farm sector. Most of these farms were established on land formerly operated by state farms (*Państwowe Gospodarstwa Rolne – PGRs*). The institution responsible for restructuring and privatising state farms, the Agency for State Property in Agriculture (AWRSP), preferred to sell or lease these holdings to new operators in one piece; as a result only a fraction of formerly state-owned land was sold to peasants in small parcels. One of the reasons for this is the location of the former state farms. Most were concentrated in northern and western Poland, where few small farms exist. In 1998, over 6700 private farms operating 100 or more hectares each were registered in Poland.

WHAT KIND OF POLICY DOES POLISH AGRICULTURE NEED?

The 'shock therapy' of the early 1990s coincided initially with a sharp drop in support for agriculture from the state budget (see Table 12.4) and with the opening of Poland's borders to international competition. Under pressure from farmers and their political representatives the government soon introduced protective measures and increased subsidies for agriculture. The 'Producer Subsidy Equivalent Index' (or PSE) increased from 5% in 1989 and only 1% in 1991 to 22% by 1997.[4] The PSE in the late 1990s was higher in Poland than in most other transforming economies. The Czech Republic and Hungary took a different path in liberalising agricultural markets: they opted for gradualism and slowly decreased agricultural support while simultaneously shifting from policies that had insulated domestic producers from foreign competition.

In Poland, over 75% of government subsidies for agriculture were used to supplement the farmers' pension fund (KRUS). These substantial subsidies are a form of social security, an income support instrument for elderly farmers rather than an agricultural policy instrument in any broader sense.

Poland did not introduce any direct payments system for farmers – the major instrument of agricultural support in the European Union. One of the most contentious elements in EU accession negotiations is to what extent Polish farmers (and farmers from other post-communist countries) should be included in CAP direct payments system.

Relatively high agricultural incomes in the EU are in large part due to high levels of money transfers to agriculture within the CAP framework. Polish and EU farm incomes are compared in Table 12.5. The fact that the average family income in EU farms is seven times higher than in Poland stems from both the EU's higher subsidisation rate and its much larger farms.

Table 12.4. State subsidies to agriculture in selected East–Central European countries, 1989–97 (Producer Subsidy Equivalent – PSE, in %)

	1989	1990	1991	1992	1993	1994	1995	1996	1997
Poland	5	-15	1	20	15	20	19	23	22
Czech Rep.	55	54	51	30	27	21	15	14	11
Estonia	80	72	57	-91	-30	-6	3	8	9
Lithuania	78	71	-259	-113	-33	-10	5	12	18
Latvia	83	77	83	-93	-38	9	8	4	8
Slovakia	56	57	44	39	35	31	25	19	25
Hungary	31	27	15	20	24	31	21	15	16
EU-12/15	40	47	47	47	49	48	49	43	42

Source: *Agricultural Situation and Prospects in the Central and Eastern European Countries*. Summary Report, European Commission, Brussels, 1998, p. 27.

Since the 1980s the EU has tried gradually to shift from the traditional agricultural policy based mostly on price and income support to a much broader and comprehensive rural policy. These changes were accelerated after the McSharry reforms of 1992. In Polish conditions it is rural policy rather than agricultural policy that is most needed since half of the rural population is not linked with agricultural production.

Table 12.5. Output and family agricultural income in Poland and the EU (ECU, unless otherwise stated)

	Poland 1996	EU-15 1995
Utilised agricultural area per farm (in hectares)	8.7	32.1
Total output	8,257	65,227
Family farm income	2,506	17,414
Family farm income excluding subsidies	2,479	9,018
Family farm income/ha	288	542
Family farm income excluding subsidies/ha	285	281

Source: *Agricultural Situation and Perspectives in the Central and Eastern European Countries – Poland*, European Commission, Brussels, 1998, p. 56.

EUROPEAN INTEGRATION

European integration is a process that should be beneficial for all partners. As far as existing EU members are concerned there have been no complaints to suggest that European integration was a mistake leading to economic deterioration in any given country. Of course within countries benefits may not have been uniformly spread and even between countries some may have benefited more than others. Within Poland the majority of peasants believe that EU accession will ruin them – they believe that they will not be able to compete against the modern and efficient farms of Western Europe. In fact the real problem facing Polish rural areas is not that a considerable part of the agricultural sector might be destroyed as a result of integration or that the financial situation of farmers might deteriorate; the threat lies rather in the possibility that a sizeable portion of the rural population and their farms will become increasingly marginalised in broader economic and social terms. Preparing for EU membership entails the creation of new institutions so that new member states and particular social groups can profit fully from integration. Polish farmers see themselves as the weak partner in confrontation with the EU's well-organised and efficient farming system. They are poorly organised, insufficiently informed and highly dispersed. Sharply declining farm incomes in the 1990s alongside strong Western competition on the Polish market provoked massive protests from the major farmers' organisations. The proportion of farmers who support Poland's accession to the EU declined from 74% in May 1996 to just 36% in June 1999 (Table 12.6).[5]

In 1998–99 Poland began to make preparations for use of pre-accession funds, in particular those earmarked for development of agriculture and rural areas. The ministry of agriculture joined in with plans for deciding on the priorities within the EU's SAPARD (Support for Pre-accession Measures for Agriculture and Rural Development) programme. From the year 2000 Poland may receive over Euro160 million per annum within SAPARD for the development of agriculture and rural areas. After joining the EU Poland should have access to both CAP and structural funds. World Bank assistance is also expected, mainly for accelerated job creation in rural areas, but outside agriculture, through investments in infrastructure and human capital development (especially increasing access to education) as well as to support the private sector in rural areas. World Bank aid will amount to approximately $100 million per annum.

Table 12.6. Polish support for EU accession (respondents' answers in per cent)

If there were a referendum in Poland on joining the EU, would you vote:	May 1996	March 1997	April 1998
For, of which:	80	72	62
Farmers	74	39	34
Entrepreneurs	94	77	75
Against, of which:	7	12	12
Farmers	3	23	32
Entrepreneurs	2	10	13
I would not take part in such a referendum, of which:			12
Farmers			10
Entrepreneurs			6
Difficult to say, of which:	13	18	13
Farmers	23	37	24
Entrepreneurs	4	13	7

Source: E. Skotnicka-Iliasiewicz, 'Członkostwo Polski w Unii Europejskiej – racje i emocje', *Stan i perspektywy wsi polskiej w przededniu integracji z Unią Europejską*, Seminar papers, Poznań, 1998, p. 43.

CONCLUSIONS

In late 1998 and early 1999 farmers' protests against the government's passive agricultural policy intensified. This was a clear expression of discontent over the sharp drop in farming incomes which left some farms (especially large pig farms) in a particularly dramatic situation. Despite widespread criticism of the form protests took, (roadblocks, mainly organised by Andrzej Lepper's '*Samoobrona*' – Self-defence Union) they forced the government to start intervention pork purchases and to prepare a broader package of rural reforms. Public opinion polls in February 1999 indicated a surprisingly high popular support for the farmers' protests. As many as 92% of people believed that the farmers were right to protest. Like the farmers themselves, most respondents blamed the government for the poor shape of agriculture. Some 71% of respondents believed that the situation had come about mainly due to the fact that the state did not care about agriculture.

It is true that the coalition government which came to power in 1997 did little to modernise agriculture and the countryside but none of the leaders of the main political parties or the farmers' unions has a realistic, comprehensive programme of action. Farmers' organisations aimed mainly to stir up dissatisfaction with the government.

In addition to having inherited inefficient economic structures from the command economy Polish agriculture is also weak because of farmers' low level of self-organisation to improve their own economic situation. Producer groups (genuine co-operatives) are only in the first stages of organising themselves and still exist on a very small scale. Farmers do not have their own representatives in EU membership negotiations, or in those dealing with Poland's eventual participation in the Common Agricultural Policy.

Agricultural and rural issues should be at the forefront in preparing a socio-economic strategy for the country in the new millennium. Rural and agricultural development demand particular attention from, and decisive action on the part of public authorities, including the government itself. The difficulty in working out and then implementing a plan for rural areas arises because it is a question with very many dimensions. Such a policy cannot be left only to the ministry of agriculture. But at the same time the problem is that there is no institution in Poland that is able effectively to fulfil the role of being both the catalyst and co-ordinator of an integrated policy for developing rural areas. In the 1990s the dominant belief was that developing the countryside should be the responsibility above all of the ministry of agriculture and food economy, but although agriculture is very important it is an ever-diminishing part of the rural economy. Most people living in the countryside support themselves principally through incomes earned outside farming. This means that agricultural policy itself cannot solve the problems of people living in rural areas.

Rural development is a much wider social problem than was previously conceived. The countryside, with 38% of the total population, is a resource for the entire nation and failure to develop the countryside will negatively affect development in all other areas of economy and society. Awareness of these interdependencies needs to be raised at all levels of Polish society and perhaps also in the EU.

NOTES

1 Estimates based on farm accounting data of the Institute of Agriculture and Food Economy in Warsaw, February 1999.

2 *Zróżnicowanie produkcji rolnej w gospodarstwach 1996–1997,* op.cit., p. 51.

3 Ibid, p. 43.

4 See *Agricultural Situation and Prospects in the Central and Eastern European Countries. Summary Report,* European Commission, Brussels, 1998, p. 27. PSE is the annual monetary value of gross transfers from consumers and taxpayers to agricultural producers at farm gate prices.

5 *Rolnicy i mieszkańcy wsi o przyszłości polskiej wsi i rolnictwa w obliczu integracji europejskiej (1999)*, a survey commissioned by the Institute for Public Affairs (unpublished). COBOS, Warsaw.

REFERENCES

European Commision (1998), *Agricultural Situation and Perspectives in the Central and Eastern European Countries – Poland*, Brussels: European Commission.

Frenkel, I. (1999), 'Struktura społeczno-demograficzna gospodarstw rolnych i jej wpływ na procesy restrukturyzacji rolnictwa – Wybrane zagadnienia' (The socio-demographic structure of Polish farms and its influence on agricultural restructuring – selected problems), *Roczniki Akademii Rolniczej w Poznaniu, CCCVIII*, p. 31.

Rolnicy i mieszkańcy wsi o przyszłości polskiej wsi i rolnictwa w obliczu integracji europejskiej (1999), (Farmers and country dwellers on the future of the Polish countryside and agriculture in view of EU entry), unpublished survey commissioned by the Institute for Public Affairs, CBOS, Warsaw.

Zróżnicowanie produkcji rolnej w gospodarstwach 1996–1997 (1998), (The differentiation of farm production 1996–1997), Warsaw: GUS.

REFERENCES

PART III

International Dimensions of Poland's Transformation

13. Poland's place in the international economy

George Blazyca

INTRODUCTION

Of the many adjustments forced on the formerly planned economies by the collapse of communism one of the most demanding was to find a new place in the world economy. How matters in this regard would develop was by no means clear in 1989 or 1990. Nevertheless the mainstream view was that full participation in the international division of labour would accelerate the domestic economic modernisation that was so badly needed. Opening up to the world economy was considered an essential aspect of transformation and became a major plank of the early 1990s 'Washington consensus'. Later, attention shifted to aspects of 'international competitiveness' as it became clear that Poland, like other candidates for EU accession, would only be admitted once it was clear that it could meet competition from EU firms. By the end of the 1990s, in the face of a mounting trade and current account deficit, concerns began to mount that while opening the economy had been a real achievement of the early 1990s Poland's international competitiveness was far from secure.

Some brave early attempts to look ahead and identify the likely location of the socialist economies in the trade and investment patterns of the future were made just as the old system collapsed. The general view was that the Central European economies would develop specialisms reflecting resource endowments. These were thought to be mainly in energy, raw materials and agriculture as well in a good stock of highly educated and skilled labour. Although rarely discussed openly, what was clearly undesirable was that countries would find international competitiveness coming to rest, precariously, on low cost and unskilled labour. With a first decade of transformation behind us, we can reconsider those early expectations in the light of experience. As we will see, not all were fulfilled and many new complications emerged. In this chapter we consider the place of Poland in the international economy, we review the major features of Polish trade (touching also on inward investment) in the 1990s, drawing attention to changes, strengths, weaknesses and challenges at the start of the new century.

POLAND'S TRADE PERFORMANCE IN TRANSITION: KEY FEATURES

For Poland, in terms of international economic reorientation, the following seem to be the major features of the 1990s transformation:

- the first and overwhelmingly clear characteristic is trade openness;
- the second is the sharp and abrupt switch from a Comecon-Soviet orbit to an EU-trajectory;
- the third is a shift in the commodity structure of trade that is somewhat more difficult to pin down precisely and generates controversy as to the depth and speed of restructuring in favourable directions especially regarding skills content of exports;
- the fourth is an increasing trade deficit – a 'structural deficit' according to some Polish experts;
- the fifth is the role of foreign capital in shaping trade flows, in particular in locking a steady import demand into new investment while not necessarily, at least by the end of the 1990s, creating a sufficiently strong exports capacity;
- the sixth, closely related aspect, is the shifting nature of the institutional-organisational aspects of foreign trading especially as shaped through liberalisation, privatisation and inward investment.

We discuss each of these developments in turn before looking at some of the wider trade related issues and debates that they feed into.

Shock therapy and trade openness

Economic shock therapy in Poland in 1990 was laced with a liberalisation that suddenly and abruptly threw the economy wide open to international trade. Poland's average external tariff fell from 18.3% in 1989 to 5.5% in 1990 (Nuti, 1996). The only real domestic economy 'defence' came via a sharp złoty devaluation which, as might be expected, slowed imports and boosted exports but to an altogether unexpected extent. In 1990 export volumes increased by 13.7% (over 1989) while imports declined by 17.9%, helping to generate a massive $3.8 billion trade surplus.[1] Within this the trade reorientation from soft to hard currency payments areas (to use the nomenclature of the old system) was dramatic: hard currency exports increased in volume by 40.5% in 1990 as soft currency exports fell by 13.3%. Despite that year's almost 12% decline in GDP hard currency imports were barely affected (down in volume by only 2.9%) while Polish consumers and producers virtually abandoned soft currency imports (down by 34.1%). Pushed by the decline and shift in domestic demand Polish exporters plainly made a considerable effort to win sales in hard currency markets. A sharp deterioration in Poland's terms of trade (to 83.7 in 1990 and then 99.2 in 1991) hints at exports made at bargain prices, 'distress sales' as some have argued.

In the years that followed, trade flows were shaped by a combination of real currency appreciation and, a little later, by domestic economic growth, both of which acted to slow exports and suck in imports. Resumption of growth in EU markets gave a later boost to Polish exports. Despite increases in the level of tariff protection (to a high of 19.5% in 1994, see OECD, 1996, p. 125) the trade balance slipped into ever-deeper deficit. The first signs of an awakening of Polish exports emerged in 1994–95, encouraging a mid 1990s view that the country was beginning to establish new lines of export specialisation that might prove long lasting. Imports meanwhile continued to grow at a fast pace – the already open economy would shortly be locked into international arrangements, especially through the Europe (EU) Association Agreement, which would ensure there could be no backtracking in this respect.

Table 13.1. Foreign trade and GDP growth in the 1990s (% annual change, volume)

	Exports	Imports	Polish GDP	EU GDP
1990	13.7	-17.9	-11.6	3.0
1991	-2.4	37.8	-7.0	1.7
1992	-2.6	13.9	2.6	1.2
1993	-1.1	18.5	3.8	-0.4
1994	18.3	13.4	5.2	2.8
1995	16.7	20.5	7.0	2.4
1996	9.7	28.0	6.0	1.6
1997	13.7	22.0	6.8	2.5
1998	9.4	14.6	4.8	2.7
1999	-2.0	4.4	4.1	2.1

Note: EU is 'EU-15'.

Sources: All data are from Polish official sources, GUS, various years including: *Informacje o sytuacji społeczno-gospodarczej kraju rok 1999*, pp. 79, 91; *Informacje o sytuacji społeczno-gospodarczej kraju rok 1998*, p. 127; *Rocznik Statystyczny Handlu Zagranicznego 1999,* p. 7; *Handel zagraniczny styczeń-grudzień 1999*, p. 2; *EC Economic Data Pocket Book* (Eurostat, no. 3, 2000).

A switch in trade orbit 'from Moscow to Brussels (and Berlin)'

In the first phase of economic transformation in the early 1990s the impact on trade flows was dramatic, indeed for some writers it was 'one of the most remarkable features of the transition' (see Carlin et al., 1999). The Comecon collapse combined with 'transformation recession' in the former CPEs led to an abrupt shift in the geography of Polish trade. As early as 1991 most of Poland's trade was with the EU and by the mid 1990s Poland had settled on an 'equilibrium' where around two–thirds of its trade was 'Brussels-centred'. In trade terms Poland has been 'EU-integrated' for most the past decade and EU membership (again in trade terms although excluding agriculture) is something of a formality, although an immensely important one.

Table 13.2. EU share in Polish trade (% of total)

	Exports	Imports	Polish GDP	EU GDP
1990	13.7	-17.9	-11.6	3.0
1991	-2.4	37.8	-7.0	1.7
1992	-2.6	13.9	2.6	1.2
1993	-1.1	18.5	3.8	-0.4
1994	18.3	13.4	5.2	2.8
1995	16.7	20.5	7.0	2.4
1996	9.7	28.0	6.0	1.6
1997	13.7	22.0	6.8	2.5
1998	9.4	14.6	4.8	2.7
1999	-2.0	4.4	4.1	2.1

Source: As for Table 13.1 above and *Rocznik Statystyczny Handlu Zagranicznego 1997*, Warsaw: GUS, 1998, p. 5.

Within this geographic trade reorientation it is no surprise that Germany has once again (as in 1938) become Poland's leading trade partner.[2] Germany has substituted itself in the position held by the Soviet Union in the first 40 post-war years. Where the Soviet Union had accounted in 1986 for 33% of Polish imports and 28% of exports, a united Germany had, in 1999, 36.3% of Poland's exports and provided 25.3% of imports. Later, mauled by the rouble crisis of 1998, Russia saw its trade with Poland collapse (Russia took only 2.5% of Polish exports, and provided only 5.7% of all Polish imports in 1999). Of course the 1999 trade shares were extremely lop-sided and, looking further ahead, Russia is bound to become once again a significant trade partner.

New export specialisms

One of the most intriguing of transformation questions was: where would Poland find a new niche in the international economy? For over 40 post-war years the country was locked into the supposedly socialist division of labour. This had several well-known peculiarities the correction of which gave clues as to likely changes. The Polish trade pattern from the 1940s through to the 1980s was 'schizoid' in that trade within COMECON marked Poland out as a relatively advanced producer, with export specialisms in the supposedly sophisticated engineering sector, while in its trade with the West the country resembled much more a developing country, with exports mainly of fuel, materials, food and items involving little sophisticated processing. One of the most damaging results was that the COMECON pattern of specialisation reinforced a growing technology gap between Poland and the West.

How would things be in the new open trading arrangements of the 1990s and beyond? What would happen to the considerable export capacities in manufacturing but where goods were uncompetitive and sold mainly in the East? No one believed that, locked into its existing resource base, there would be any dramatic short-term shift in export profile. Immediate trade gains in the West might be achieved through keen selling and by adrenaline-like injections of marketing but substantial change needed a new product profile and that, in turn, needed new investment. Moreover, EU import restrictions on goods where a country like Poland might otherwise have quickly increased sales (especially steel) would also shape new trading patterns. In 1990 a group of Western economists looked ahead to possible emerging specialisms in the formerly socialist bloc (see *Monitoring European Integration*, 1990). Their reasoning led them to conclude that resource endowments would give the East some short– and medium–term comparative advantage in energy, agriculture and 'skill-intensive light manufacturing … probably higher up the skill ladder'.

What did happen to Poland's export profile in the 1990s? There is no doubt that the export structure *has* changed but the critical questions are: to what *extent* and at what *pace*? Is Poland building an export capacity that will permit it to sustain the fast GDP growth (with its strong imports consequences) crucial for early EU membership. It will perhaps be little surprise that in examining these issues optimists find an acceptably fast pace of export restructuring into the higher skill end while pessimists emphasise technological deterioration and slow progress. Later we return to the more macro considerations, but first we examine in greater detail the Polish exports profile in the 1990s.

The dominant export sector throughout the post-war period viewed through the SITC 'section' classification was the large machinery and transport equipment industry (SITC-7). In 1985 it accounted for 39.4% of total exports, falling in 1990 to 26.2% and then increasing slightly to 30.3% in 1999.[3] The share of mineral fuels in exports has fallen steadily while food and animals held a fairly steady 10% of exports in the 1990s, at least until the 1998 Russian crisis. The striking growth in exports appears in the two sectors of manufacturing, 'manufactures classified by material' and 'miscellaneous manufactures'. While the growth of manufactures in exports is generally welcome the question that remains is: how far up the skills ladder has it taken Poland? Some observers have detected real progress in this regard while others see much less evidence of substantial transformation. Among the former, a careful study by Kamiński (1998) notes 'spectacular' trade reorientation in the early 1990s by geography and by commodity alongside a 'significant improvement in the capacity of Polish firms to compete internationally'. Within Poland however it is not hard to find those who tend to a much more cautious view.[4]

Table 13.3. Total exports by SITC section (% share, current prices)

	1985	1990	1999
0. Food & live animals	7.5	10.9	8.5
1. Beverages & tobacco	0.7	0.5	0.4
2. Crude materials (inedible except fuels)	7.2	6.8	3.1
3. Mineral fuels	15.7	10.7	5.0
4. Animal & vegetable oils	0.2	0.2	0.2
5. Chemicals and related products	6.1	9.2	6.2
6.Manufactured goods, classified by material	15.0	23.0	25.5
7. Machinery & transport equip.	39.4	26.2	30.3
8. Misc. manufactures	6.8	7.5	20.9
Total (incl. others)	100.0	100.0	100.0

Sources: GUS, *Rocznik Statystyczny Handlu Zagranicznego 1999*, p. 12; *Handel zagraniczny styczeń-grudzień 1999*, p. 2.

To throw some light on this we explore the export basket more closely. We begin by identifying the 'successes' – those industry branches where the ratio of exports to total sectoral production is increasing faster than the average. We also review the literature on export factor content. Finally we take a detour, for purposes of illustration, to Polish–German trade on the grounds that the export profile in relation to Poland's largest (and surely demanding) customer may give us clues as to the direction that export restructuring is taking.

One way of identifying changing export specialism is through the shifting share of exports in any sector's production compared to the average across all industry. Table 13.4, based on Polish research (Lubiński and Marczewski, 1999), shows that the great sectoral export success of the 1990s, measured by *changes* in the exports to production ratio, was in wood and paper, followed by light industry, construction materials then metals, while the electrical and mechanical engineering sector shouldered the brunt of export restructuring losses. The authors believe that export specialisation gains in light industry were achieved 'almost exclusively due to the outward processing trade in the clothing sector' while wood and paper successes came from furniture (with outward processing again a strong feature). In their view industry exported more but 'the greatest progress was in those *labour intensive branches* and was based on the *shallow processing of raw materials*. The situation of capital intensive industry, using highly skilled labour, mainly in electrical and mechanical engineering, deteriorated' (our emphasis).

Table 13.4. Export specialism by industry branch, 1989–97 (ratios, % of branch production exported in relation to average % for all industry)

	Export specialisation		Change in specialisation
	1989	1997	1997/1989
Fuel and energy	0.5	0.5	1.00
Metallurgy	1.2	1.5	1.25
Electrical & mechanical engineering	1.9	1.1	0.58
Chemicals	1.0	1.2	1.20
Construction materials	0.5	0.8	1.60
Wood & paper	1.0	1.7	1.70
Light industry	1.6	2.6	1.63
Food industry	0.6	0.6	1.00

Note: The data should be interpreted with care since in 1997 outward processing is estimated in gross terms but in 1989 in net terms. This adjustment exaggerates 1997 exports especially in light industry. But few doubt that Polish trade specialisms have moved in the direction indicated. Note also that the sectoral classification used here is the old Polish branch system and not the SITC.

Source: Own estimates based on data in Lubiński and Marczewski (1999).

The Kamiński story on exports is much more upbeat. His study of emerging trade specialism in the period to 1995 points to 'spectacular reorientation' with manufacturing as the top export performer and factor content shifting up the skills ladder. Given that the pace and intensity of restructuring has become an important issue across transforming economies it is interesting that Kamiński's evidence, depending on how it is presented (see Table 13.5), can point to dramatic change taking place *either* in the very early transformation period (1989–91) *or* in the later (1991–95) phase. For example, an examination of exports at the four-digit level (807 subgroups in all) seems to show greater gains in moving to 'better' exports, in diversifying the export basket, over the period

1989–91 rather than 1991–95. But when exports are judged by factor intensity it seems that most change took place in the later period. Kamiński believes that while export expansion in the early transition period 'was driven mainly by unskilled labour-intensive manufactures', in the later period 'a discernible shift toward human capital intensive products seems to have occurred' so that 'the *emerging engines of growth* [our emphasis] seem to be capital-intensive and technology-intensive sectors'. Of course this is to explore the *direction* of (factor intensity) change in an export basket where even in Kamiński's account unskilled labour-intensive and resource-intensive products predominate. Similar research by Alan Smith (1999) emphasises the role of labour-intensive products in explaining the *growth* of Polish exports to the EU-12 in the early 1990s. According to Smith almost half of the increase in those exports over 1988–94 came from labour-intensive products (47%), then from resource-intensive production (29%) and human capital intensive production (24%).[5]

As we noted earlier the evidence on the *pace* of export restructuring in the early 1990s seems mixed. Kamiński's optimism co-exists alongside the doubts of others, especially writers in Poland. If the pessimists are right then in the early 1990s the tilt in export profile towards unskilled labour was greater than might have been expected given the view that Poland inherited from the centrally planned system a highly qualified labour force. This may have been one of the greatest misjudgements in assessments of the legacy of central planning. Moreover Poland's late 1990s trade problems allow some doubt as to whether the capital- and technology-intensive 'engines' continued to operate at full steam in the years that followed. Although Alan Smith's assessment of ability to withstand competition within the EU meant that he located Poland in the 'second league' of accession candidates he was ready to be optimistic, suggesting that the 1996 position may not have fully captured changes in economic structure 'currently taking place' and which might permit in due course a movement to the first group of stronger economies (Slovenia, Hungary and Czech Republic). More recent studies of the longer 1990s experience are also helpful here. Marzenna Weresa's (1999) survey of trade and investment flows over 1991–98 using data on revealed comparative advantage suggests that the period actually consists of two substantially different episodes: an early period (1991–95) when noticeable exports restructuring took place and a later period (1995–98) of much less change.[6] At first sight this looks odd, given that the early period had little FDI, the later period much more. But as Weresa herself suggests, time lags are likely to be important here: the FDI surge of the late 1990s may mean that a new period of substantial export restructuring was about to begin. The earlier period may reflect, as has been hinted above, the desperate marketing push induced by the 'shock' of lost domestic and COMECON markets and the sudden appearance of the 'hard budget constraint'.

Table 13.5. Reorientation in trade with the EU, 1989–95

	1989	1991	1995
Revealed comparative advantage (RCA)[a] across 807 SITC four-digit subgroups:			
No. of *manufacturing* products in the top ten	3	5	6
No. of *product categories* with RCA greater than unity	203	230	211
No. of *manufacturing product categories* with RCA above unity	124	137	139
	1994	1996	1998
Factor content of exports (% composition of exports)			
Natural resource-intensive	38.3	29.9	26.7
Unskilled labour-intensive	29.1	30.0	28.1
Technology-intensive	13.5	17.3	18.5
Human capital-intensive	19.0	22.7	26.6

Note: [a] RCA is defined as the ratio of the share of any product in a country's exports to the share of that product in world (here EU) trade. An RCA greater than one indicates comparative advantage.

Sources: Kamiński, 1998; *Gazeta Wyborcza*, 26 May 2000

A closer look at export restructuring: Poland's trade with Germany

As the focus of trade has shifted from East to West so Polish producers have had to meet much tougher market tests. A close examination of Polish–German trade in the late 1990s may therefore give us clues as to the pace, extent and direction of export restructuring in transformation. Germany, as noted earlier, is Poland's principal trading partner and had in 1998 36% ($10.2 billion) of total Polish exports. By SITC section, Poland generated small trade surpluses in food, crude materials, mineral fuels, a much larger surplus in 'miscellaneous manufactures' (SITC 8, $1.9 billion) but very large deficits in each of chemicals (SITC 5, $1.5 billion), 'manufactures' (SITC 6, $375 million) and machinery and equipment (SITC 7, a $2.6 billion gap). Within the impressive SITC 8 surplus, closer inspection reveals that the great Polish success story of the 1990s has been in furniture ('*meblujemy UE*' – 'we are furnishing the EU', as the Polish expression has it) with export sales in 1998 of almost $1.1 billion, accounting for more than 10% of all exports to Germany. Adding in clothing yields exports worth approximately the same, another $1.1 billion. In SITC 7 in 1998 the champion Polish sector was ships (exports worth $739 million). In this, generally higher skills-based sector, there were signs also of emerging specialisms in motor vehicles (exports worth \$500 million). SITC 6 manufacturing contains less highly processed items: plywood and wood products accounted for \$436 million of export sales, yarns and textiles for \$370 million, metals, steel bars and structures for \$540 million.

Table 13.6. Polish–German trade by SITC grouping, 1998 (\$m, current prices)

	Exports	Imports	Balance
Food & live animals	537.4	457.7	79.7
Beverages & tabacco	4.4	20.4	-16.0
Crude materials	367.5	207.0	160.5
Mineral fuels	424.9	195.8	229.1
Animal & vegetable oils	9.6	80.0	-70.4
Chemicals	313.0	1,795.8	-1,482.8
Manufactured goods, classified by material	2,799.0	3,173.7	-374.7
Machinery & transport equip.	2,825.5	5,483.3	-2,630.8
Misc manufactures	2,922.6	1,001.8	1,920.8
Total (incl. others)	*10,233.3*	*12,441.1*	*-2,207.8*

Source: GUS, *Rocznik Statystyczny Handlu Zagranicznego* (1999, p. 91).

We can summarise this in a slightly different way, section by section, picking out, admittedly impressionistically, what appear to be Polish export strengths from the 1998 data as follows:

- in crude materials, 'wood, simply worked' accounts for one–third of all Polish exports to Germany;
- in mineral fuels, coal and coke account for 83% of sales;
- in chemicals it is hard to see any distinct Polish specialisation but it is fairly evident that Germany, with its long traditions in this sector, does well in sales to Poland at the high end of the technological scale;
- in manufacturing (SITC 6) the top 10 Polish exports, none sophisticated, account for 65% of exports in the sector;[7]
- in machinery and equipment, ships account for 26% of exports but it seems that new Polish specialisms are emerging in cars, TVs and perhaps also in spare parts (the FDI link here may be beginning to be activated);
- and finally in 'miscellaneous manufacturing' furniture and clothing account for an overwhelming 80% of the sector's total exports.

Table 13.7. Major exports to Germany, an impressionistic comparison of 1998 and 1989

	1989 ($'000)	1998[a] ($m)
1. Furniture	61	1,084
2. Plywood and wood products	20	437
3. Men and boys clothing	9[b]	462
4. Women and girls clothin	-	667
5. Footwear	14	84
6. Yarn and textiles	19	371
7. Coal and coke	100	354
8. Copper	235	179
9. Steel bars and structures	59	362
Sub-total	517	4,000
Total exports to Germany	1,907	10,200

Notes: [a] at three-digit SITC product group level; [b] men and women combined.

Sources: GUS, *Rocznik Statystyczny Handlu Zagranicznego* (1999); *Handel Zagraniczny* (1990).

Another impressionistic 'before and after' comparison with export structures in the old system, made difficult because of changing trade nomenclature not to mention political geography, nevertheless reveals clearly the abrupt change in the 1990s fortunes of the Polish furniture and clothing sector. Motor vehicles, domestic electrical appliances and consumer electronics, almost totally absent in the 1989 export profile, also begin to make an appearance by the late 1990s.

Liberalisation in the 1990s evidently had a dramatic effect on trade as Polish business (private and public) responded to market signals and became embedded in new contractual arrangements, especially in the 'outward processing trade' (OPT). This was particularly a feature in clothing and furniture. The key question here is: how long lasting will such arrangements be? If OPT is based essentially on cheap labour then its further relocation is to be expected. If on the other hand the Polish producers of clothing and furniture do succeed in moving up a skills ladder, all need not be so gloomy. It seems unlikely however that they will achieve this without some assistance, perhaps drawing on the lessons of successful Western experience in developing networks, 'clusters' and co-operative arrangements between firms. The early strength of Polish economic transformation in the 1990s (based largely on the explosion in small-scale entrepreneurial activity – although whether this was so in clothing or furniture looks worth further research) can easily turn into a weakness as initial energies are spent. Polish enterprises, unless absorbed within the structure of international firms, are likely to meet barriers to growth and consolidation (lack of resources, lack of market intelligence, high interest rates, lack of innovation, shortages of appropriately skilled labour), to overcome which some policy intervention is probably needed.

The external balance: a 'structural' trade deficit

By the end of the decade the trade restructuring pessimists seemed to have grounds for their doubts. The evidence most often cited in this respect is the country's fast-growing trade deficit, the bulk of which, as would be expected, arises in EU trade. Płowiec (1997, p. 608) calls this a 'structural deficit' because it 'cannot be liquidated other than through a real change in the export structure favouring a growing share of highly processed and technology intensive goods'.

The trade imbalance deepened in the second half of the 1990s and was the main component in a current account deficit that by 1999 was (at 7.6% of GDP) at, if not beyond, what would normally be labelled a dangerous threshold. For some however the deficit was the healthy and visible sign of an economy re-tooling to meet new challenges in the face of chronic shortages of domestic investment. In a contribution to the debate in Poland one expert noted that the trade deficit was 'completely acceptable … so long as we want to import capital the deficit is inevitable … the deficit is healthy, essential' (see Lutkowski in *Aktualne tendencje …*, 1999, pp. 177–8). If effective restructuring was taking place then there would indeed be little cause for concern. However throughout the 1990s and especially towards the end of the decade observers of economic developments in Poland (including the international agencies) seemed to be focusing greater attention on deficiencies in the microeconomic mechanism. The late 1990s combination of growing weakness in key macro areas (current account, inflation, unemployment) with the suggestion of problems at the micro level looked decidedly awkward and unfortunate. After all, one lesson of the late 1990s crises in Southeast Asia, the Czech Republic and Russia was surely that the market eventually exposes such weaknesses. If micro mechanisms were failing to function properly then vulnerability to crisis and investor flight could become a real danger.

It is worth noting here another well-known Polish trade phenomenon of the (early) 1990s, the vigorous informal, 'cross-border' or 'suitcase trade'. This peaked in 1995 with net exports of $7.2 billion, but was shaken very badly by the Russian crisis of 1998. Its inevitable decline in the years ahead removes another 'safety mechanism' that would otherwise compensate for difficulties in the balance of formal trade flows.

Table 13.8. Top 20 Polish products exported to Germany in 1998

	1998 ($m)
1. Furniture and parts	1,083.7
2. Ships	738.5
3. Women & girls' clothing	666.9
4. Men & boys' clothing	461.5
5. Manufactures of base metals n.e.s.	362.6
6. Wood manufactures n.e.s	303.8
7. Goods vehicles	278.3
8. Cars	228.9
9. Equipment for electricity distribution	224.9
10. Iron, steel or aluminium structures	211.3
Sub-total (1–10)	*4,560.4*
11. Motor vehicle parts	187.8
12. Coal	179.5
13. Copper	178.6
14. Coke	174.9
15. Made up textiles	154.9
16. Electrical switchgear	153.1
17. Iron and steel bars rods etc.	150.3
18. Veneers	132.0
19. Clothing not elsewhere specified	124.7
20. Preserved fruit	119.2
Sub-total (10–20)	*1,555.7*
Total (1–20)	*6,116.1*
Total exports	*10,233.3*
(1–20) as percentage of total exports	*59.8*

Note: n.e.s. = not elsewhere specified.

Source: GUS, *Rocznik Statystyczny Handlu Zagranicznego 1999.*

FDI and trade

A new and positive feature of the Polish export structure is the emergence of sectors (cars, consumer durables, components) whose existence is shaped largely by the activities of MNCs. If at the end of the 1990s their presence was still relatively modest one should remember that the country only began to attract FDI on any significant scale from the mid 1990s. Estimates of the FDI flow into Poland vary considerably depending on sources used. All however point to the same broad trends showing a weak early 1990s start and steady growth from the mid 1990s. The OECD (1998, p. 133) recommends as the more accurate measure FDI on an accruals basis in the balance of payments statistics and notes inflows worth $1.9 billion in 1994, $3.7 billion in 1995 and $4.5 billion in 1996. The Polish central bank estimates that inflows were worth $5bn in 1998 and $6.6 bn in 1999 while the inward investment agency (PAIZ), from its surveys, believes that 1998 saw FDI soar to just over $10 billion. It is worth noting however that PAIZ figures are exaggerated by inclusion of profits reinvested in Poland and in-kind investment contributions. Nevertheless the surge in fixed capital inflows since 1995 means that Poland is, in absolute terms, the regional leader in attracting FDI although it still lags in FDI per capita where it ranks sixth among Central European economies. With its large domestic market, low labour costs, easy access to the EU market, a string of investment-pulling privatisations in the pipeline (for 2000–02), the signs were that Poland, barring any major economic or political upset, could expect to move speedily up the FDI league table. The sectoral destination of FDI confirms the strong interest of foreign investors in domestic demand. The FDI stock in manufacturing was heavily skewed towards sectors where demand was strongly growing: at end 1997 foodstuffs had 24.6% of the total stock, cars 14.8%, chemical products 10.6%, and wood and paper virtually the same.

Table 13.9. The trade and current account balance in the late 1990s

	1995	1996	1997	1998	1999
Trade balance[a]	-6.2	-12.7	-16.6	-18.8	-18.5
Of which, with EU	-2.7	-7.5	-10.5	-11.8	-10.5
as %	43.0	59.0	63.0	63.0	57.0
'Informal' trade balance[b]	7.2	6.4	6.0	6.0	3.6
Current account[b] ($billion)	5.3	-1.4	-4.3	-6.9	11.7[c]
% of GDP	4.6	-1.0	-3.2	-4.6	7.6[c]
FDI inflow[b] ($billion)	1.1	2.8	3.1	5.0	6.6[c]

Notes: [a] The trade data reported here for each year are from GUS on a 'customs basis' and differ from trade data reported by the central bank on a payments basis; [b] National Bank of Poland balance of payments data; [c] initial data.

Source: As for Table 13.1, *Rzeczpospolita*, 2 February 2000.

As noted above, the welcome acceleration in FDI inflow in the late 1990s was accompanied by the intensive importing activity of foreign-owned firms. The data (see Weresa, 1999; GUS) are patchy but suggest that MNC imports have been running in the 1990s at around twice the rate of exports with the gap widening – at least up until 1997. In 1994 foreign-owned firms had imports of $7.1 billion and exports of $4.3 billion. Three years on, in 1997, they had imports of $25.1 billion and exports of $13.5 billion. At the end of 1998 they accounted for 48% of Polish exports and 53% of imports, up from 25% and 33% in 1994. Looked at in another (politically provocative) manner, foreign-owned firms were responsible for 61% of the country's 1998 trade deficit. A slippage from 1994 through to 1997 in export sales as a proportion of their total revenue (from 15.6% to 13.8%) also caused some concern, suggesting that foreign investor firms in Poland had their sights increasingly set on the domestic economy, seduced (like domestic firms showing lack of interest in exports) by its strong growth. Foreign-owned firms are undoubtedly active exporters; the only problem is that they are even more active importers. The council for socio-economic strategy (Rada Społeczno-Gospodarczej, RSSG – a government sponsored but independent think tank) in summing up its January 1999 seminar on trade and FDI noted of foreign firms in Poland that 'one cannot observe any more intensive activity in favour of creating a productive capacity with a clear pro export orientation' (see *Aktualne tendencje* ..., 1999, p. 50). Once again it is worth noting that more recent research identifies clearer signals of more encouraging developments, especially in the sectors where MNC activity is strong (motors and telecoms), so it may be that substantial improvement in trade performance is in sight.[8]

Table 13.10. FDI in Central Europe, 1998

	Total stock ($bn)	Stock per capita ($)
Poland	**30.7**	**793**
Hungary	22.5	2,205
Russia	10.3	70
Czech Republic	9.0	873
Romania	3.8	167
Croatia	2.9	604
Ukraine	2.6	50
Slovenia	2.4	1,200
Estonia	2.1	1,312
Latvia	1.9	760
Slovakia	1.7	320
Lithuania	1.5	405
Bulgaria	1.4	166

Source: Rzeczpospolita, 24 June 1999.

In the longer run FDI will play a critical role in reintegrating Poland into the world economy and into the production organisation of the international firm. In the short to medium term however dangers abound. Experience shows that

MNCs have a hefty import propensity in the early stages of new investment. They have, not surprisingly, also tended to be particularly active in sectors where domestic demand has been growing fastest. Strong inward investment is badly needed for continued economic modernisation. For the future the Polish authorities must do what they can to maintain that inflow while also encouraging MNCs into export while trying to 'capture' within the country more of the internal activity of the international firm. The EU accession trajectory combined with strong, but balanced, economic growth is probably the strongest bait for continued FDI inflow. Risks of upset to any of these elements are likely to dent MNC interest in the country with extremely damaging results for overall economic modernisation.

Institutional aspects of trade restructuring

The institutional structure underpinning foreign trading relationships has also undergone great change in the 1990s. In the old system foreign trade was a state monopoly. In 1988 some 30 specialised foreign trade organisations (FTOs) together with 19 other state firms accounted for almost 90% of all exports and imports.[9] In 1990 the private sector had only a small proportion of exports (4.8%) but was already becoming enthusiastically engaged in imports with 14.3% of the total. Liberalisation opened the door to traders and new private businesses immediately jumped in. By the late 1990s the institutional-organisational set-up in foreign trade was, through the combined process of new business creation, privatisation of state concerns and inward investment, thoroughly transformed. In 1999 the private sector's share in trade had jumped to 81% of exports and 87% of imports. Another striking feature is that exporting, although in private hands, remains a highly 'selective' and concentrated activity. The top 200 exporters are said to be responsible for around half of total exports (Lubiński and Marczewski, 1999, p. 53). To put it another way some 60% of firms are not involved in export and, of the 40% that are, only 8% are 'strongly' active (Płowiec, 1997, p. 606). In an interesting comparison of firms' export propensity across Spain, Poland and Romania, Carlin and her colleagues (see Carlin et al., 1999) found that while most Spanish firms are involved to some degree in export, in Poland and Romania 'many firms do not export at all'. Of 2.7 million legally registered firms only 42,000 were said to be involved, in 1999, in exporting.[10] If the early 1990s' foray into trade was spontaneously released by liberalisation, then the questions for a country like Poland are: how to sustain it beyond that basic stage, and how to attract more firms into exporting? Some Polish specialists note gloomily that Polish firms are losing the competitive struggle against import competition and barely holding on to exports. One contributor to the debate reported for example that while import penetration had risen from 24% to 31% over 1994–97 the share of exports in sales revenues had stuck at 14% over the same period, adding: 'greater difficulties in selling on the domestic market are accompanied by difficulties on foreign markets. If this process continues one can count on enterprises being pushed out of the market' (*Aktualne tendencje* ..., 1999, pp. 78–9).

SOME WIDER ISSUES

Not exporting strongly enough, importing too enthusiastically

Poland, well into post-communist transformation, is by no means an intensive exporter. Its exports were worth $309 per capita in 1985, some 78% of the world average of $398. By the late 1990s they had more than doubled (to $730 in 1998) and, with the world exports growth somewhat dented by turbulent international conditions, Poland's export 'intensity' jumped to 85% of the world average in 1998, a proportion that is likely to slip in 1999–2000. In comparison with the other leading transition economies, admittedly much smaller and so for size reasons likely to be disproportionately strong traders, Polish exports per capita are low. In 1998 the Czech figure was $2561 and the Hungarian $2275. Poland looked to be much closer to the country group containing Belarus and Bulgaria with $714 and $602 respectively than to the premier division of EU aspirants. Poland's share in world exports did increase in the 1990s (from 0.4% in 1990 to 0.6% in 1998) but the growth in imports share was much faster (from 0.3% to 0.9%). The changing snapshot shows a country reintegrating in the world economy but with some way to go before it recaptures even its pre-World War II position of around 1% of world trade.[11] The fast pace of import growth is by far the strongest feature on the Polish trade scene. In the mid 1980s Poland had imports of $291 per capita (1985), a figure equivalent to 71% of the world average of $413. By 1998 it was $1217, exceeding (by 35%) the average world figure ($902). Poland's import thirst in relation to other transforming economies is striking. The relationship between imports and exports showed explosive growth from the mid 1990s, the Polish experience closer, among EU countries, to that of Portugal than of Spain, a country more similar to Poland in size. Ireland, a country whose foreign trade pattern is shaped by very strong FDI penetration, reveals, as might be expected, the opposite tendency, a remarkably strong export orientation.

Vulnerabilities may increase

An added problem for the early years of the new decade is that Poland must service a growing burden of debt repayment following the restructuring deals of the early 1990s. Agreements with official creditors in the Paris Club (1991) and with private creditors in the London Club (1994) included generous debt forgiveness packages carefully crafted to create a breathing space to build a strong export capacity. In each case around 50% of obligations were written off: remaining debt was to be repaid to the Paris Club by 2014 and to the London Club by 2024. London Club debt service obligations do not start until Paris Club creditors are repaid. The result however is that repayments grow steadily in the first decade of the twenty-first century. It seems likely that the debt service to exports ratio will increase markedly but even at the 11% figure suggested below it poses no special danger. Many countries safely manage higher debt burdens.

Table 13.11. The imports/exports ratio

	1995	1996	1997	1998	1999[a]
Poland	125.1	152.0	164.3	166.7	165.8
Czech	116.7	126.5	119.3	109.3	105.1
Hungary	120.2	115.5	111.2	111.7	113.0
Spain	125.4	119.3	117.7	121.8	129.6
Portugal	143.1	142.9	146.0	155.3	155.7
Ireland	74.1	73.8	73.3	69.0	65.7

Note: [a] average in first three quarters, except for Portugal and Ireland where average is over two quarters.

Source: Informacje o sytuacji społeczno-gospodarczej kraju rok 1999, Warsaw: GUS, 2000, p. 97.

Table 13.12. Debt service obligations, 1997–2005 ($ billion)

	1997	1998	1999	2000	2001	2002	2003–5
Total debt service	2.3	2.3	2.4	2.8	2.9	3.3	4.2
Exports[b]	27.2	30.1	26.4	27.7	30.5	33.6	37.0
Informal' net exports[b]	6.0	6.0	3.6	3.0	2.0	1.0	0.0
Debt service/all exports (%)	6.9	6.4	8.0	9.1	8.9	9.5	11.4

Notes: [a] annual average; [b] debt service payments are from the Ministry of finance. Trade estimates are ours. We assume that informal trade gradually vanishes and the exports increase by 5% in 2000 and 10% per annum thereafter.

Sources: GUS, press reports.

The problem is rather the existence of yet one more factor that may increase investor nervousness in the future. The danger is compounded by the marked increase in the final years of the 1990s in enterprise (and to a much smaller extent municipal) foreign currency indebtedness. At end 1999 it was estimated that firms' foreign currency debts totalled around $22 billion, of which half was thought to be the borrowing of Polish subsidiaries from foreign parent companies on unknown terms and maturities. The other worrying feature is speculative ('hot money') inflows which, in early 2000, were estimated (*Rzeczpopolita*, 24 April 2000) to be running at the rate of around $15 billion per annum, equivalent to 60% of official international reserves.

Trade disequilibrium and slower economic growth: impact on EU entry prospects

The 'market' is said to get 'fidgety' when a country's current account deficit reaches 5% to 6% of GDP. Poland's 7.6% deficit in 1999 should by this reckoning have triggered some serious upset. That none transpired, at least up until the time of writing in mid 2000, was ascribed to a range of factors including confidence in Polish macroeconomic management, the high level of foreign currency reserves, the unusual 'transformation economy' feature of continued attractive privatisation prospects, and the knowledge that the share of speculative capital was still relatively small. Nevertheless in 1999–2000, as the economy's internal and external balance slipped, the monetary authorities tried to restore order in the only way they could – by raising interest rates. Higher rates slow imports and inflation but also restrain GDP growth. Yet fast GDP growth is crucial to closing the gap with the EU and has always been viewed as critical to the speed of EU accession. There are other complications too. Increasing the interest rate differential with the rest of the world makes investment in Polish securities more attractive so adding further upward pressure to already strong real appreciation of the currency, with adverse effects on the trade balance. It also raises the likelihood of greater hot money inflows. The overall impact of these various forces is always hard to determine but in the new decade the Polish economy seemed to be surrounded by just the sort of unwelcome and multiplying uncertainties that could hit the EU accession process. [12]

Trade debates in Poland

Another key accession issue is that one of the enlargement criteria focuses explicitly on the 'ability to withstand competition within the EU'.[13] While, as we noted above, Smith was prepared to be generously optimistic in his view that Polish competitiveness, although hardly strong in the mid 1990s, could have been on an upward trajectory, boosted in part by accelerating inward investment, others had grave doubts. The sharply deteriorating trade and current account situation in the later 1990s stimulated discussion within Poland on how to interpret the economic signals and devise appropriate policy. At one level the persistent and deep trade deficit showed already who was winning and losing the competitive struggle as trade barriers fell. The news for Poland was not good. A deficit in EU trade of around $10 billion per annum represented, as some Polish specialists began to note, substantial EU job creation. By May 2000 it was a point that President Kwaśniewski took with him on an official visit to France. He explained to readers of *Le Figaro* that 'we estimate that thanks to exports to Poland over a million people in Europe have jobs' (*Rzeczpospolita* ,16 May 2000).

The first thing that should be said about the Polish trade debate is that there appears to be no significant push for imports to be restrained in any more active way than at present applied; that is, indirectly through restrictive monetary policy. The view surfaced in 1999–2000, but only just, that if deterioration were to continue then Poland might have a right, and find it useful, to appeal to exceptional (balance of payments) clauses in international agreements to take direct action on imports. This minority position has been put by some but the great weight of opinion is that the best way to correct the trade imbalance is by concerted pro-exports effort rather than by any anti-imports action. Within this broad view it is possible to detect two diverse approaches: one is decidedly 'liberal' and argues that more successful export restructuring has been handicapped by a general slowdown in reform pace and growing statism (perhaps 'cronyism' is a more accurate label); the other is markedly more interventionist and argues that Poland has been slow to learn and copy the pro-export strategies of the developed market economies and the EU in particular. The policy implications are correspondingly diverse: Polish liberals argue for faster privatisation, stronger anti-inflation policy and a more restrictive fiscal stance, and pin much hope on real exchange rate appreciation automatically to restructure the economy; the interventionists focus attention on the need for activity to promote exports, better trade insurance, lower interest rates, greater commitment from the financial sector, tax reliefs on export orientated investment, more state spending on R&D to push exporters up the skills ladder, policies to encourage the SME sector to get into exports, and so on.

And back to the EU accession process

This discussion, or at least its second current, reflects a wider point in that there is a strong feeling that the trade asymmetries built into EU 'Europe Association' agreements of the 1990s while on the surface favouring Poland in reality favoured EU producers. As one observer put it, 'the calendar for liberalisation was simply the reverse of Polish export possibilities, chiefly over 1992–95. Where we had a comparative advantage resulting from low labour costs we had delays in gaining access to markets' (see *Aktualne tendencje* … , 1999, p. 182).

Meanwhile, few could have doubted that, notwithstanding the most heroic attempts at restructuring, Polish firms, no matter their ownership form – whether state owned, newly privatised or just new... were at a severe organisational disadvantage in comparison with EU enterprises. The resulting trade deficit, persistent over the medium term, is taken to confirm this and the argument follows that Poland is doubly disadvantaged in that it has not benefited from a strong flow of EU structural funds to help create the basis for future export growth. Another variant of this at the level of policy formulation is that Poland has simply been disadvantaged by the country's lack of, and lack of familiarity with, the sophisticated trade policies that exist in the EU that can be speedily called in to service when needed (especially use of non-tariff barriers). This helps fuel the view that the EU seems to be pressing on candidate countries a fairly pure version of liberalism notwithstanding those countries' needs for more sensitive treatment. The apparent inability or unwillingness of the European Commission to discern the real 'asymmetric' needs of the candidate countries in this regard has the potential to do great damage to the accession process. The decline in support for EU membership and the growth of euroscepticism in Poland, although by no means severe, should give pause for reflection. Between 1994 and early 1999 the proportion of the population in favour of EU entry fell from 77% to a low of 55% although it did climb again to 59% by May 2000. Meanwhile over the same period the 'no' vote increased from 6% to a fairly stable 26% (see CBOS, 1999, 2000).

It may be almost inconceivable that the EU accession process could be derailed. In mid 2000 negotiations were in full swing although about to meet the more difficult areas of agriculture, capital and labour mobility. The Polish authorities continued to push January 2003 as the preferred entry date and most of Polish society remained committed to entry. On the other hand the EU trade deficit was causing growing concern and for the first time began to be equated with Polish jobs lost.[14] The domestic political calendar with a presidential election in late 2000 and parliamentary elections soon after created room for the amplification of dissenting voices. Brussels appeared to be stiff and unyielding on Polish needs. A storm might not come, but some ominous clouds gathered on the horizon.

CONCLUSION

What does our overview and survey of Poland's international economic relationships in the 1990s tell us? There was undoubtedly a remarkable and sudden early 1990s shift in the geography of Polish trade. The commodity structure of trade has changed too and most noticeable is the shift in exports towards manufactures embodying relatively unskilled labour in which the outward processing trade (especially in furniture and textiles) played a major role. The signals that the export mix moved up the skills ladder are not so clear cut but may reflect the delayed arrival of FDI with better results on the horizon. Poland's EU trade deficit has increased sharply, a permanent (some would say 'structural') feature of the late 1990s. Meanwhile, as FDI flows kicked-in in the second half of the 1990s the imports effect was immediately noticeable, the exports impact less immediately clear. Optimists saw signs of healthy restructuring as MNCs began to shape trade flows. The pessimists worried, especially when the current account deficit rose to more than 7% of GDP, and argued for much clearer 'exports policy'.

If, beneath the noise of the immediate statistical data, export restructuring did accelerate in the late 1990s and into the early years of the new decade then economic imbalances will diminish and the trade problems will correct themselves. But if this is not happening, if the micro-level restructuring is slower, then Polish vulnerability to investor flight will grow – at least in that interval (which could be longer than the 6 to 8 years sometimes identified by the Polish authorities) before the złoty merges into the euro zone.

The external account highlights a major area of economic weaknesses and few doubt that action is needed. The policy debate in the country points to the need to catch up quickly with Western experience in export promotion in terms of a wider panoply of fairly orthodox pro-export initiatives but which Poland perhaps neglected in the first 'liberal' phase of transformation in the 1990s. If the trade and current accounts situation deteriorates further, direct action to stem imports cannot be ruled out but that would clearly have wider economic and political significance. Given the scale of the Polish trade problem it is surprising in retrospect that the European Commission has not taken a much more active role in trying to shape and stimulate a stronger Polish export capacity. This is especially so in view of the Eldorado of the Polish market that suddenly appeared for EU producers in the 1990s.

Finally, it is worth commenting on a more institutional feature of 1990s' trade developments. When Poland's *planned* trade collapsed it was replaced by highly *spontaneous* activity. This saw a fast-growing private sector (especially on the import side) and state firms shifting into 'distress sales' in 1990 before largely contenting themselves with a strongly growing domestic market in the 1990s. From the mid 1990s trade flows started to be shaped by the *deliberate* actions of the international firm. Throughout the 1990s governments played virtually no role at the micro level in shaping trade (forwarding a trade policy through macro stabilisation, privatisation and the negotiation of liberal international trading arrangements). For many this was as it should be. On the other hand, perhaps the growing trade problems of the later 1990s show that in the flow of trade 'regimes' from *planned* through *spontaneous* to *MNC-managed* there is also a need for the state to re-engage by building the institutions and developing policies that will do something for exports before the need arises to take more drastic steps to curb imports.

NOTES

1 These data and those that follow are from *Rocznik Statystyczny 1991*, Warsaw: GUS, 1991, pp. 379–80.
2 In 1938, of course with quite different borders than today, Germany took 24% of Polish exports and provided 23% of imports while the (autarchic) USSR took 0.3% of Polish exports and provided 0.8% of imports.
3 In current prices. It is worth noting that the restructuring process seems much stronger in the Czech Republic and Hungary where the SITC-7 export share rose from 28% and 25% in 1994 to 42% and 52% respectively in 1998, *Rocznik Statystyczny1999*,Warsaw: GUS, 1999, pp. 699–780.
4 Urszula Płowiec (1997, p. 606), for example, complains of a 1990s commodity structure in exports where over 90% of goods comprise 'agricultural produce, raw materials and labour intensive products with a large share of low qualified labour' and only around 5% embody 'advanced technology'.
5 Note that Kamiński breaks down products into four groups: natural resource-intensive, unskilled labour-intensive, technology-intensive and human capital-intensive, while Smith's methodology differs. He uses a three-way classification of human capital-intensive, resource-intensive and labour-intensive.
6 She notes that the correlation coefficient across RCAs between 1991 and 1995 is 0.67, indicating some change in profile, as compared to 0.94 in 1995–98, suggesting barely any change.
7 Poland's top 10 export earners, at three-digit 'group' level, in SITC 6 in 1998 are shown below:

		$m
699	Manufactures of base metals, not elsewhere specified	363
635	Wood manufactures not elsewhere specified	304
691	Iron, steel or aluminium structures	211
682	Copper	179
658	Made-up articles of textile materials	155
676	Steel bars, rods, sections	150
634	Veneers, plywood	133

661	Lime, cement, fabricated construction materials	106
651	Textile yarn	97
641	Paper and paperboard	73
Sub total		*1,816*

Source: *Rocznik Statystyczny Handlu Zagranicznego 1999*, Warsaw: GUS, 1999, pp. 204–31.

8 Research by Kamiński for the World Bank, reported in *Gazeta Wyborcza,* 26 May 2000.

9 From Lubiński and Marczewski, 1999, p. 52. Some FTOs, after privatisation, managed to transform themselves into successful conglomerates, often initially stimulated by backward integration. The Elektrim enterprise is probably the best example (power, communications, electrical engineering) but others had a harder time. See Chris Bobinski, 'Poland's exporters find a new lease of life', *Financial Times,* 1 December 1993.

10 'Tylko 42 tysiące firm', *Rzeczpospolita,* 18 May 2000.

11 *Mały Rocznik Statystyczny 1939*, Warsaw: GUS, 1939, p. 164.

12 Political uncertainties also exist and are discussed in this volume by Szczerbiak and Bobiński.

13 The enlargement criteria were set out at the Copenhagen summit of the EU in June 1993 as follows: 'Membership requires that the candidate country has achieved stability of institutions guaranteeing democracy, the rule of law, human rights and respect for and protection of minorities, the existence of a functioning market economy as well as the capacity to cope with competitive pressure and market forces within the Union. Membership presupposes the candidate's ability to take on the obligations of membership including adherence to the aims of political, economic and monetary union' (quoted in Henderson, 1999).

14 As one Polish economist put it, 'after reaching a current account deficit of around 7.2% of GDP in 1999 this indicator must decline significantly in 2000. If that doesn't happen it will mean that foreign capital is not creating the hoped for competitive capacity in Polish enterprises and the economy may find itself paralysed at the ceiling of the current account deficit and incapable of moving from it. Polish consumers will be creating jobs for foreign workers' see Noga, 2000).

REFERENCES

Aktualne tendencje w Polskim handlu zagranicznym: wnioski dla polityki ekonomicznej (1999), (Actual tendencies in Polish foreign trade: conclusions for economic policy), Rada Strategii Społeczno-Gspodarczej, Raport nr 35, Warsaw: Sierpień.

Carlin, W., Estrin, S., Schaffer, M. (1999), *Measuring Progress in Transition and Towards EU Accession: A Comparison of Manufacturing Firms in Poland, Romania and Spain,* Centre for Economic Reform and Transformation, Heriot-Watt University, Discussion Paper no. 99/02, January.

Centrum Badania Opinii Społecznej (CBOS) (1999), *Poparcie dla integracji Polski z unią europejską* (Support for Polish EU integration), Warsaw: CBOS. (2000) *Polacy, Węgrzy, Czesi, Litwini i Ukraińcy o integracji z Unią Europejską*, (Poles, Hungarians, Czechs, Lithuanians and Ukrainians on EU integration), Warsaw: CBOS.

Economic Survey of Poland 1997, Paris: OECD (1996).

Economic Survey of Poland 1998, Paris OECD (1998).

Henderson, K. (1999), 'The real challenges of EU eastward enlargement', paper delivered to the BASEES conference, Cambridge, March.

Kamiński, B. (1998), 'Poland's transition from the perspective of performance in EU markets', *Communist Economies and Economic Transformation*, 10 (2).

Lubiński, M. Marczewski, K. (1999) 'Handel zagraniczny Polski w okresie transformacji' (Polish foreign trade in the transformation period), *Ekonomista,* 1–2.

Monitoring European Integration: The Impact of Eastern Europe (1990), London: Centre for Economic Policy Research.

Noga, A. (2000), 'Model ostrzegawczy dla Polski', (A warning model for Poland), paper presented to the seminar organised by Instytut Finansów w Wyższej Szkole Ubezpieczeń i Bankowości, Hotel Forum, Warsaw: 31 January.

Nuti, D.M. (1996), 'Inflation, interest and exchange rates in the transition', *Economics of Transition*, 4 (1).

Płowiec, U. (1997), 'Handel zagraniczny Polski pod koniec lat 90. – problemy i wyżwania' (Polish foreign trade at the end of the 1990s – problems and challenges), *Ekonomista,* 5–6.

Smith, A. (1999), 'The competitiveness of East European exports in EU markets', paper presented to the workshop, *Poland and the Transformation in Europe: The Role of FDI*, School of Slavonic and East European Studies, University of London, November.

Weresa, M. (1999), 'Foreign direct investment and trade patterns: theory and evidence from Poland', paper presented to the workshop, *Poland and the Transformation in Europe: The Role of FDI*, School of Slavonic and East European Studies, University of London, November.

14. Poland – European Union: the economics of accession

Witold M. Orłowski

INTRODUCTION

On 30 March 1998, eight years after the beginning of the radical programme of economic reforms aimed at its transformation into a market economy Poland embarked on formal EU entry negotiations. The integration and accession programme was supported by of all the major political forces in the country and, at least initially, by the overwhelming majority of the population. Poland had started its drive towards the world's largest and probably most significant regional integration block.

The reasons for applying to the EU were both economic and political. After having passed through the initial liberalisation shock, connected with the stabilisation effort, the economy started a search for a new path of sustainable growth. Soon it became obvious that, in order to grow, the Polish economy needed wide access to West European markets, some way of reducing the perceived risks of investment and easier access to foreign financing. What was even more important, however, was that Poland needed a new anchor for political and social stability. EU membership meant not only a broader economic co-operation it also implied leaving the grey zone where the potential always existed for economic, social and political instability, and moving instead to a conclusion of the transition process.

The enlargement to the East also represents an unprecedented challenge for the EU. Never before in its history has the organisation had to include so many new members with such large disparities in development levels as compared to existing EU members. As the resources that can be spent on the enlargement are reduced their rational use becomes a priority. Enlargement therefore also requires a 'transition' for the EU itself: one that involves reforming the least efficient and most costly common policies, enhancing the efficiency of EU institutions, increasing the flexibility of markets to adjust to new economic conditions. Nevertheless, the price is worth paying: if the enlargement goes smoothly both parts of Europe can be reintegrated and a potentially explosive economic and social imbalance between the two regions can be reduced or even eliminated.

POLAND AND WESTERN EUROPE IN A HISTORICAL PERSPECTIVE

In discussing Polish EU membership we deliberately use the word 're-integration' rather than 'integration'. One may point to the fact that since the pre-industrial revolution in the sixteenth and seventeenth centuries Poland – like the other Central European countries – was a part of the European world-economy. The partitions of Poland, and the loss of independence for the whole of the nineteenth century, meant that various parts of the country participated in the economic life of Europe as integral elements of other national economies (see Gorzelak, chapter 11 in this volume). Nevertheless, the Polish provinces of the three empires (Russia, Austria and Germany) were involved in modern European industrialisation. When independence was regained after World War I the country managed to merge separate provinces of the three empires into one national economy. Poland was undoubtedly poorer than the West European countries, partly due to its dualistic economic structure (the Eastern half of Poland was predominantly agricultural and poorly developed; again Gorzelak takes up these issues). But Poland did have a functioning market economy, a developed legal framework and market institutions. Polish GDP per capita in the late 1940s, after post-war reconstruction, was estimated by the UN at only 6% below that of Italy, and almost 40% above Spain (see United Nations, 1950).

The situation changed dramatically during the 40-year long 'central planning' period. Then the economy was insulated from international markets and developed in a semi-autarchic way (sometimes also described as an extreme case of development through import substitution). Market economy institutions, the associated legal framework, as well as the spirit of private entrepreneurship, were deliberately destroyed by the communist rulers and replaced by an inefficient and eventually chaotic and anti-developmental system of central planning. In sharp contrast with optimistic statistics on economic growth the command economy was not able to deliver its promised fast development on a sustained basis. On the contrary the development gap between Poland and the West European countries grew to an unprecedented extent (see Figure 14.1). [1]

Figure 14.1. Relative GDP per capita in Poland and in various regions according to purchasing power parity (PPP) in 1950 and during 1990s

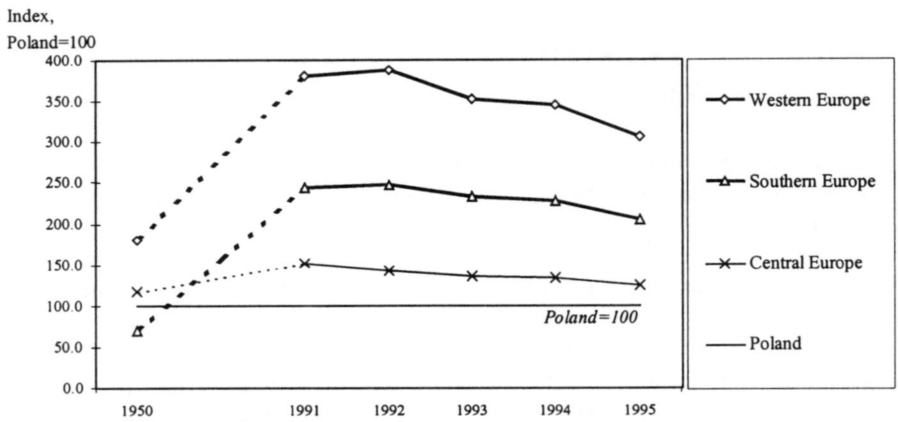

Western Europe: Germany, France, Italy, UK
Southern Europe: Spain, Portugal, Greece
Central Europe: Poland, Czech Rep., Slovakia, Hungary

Source: Estimates for 1950 based on UN data, OECD

Poland was not the only country suffering because of the separation from its natural economic partners. Over the 40-year post-war period not only were the economies of all the Central European countries dwarfed by Western Europe but even Southern Europe, once much poorer, greatly outperformed Central Europe. The gap was not only in real income but also in the institutions, legal framework, technology, human capital development, and ability to compete on the world market. After over 40 years of central planning Central European economies were left in disastrous shape. It was almost as if the war had continued there for a long period after the West started reconstruction and embarked on successful development. Obviously, there was some success in industrialisation, social development, literacy, health and urbanisation. The progress, however, was insufficient to secure convergence towards West European standards. Only the peaceful political, social and economic breakthrough of 1989–90 brought to an end the process that had seen the development gap between Poland and the West continuously grow wider. Reintegration started with rebuilding long-term economic ties and the next logical step on this road was to join the EU.

POLAND'S DRIVE TOWARDS EU MEMBERSHIP

EU membership was declared to be a policy objective by the Polish government as soon as such a move became politically feasible. However, the way forward, as it seemed in 1989, was pretty long. In 1989 Poland was still treated as a non-market economy that needed and received EU support in the form of development assistance (through the Phare programme), emergency deliveries of food, and some trade concessions (preferential tariff rates for Polish imports in line with the Generalised System of Preferences – GSP). It was only during the first months of 1990 that the idea emerged that Poland should start negotiating an association agreement with the EU (see Kawecka-Wyrzykowska, 1999). That association agreement, or the 'Europe agreement' as it became known, was finally signed in December 1991. It called for the full bilateral liberalisation of trade in industrial goods over a 10-year period, some concessions in the case of other products, namely food, and for limited liberalisation with respect to flows of services and capital. A special financial scheme was granted for EU development assistance under the Phare programme, and a framework was set up for economic, political and cultural co-operation. Despite Polish efforts the EU did not want to make any clear declaration concerning future membership prospects. Finally, in a compromise formula, the EU agreed only to note Poland's unilateral declaration of its wish to join the Union.

In the period that followed, the EU's position towards Eastern enlargement began to evolve in a more promising direction. During the Copenhagen summit in 1993 an invitation was issued to the Central and Eastern European countries (CEECs) that wished to join, together with a set of criteria that had to be satisfied by the time of accession. Those criteria insisted on the existence in applicant countries of stable democracy and the rule of law, functioning market economies able to cope with competitive pressure in the Union, and the ability to adopt and implement the *acquis communautaire*. A serious potential danger for enlargement was created by adding an additional criterion, namely, the Union's ability to accept new members. This linked enlargement to the progress of internal EU financial and institutional reform.

Based on the Copenhagen criteria Poland formally applied in 1994 to join the EU. Three years later the European Commission issued a favourable opinion on the application (see European Commission, 1997) and negotiations on entry conditions started in March 1998. Here one should point to some specific features of the negotiation process:

- the negotiations are not between competitors but among the present and future members of the same club. For this reason both sides are interested in an applicant's successful entry into the single market. If in the future an applicant like Poland became stuck with poor economic performance, such as difficulties with the balance of payments, the EU would be forced to provide financial support (as was the case with Greece in the 1980s);

- the negotiations are not 'negotiations' in the traditional sense of the word. To enter the EU Poland has to accept the *acquis communautaire* in full (concessions would be minimal and extremely difficult to obtain), in other words, Poland must accept EU rules;
- those issues that can be negotiated include: the possibility of transition periods in implementing some parts of the *acquis* (particularly the most costly ones); the possibility of introducing transition periods during which Poland would not take full advantage of some membership rights; procedures regarding Poland's involvement in certain common policies of the Union; the extent of financial support for Poland resulting from participation in the sharing of structural funds.

Despite the fact that the negotiations are expected to be difficult, it is possible that Poland will be accepted as a member state relatively soon. The target date, as set by Poland, is to finish the negotiations by the year 2001 and to enter the EU in 2003. However, meeting such a timetable (which the EU calls 'very ambitious') would require a huge adjustment effort from both sides as well as a strong political will. In their absence the negotiations may take much longer.

CHALLENGES OF EU MEMBERSHIP

What costs and benefits should Poland, and the EU, expect if Poland eventually joins the club? The rationale for enlargement seems to be more evident on the Polish side. First, as an EU member Poland will get irrevocable and unlimited access to the West European market. Given the huge differentials in wage levels between Poland and its Western neighbours, this should create tremendous business opportunities for both domestic and foreign investors. Second, EU membership will greatly reduce the investment risk, encouraging long-term capital flows to Poland (see Baldwin et al., 1997). Third, membership will help Poland in developing a stable, market-friendly legal framework that will encourage long-term investment. Fourth, Poland, as an EU member, will be eligible for generous structural aid, and Polish agriculture will gain at least some of the Common Agricultural Policy (CAP) benefits.

But EU membership also involves costs for Poland. In adjusting to the demands of the single market Polish producers will have to meet EU product norms, ensuring that a product manufactured in Poland satisfies EU consumer protection rules (as it can be sold everywhere in the EU). Competitive pressure will also greatly increase on the 'domestic' market and the freedom to support Polish firms with public assistance will be severely restricted. Both phenomena will force Polish firms to adjust, making them boost investment and productivity if they are to survive. Even more challenging, Polish firms will have to make additional investment to ensure that EU environmental or social protection norms are satisfied.

In a nutshell, the costs for Poland may be threefold. First, the accelerated restructuring and modernisation of the economy, reinforced by intensified competition, may push up unemployment, particularly if the adjustment capacity of domestic firms is low and labour market flexibility poor. This problem has a sharp spatial dimension since some regions – particularly those with ailing industries – may be much more strongly hit than others. Second, Poland may be forced to introduce costly legislation that will impair the long-term growth of competitiveness and productivity. One example is the high level of social protection, leading to higher labour costs and reduced market flexibility. Another is an EU inspired, CAP supported, protectionist policy in agriculture that slows structural changes. Fortunately, it seems that the scale of such negative phenomena will not be too great.[2] Finally, Poland may have to adopt some costly regulations that do not easily fit with the current preferences of society. A good example is the environment. The rich EU countries run very costly environmental policies. Although the need to spend more on environmental protection in Poland is obvious, at the current level of its income Polish society would probably prefer to have less costly environmental policies than these of the EU. This is especially true if one assumes, as a rule of thumb, a '20–80 principle': 20% of expenditure on environmental protection, if well targeted, may yield 80% of the potential improvement.[3] This may be particularly valid in Poland where environmental pollution is much more severe than in the EU and where existing Polish environmental policies, putting more stress on concentrating resources on particular uses and being more market-based, seem better suited to Poland's needs than the EU environmental *acquis*.

The effects of enlargement for the EU include, on the benefits side, faster economic growth due to expanded trade and investment links, better allocation of resources, and – last, but not least – a more stable, more prosperous neighbour. On the costs side the EU should mainly count the increased burden of financial transfers.

EU membership is obviously a challenge for the Polish economy and society but the country is relatively well prepared to face such challenges (although several sectors of the economy may face tough problems). [4] The real shock that Poland had to absorb in 1990–91 was much more dangerous than economic liberalisation due to EU accession. In 1989 the economy was close to collapse, Polish firms lacked adjustment capabilities and domestic products could not compete on world markets. Despite this, Poland undertook the most radical programme of systemic reforms in Central and Eastern Europe. The liberalisation, stabilisation and elimination of obstacles to entrepreneurship brought results quite quickly. In 1998 Polish GDP was around 29% above its pre-reform level while only Slovenia among other transition economies even approached the 1989 GDP level.[5]

The liberalisation shock connected with EU membership will not be of the same scale, and should not lead to any serious growth slow down (see Czyłewski et al., 1998). One should remember that due to the Europe Agreement the liberalisation of flows of goods, services and capital between Poland and EU was, by the late 1990s, more significant than it had been in the case of the Mediterranean countries even a few years after their accession. This was particularly true in financial markets, which were jealously protected by the South Europeans for long years after EU accession (in Greece the last restrictions were removed only in 1994). In sharp contrast Poland, while joining the OECD in 1996, agreed on almost full liberalisation of capital flows and, from 1999, permitted foreigners almost unrestricted access to domestic financial markets (that does not mean, however, that they do not need licences, if such a licence is required by a Polish firm).

Despite the bargaining that goes on in accession negotiations and despite some obvious adjustment costs, speedy economic liberalisation is not the critical factor in EU accession. The real challenge for Poland is to maintain, after joining the EU, fast and sustainable economic growth. That requires the conclusion of structural reforms started during the 1990s, reforms such as those in privatisation and enterprise restructuring, structural reforms of the public sector, improved functioning of market institutions and public administration, liberalisation of the labour market to make it more flexible. The burden of taxation should be lowered and the state should limit its too extensive role in the economies so liberating more resources for the private sector. Economic and legal stability needs to be secured to attract long-term foreign capital.

CONDITIONS FOR REAL CONVERGENCE

The biggest challenge for the Polish economy is therefore to use EU membership as a vehicle to accelerate economic growth. The key issue for the country is whether EU membership will generate 'real economic convergence', that is, the ability of a less developed country to grow faster so that, over time, the initial gap in GDP per capita diminishes. Neoclassical economic theory explains what should happen in the following development mechanism. In poor countries labour is relatively cheap and in plentiful supply while capital is scarce and relatively expensive. As capital is expensive, its marginal return, its price, must be high. This implies that investment in the poorer country brings higher returns than in the richer countries where capital is less expensive and abundant. This, in turn, creates an incentive to shift capital from richer to poorer countries leading to higher growth rates in the latter.[6] But this mechanism does not work equally well in every situation. Certain conditions must be fulfilled. It requires an open economy, a stable legal and social framework, limited market distortions, a stable and transparent macroeconomic policy, efficient financial markets and that domestic producers have sufficient adjustment capabilities. Will EU membership help in ensuring that such a mechanism functions in Poland?

Table 14.1 shows the distance in level of economic development between Poland and the EU. The development gap can be measured in different ways. The first is simply to compare GDP per capita in Poland and in the EU-15. Of course to do this properly we need to allow for differences in price levels or more generally in the purchasing power parity (PPP) of the different currencies involved. If the average price level in one country is lower than in another then the same nominal value of GDP translates, in fact, into more goods and services being available in the former (the prices of services vary particularly markedly among countries). Table 14.1 shows that Polish GDP per capita, adjusted for differences in PPP, represented in 1996 only 38% of the EU-15 average. The richest EU members had income levels 2.5 to 3 times greater than in Poland. Even in the poorest EU member states, Greece and Portugal, income levels exceeded that in Poland by some 80%.

Another way of looking at the development gap is to calculate a time distance: the number of years of economic growth needed to catch up and reach the same income level. As can be seen from Table 14.1. Poland's 1996 GDP per capita was reached by EU members, on average, 32 years earlier. As simple arithmetic shows, even under the most optimistic assumptions, as for example a long-run GDP growth of 6%, and given the fact that economic growth is going to continue in the EU-15 as well (see Baldwin, 1994), a similar number of years will be needed for Poland to reach a GDP level comparable with the EU-15. The time needed to close the gap obviously depends on the ability of the Polish economy to maintain fast economic growth.

In the history of EU enlargement to date one can make only one strong case where convergence has occurred (the Irish example). The Irish Republic joined the EU (at that time the EEC) in 1973 when its GDP per capita was 60% of the EU-15 average. During the 1970s and 1980s its GDP increased only slowly and in 1989 it reached 68% of the EU average. But in the 1990s Irish GDP growth accelerated in relative terms and in only 8 years by 1997 it managed to reach the EU-15 average.

On the other hand, a counterexample can be found in the case of Greece. Greece joined the EEC in 1981 when its per capita GDP was close to the Irish at 66% of the EU-15 average. But in the years that followed Greek GDP per capita did not change a great deal in relation to the EU-15 and it still remained at 66% of the EU average even in 1997. It is evident that in this case no real convergence occurred.

Table 14.1 The economic development gap between Poland and the EU

	GDP per capita in 1996 (purchasing power parity)		Year in which 1996 GDP level of Poland was	Distance in years	Average growth rate between the year in column (c) and 1996
	EU-15 =100	Poland= 100	attained		
	(a)	(b)	(c)	(d)	(e)
Luxembourg	163	429	1957	39	3.8
Denmark	114	300	1954	42	2.7
Austria	113	297	1960	36	3.1
Belgium	113	297	1957	39	2.8
Germany	111	292	1963	33	3.3
France	105	276	1962	34	3.0
Netherlands	105	276	1964	32	3.2
Italy	102	268	1964	32	3.1
Sweden	101	266	1953	43	2.3
UK	98	258	1956	40	2.4
Finland	96	253	1964	32	2.9
Ireland	94	247	1977	19	4.9
Spain	78	205	1971	25	2.9
Portugal	69	182	1980	16	3.8
Greece	67	176	1977	19	3.0
EU-15	*100*	*263*	*1964*	*+32*	*3.1*
Poland	*38*	*100*	*1996*	*-32*	-

Source: Author's calculations based on Eurostat and OECD data.

The different macroeconomic and structural policies followed by each country can easily explain the diverse results obtained (real convergence for Ireland, none for Greece). Both countries enjoyed huge EU transfers, which were of similar magnitude if related to GDP (around 6%, well above the maximal ceiling of 4% of GDP budgeted by the EU for the Eastern enlargement). However, while Greece used the transfers mainly for maintaining high consumption levels, Ireland channelled them into investment (particularly after Irish economic policy experienced a dramatic shift in the mid 1980s). The consumption to GDP ratio in Greece, at the end of the 1990s still the highest among the OECD countries, was close to 93% in 1990. In Ireland on the other hand the consumption/GDP ratio ranks among the lowest in the OECD (second lowest after Korea) and, since the mid 1980s, did not exceed 74%. The main macroeconomic device accommodating high consumption in Greece was the huge fiscal deficit, reaching almost 20% of GDP in the late 1980s (see Orłowski, 1999). At the same time Ireland, after fiscal adjustment in the mid 1980s, balanced its state budget. Thus, prudent Irish macroeconomic policy from the mid 1980s created a low-inflation, low-taxes, saving- and investment-promoting environment, and attracted significant foreign investment. It is this that is mainly credited for the countries economic success (see European Commission, 1996). In sharp contrast Greece, during the 1980s, displayed a total inability to create a stable framework for economic growth. Greece's indecisive economic policy resulted in a relatively high rate of inflation (between 14% and 22% per annum in the 1980s). It was not until the mid 1990s that inflation was gradually reduced to single figures as a result of co-ordinated fiscal and monetary policies.

Apart from fiscal policy one should not overlook the impact of the different structural policies pursued in the two countries. Irish enterprises proved to be more competitive and better able to adjust perhaps because the economy was quite rapidly liberalised and remained predominantly private. In Greece however the authorities pursued, in the 1980s, a policy of nationalisation of large firms, pushing up the share of public enterprises in (non-agricultural) GDP to over 20% (as compared to between 5% and 10% in Ireland).

The long-term economic performance of Greece and Ireland in the EU sheds some light on what are likely to be key determinants of real convergence also in the Polish case. Clearly, a prudent macroeconomic policy that encourages saving and long-run investment is at the core of success. The main challenge, therefore, is to resist strong pressures for a rapid increase in consumption once large EU development assistance and private capital begin to flow. The simplest mechanism conducive to boosting consumption works through greater public spending – both increased government consumption and higher transfers to households. Given the relatively cheap and easily available financing of the fiscal deficit post-EU accession those pressures may be hard to resist.[7] The inability of Greece to maintain high saving resulted in sluggish economic growth and general social disappointment with the integration process.

Another lesson from the experience of Greece and Ireland concerns structural policy. Not only is it important to mobilise sufficient domestic saving through appropriate macroeconomic policies but it is critical also to invest efficiently (Girard and Hurst, 1994, point to huge differences among countries in investment efficiency). Achieving the right structural policy, aimed at promoting the efficiency of financial markets and at increasing the adjustment capabilities of domestic firms, mainly through privatisation, demonopolisation and restructuring, is a key issue. The less advanced these processes are at the moment of joining the EU, the higher the risk that Poland will not be able to make good use of the available capital, and so will fail to converge with the EU.

Another question is the extent to which the adoption of the EU's legal framework and market regulation may contribute to Polish economic growth. Generally speaking, the *acquis communautaire* is a package of regulations governing the functioning of the EU's single market, where barriers to the free flow of goods, services and productive factors (labour and capital) are lifted, and where uniform principles of market organisation are introduced (embracing competition law, state aids, consumer rights, environmental protection, support for regions, and so on). Each element of the *acquis* will have a tremendous impact on Poland's economy and society. The *acquis* represents a well-developed, coherent set of laws that support economic development. Implementing the *acquis* in Poland may contribute to speeding up real convergence. Indeed some suggest (see Barbone and Zalduendo, 1997) that the combination of the acceptance of the EU legal order, correct macroeconomic policies and a high saving rate may shorten the process of real convergence for Poland to around 20 years).[8]

Modern growth theory suggests that the most important single factor contributing to real convergence is human capital. Investment in human capital (learning and experience) plays a crucial role in fostering long-term growth. In other words, it is not machines that generate GDP, it is the people who produce machines and other outputs. Human capital in Poland is not as highly developed as is often assumed. If Poland wants to maximise the chances for real convergence then this type of investment should be strongly promoted. Table 14.2 gives an indication of the scale of investment in human capital (in a broad sense) in Poland compared to selected EU members.

Despite the fast progress that was observed in Poland during the 1990s the proportion of students in the population in the mid 1990s was still much lower than in the majority of EU countries (although, surprisingly, it was close to that of Ireland). Polish R&D spending as a proportion of GDP, albeit lower than the EU-15 average, was comparable with that of Spain. The quality of education and scientific research is another important issue, as the educational patterns inherited from communist times did not fit the needs of the market economy. In-depth reforms in education and research, as well as securing sufficient funds to finance them, will play a crucial role in maximising Poland's chances for real convergence (Orłowski, 1998b).

Table 14.2. Investment in human capital in Poland and selected EU countries

	Full-time students enrolled in tertiary education per 100 in the 5–25 years age bracket			Spending on R&D as % of GDP (1994)
	1990	1994	1996	
Greece	-	8.6	-	0.49
Ireland	4.4	6.2	-	1.41
Portugal	-	7.6	-	0.63
Spain	7.5	10.1	-	0.85
UE-15	7.6	9.1	-	1.95
Poland	2.9	5.1	6.5	0.82

Sources: GUS, OECD.

Figure 14.2. GPD per capita in regions of Poland (purchasing power parity, EU-15=100)

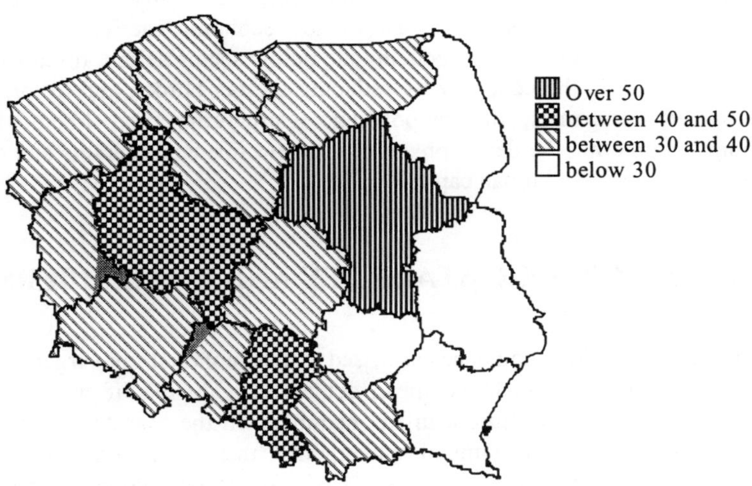

Sources: ZBSE, NOBE.

Another question is: what role may be played by development assistance from the EU? As Figure 14.2 shows, Poland's entire geographic area qualified (at the end of the 1990s) for support from EU structural funds.[9] Only Mazovia, centred on Warsaw, the most highly developed and the most dynamic region of the country, inhabited by some 13% of Poland's population, looked likely to reach the threshold level of 75% of EU average GDP per capita over the next 10 years while the rest of the country looks likely to remain eligible for significant EU transfers.

Poland, as EU member, will presumably be entitled to development assistance reaching probably as much as Euro7–8 billions annually by the year 2006. These funds may help in developing infrastructure, promoting rural development and creating new jobs. The EU experience to date shows, however, that even the most generous structural fund transfers cannot solve a country's problems unless the right economic policies are pursued and markets are flexible. The most striking example of the failure of transfers to improve economic performance (due to a lack of appropriate domestic policy) is Greece, a country that received one of the highest levels of transfers in relation to GDP. One can easily find other examples of this type, especially at sub-national level, from the chronically underdeveloped Italian Mezzogiorno to Spain, where unemployment in some regions exceeds 30%. In a nutshell, structural funds may help a country to enter the path of real convergence, but by no means will it guarantee it.

All of this means that the economic policy that can promote Poland's chances of convergence should focus on maintaining responsible macroeconomic policy aimed at creating a stable framework for economic activities, promoting domestic savings, in particular reducing the public sector deficit, diminishing the role of the state in the economy by reducing the tax burden and by privatising state-owned companies, demonopolising, restructuring and liberalising the economy, promoting the development of efficient financial markets and creating incentives to invest in human capital.

MACROECONOMIC STABILITY AND EU MEMBERSHIP

Another problem that should be discussed is the 'nominal convergence' of the Polish economy, by which we mean achieving a degree of macroeconomic stability similar to West European EU members. In the Maastricht treaty most EU countries agreed that nominal convergence, that is, the introduction of the common currency, would create a new basis for deeper economic integration. Economic and Monetary Union (EMU) became part of the *acquis* although the UK secured its famous 'opt-out' clause. This means that Polish EU membership of Poland must also entail involvement in EMU (it seems that a permanent 'opt-out' is excluded). Although a country does not have to accept the principles of EMU at the very moment of accession it is assumed that new EU members will accept them over time (European Commission, 1997). But it is obvious that so far as a country remains outside the euro area some room for manoeuvre in fiscal and monetary policy, albeit restricted, will still exist.

The Maastricht criteria are generally considered to be a set of orthodox rules for the conduct of fiscal and monetary policy (although based on some arbitrarily chosen thresholds). The final objective of EMU is to create a stable macroeconomic framework of very low inflation, no exchange rate risk, sustainable fiscal positions of governments, and totally free movement of capital. The main benefits of monetary union include: elimination of exchange rate risk (this should be an incentive for long-term EU-wide economic ventures), price stability, elimination of unjustified price differences between markets, lower foreign exchange reserve needs, and dynamic growth effects due to improved microeconomic efficiency (Gros and Thygesen, 1992).

The situation becomes less clear when the discussion concerns an economy in transition such as Poland's. There are reasons to believe that the adjustment costs on the road to monetary union may be significantly higher than in the case of West European countries because of the lower adjustment capabilities of economic agents. Another factor that makes the adjustment difficult is the unfinished process of 'corrective' inflation, that is a need for a faster than average growth of prices that were suppressed in the communist economy (notably some services and energy prices). However, once those costs are absorbed the gains may be even greater than in the developed market economies. Accepting EMU principles, and even more, joining the euro area, means a massive 'import' of economic stability, an incentive to increase savings and investment. Particularly strong incentives will be created for export-orientated foreign investment. In a nutshell, a much more stable and predictable economic environment should pay off in faster economic growth.

On the other hand, some dangers clearly exist. The low adjustment capabilities of economic agents may impose high costs (for example in adjusting to external shocks) and an unreformed (or insufficiently reformed) public sector may damage the government's fiscal position. If factor markets are not flexible enough social costs may also be excessive and expressed in a sharp increase in unemployment. All these factors may be eliminated, or at least limited, by the continuation of appropriate structural policies and reforms.

Figure 14.3 shows the path of nominal convergence of the Polish economy during the 1990s. The most characteristic feature is a steady improvement in macroeconomic stability, particularly noticeable in the gradual fall in the inflation rate, while maintaining a reasonably good fiscal stance.

It is worth noting that the distance that Poland had to travel to fulfil the most important Maastricht criteria (inflation and fiscal balance) was, in 1999, significantly shorter than for the Iberian countries in 1992 (7 years before they finally joined EMU; Poland also wishes to join the single currency area within a 7-year period). The deficit target of 3% of GDP was missed only marginally, while the ratio of the public debt to GDP, at around 45%, is much lower than in the majority of the EMU members. Over the past decade Poland managed to reduce the annual inflation rate from over 1000% in the first half of 1990 to some 6% by mid 1999. Although a discussion is always possible on whether more could have been achieved, Poland had managed to get close, in the late 1990s, to inflation rates observed in Western Europe.

Figure 14.3. The nominal convergence of the Polish economy, 1991–99

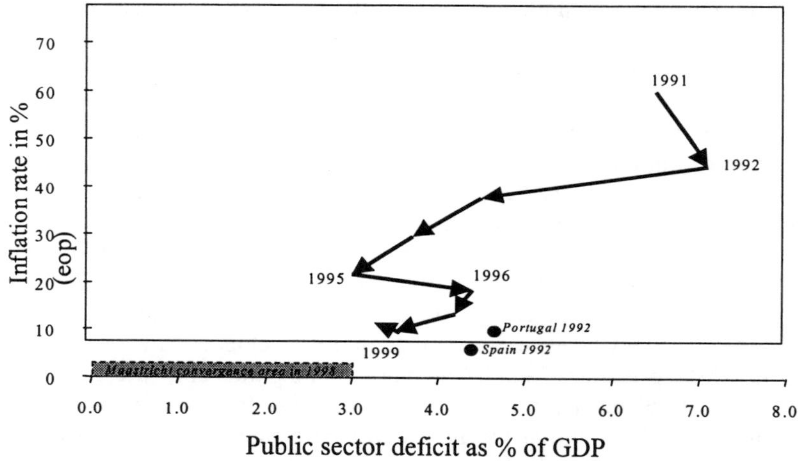

Source: GUS, MoF

The relative success of the anti-inflationary policy does not mean that the disinflation process will continue without any pain in the years ahead. If we assume no revolutionary changes or breaks in trends in the world economy then over the next 7–10 years Poland will have to all but eliminate inflation. That means breaking 'inflationary inertia', which involves dismantling the open or hidden indexation mechanisms embedded in the economy. The economic policy issues connected with the drive towards EMU can be summarised as follows:

- disinflationary policy should concentrate on fighting inflationary inertia through breaking the indexation mechanisms in the economy. These exist in the high inflationary expectations of economic agents mainly in the form of the wage indexation mechanism (expected growth of wages to compensate for inflation). Another indexation mechanism that played an important role during the 1990s but which was eliminated in 2000 was the exchange rate indexation (steady nominal currency depreciation built into the crawling-peg and crawling-band exchange rate regimes);

- fiscal and monetary policies should be co-ordinated and built around eliminating inflation. The medium-term plans of the government, aimed at balancing the budget by the year 2001, mainly through curbing consumption and cash transfers to households (Ministerstwo Finansów, 1999) begin to set out a suitable fiscal policy. Achieving a balanced budget, however, requires success with the 1999 pensions reform as well as the continuation of structural reforms in other parts of the public sector;
- the medium-term targets of monetary policy include reducing inflation to rates compatible with EMU rules. However if disinflationary policy is based mainly on monetary policy, and the indexation mechanisms are still in place, the effort to reduce inflation may impose heavy recessionary costs. Only recession and a drastic deterioration of the financial situation of firms will force employees to accept a decline in real wages. It is evident that disinflation based mainly on the use of monetary tools is constrained by considerations of political economy (the willingness of policy makers and workers to put up with recession);
- one solution to this problem is an increase in the credibility of macroeconomic policy. If economic agents believe that the government's zero-inflation target *will* be met the indexation process may be arrested and inflation fall to the desired level;
- a strong domestic currency enhances the credibility of macroeconomic policy while the risk of a major foreign exchange crisis (and devaluation) as experienced by Hungary in 1995 or the Czech Republic in 1997 is always a serious blow to long-run policy credibility and makes the disinflation process longer and more painful. In the 1990s Poland was the only large CEE economy to escape any serious financial and foreign exchange crisis, an achievement purchased at the price of policy to cool domestic demand in 1997–98. Macroeconomic policy must therefore be cautious enough to avoid such crises in the future (see Hausner et al., 1998).

A question that may arise is whether Poland can speed up nominal convergence by an immediate move of fixing the exchange rate of złoty against the euro, or even by the unilateral adoption of the euro as a domestic currency (without any permission from the European Central Bank).[10] It seems, however, that such a move would be premature. The significant inflationary differentials between Poland and the euro area would continue even after the adoption of the euro, especially in the non-tradeable sector. This statement is not in conflict with the long-term trend of the real appreciation of złoty, caused by the well-known Balassa-Samuelson effect. Continuous wage inflation, combined with the rapid hardening of the macroeconomic environment, could lead to deep recession. Polish firms in the tradeable sector would be forced to adjust by restructuring and finding deep productivity gains which probably only some could achieve. Therefore, the cost of an attempt to find a shortcut to the euro could be tremendously high.

Provided that macroeconomic policy remains prudent, increased policy credibility is therefore the crucial factor in Poland's drive towards EMU. One may also point to the fact that – as was the case in the Iberian countries – the *declared intention* itself, to join the Euro area, may help in this respect. The impact of EMU on rapidly growing confidence in the macroeconomic policy of the Iberian countries is an important example in two ways. First, in the long-term, the prospects of EMU membership created confidence in future price stability, the result of exchanging a weaker domestic currency for a stronger euro (in the more stable economies such as Germany the problem was quite the opposite). Second, in the short and medium term, the disinflationary policy issue boiled down to one question: will the country qualify for EMU membership? It can be claimed that whatever the general level of confidence in domestic institutions and economic policies in those countries there was little doubt about the political will of governments to join the 'hard core' of EU integration. Hence, the long-term problem of macroeconomic policy credibility was replaced by a short-term problem of the political determination to qualify for EMU, and this qualification was easy to measure (due to the precise conditions set by the Maastricht treaty), and connected with emotional rather than economic motivations (national pride).

If Poland follows this road, and provided that macroeconomic policy remains sensible enough to prevent any major setback to exchange rate stability, the aim to join EMU by the year 2006–07 seems quite realistic. Modern economics generally rejects any possible long-run trade-off between inflation and GDP growth (although it may exist in the short run). The modern growth paradigm, embodied for transition economies in 'the Washington consensus', points to low inflation as a factor promoting long-term growth. This means that nominal convergence may also help in achieving real convergence. Obviously, one should bear in mind that the link between low inflation and faster GDP growth is not simple. As the recent Russian crisis shows, sustainable low inflation cannot be achieved at a price of building up other imbalances and requires an adequately prudent macroeconomic policy.

ACCESSION NEGOTIATIONS: THE MOST SENSITIVE AREAS

The most important issues connected with Poland's EU membership, real and nominal convergence, will not be the most discussed items during entry negotiations. The most sensitive economic areas of the negotiations will most likely encompass agriculture and the free movement of labour. The freedom to buy land, although important from the political and social point of view (mainly due to the existing fears about a massive German buy-out of land in western parts of Poland), does not seem to be a really important issue from the purely economic point of view. On the other hand, agriculture and labour are two critical issues and we review them below.

The problem with Polish agriculture is complex, mainly due to the interaction of two unfortunate factors. On the Polish side there is low efficiency due mainly to excessive rural employment. On the EU side the problem is an excessively protectionist agricultural policy that results in huge fiscal costs, disrupts trade, and slows structural change (badly needed in Poland). Full involvement in the Common Agricultural Policy (CAP) would require multi-billion transfers, mainly in the form of direct income support for Polish farmers. As a result, the initial position of the EU is that Polish farmers should be cut off from the bulk of direct support. It is hardly surprising that Poland's negotiating position is different: without such full support already less-efficient Polish farmers will not be able to compete on equal terms with West European farmers. From a longer-term perspective however the problem does not look insoluble. Some compromise can probably be found. The pressure for CAP reform should lead, over time, to its liberalisation (lowering the level of protection and price support) making the 'unequal terms of competition' less of a problem. On the Polish side, the gradual outflow of labour from agriculture, and a sensible policy of rural development, may help in promoting efficiency growth in agriculture. Moreover the problems of Polish agriculture are not so unprecedented as we tend to think. Although the sector employs around 25% of the total labour force a similar share was recorded in Italy in the mid 1960s, in Spain in the early 1970s, and in Portugal in the early 1980s. In the late 1990s agriculture in those countries employed respectively 7%, 8% and 12% of the labour force. The problems of agriculture cannot be solved in the short run, but eventually market pressures, albeit temporarily modified by agricultural policies, are likely to prevail.

A separate problem is connected with food prices. Prices of basic agricultural products are supported in the EU at a level some 60% above world market levels. In Poland the price level is, on the average, only around 30% above the world level. That does not mean, however, that joining the EU and the CAP will necessarily trigger huge hikes in Polish food prices. This is unlikely due to the combination of gradual CAP liberalisation, leading to a lower level of price support in the EU, and real złoty appreciation, leading to increases in Polish food prices in terms of world currencies even before joining the EU.

The free movement of labour is treated as a danger for Western European labour markets, mainly in Germany and Austria. Is fear of a massive emigration justified? The answer seems to be 'only partly'. First, the history of previous EU enlargements does not confirm the hypothesis that opening borders for the free movement of labour leads to high flows of migrants from poor to rich countries. Historically, the creation of the single market, unifying regions that even today range in their per capita GDP from ratios of 1 to 7.5 (or from 1 to 5 if the numbers are adjusted for differences in purchasing power), led to much less migration than expected. Relatively limited labour mobility may be explained by a mix of various cultural, social, linguistic, economic and institutional factors. Second, the successful development of Poland, and its income growth, may reduce the differentials between Poland and Western Europe over time. The Polish wage level relative to wages in western *Länder* of Germany increased from 2% in 1989 to 6% in 1990 and 15% in the late 1990s. If the purchasing power of currencies is taken into account Polish wages are around 30% of the German level. Thus, differences remain but progress in narrowing them is quite fast. Third, the Polish experience also suggests that it may be misleading to consider current income relativities and the relaxation of legal obstacles as the only variables explaining the propensity to migrate. The highest emigration from Poland to the West happened during the 1980s when the command economy collapsed and when emigrants faced serious formal hurdles (restrictive visa policies). During the 1990s the propensity to emigrate fell considerably despite significant liberalisation (visa-free travel). Of course, income differentials shifted favourably during the 1990s but one may also argue that a general improvement in economic and social development prospects in Poland helped.

Does this mean however that a fear of huge emigration is without foundation? Certainly not. The potential extent of emigration from Poland to Western Europe in a unified labour market is estimated at around 400,000 people over a 7-year period (in the scenario of successful Polish development, Orłowski and Zienkowski, 1998b). Obviously, if the positive scenario does not materialise the risk grows – independently of whether Poland joins the EU labour market, or not.[11] This would not destroy West European labour markets but could cause some damage. Therefore transition periods with restricted labour mobility are probably unavoidable. The West Europeans should keep in mind, however, that the real nature of the unemployment problem in the majority of EU countries is not immigration but the inflexibility of their own labour markets. If these markets are reformed and liberalised the risks will greatly diminish.

CONCLUSION

Poland's integration with the EU can be seen as a process of recreating traditional economic links brutally cut off for dozens of years for political reasons. If one applies such optics, all the current costs and challenges for both sides are relatively small and short-lived. Moreover, the process of Polish EU accession is just one piece of the Europe-wide drive towards unity and by no means the most costly or difficult one.

Obviously, challenges do exist and do matter. Nevertheless, with a positive approach from both sides and with continuing economic growth in Poland, even the most sensitive problems, like the modernisation of the Polish agriculture and the freedom of movement of labour, can be solved. The biggest challenge for the Polish economy is to use EU membership as a vehicle to accelerate economic growth and to achieve, over time, real convergence with the West. A nominal convergence, albeit important, if generated by a wise macroeconomic policy can only help in achieving fast, sustainable, long-term GDP growth

NOTES

1 A clear contradiction exists between the officially published data for the period 1950–90, suggesting that the long-term GDP growth rate in Poland (around 4% per annum) exceeded that of Western Europe, and the easily observable increase in economic distance between the two. The communist period growth rate was overestimated for a number of reasons: the different methodology used, which excluded services from the analysis; underestimation of price deflators; overlooking product quality deterioration; and – last but not least – by deliberately falsified data (mainly at the level of enterprises interested in overstating output volume). An 'implicit' growth rate for Poland in 1950–90, calculated as the rate consistent with changes in the relative GDP levels vis-à-vis Western Europe, is equal to around 1.2–1.5% a year.

2 There seems to be a general misunderstanding of the impact of the *acquis* on the labour market. The point is that the majority of misguided social policies are set on the national rather than on the EU level.

3 Examples may be found in the World Bank study (World Bank, 1997).

4 For the analysis of the sectoral impact of the EU membership see: Czyłewski et al. (1998).

5 The final estimates of the Research Centre for Economic and Statistical Studies of the Central Statistical Office and Polish Academy of Sciences (to be published).

6 The same result – faster growth in the poorer country – may be obtained, in theory, even without capital imports, but due to the characteristics of the neoclassical production function (diminishing returns to scale). In an economy that does not have much capital each saved and invested unit of capital gives higher production growth than in a developed economy. Therefore there is no need to borrow capital from abroad; with the same savings rate, a less developed economy will be growing faster than a developed economy.
7 The declared medium-term plans of the Polish government call for balancing the budget even before the EU accession (Ministerstwo Finansów, 1999) and therefore follow the Irish rather than the Greek example.
8 Most authors, when talking about the time period necessary for convergence, take as a threshold 75% of the EU-15 average GDP per capita level, the level that triggers support from structural funds (Baldwin, 1994; Barbone and Zalduendo, 1997).
9 The majority of the EU development funds is spent under so-called Objective 1 (assistance for regions lagging behind in development). The formal threshold for qualifying the region as covered by Objective 1 is a GDP per capita level below 75% of the EU average.
10 A discussion on this issue started recently after the publication in the daily *Rzeczpospolita* by two well-known economists Andrzej Bratkowski and Jacek Rostowski (Rzeczpospolita, 26 April 1999).
11 As the simulations show, with no improvement in the income relations between Poland and Germany, the potential for migration grows to more than 1 million persons (see Orłowski, and Zienkowski, 1998b).

REFERENCES

Baldwin, R.E. (1994), *Towards an Integrated Europe*, London: Centre for Economic Policy Research.
Baldwin, R.E., Francois, J.F. and Portes R. (1997), 'The costs and benefits of eastern enlargement', *Economic Policy,* no. 24.
Barbone, L. and Zalduendo, J. (1997), 'EU accession of Central and Eastern Europe: bridging the income gap', World Bank Policy Research Working Paper, no. 1721, Washington, DC: World Bank.
Czyłewski, A.B., Orłowski, W.M. and Zienkowski, L. (1998), *Średniookresowe efekty członkostwa Polski w Unii Europejskiej* [Medium-term effects of the Poland's membership in the EU], Łódż European Instituteż
European Commission (1996), 'Annual economic report for 1996', *European Economy*, no. 61/1996.

European Commission (1997), *Agenda 2000: Commission Opinion on Poland's Application for Membership of the European Union (avis)*, Brussels: European Commission.

Girard, J. and Hurst, C. (1994), 'Investment and growth: quality versus quantity', *EIB Papers*, no. 23/1994.

Gros, D. and Thygesen, N. (1992), *European Monetary Integration*, London: Longman.

Hausner, J., Moeody, M., Wilkin, J. Wojtyna, A. and Zirk-Sadowski, M. (1998), *Przystąpienie czy integracja? Polska droga do Unii Europejskiej* (Accession or integration? Poland's road to the EU), Warsaw: Friedrich Ebert Stiftung.

Kawecka-Wyrzykowska, E. (1999), *Polska w drodze do Unii Europejskiej* (Poland on its way to the EU), Warsaw: PWE.

Ministerstwo Finansów (1999), *Strategia finansów publicznych i rozwoju gospodarczego Polski 2000–2010* (Strategy of the public finance and of economic development of Poland, 2000/2010), Warsaw: Ministerstwo Finansów.

Orłowski, W.M. (1998a), *The Road to Europe. Macroeconomics of Accession to the European Union*, Łódź European Institute.

Orłowski ,W.M. (1998b), 'Poland and the European Union: conditions for real convergence', *Research Bulletin RECESS/ZBSE*, no. 4/1998.

Orłowski, W.M. (1999), 'Real exchange rate and growth after EU accession: the problem of transfer and capital inflow absorption', in H. Gabrisch and R. Pohl (ed.), *EU Enlargement and its Macroeconomic Effects in Eastern Europe*, London: Macmillan Press.

Orłowski, W.M. and Zienkowski, L. (1998a), 'Estimate of the level of development and internal economic differences in the 16 new voivodships', *Research Bulletin RECESS/ZBSE*, no. 4 1998.

Orłowski, W.M. and Zienkowski, L. (1998b), 'Potential size of emigration from Poland after joining the European Union: an attempt of a forecast', *Research Bulletin RECESS/ZBSE*, no. 2/1998.

Piskorz, W. and Plewa, J. (1995), 'The costs of integration of Polish agriculture with the European Union', paper presented to the Annual Meeting of American Agricultural Economics Association, 6–9 August 1995, Indianapolis.

United Nations (1950), *National Income Statistics 1938–48*, New York: United Nations.

World Bank (1997), *Poland: Reforms and Growth on the Road to the EU*, Washington, DC: World Bank.

15. Can Polish politicians work together on EU accession?

Christopher Bobiński

THE BRISTOL APPEAL (*APEL BRISTOLSKI*)

On the afternoon of 11 May 2000 in Warsaw's exclusive Bristol Hotel, a room full of people invited to a meeting of all seven of Poland's former post-1989 prime ministers waited expectantly for the event to begin. There was a certain tension in the air. The prime ministers were to sign an appeal calling on all of Poland's politicians to co-operate closely on issues related to the country's membership of the European Union and many of the invited spectators thought, rightly as it turned out, that such a common appeal was impossible, given divisions in Poland on EU matters. As the time for the meeting to start came and went, four prime ministers – Tadeusz Mazowiecki (1989–90) and Hanna Suchocka (1992–93) from the Freedom Union (UW), then in the governing coalition with the Solidarity Electoral Action (AWS) and Józef Oleksy (1995–96) and Włodzimierz Cimoszewicz (1996–1997) from the opposition Left Democratic Alliance (SLD) waited in an anteroom for their remaining colleagues to arrive. A fifth, Jan Krzysztof Bielecki (1990–91) also from the Freedom Union and then a director at the European Bank of Reconstruction and Development in London, had agreed to sign the appeal but could not be at the meeting in person. The sixth, Waldemar Pawlak (1993–95) from the Polish Peasant Party (PSL), pleading an urgent meeting elsewhere, called at the last minute to say he could not come. That left Jan Olszewski (1992) from the right wing Movement for the Reconstruction of Poland (ROP) to wait for. 'I think he's coming,' Tadeusz Mazowiecki told the editors of the *Unia & Polska* magazine, the organisers of the event. 'We ordered a car together, from parliament so he certainly intended to come.' As the minutes passed the four prime ministers present debated whether to sign the appeal at all. Hanna Suchocka was initially the most sceptical. 'If we go in like this and sign the appeal then we'll send a signal that the next coalition in Poland will be made up of the SLD and the UW,' she said. Tadeusz Mazowiecki was more sanguine about the implications. Calmest of all were Oleksy and Cimoszewicz who did not hesitate. 'Let's do it,' Cimoszewicz finally said as Olszewski still failed to show. Despite Suchocka's misgivings the four went into the meeting room to sign what came to be called the Bristol Appeal (*apel Bristolski*).

The meeting marked the culmination of an initiative taken by *Unia & Polska* magazine at the beginning of 2000. It was designed to explore how far it would be possible to take an all-party consensus on Polish membership of the European Union. The review, founded in 1998 and devoted to analysing the implications of Polish membership of the EU both for Poland and the EU, had even gone so far as to suggest that an all-party coalition government should be formed for the time that it takes to get Poland into the EU. The reasoning behind this proposal was that the challenge of meeting EU membership criteria in the spheres of legislation, administrative change, microeconomic adjustment and transformation of politically sensitive sectors like the steel and coal industries and agriculture, was so great that it could not be borne by one party or even a coalition composed of parties from one side of the political spectrum alone. Rather, the magazine argued, it needed a coalition of all the parties to achieve the effort needed if Poland is to be ready by the 'EU – compatible' target date (31 December 2002) the country has set itself.

There was another aspect to the argument for a coalition, or at least for a switch, for a time at least, from adversarial politics to the politics of co-operation. This derives from the fact that Poland's own entry negotiations, which started in 1998, are set to run till 2001 if the country's accession date is to be met. The culmination of the negotiations will thus come together with a series of elections. These started in October 2000 with the presidential election, followed in 2001 by national parliamentary elections, then by local government elections, all capped by the referendum on EU membership. The elections could delay the drive towards EU membership unless a consensus on the question could be struck. There could be nothing worse for Poland's EU negotiators, led by Jan Kułakowski, than for their efforts to be accompanied by a vociferous campaign in which their every move was debated by one or other side of the political spectrum. In addition, if the opinion polls are to be believed, the former communists from the SLD are set to do well in coming elections while the Solidarity – based right-wing AWS looks likely to find itself in opposition. Given that the SLD in government would take responsibility for conducting EU policy, the AWS could be pushed into questioning any accession treaty the government negotiates, creating the possibility of the AWS veering towards a hard right that is already against membership. Thus AWS, together with the PSL, could find themselves urging a no vote in the membership referendum, taking the opponents of Polish EU membership dangerously close to 50%.

Unia & Polska reasoned that the politics of coalition or at least co-operation could help to avoid such a scenario. Co-operation between government and opposition before parliamentary elections on EU-related issues would limit the possibility of either side picking a fight over the EU question during the election. It would also oblige both winners and losers to work together after the election. Thus *Unia & Polska*, building on the precedent of a meeting and a common photograph of the seven former premiers taken on the day in 1999 that Poland joined Nato, decided to ask all seven in separate interviews whether, metaphorically, such a common, EU-related picture was possible.[1]

SEVEN PRIME MINISTERS ON EUROPE

The first to be interviewed was Jan Olszewski, a lawyer who had defended many oppositionists in political cases under the communists and had, after independence in 1989, staked a place for himself on the nationalist right of the political spectrum. His short term in office came to a dramatic end in June 1992 when Antoni Macierewicz, his interior minister, moved to reveal the names of former police informers in parliament and in government. Alarmed by these developments and with the active encouragement of the then President Lech Wałęsa, parliament brought down the Olszewski administration. Olszewski told us that there was no alternative to Polish membership of the EU – 'either we integrate with Western Europe or we find ourselves in the Russian sphere of influence'.[2] But he also cautioned that the target date of 2003 was quite unrealistic: 'We now all know that Polish accession on January 1, 2003 is quite impossible. It appears that only the Polish government believes in this date … I think that membership is a matter of a decade.' Olszewski further explained that the government strategy should be changed: 'We are currently spending enormous amounts of money to be ready at the end of 2002 … This is a suicidal strategy as it aims at an unrealistic target.' Instead, Olszewski suggested that Poland should first co-operate with other Central European applicant countries and concentrate on modernising and growing their economies, with membership postponed until their economies were stronger. Polish membership was impossible in the near future simply because of the costs to the present member states. Finally, Olszewski grudgingly admitted that policy on Europe *should* be co-ordinated but cautioned that a 'serious discussion' on this policy had first to take place. In the event, Olszewski failed to turn up at the Bristol meeting, explaining that jet lag following his return from the USA the previous day meant that he had overslept. He also refused to sign the Bristol appeal, saying that it was too 'euroenthusiastic'. In a separate declaration he wrote that economic factors meant that a majority of EU leaders were against early enlargement. Thus what was needed was an effort to change their minds, not 'one-sided demonstrations of enthusiasm in respect of fulfilling the criteria for EU membership' by Poles.

Next came Włodzimierz Cimoszewicz, who headed a coalition between his own former communist SLD and the PSL as prime minister between 1996 and the elections in the autumn of 1997 which were won by the AWS and the Freedom Union. Cimoszewicz pointed out that demonstrating national unity in the case of Nato was much easier than in the case of EU membership:[3] 'Nato was a matter of security that didn't impinge on the economic interests of major social groups in the country. EU membership is more complex.' Cimoszewicz also doubted that a 'government of national integration' was possible: 'My reading of Polish politics tells me that even an issue of the highest priority like joining the EU is not reason enough to serve for working towards national reconciliation and agreement.' Nevertheless he saw the need for working towards an informal 'pro-European party' which would draw recruits from every political parish. Cimoszewicz also recognised the danger that today's governing parties would contest EU membership once in opposition: 'This is why we need politicians from opposing political camps to show the courage to make common declarations demonstrating their pro-European intent.'

Unia & Polska followed up with an interview with Jan Krzysztof Bielecki. Bielecki was originally an underground Solidarity activist from Gdańsk who in 1990 was asked by President Lech Wałęsa to form a government after Tadeusz Mazowiecki resigned on losing his bid for the presidency. At the time Bielecki was a member of the free market Liberal Democratic Congress (KLD), later a part of the Freedom Union. Bielecki, at the EBRD since the mid 1990s, takes an active interest in Polish politics. He was also for a time, in the Suchocka government, the head of the EU integration unit. In his interview Bielecki stressed that Poland's drive for EU membership should be based on support at the grass roots.[4] He argued that already, in February 2000, people in local government were well aware that there were funds to be had from the EU. These funds, they also believed, could resolve their local problems. If there are any coalitions to be made they should be constructed at the local level and should be aimed at solving very concrete problems. Then and only then would national politicians become aware that, if they failed to work for EU membership, people would hold them responsible for the loss of financial and other opportunities. The only thing that can mobilise national politicians, according to Bielecki, is fear of losing their elected posts as a result of a backlash of this kind. He also warned that couching the drive for EU membership in terms of a 'national challenge' would be of no use. Nevertheless Bielecki argued for a maximum of co-operation between the parties in parliament on the issue of pushing through EU related legislation.

Bielecki was followed by Józef Oleksy from the SLD who headed a coalition government with the PSL in the mid 1990s.[5] He was forced to resign in the wake of unsubstantiated allegations put forward at the end of his term in 1995 by President Lech Wałęsa accusing the SLD politician of having acted as an informer for the Soviets. Oleksy, who has made the issue of EU integration one of his specialities, declared that the SLD was happy to work with the government on EU-related legislation as long as the draft laws sent to parliament for consideration contain no flaws: 'We will not tolerate in the name of co-operation projects which contain errors and which have not been consulted on properly … .' 'Nevertheless we are ready,' he added, 'to co-operate with the government, support it and speed up the legislative process.'

When *Unia & Polska* talked to Hanna Suchocka she was justice minister in the AWS–UW coalition government headed by Jerzy Buzek. Of the seven politicians interviewed she was the only serving cabinet official. She had headed a coalition of Solidarity, based parties from 1992 to 1993, when an ill-advised vote of no confidence put by representatives of the Solidarity trade union itself saw her administration lose its majority. This opened the way to the 1993 elections that brought in the SLD–PSL coalition. We asked Suchocka directly if there was a possibility of a consensus being reached between all the parties before and after the parliamentary elections expected in 2001.[6] She replied that the logic of election politics would mean that the parties would tend to underline how they differed on EU issues, *not* how they agreed: 'I can well imagine the development of a race to show who is most pro-Polish, who is the best qualified to defend our national interests in entering the EU. Then I think it will be difficult to find a common platform.' She added that the issue evoked significant emotions: 'If we could achieve agreement on, in my view, the crucial issue, the future of agriculture, then we could lobby for Polish entry together. But every discussion on this subject generates incredible emotions and mutual accusations even amongst us former premiers.'

Waldemar Pawlak, from the Polish Peasant Party (PSL), alone of the seven had been prime minister twice: once, briefly, in 1992 when he had unsuccessfully attempted to put together a government in the wake of the collapse of the Olszewski administration and then from 1993 to 1994 as the first leader of the SLD–PSL coalition. Pawlak, who has since demonstrated scepticism towards the EU occupies a special place in this story as it was he who in 1994 actually submitted to Brussels Poland's formal application for membership. Nevertheless our interview never got around to the problem of co-operation between the parties because the former PSL leader concentrated his remarks on the need to adopt a tougher stance in EU talks:[7] 'Let's start from the fact that our present capitulationist position on the EU is pathetic,' he said, adding that Poland's trade deficit in the EU's favour means that Brussels and the member states have no intention of allowing the country to join soon so there is no point in having Poland speed up its efforts to join by 2003. He continued: 'If we rush to join then the only way we can meet this target is by capitulating all the way down the line'. Pawlak's main argument was that if Poland joined at the wrong moment then the country's economy, including its agriculture, would be destroyed by competition from West European companies. He suggested that an alternative to EU membership could be closer links with the US or with countries in the Far East. Nevertheless Pawlak did not entirely negate the advantage of joining the EU in time: 'I am a pragmatist and am against capitulation. I will make my mind up on the issue when I see what the terms of membership are.'

The general tenor of our interview meant that we had scant hope of Waldemar Pawlak turning up at the Bristol or of his signing the appeal. That indeed was the case. Moreover, not only did Mr Pawlak fail to sign but, in contrast to Jan Olszewski, he did not take the trouble to explain why. Evidently Mr Pawlak felt that his potential voters are in the countryside and the small towns and that there was no point in justifying his actions to an urban audience.

The final interview in the series, with Tadeusz Mazowiecki, independent Poland's first prime minister from 1989 to 1990, was published in an issue of *Unia & Polska* devoted to the annual European Meeting organised by the Robert Schuman Foundation, a Polish non-governmental organisation.[8] Indeed the timing of the Bristol Appeal was linked to that of the 'European Days', a set of seminars and street events designed to inform people about the EU. Mazowiecki, who heads the European Integration Committee in the Sejm, agreed that EU issues should be ring-fenced and taken out of the general run of political exchange between governing coalition and opposition. He added that all sides should accept the principle of co-operation between government and opposition and that this should be accepted by every successive administration. This was needed, Mazowiecki said, because the process of accession was a long one and would involve more than one government administration. Thus there needed to be continuity: 'I cannot imagine a situation in which the political set-up changes and the new coalition or the new opposition questions the point of going ahead with European integration.'

CO-OPERATION OR DISSENT OVER EU ISSUES?

In the event, five former prime ministers, including Hanna Suchocka, signed the Bristol Appeal which called for 'all political and social groups at the national, regional and local level to work towards a common pro-European platform'. It also called for 'common actions in parliament designed to ensure that laws needed to make Poland conform to the legal system of the European Union are passed in time'. The document appealed to society at large to 'take part in furthering a cause which will ensure a secure place for Poland on our continent and will allow our country to further its national interests together with other European states, members of the European Union'.

The appeal seemed to show that on EU issues the Freedom Union and the left-leaning Democratic Alliance were the two groupings which could work together. The fact that Waldemar Pawlak failed to sign faithfully reflected majority opinion in his PSL, led, at the time of writing, by Jarosław Kalinowski, that the EU would bring more harm than good to the countryside. Indeed, as of mid 2000, only a minority of the PSL saw benefits flowing from Polish membership and participation in the Common Agricultural Policy. Jan Olszewski's stance also pointed to the possibility that despite its verbal support for EU membership the political right could well develop into a significant eurosceptic force, making the possibility of a national coalition a distant one.

Indeed, on 9 July 2000 Marian Krzaklewski, the AWS presidential candidate sounded a warning note in a major election speech which bode ill for the prospect of building a national consensus on the EU in Poland. Krzaklewski sought to draw a clear line between his own vision of Polish European policy and that represented by the SLD and what the AWS leader called the 'ideological' wing of the Freedom Union. Speaking in Warsaw's circular Porczynski gallery he said:

> The AWS and a major part of responsible politicians in the Solidarity camp see integration in the EU as a practical aim for Polish policy. It is designed to secure prosperity for Poles, to open European Community markets for our products and to ensure that Polish industry and farming enjoy similar conditions to those which producers have in the present member states. Also to create additional guarantees of external security. If however integration with the EU is seen as an ideological aim, then negotiating to defend Polish political and economic interests becomes less important. Then the main aim is to take part in a specific 'cultural revolution' designed to implement the ideological project of creating a new European identity. The adoption of such an ideological approach means that the modernisation of the Polish economy, solving social problems, the fate of Polish agriculture – in short the defence of the national interest – ceases to be the main aim, also in the context of European integration and is relegated to being merely a problem which has to be marginalised.
>
> Those who support the idea of treating Poland's integration with the European Community as an ideological aim think that a natural coalition for realising this purpose can only be a coalition of the SLD and the left wing of the Freedom Union. The post-communists are further motivated by their opportunism which they developed in the time of the Polish People's Republic. The post-communists in reality treat Brussels as a new Moscow, the EU as a new Comecon and their policies – also in the international sphere – as no more than a form of looking for sponsors for their own careers.[9]

The speech set the stage for a fundamental cleavage in Poland's EU policy and seemed to foreshadow the development which *Unia & Polska* had sought to head off. Krzaklewski suggested in no uncertain terms that an SLD government would not negotiate with the EU to defend Poland's national interests but would agree to Brussels' terms in the name of some 'ideological aim' and in its own personal interests. The conclusion looked clear. If the AWS were to find itself in opposition then its primary duty would be to fight the way the negotiations were conducted at every turn and then call on its supporters to oppose in the referendum any accession treaty a future SLD government might sign.

At the same time the AWS government headed by Jerzy Buzek, which in June 2000 lost its Freedom Union partner and had thus become a minority administration, showed every sign of pressing ahead with pro-EU policies. In contrast to Marian Krzaklewski's electioneering stance it also showed a willingness to work together with the opposition at least on EU accession. This reflected more than a division of roles between two Solidarity leaders. As prime minister, Jerzy Buzek's primary task became one of keeping the minority government in power for as long as possible and maintaining a stable backdrop against which Marian Krzaklewski could conduct a presidential campaign aimed at mobilising the post-Solidarity vote against what he termed the post-communist threat. It also showed a more down to earth pragmatic approach on the part of Jerzy Buzek, who seemed to have come under the influence of Jacek Saryusz-Wolski, a single-minded pro-European who in April 2000 became the minister in charge of the European Integration Office (UKIE). Buzek seemed to have become convinced that the adoption of a policy aimed at bringing together government and opposition on the European issue would add legitimacy to an administration that could not count on an automatic majority in parliament.

Working at first behind the scenes, Saryusz-Wolski managed to persuade parliament to establish a special committee, the European Law Committee (an earlier proposal to call it the Grand Committee was dropped), whose sole aim was to push through the necessary EU legislation as quickly as possible. The committee, set up in July 2000, was viewed by many as the first step to a closer relationship between government and opposition. In another conciliatory move the SLD was invited by Premier Buzek to send observers to meetings of the Committee of European Integration (KIE), a government body with the final say on EU policy before policy is approved by the council of ministers (cabinet) itself. The invitation was accepted. In a symbolic gesture, Jan Kułakowski, the government's chief EU negotiator, met with the SLD's foreign policy and EU affairs committees. The government and SLD opposition also began to move towards a consensus on the issue of keeping in post, for continuity, key officials in the negotiating team even after the 2001 parliamentary elections.

At the same time it remained unclear how willing the SLD would be to work with the opposition in the event, as seemed likely from the perspective of summer 2000, of its winning the next parliamentary elections. Indeed it was clearly in the SLD's interest, in the run-up to the general election, to be seen to be the party of conciliation and co-operation. After all, the SLD could expect that the AWS and Freedom Union parties would be campaigning on the argument of the need to save Poland from a post-communist monopoly in which both the presidency and the government were held by people with their roots in the communist past. Thus it would be very much in the interest of the SLD to argue that after the election it was ready to share power with other parties.

Nevertheless when questioned on this the SLD party leader, Leszek Miller, restricted himself merely to saying: 'We had to wait more than two years before the government was ready to talk to us on the EU issue. After the next election we will immediately have proposals for the opposition.'

There was however another factor in the equation – President Aleksander Kwaśniewski himself. When asked by *Unia & Polska* what were the chances of inter-party co-operation he replied:

> It would certainly be a good thing if we could create a climate of co-operation over the EU issue. It would be good if there was a constant, public dialogue between the main political groups on negotiation issues. I doubt however that this will happen. The present government headed by Jerzy Buzek, despite its declarations, is not trying to achieve this. Would another government try harder to achieve it? I don't know and I would be careful on this issue. All governments fall prey to the same tendencies: a belief in their own omnipotence and lack of contact with anyone else. I don't know if Leszek Miller's administration would in this sense be any different from Jerzy Buzek's. However the need to conduct integration activities in concert definitely exists. Thus the President has to do what he can to achieve this.[10]

Aleksander Kwaśniewski was speaking before the AWS–UW coalition broke up. In June 2000 as the crisis leading to the break up developed the president returned to the issue at a press conference in Poznań.[11] He caught his own advisers by surprise when he proposed a three-point plan for co-operation on the EU issue. First, he urged the establishment of a special committee in parliament designed for speedy passage of EU-related legislation. Second, he suggested that the Polish EU negotiating team should contain observer-advisers from the opposition. Third, he argued that competent members of the negotiating should be kept on after elections irrespective of the political hue of the government of the day. President Kwaśniewski's suggestions were received with a certain amount of reserve by government supporters. His idea that representatives of the opposition should take part in the work of the negotiating team was deemed to be impossible from the constitutional point of view. However the President's remarks signalled clearly to Leszek Miller that his former party colleague was a supporter of a conciliatory approach to the opposition, at least on EU-related issues.

CONCLUSIONS

It is difficult to measure what in fact was achieved by *Unia & Polska's* series of interviews or its 'Bristol Appeal', its intervention attempting to promote wider co-operation on EU matters. The magazine's readership embraces officials and politicians who are directly involved in EU affairs as well as academics and students who teach and study the subject. Nevertheless, in the first half of 2000, it was the only Polish publication to discuss openly the need for a broader political approach in facing up to the demanding challenges of adapting to EU membership. Unbeknown to the editors of *Unia & Polska* the government's Europe Committee chief, Jacek Saryusz-Wolski, was also working on this with a proposal for a parliamentary 'special committee for Europe' to speed EU legislation.[12] Saryusz-Wolski was also trying hard to persuade Jerzy Buzek of the merits, for EU accession, of a domestic politics of co-operation.

The future mood within Poland on EU membership will certainly be affected by the position taken by the European Commission and the member states on Poland's application. Clear signals from the EU that it does not want Poland in the Union will fuel domestic opposition to membership. But a delay in membership need not be so damaging provided it is accompanied by a *firm* perspective of accession. Indeed that would be in tune with the popular mood in the country, a mood that sees a minority in favour of joining the EU as soon as possible (29% in May 2000 according to opinion polls) and a majority (58% according to the same poll) wanting membership later, when Poland is ready.[13]

The EU accession process and its internal politics hinge, in Polish circumstances, particularly on rural/agricultural matters. It is important that a serious effort is made in Poland to formulate, in conjunction with the EU, a viable policy on rural development. This would let the Polish Peasant Party (PSL) swing behind the EU cause and help persuade the rural population of its merits. The AWS, despite Marian Krzaklewski's divisive attitude, also has to be encouraged to rethink its attitude to Poland's future role within the EU. This should include a proper debate over the sovereignty issue. Will entry into the EU mean, as some suggest, a detrimental loss of sovereignty ('Don't let them move the capital from Warsaw to Brussels', say the posters put up by nationalist opponents of the EU) or will it lead rather to an advantageous 'pooling' of sovereignty, giving Poland an influence in shaping the policies of an entire continent, one large enough to play a leading role on the world stage?

Unless these two conditions are met, and the PSL with the AWS are won over to a more consistently positive view on the EU, the opposition to Poland's membership will remain strong, perhaps coming dangerously close to the 50% mark that would make the outcome of the referendum on membership, to say the least, uncertain.

NOTES

1 All the interviews were published in 2000 in issues of *Unia & Polska*. The majority were conducted by Krzysztof Bobiński and Marek Saryusz-Wolski. One interview, with Hanna Suchocka, was conducted by Krzysztof Bobiński and Natalia Syrzycka-Mlicka.

2 See *Unia & Polska*, 24 January 2000 for the full interview.

3 See *Unia & Polska*, 7 February 2000.
4 See *Unia & Polska*, 21 February 2000.
5 See *Unia & Polska*, 6 March 2000.
6 See *Unia & Polska*, 3 April 2000.
7 See *Unia & Polska,* 17 April 2000.
8 See *Unia & Polska*, 15 May 2000.
9 *Gazeta Wyborcza*, 11 July 2000.
10 See *Unia & Polska*, 15 May 2000.
11 The account of the Kwaśniewski press conference was reprinted in *Unia & Polska*, on 26 June 2000.
12 The first formal meeting between Saryusz-Wolski and the chairman of the Sejm, Maciej Płażynski, took place on 17 April 2000.
13 When asked: 'Should Poland first modernise its economy and only then join the EU?', some 58% of those surveyed in May 2000 agreed as compared 48% in April 1997. On the other hand the proportion of the population in favour of the 'speediest entry' fell from 40% in April 1997 to 29% in May 2000. Nevertheless had an entry referendum been held in May 2000, 59% would have voted 'yes' and 25% 'no'. It is interesting to note that the pro vote has oscillated over the period May 1999 to May 2000 between 55% and 59% while the anti vote has held remarkably stable at 25–26%. See *Polacy, Węgrzy, Czesi, Litwini i Ukraińcy o integracji z Unią Europejską* (Warsaw: CBOS, June 2000).

Index